W9-ALT-007

Second Edition

FUNDAMENTALS OF PROGRAMMING LANGUAGES

COMPUTER SOFTWARE ENGINEERING SERIES

ELLIS HOROWITZ, EDITOR
University of Southern California

WAYNE AMSBURY
Structured BASIC and Beyond

JEAN-LOUP BAER
Computer Systems Architecture

PETER CALINGAERT
Assemblers, Compilers, and Program Translation

M. S. CARBERRY, H. M. KHALIL, J. F. LEATHRUM, J. S. LEVY
Foundations of Computer Science

SHIMON EVEN
Graph Algorithms

W. FINDLAY and D. A. WATT
Pascal: An Introduction to Methodical Programming, Second Edition

ELLIS HOROWITZ and SARTAJ SAHNI
Fundamentals of Computer Algorithms

ELLIS HOROWITZ and SARTAJ SAHNI
Fundamentals of Data Structures

ELLIS HOROWITZ
Fundamentals of Programming Languages

ELLIS HOROWITZ
Programming Languages: A Grand Tour

TOM LOGSDON
Computers and Social Controversy

IRA POHL and ALAN SHAW
The Nature of Computation: An Introduction to Computer Science

ARTO SALOMMA
Jewels of Formal Language Theory

DONALD D. SPENCER
Computers in Number Theory

JEFFREY D. ULLMAN
Principles of Database Systems, Second Edition

SECOND EDITION

FUNDAMENTALS OF PROGRAMMING LANGUAGES

ELLIS HOROWITZ
University of Southern California

COMPUTER SCIENCE PRESS

Computer Science Press, Inc.
11 Taft Court
Rockville, Maryland 20850

1   2   3   4   5   6   87   86   85   84

Library of Congress Cataloging in Publication Data

Horowitz, Ellis.
   Fundamentals of programming languages.

   Bibliography: p.
   Includes index.
   1. Programming languages (Electronic computers)
   I.Title.
   QA76.7.H67 1983b 001.64'24 83-15369
   ISBN 0-88175-004-2

Dedicated to
Maryanne, Ruth, Edward,
Cecile, Mom and Dad.

CONTENTS

PREFACE .... **xi**

1. **THE EVOLUTION OF PROGRAMMING LANGUAGES** **1**

1.1 Early History 3
1.2 Early Modern History 5
1.3 FORTRAN and ALGOL 60 9
1.4 The Stormy '60s 13
1.5 Advances in the '70s 22
    Concepts Discussed in This Chapter 29
    Exercises 30

2. **THE CHALLENGE OF PROGRAMMING LANGUAGE DESIGN** **33**

2.1 Criteria for Language Design 35
2.2 Some Possible Solutions 40
    Concepts Discussed in This Chapter 45
    Exercises 45

3. **DEFINING SYNTAX** **47**

3.1 The Character Set 47
3.2 BNF 51
3.3 Syntax Graphs 57
3.4 Syntax and Program Reliability 63
    Concepts Discussed in This Chapter 72
    Exercises 72

4. **VARIABLES, EXPRESSIONS AND STATEMENTS** **77**

4.1 Variables and the Assignment Statement 77
4.2 Binding Time and Storage Allocation 82
4.3 Constants and Initialization 86

4.4	Expressions	89
4.5	Conditional Statements	93
4.6	Iterative Statements	97
4.7	The GOTO Statement and Labels	101
4.8	A First Look at Ada	105
	Concepts Discussed in This Chapter	108
	Exercises	109

5.	TYPES	117
5.1	Data Types and Typing	117
5.2	Enumerated Data Types	119
5.3	Elementary Data Types	121
5.4	Pointer Data Type	132
5.5	Structured Data Types	137
5.6	Type Coercion	149
5.7	Type Equivalence	151
5.8	A Look at Ada and Types	154
	Concepts Discussed in This Chapter	159
	Exercises	160

6.	SCOPE AND EXTENT	165
6.1	The Basics	165
6.2	Run-time Implementation	175
6.3	An Extended Example	183
6.4	Binding, Scope and Extent Revisited	185
6.5	A Look at Ada and Scope	191
	Concepts Discussed in This Chapter	195
	Exercises	196

7.	PROCEDURES	199
7.1	General Features	199
7.2	Parameter Evaluation and Passing	202
7.3	Call-By-Name	205
7.4	Specification of Objects in a Procedure	207
7.5	Aliasing	213
7.6	Overloading	214
7.7	Generic Functions	217
7.8	Coroutines	221
	Concepts Discussed in This Chapter	226
	Exercises	227

8.   DATA ABSTRACTION 233

8.1   An Introduction 233
8.2   MODULA 237
8.3   Euclid 243
8.4   Ada 247
8.5   SIMULA 67 251
8.6   Abstract Data Types 256
        Concepts Discussed in This Chapter 262
        Exercises 262

9.   EXCEPTION HANDLING 265

9.1   Design Issues 265
9.2   PL/I ON-Conditions 269
9.3   Exception Handling in CLU 273
9.4   Exception Handling in MESA 275
9.5   Exception Handling in Ada 278
        Concepts Discussed in This Chapter 284
        Exercises 284

10.   CONCURRENCY 287

10.1 Basic Concepts 287
10.2 Semaphores 291
10.3 Monitors 295
10.4 Message Passing 302
10.5 Concurrency in Ada 306
        Concepts Discussed in This Chapter 320
        Exercises 320

11.   INPUT-OUTPUT 325

        Concepts Discussed in This Chapter 339
        Exercises 340

12.   FUNCTIONAL PROGRAMMING 343

12.1 What is Functional Programming 343
12.2 The Basics of LISP 346
12.3 The LIST Interpreter 355
12.4 FUNARGs and FEXPRs 361
12.5 The PROG Feature 364

12.6   Delayed Evaluation 368
        Concepts Discussed in This Chapter 371
        Exercises 371

13.   **DATA FLOW PROGRAMMING LANGUAGES** 373

13.1   The Data Flow Model 373
13.2   Language Design Goals 381
13.3   VAL—A Data Flow Programming Language 384
        Concepts Discussed in This Chapter 392
        Exercises 393

14.   **OBJECT ORIENTED PROGRAMMING LANGUAGES** 395
        Chapter 14 was written by Tim Rentsch.

14.1   History 396
14.2   Division of Smalltalk into Programming Language
        and User Interface 396
14.3   Smalltalk: Object Oriented Programming Language 397
14.3.1 Objects 398
14.3.2 Messages 400
14.3.3 Methods 402
14.3.4 Classes 403
14.3.5 Control Structures 404
14.3.6 Classes Compared to Abstract Data Types 406
14.3.7 Inheritance and Subclassing 406
14.4   Smalltalk: Object Oriented User Interface 411
14.5   Design Principles 415
        Concepts Discussed in This Chapter 418
        Exercises 418

REFERENCES 421

INDEX 433

PREFACE

"...I always worked with programming languages because it seemed to me that until you could understand those, you really couldn't understand computers. Understanding them doesn't really mean only being able to use them. A lot of people can use them without understanding them."
Christopher Strachey

The development of programming languages is one of the finest intellectual achievements of the new discipline called Computer Science. And yet, there is no other subject that I know of, that has such emotionalism and mystique associated with it. Thus, my attempt to write about this highly charged subject is taken with a good deal of caution. Nevertheless, in my role as professor I have felt the need for a modern treatment of this subject.

Traditional books on programming languages are like abbreviated language manuals, but this book takes a fundamentally different point of view. I believe that the best possible way to study and understand today's programming languages is by focusing on a few essential concepts. These concepts form the outline for this book and include such topics as variables, expressions, statements, typing, scope, procedures, data types, exception handling and concurrency. By understanding what these concepts are and how they are realized in different programming languages, one arrives at a level of comprehension far greater than one gets by writing some programs in a few languages. Moreover, knowledge of these concepts provides a framework for understanding *future* language designs.

This approach to the study of programming languages is analogous to the way natural languages are studied by linguists. According to the linguists Victoria Fromken and Robert Rodman, (in *An Introduction to Language*, Holt-Rinehart-Winston), "a linguist attempts to find out the laws of a language, and the laws which pertain to all languages." In their book they try to identify the universals of syntax, semantics, and phonology (sounds). But unlike the linguists who see their role as identifying these universals, computer scientists can hope for more. The study of the nature of programming languages can lead both to better understanding of existing languages and also to superior language designs in the future. The approach taken here hopes to support those goals.

When Jean Sammet's book *Programming Languages: History and Fundamentals* first appeared, with its famous cover of the Tower of Babel of programming languages, FORTRAN and COBOL were overwhelmingly used in scientific/commercial computing, and in academia FORTRAN was preeminent. ALGOL60, PL/1, BASIC and others were all being used, but they only accounted for a small percentage of the programs written in a higher level language. Today the situation is far more diverse. Pascal and its derivatives are making major inroads in academic and microprocessor use. PL/1 usage has increased substantially. The successful UNIX operating system has given us a cadre of programmers who know their (A, B and) C. APL continues to attract a devoted body of followers who use it to solve every type of computing task. And, many other languages continue to be used. To further compound this diversity, new languages loom on the horizon with the definite possibility of their becoming very important. I'm thinking in particular of the new U.S. Department of Defense sponsored language called Ada. The Tower of Babel of '69 which seemed to capture our sense of frustration over the proliferation of languages has today grown even larger. Thus, it becomes ever more essential that when we study the subject of programming languages we concentrate on the fundamental concepts and issues.

Is a comparative study of programming languages possible? The imperative programming language has now been with us for over 25 years. Many of its concepts are well-understood. Other concepts, though still controversial, assume a very similar form when the decision is made to incorporate them into a language. Thus, it is possible to present a great deal about these languages in an analytical manner. Other concepts such as exception handling and concurrency are newer and hence less well-understood. A treatment of these topics can only hope to present the issues and point out the strengths and weaknesses of existing language features which support these concepts, but it cannot provide all the answers.

Though much work has been done on imperative programming languages, one must not overlook the area of functional programming languages. As a radically different model of programming they *must* be studied. Moreover, the continuing success of LISP indicates that programming languages based on these ideas have practical as well as theoretical merit. Nevertheless, the bulk of the research on and development of programming languages has been in the imperative school and that is necessarily reflected here.

This book follows the guidelines which were stated by the ACM Curriculum Committee for the design of the course CS 8, "Organization of Programming Languages." See the *Communications of the ACM*, March 1979 for complete details. It is appropriate for undergraduate computer science majors who have had one year of programming. Knowledge of Pascal is desirable, but PL/1, ALGOL60, ALGOL68 or something similar are adequate substitutes. The book has also been used successfully in a first year graduate course whose objective was to survey the important features of current languages.

I have taught a course based on this book to two different audiences. The first group consisted of sophomores and juniors with Pascal and data structures in their background. I had a lab in which the instructors first taught PL/1 and then LISP. Programming exercises were included. In the lectures I worked straight through the book, selecting many of my examples from PL/1 and Pascal. I recently replaced PL/1 by Ada. The second group consisted of seniors and graduate students in computer science. There was no laboratory. Instead each student was given responsibility for a different aspect of a programming language. For example one student presented an overview of Ada, another discussed Ada packages and another Ada tasks. There were Pascal, APL, ALGOL68 and Euclid experts and they all lectured on the salient features of their respective programming languages. By working closely with each student I felt I was able to maintain a consistently high level of presentation.

When discussing a programming language, it often becomes essential to refer to its defining document. This caused me to put together a set of language reference manuals for my classes. In addition I found it educational and entertaining to include a variety of articles by well-known researchers. This effort eventually led me to produce an anthology of source material which I am publishing jointly with this text.

It is called *Programming Languages: A Grand Tour.* It contains some classic papers such as the "ALGOL60 report," some controversial papers such as "Can Programming be Liberated from the von Neumann Style?" by John Backus, plus overviews of Pascal, Concurrent-Pascal, Ada, MODULA, C, ALGOL68, CLU, Euclid, FORTRAN77, LISP, and APL. In addition it contains the complete language reference manuals for Ada, ALGOL60, ALGOL-W, C, and MODULA. I hope the reader and instructor will find the anthology a useful reference and adjunct to this text.

A few sentences about Ada seem appropriate. During the time I was writing this book, I watched Ada grow from a requirements document to a standardized programming language. As I studied the language, I began to incorporate it into my classes. Now I observe that many of my examples come from Ada. My main justification is because Ada is one of the very few languages which has included, in some way, most of the language features I wish to discuss. Therefore, it provides a common thread for examples. This use of Ada caused me to reprint the entire Ada language reference manual in the accompanying anthology. Ada will doubtlessly gain a significant share of the programming language market. Its use here is not an endorsement, but the recognition of its scope and its growing importance.

Many people have contributed their efforts to the improvement of this book and I would like to acknowledge their assistance. Of primary help were the students who attended my classes at USC and at the Technion in Israel. John Guttag and Barbara Liskov of MIT through their own course on programming languages were an inspiration. Several people provided in-depth reviews including Richard Gillmann, Paul Hilfinger, David Jefferson, and Richard Schwartz. Their insights supplied a great deal of guidance to me for which I am grateful. Students Alfons Kemper, Georg Raeder, Simon Wegner, and Ronald Williamson also supplied helpful remarks. Brian Reid and Ray Bates helped me with the text preparation system, Scribe. And I thank USC's Information Sciences Institute for access to their facilities.

The study of programming languages is fascinating but not easy. I hope that this book sets people looking and thinking in the right direction.

Numerous suggestions for improvements have been incorporated into this new edition. Thanks go to David Watt, Ira Steven, and to anonymous reviewers.

Ellis Horowitz
University of Southern California
1983

ACKNOWLEDGMENTS

I would like to officially acknowledge and thank the following people and organizations for granting me permission to reprint various programs and algorithms: Table 1-2 comes from [Knuth 78] and is reprinted by permission of the author. Table 6-9 comes from [Johnston 71], reprinted by permission from the author; Table 7-6 reprinted by permission of the author Bob Schwanke; Tables 8-6 and 8-7 come from [Chang 78] reprinted by permission of the authors; Table 9-3 comes from [Liskov 79] and is reprinted by permission of the author; Table 10-4 comes from [Holt 78] and is reprinted by permission of the author; Table 10-5 comes from [Brinch-Hansen 75] and is reprinted by permission of the author; the three examples of VAL programs come from [Dennis 79] and are reprinted by permission of the author; Tables 9-3, 7-7, 10-10, 11-6 and 11-8 all come from [Ada 80]. Figure 1-4 was originally conceived and appeared as the front cover of the Jan. 1961 issue of *C.ACM* and is reprinted by their permission; Figure 7-4 comes from [Jensen-Wirth 74]; Table 12-1 comes from LISP] reprinted by permission of the author.

Chapter 1

THE EVOLUTION OF
PROGRAMMING LANGUAGES

"And the Lord said, 'Behold, they are one people, and they have all
one language; and this is only the beginning of what they will do.'"
Genesis 11:6

A *programming language* is a systematic notation by which we describe
computational processes to others. By a computational process I mean
nothing more than a set of steps which a machine can perform for
solving a task. To describe the solution of a problem to a computer, we
need to know a set of commands that the computer can understand and
execute. Given the diversity of tasks that computers can do today,
people naturally find it surprising that the computer's built-in abilities
are so primitive. When a computer comes off the assembly line, it will
usually be able to do only arithmetic and logical operations, input and
output, and some "control" functions. These capabilities constitute the
machine language of the computer. But because this language is so far
away from the way people think and want to describe solutions to
problems, so-called *high-level programming languages* have been
conceived. These languages use less primitive notations than machine
language, and hence, they require a program which will interpret their
meaning to the computer. This program is not generally part of the
computer's circuitry, but is provided as part of the *system software* which
is included with the computer. The purpose of this book is to study
how these programming languages are designed to meet the needs of

the human and the machine.

The concept of a programming language is relatively new, and it is rather surprising that there is almost no early historical evidence of the development of notations for computational processes. Over many centuries, mathematicians have developed highly sophisticated notations for describing static, functional relationships. The well-known binomial theorem or the famous Fourier transform are just two examples. But as far as is known, no formal notation for describing computational processes was ever devised until modern times. As we shall see, natural language and an informal style were usually adopted whenever a need would arise.

The development of the modern digital computer has given a great stimulus to the development of notations for processes. Thus a programming language is usually taken to mean a notation for describing computational processes to a computer. But as people must create and modify their programs and read the programs written by others, a programming language must be intelligible to human and machine alike.

It would be convenient if I could use a single programming language to describe all of the concepts I wish to discuss. However, this is infeasible because no single language contains all of the essential elements in the proper form. Therefore, throughout this book I will feel free to mention features of different languages whenever it seems appropriate. However there are two languages which will be used repeatedly. These are Pascal and Ada. Recently Pascal has become the *lingua franca* or common tongue of the computer science academic community. Moreover it is a language which has been very successful at integrating a small set of features into a powerful and efficient programming tool. The second language from which I will draw many examples is Ada. To some this might seem premature, for as I am writing this, there is not a single Ada compiler generally available. Nevertheless, the documentation for Ada is readily available, [Ada 79ab, 80], and new Ada primers are being published at a rapid pace. One does not have to know Ada in advance to read this book, and in fact a study of this book will serve in part as a primer for the Ada language. As Ada contains virtually all of the features which are considered essential in a modern programming language, it makes sense in the '80s to use it for examples.

In Chapter 2 we will launch into the controversial subject of how to judge the quality of a programming language. But first it will be instructive to examine at least a brief history of the development of programming languages in order that we might better understand the recent progress that has been made and the situation we find ourselves in today.

1.1. Early History

The earliest known algorithms were discovered written on clay tablets which were unearthed by archaeologists. These tablets date between 1500-3000 B.C.,and so they are approximately 3,500 to 5,000 years old. They were found in the area called Mesopotamia (Iraq) near the ancient city of Babylon, which is near the modern city of Baghdad. The Babylonians used the sexagesimal number system, radix 60, and from their work came our current notions about hours, minutes and seconds. They also used a form of floating point notation so that the three digit sexagesimal number 8, 50, 36 could stand for

$$8 \times 60^2 + 50 \times 60 + 36 = 31,836$$

or for

$$8 \times 60 + 50 + 36/60 = 530.6$$

or in general for

$$8 \times 60^k + 50 \times 60^{k-1} + 36 \times 60^{k-2} = 31,386 \times 60^{k-2}$$

Using base 60, multiplication and division can be done fairly easily, and estimating the magnitude within a factor of sixty is not too hard.

In addition to producing mathematical tables, the Babylonians could solve algebraic equations. They did this by giving an "algorithm" which computed the solution. Interspersed among the algorithm's steps were calculations on actual numbers, even though the algorithm was a general one. At the end they placed the phrase loosely translated as "This is the procedure." This is perhaps the first appearance of a programming language notation.

Their algorithms did not however have conditional tests such as "if x < 0 then branch" because the Babylonians did not know about negative numbers or even about zero. To express more than one possibility they would repeat the algorithm as many times as was needed. Algorithms which involved iteration were expanded out for several steps until the given problem was solved. Donald Knuth in his article on ancient Babylonian algorithms, [Knuth 72], gives an account of several of these. One example is given here (slightly altered) from his paper:

"One shekel has been invested; after how many years will

the interest be equal to the initial capital?

You should proceed as follows:Compound the interest for
eight years. The combined total (capital and interest)
exceeds 2 shekels. What can the excess of this total
over the capital plus interest for three years be
multiplied by in order to give the four total minus 2?
8, 50, 36 (months). From four years subtract 8, 50, 36
months, to obtain the desired number of full years and days.

This is the procedure."

The problem is to find out how long it takes to double your
investment in units which were used in biblical times. The example
assumes an interest rate of 10%. Since

$$1.95 = 1.1^7 < 2 < 1.1^8 = 2.14$$

the answer lies somewhere between 7 and 8. The Babylonians realized
that in any year the growth is linear, so they used interpolation to get
the number of months less than four years using the formula

$$12(1.1^8 - 2)/(1.1^8 - 1.2^7) = 8.84$$

which is, in sexagesimal 8, 50, 36 or just the number given in the
algorithm. The general procedure that the Babylonians were describing
consists of forming powers of $1+r$, where r is the interest rate until you
find the first value of n: $(1+r)^n > 2$. Then calculate

$$diff = 12((1+r)^n - 2)/((1+r)^n-(1+r)^{n-1})$$

and the answer is "n years minus *diff* months."

Though other ancient people developed advanced mathematical
concepts and notation, no one improved upon the Babylonians for
developing a notation which could be used to describe computational
processes. But one other person worth mentioning in this section is
Euclid, who lived in Greece about 300 B.C. In his *Elements*, Book 7,
Propositions 1 and 2, Euclid states an algorithm for computing the
greatest common divisor of two integers. Though his method was given
fifteen hundred years after the Babylonian tracts were made, it has
become known as the oldest algorithm. To describe it, Euclid used his
native language. Because zero was still not recognized and even the
number one was not regarded as a legitimate divisor, Euclid was forced
to duplicate his method to handle these special cases. The algorithm in

English, but as Euclid originally proposed it,can be found in [Knuth 69].
Though the algorithm included iteration, its form progressed very little
over the Babylonians' as a notation for describing computational
processes. More importantly, its use was merely an isolated instance,
rather than a step in a continuing process of development of a formal
notation for expressing algorithms.

1.2. Early Modern History

The next group of researchers we examine are those 19th and early
20th century scientists who were interested in machines for
computation.

The first of these is Charles Babbage (1792-1871) who,between 1820
and 1850,designed two machines for computation. One relied on the
theory of finite differences and so he called it his *Difference Engine.* The
other embodied many of the principles of a modern digital computer,
and this he called his *Analytical Engine.* Neither of these machines was
ever completed, but remnants of both can be seen today at the Science
Museum in London. Figure 1-1 shows part of the latter device. The
Analytical Engine had an architecture which was remarkably similar to
today's computers, as can be seen in Figure 1-2.

One concept it lacked was the idea of a stored program, i.e., the
program and data both being kept in the computer's memory. Instead
there existed variable cards and operation cards which were input and
caused the machine to operate. Programs were written by placing on
operation cards a sequence of desired operations and placing the data on
the variable cards. In essence programs were written in machine
language. One of the people who collaborated with Babbage was Ada
Augusta, Countess of Lovelace, the daughter of the famous poet Lord
Byron. She has recently been recognized as the first programmer and
the new programming language,developed under the sponsorship of the
United States Defense Department,is named in her honor, [Ada 80].

Figure 1-3 shows a program written by her for Babbage's Analytical
Engine. The problem is:Given m, n, d, m', n', d',determine the values
of x, y, which satisfy the two linear equations

$$mx + ny = d$$
$$m'x + n'y = d'$$

The answers are easily verified to be

$$x = (dn'-d'n)/(mn'-m'n) \quad y = (d'm-dm')/(mn'-m'n)$$

Courtesy of IBM Corp.

Figure 1-1: The "Mill" for Babbage's Analytical Engine

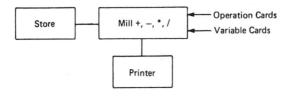

Figure 1-2: Schematic Architecture of Babbage's Analytical Engine

In Figure 1-3 we see the program that Lady Lovelace wrote to solve this problem. First, one sees three types of variables: the variables containing the input, the working variables and the result variables. The variables v0, v1, v2, v3, v4, v5 are respectively assigned the input values m, n, d, m', n', d'. Variables v6 - v14 are used for temporary storage while v15 and v16 are used for the results. Each operation is numbered, in this case 1, 2,..., 11, and the corresponding operation appears in the second column. Whenever the value of a variable is used, that value is restored to the variable unless it is perceived that it will be used no longer. In the latter case, a zero is substituted. At the end of the program, every column should contain a zero except for the result variables. We see that variable v0 = m is changed to zero after operation 5 and that v11 = dm' is set to zero after operation 9.

Another interesting facet of the Countess' program is her use of superscripts on the variables v0,...,v16. These superscripts indicate the number of changes in value that a variable has undergone. Each new value causes the superscript to be increased by one, but a zero value causes the superscript to also become zero. But if this variable now assumes a nonzero value, its new superscript is not one, but resumes at one more than its previous nonzero value. To determine how often any single quantity is used during the program, one need only scan its column. In Figure 1-3 we see that all the input data and temporary storage is used twice except for mn' - m'n, which is used three times.

When one reads the works of Babbage and Countess Lovelace, it is clear that they grasped the immense potential of their invention. Anticipating the field of study we now call *analysis of algorithms*, Countess Lovelace stated

"In almost every computation a great variety of arrangements for the succession of the processes is possible, and various considerations must influence the selections amongst them for the purposes of a

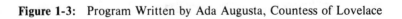

Figure 1-3: Program Written by Ada Augusta, Countess of Lovelace

calculating engine. One essential object is to choose that arrangement which shall tend to reduce to a minimum the time necessary for completing the calculation."

The above quote and the example program came from Note D of "Sketch of the analytical engine invented by Charles Babbage" by L.F. Menabrea, by Ada Augusta, Countess of Lovelace.Reprinted in *Charles Babbage and His Calculating Engines*, edited by Philip and Emily Morrison, Dover, N.Y., 1961.

A Leap Forward

The 1930s and 1940s witnessed a creative explosion in programming notations. Some of these were theoretical in the sense that they were not intended to be used for actual calculations on a real computer. Table 1-1 mentions just a few.

> Zuse's Plan Calculus
> Turing's Turing Machine
> Church's Lambda Calculus
> Aiken's Mark I
> Von Neumann's Flow Diagrams

Table 1-1: Early Pioneers of Programming Language Notations

Many others did important work, and some even developed compilers for their languages. However, it was not popular at that time to give names to their languages. Knuth and Trabb-Pardo in "The Early Development of Programming Languages," [Knuth 78], give an excellent introduction to the work of these people and show how a "typical" program might have looked if coded by the various language developers. Unfortunately most of this research was unknown to the early developers of the modern digital computer.

1.3. FORTRAN and ALGOL60

As this is an abbreviated history, we now jump forward in time to the middle 1950s and the development of FORTRAN. A group at IBM in New York headed by John Backus was investigating the possibility of a so-called algebraic language translator. The great question in many people's minds at that time was not whether such a language could be designed and compiled, but if it would be terribly inefficient. This concern had a great impact on the design of the language, and today we find that, as a result, many FORTRAN compilers generate very efficient code. FORTRAN 0 (for FORmula TRANslation) was first designed about 1954, followed by two and one-half years of building the compiler. It was not the FORTRAN we know today. There were no FORMAT statements and no user defined functions. The conditional statement had the form

IF(cond) TRUE, FALSE

where TRUE and FALSE were replaced by statement labels. Variables of at most two characters were allowed, which was an innovation for its time.

As the compiler for FORTRAN 0 was nearing completion, FORTRAN I and FORTRAN II were being designed. FORTRAN, [Backus 57], once it was released, soon became immensely popular, in large measure due to IBM's sponsorship, who supplied it for free. In fact, the language became so firmly entrenched that no one imagined how difficult it would be to move the programming community to the newer and (possibly) better languages which would soon be developed.

In Knuth and Trabb-Pardo's excellent article on early programming languages, they hypothesize what a typical program would have been like and how it would have looked. In Table 1-2 we have borrowed their FORTRAN II and ALGOL60 versions. Their program doesn't do very much, but it involves looping, arrays and subscripting, a function, and input/output and, therefore, shows many of the salient features of the language.

In the FORTRAN version many of the characteristic features of modern day FORTRAN are clearly visible.

□ There is a set of fixed fields, including columns 1-5 for the label, 6 for continuation, 7-72 for the statement, and 73-80 for an optional sequence number.

□ Typing is implicit; all variables whose name begins with I, J, K, L, M or N are assumed to be of type INTEGER and otherwise they are of type REAL.

□ The arithmetic IF statement provides for branches on negative, zero or positive.

□ The DO statement existed but by today's standards had several peculiarities and limitations including: it always executed once, it could only count up, and limits had to be either constants or simple integer variables. The new ANSI 77 FORTRAN standard has improved on all of these deficiencies.

□ FORMAT statements gave control over input/output and introduced the use of the H for (Hollerith) character strings.

□ A feature for commenting was provided.

In Table 1-2(b) we see the same procedure written in ALGOL60. Here we see many concepts of modern programming languages appearing for the first time.

□ No fixed fields but free format was adopted.

□ Certain identifiers were reserved and indicated by boldface; in fact a publication language was defined which helped ALGOL60 to become for many years the only language in which algorithms were communicated in the literature.

□ Explicit typing of all identifiers was required.

□ A considerably more general iteration statement was adopted.

□ The concept of block structure was introduced permitting a close association between variables and the text which uses them.

□ Character constants delimited by quotes were allowed, and many other features were introduced such as recursive procedures, value parameters, call-by-name, and dynamic array bounds.

ALGOL-Like Languages

It is hard today to appreciate the substantial influence that ALGOL60 had on the community of people interested in programming languages. The ALGOL60 report, [Naur 63], took the form of a holy document which was carefully scrutinized, analyzed, but rarely modified. Perhaps the strongest indication of this influence was the term *ALGOL-like* which was soon applied to many subsequent language developments. To be ALGOL-like was to be O.K.; it served to say that this new language, at least in spirit, adopted the major features of ALGOL60, and possibly (but not always) improved upon them. In textbooks and research articles which communicated new algorithms, the description language might be informal but was almost certainly ALGOL-like. So, one might well ask: what are the characteristics which make a language ALGOL-like? There are six features which seem pertinent to answering this question.

□ It should be an algorithmic language for describing computational processes;

□ It is imperative, i.e. the algorithm is conveyed as a sequence of changes to the store;

```
C   A HYPOTHETICAL PROGRAM IN FORTRAN
    FUNF(T) = SQRTF(ABSF(T)) + 5.0*T**3
    DIMENSION A(11)
1   FORMAT(6F12.4)
    READ 1,A
    DO 10 J = 1,11
    I = 11-J
    Y = FUNF(A(I+1))
    IF(400.0-Y)4,8,8
4   PRINT 5,I
5   FORMAT(I10, 10H TOO LARGE)
GO TO 10
8   PRINT 9,I,Y
9   FORMAT(I10, F12.7)
10    CONTINUE
    STOP
```

(a) A Typical FORTRAN Program

```
begin integer i, real y; real array a[0:10]
  real procedure f(t);  real t; value t;
      f := sqrt(abs(t)) + 5 x t ↑ 3;
  for i := 0 step 1 until 10 do read(a[i]);
  for i := 10 step -1 until 0 do
      begin y := f(a[i]);
          if y > 400 then write(i, 'too large')
                     else write(i,y)
      end
end
```

(b) A Typical ALGOL60 Program

Table 1-2:   The Same Program Written in FORTRAN II and ALGOL60

[Knuth 78]

▫The basic units of computation are the block and the procedure;

☐ It has the notion of type and type checking;

☐ It uses the lexical scoping rule;

☐ It assumes compilation.

It is not fruitful to speculate for long on why ALGOL60 failed to become more widely used. Surely its lack of standard input/output and its use of the call-by-name parameter passing mechanism served to discredit it. IBM's lack of support also played a role. From today's point of view we can observe some of the language's weaknesses. One lack is the inadequate type checking system. Another is the inability to define new types such as is done today using, for example, a record feature. A single change in the program causes the entire program to be re-compiled. There is no abstraction mechanism for data as there is for control (the procedure). The scope rules prevent one from adding a facility such as a string processing package and making it generally available without enclosing everything else in the same block. Nevertheless, for the decade of the '60s, ALGOL60 remained the dominant standard with which all subsequent languages were compared.

1.4. The Stormy '60s

In the early 1960s as the notion of a compiler was developed and many translation problems were solved, an exponential growth in new programming languages resulted. According to Jean Sammet, a chronicler of this period, "Over two hundred languages were developed over the next decade, but only thirteen of them ever became significant either in terms of concept or usage." This explosion of languages and dialects led to the now famous programming language *Tower of Babel* which appeared on the cover of Sammet's book, (see Figure 1-4).

In 1959 the U.S. Department of Defense began to perceive the need for a single language which would be used by all of the military branches. They convened a group of professionals from government, industry and private consultants to design such a language. In late 1959 the COmmon Business Oriented Language, or COBOL was designed and named. By late 1960, working COBOL compilers were produced by RCA and Remington-Rand-Univac. The cooperation between government and industry proved to be a powerful force favoring the acceptance of COBOL by the computer-user community. During the '60s and '70s it was believed (though unproven) that the majority of programs written in a higher level language were done in COBOL,

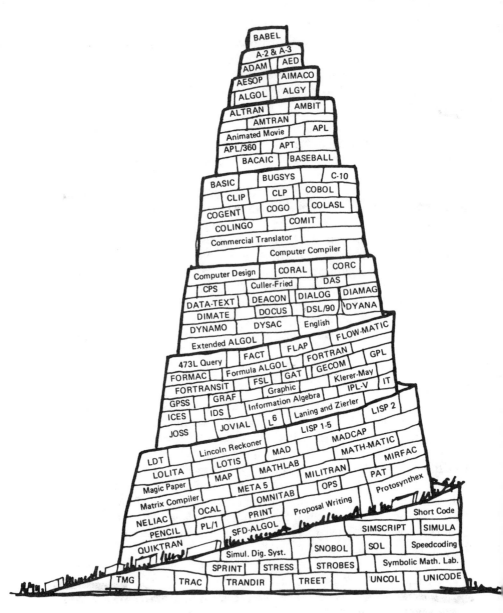

Figure 1-4: Tower of Babel

Concept of the Tower of Babel to represent a large set of
programming languages is due to *C.ACM*, a publication of ACM.

[COBOL 72].

COBOL introduced several new concepts into the field of language design. One is the idea of a data description (the so-called DATA division) which is machine independent. This in turn led to the concept of database management systems. A general IF-THEN-ELSE statement was provided, as was the concept of noise words to improve readability. There was the desire to provide a language which made significant use of English so that non-technical people could understand programs. Thus one can write

SUBTRACT COSTS FROM GROSS-SALES GIVING NET-INCOME

which is equivalent in COBOL to

COMPUTE NET-INCOME = GROSS-SALES - COSTS

In the late 1950s, programming languages were developed for a well-defined application. FORTRAN and ALGOL60 were said to be languages for describing numeric computations. COBOL claimed business data processing as its chief domain of application. But over time, people came to realize that many computing tasks were common to all applications. Thus, ALGOL60, FORTRAN, COBOL and subsequent languages came to be known as *general purpose*, meaning that they were considered to be satisfactory for solving a wide variety of programming problems. Of course, all of these languages are *universal*, i.e. capable of computing all computable functions. But that is not really the point. Experience showed that a programming language designed for a special purpose would soon be asked to describe a much broader range of computations. Thus, the '60s saw designers move from the development of special purpose to general purpose programming languages.

Though FORTRAN and COBOL became the standard languages for scientific and commercial applications, ALGOL60 continued to inspire further language experimentation. Two ALGOL-like languages of great interest were ALGOL-W and Euler, both developed by Niklaus Wirth, [Wirth 66, 66b]. ALGOL-W experimented with a new parameter passing method called value-result, and introduced the **case** statement, records and pointers. Euler tried to promote procedures as objects and introduced the technique of simple precedence parsing. Wirth's later attempt at an ALGOL-like language, Pascal, was destined to become the most successful of these three languages.

In the early '60s a language totally unrelated to ALGOL60 was developed by Dr. Kenneth Iverson at IBM, [Iverson 62]. His goal was to devise a powerful, yet compact notation for computation which incorporated many concepts from mathematics. His language was described in a now famous book called *A Programming Language* (Wiley, 1962). For many years the language remained strictly on paper, at least partly due to its nonstandard character set, (see Section 3.1). In the mid-60s Iverson, Falkoff and others used APL to formally describe the new IBM/360 family of computers. This success and other factors eventually led to an implementation of the language. This first implementation caused many new questions to be addressed, such as how to express the language as a sequence of characters, what character set to use, the scope of names, and how formally to define a function; see [Falkoff 73]. Once again the APL language evolved and today a great many implementations are flourishing. Despite the fact that APL violates many of the sacred tenets of modern programming theory, it has proved itself to be a very robust and versatile language.

Another language development which was not in the ALGOL60 style was begun in the late 1950s by John McCarthy and his fellow workers at MIT. McCarthy was a member of the ALGOL60 design committee and so it is surprising that his creation LISP, [McCarthy 60, McCarthy 65], was so radically different. The application domain for LISP was to be artificial intelligence. Problems from this research area motivated McCarthy and his coworkers to design a conceptually simple language for handling symbolic expressions. Their result introduced many new concepts into programming languages. They devised a uniform representation for data and programs, the so-called S-expression. They introduced a new form of the conditional expression, the use of prefix form for operators, and recursion as the fundamental control structure. Garbage collection was adopted in preference to explicit erasure or reference counting. And they eschewed the notion of side-effect which is so central to imperative programming languages. Why has LISP survived for so long? The question is not easily answerable. Surely the use of recursive conditional expressions, the list as the unifying data structure, and the uniformity of data and program account in part for its success. Moreover, its compact and clear semantics make it an ideal tool for studying programming. Of course, most of the versions of LISP which are in use today offer variables and side-effects. Despite many attempts at a successor, no one has been able to come up with an improved blend of features. All this makes LISP an indispensable object of study in any book on programming languages, and we will investigate it closely in Chapter 12.

Another language which was developed outside the ALGOL60 tradition is SNOBOL, developed by Farber, Griswold, and Polonsky while they were at Bell Telephone Laboratories in the mid-60s, [SNOBOL 64]. Their idea was to design a language whose main strength was in processing string data. The language they produced was somewhat unusual in form, but contains many sophisticated and powerful string processing facilities. The language was modified in versions SNOBOL2 and SNOBOL3 and its present form, SNOBOL4, was given an excellent macro implementation which helped it to spread further. Its use was then encouraged by an excellently written primer, *The SNOBOL4 Programming Language* by Griswold, Poage, and Polonsky (Prentice-Hall, 2nd ed., 1971).

With FORTRAN and COBOL firmly entrenched and APL dormant, IBM in the mid-60s launched a major language design effort. This new language, PL/1, was to be the replacement for FORTRAN and COBOL and would be ready in time for IBM's new family of computers, the 360 line. Borrowing from FORTRAN, COBOL and ALGOL60, the language included block structure, recursive procedures, and COBOL-like structures (records). Also, it introduced two major concepts which had not yet appeared in any major programming language. The first was an exception handling facility. This allowed the programmer to associate commands with particular predefined and unusual conditions. If a command is enabled and its corresponding condition arises, then normal processing is temporarily halted and control is transferred to another part of the program. Conditions such as divide-by-zero, arithmetic overflow, or arithmetic underflow are typical examples. We will discuss exception handling in Chapter 9. A second major new feature was called multi-tasking. It was an attempt to inject features for describing parallelism. This idea has recently been worked on a great deal, and it is discussed in Chapter 10.

As the second half of the '60s arrived, the language SIMULA was appearing, [Dahl-Nygaard 66, Dahl 68b]. Developed by Dahl and Nygaard in Norway, this language was ALGOL60 based and had simulation as a major application domain. One important feature which it introduced was the *class* concept. Here a group of declarations and procedures are collected together and treated as a unit. Objects of the class can be generated, and they have a life which is independent of the block in which they were created. This is especially useful for applications involving simulation. The class concept is now viewed as the father (or mother) of data abstraction, the topic dealt with in Chapter 8.

The graph in Figure 1-5 shows the ancestry of some well-known programming languages. One sees that there are two large trees plus a lot of small bushes. All of the languages which have FORTRAN as

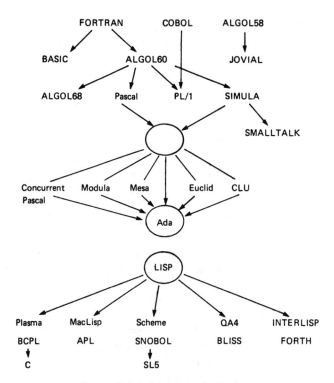

Figure 1-5: Language Pedigrees

their root, plus COBOL, are called *imperative*. An imperative language is one which achieves its primary effect by changing the state of variables by assignment. All of these languages have in common a fundamental dependence upon variables which contain values and assignment of values to variables, usually by an explicit assignment operator. Backus, in his Turing lecture [Backus 78], has pointed out that the design of these languages was largely influenced by the underlying von Neumann machine they were to be run on. By this he means that the architecture of a single central processing unit coupled to a memory led obviously to associating memory locations with variable names. Collectively, the variables describe the state of computation at any point in time. This idea of how to do computing has become so widely accepted that many people cannot imagine doing it any other way.

The second group of languages, which includes LISP, is called *applicative*. An applicative language is one which achieves its primary effect by applying functions either recursively or through composition. The result of these functional applications are values which are (hopefully) the answers we are expecting. For the past twenty-five years, imperative languages have received the most attention. That fact is reflected in the outline of this book, which spends a major portion of its time discussing language design issues for imperative languages. Perhaps the next decade will see a swing of interest towards applicative languages, for many believe that they are better suited to exploit the vast potential of computing power offered by the new, cheap computing hardware.

Why don't the imperative languages allow us to exploit the potential of parallel computation? They are intrinsically designed for sequential execution. And why haven't the newer imperative languages led to substantial gains in programming productivity? The fundamental reason is that too much of the programmer's effort is spent on keeping track of the variables which comprise the state of the program. This need to focus on the variables comes from the one word-at-a-time processing of von Neumann machines. To see this better consider how a von Neumann machine must add the values of two variables and store the result in a third. It must

□ retrieve the address of variable one from memory;
□ retrieve the value at the address of variable one;
□ retrieve the address of variable two from memory;
□ retrieve the value at the address of variable two;
□ add the two numbers;
□ retrieve the address of variable three from memory;

☐ store the result into the memory at the address of variable three.

Thus, a simple addition requires an overhead of six trips to the memory.   This example points out the fact that a great deal of information has to cross the line between the central processing unit and the memory for real computation to be done.   This is one view of what Backus has called the *von-Neumann bottleneck.*   At the programmer's level, the bottleneck appears to be due to the fact that there are too few ways to operate on more than just single variables. More about this topic in the next chapter.

In order for any new form of computer architecture to be successful, it must have a programming language which is natural for the user while producing efficient programs.   Several new models of computing which naturally incorporate parallelism have appeared together with supporting programming languages,   in particular Arvind and Gostelow's work [Arvind 77a, 77b], Backus' Functional Programming Systems [Backus 78], and Dennis' dataflow language, VAL, [Dennis 79].

Returning to the evolution of imperative programming languages, there seem to be only a few general categories under which we can group all of the facilities for describing data and flow of control; see [Horning 79b].   The first of these is the *ability to join together* a list of statements.   These statements may be either so-called declarations or executable statements. In ALGOL60, the **begin-end** is the means for accomplishing this process.   The second category is a means for *describing groups of data.*   Typical facilities in a modern programming language would include arrays and records.   The third category would be mechanisms for *describing flow of control.*   In pure-LISP, the two mechanisms are the conditional statement and recursion.   Modern imperative programming languages include some form of these features and, in addition, they contain several forms of iteration such as a **while** and **for** statement.   Another form of control flow would be an exception handling facility.   A fourth concept is a *mechanism for abstraction.*   The procedure is the classical form of abstraction.   A more recent form of abstraction unit is the package of Ada.   Here is an attempt to group together a data abstraction as a set of related declarations and procedures.   The final major category of imperative programming languages is the *concurrency facility.*   This implies a means for delineating processes plus methods for synchronizing communication between processes and for nondeterministic choosing between alternatives.

The evolution of the imperative programming language has led to the refinement of these five basic categories and their incorporation into a single language. ALGOL60 led the way with **begin-end** for grouping, **if-then-else** for selection, **for** and **for-while** for iteration, and procedures for abstraction. PL/1 followed, adding structures as a form of data encapsulation and features for exception handling. Ada has developed tasks for concurrency, packages for abstract data types, and has a complete range of facilities satisfying all of the other categories.

The Coming of Pascal

After the ALGOL60 development committee finished its work, responsibility for the language was turned over to the IFIP Working Group 2.1. That group continued to refine the specifications of the language and subsequently released a document which makes mostly minor changes to the language and clears up a number of confusions and ambiguities; see [de Morgan 76a]. One consequence of these modifications is that the new version of ALGOL60 is now closer to most existing implementations, [de Morgan 76b]. Soon after the development of ALGOL60, this IFIP working group decided to begin work on a successor to ALGOL60, one which would be far better and not perpetuate the mistakes of the earlier attempt. The result of this effort first appeared as a report in 1968, and the language was termed ALGOL68, [van Wijngaarden 68]. It was immediately perceived to be a substantially different language than ALGOL60. More importantly, there was a substantial dissenting minority report from the committee which protested the publication of the ALGOL68 report in 1968. Many of them insisted that the report was too difficult to be read and understood, even by accomplished programmers. Hindsight has proven this objection to be correct. A revised report was worked on and was eventually released in 1975. Nevertheless ALGOL68 introduced many new and interesting concepts and showed how the principles of generality and orthogonality (see Chapter 2 for an explanation) could be applied to a language design. One of the dissenting members of the ALGOL68 committee was Niklaus Wirth, who went on to produce another language of his own called Pascal.

The Pascal design goals centered around the idea of providing a few, nicely integrated features which were compilable into efficient code. These two design goals were admirably achieved. Other facets of Pascal which made it attractive were its data structuring facilities, in particular its user defined data types. Another attractive feature was that Pascal was given an axiomatic definition by Hoare and Wirth [Hoare-Wirth 71]. The growing software crisis and the interest in program verification made Pascal the obvious candidate for talking about such issues.

Of course, even Pascal has blemishes. On the negative side, aliasing (see Chapter 4 for a definition) is possible. The use of pointers, though improved over PL/1, still offers dangerous possibilities, and the typing system has some anomalies (see Chapter 5). For example, all enumerated types are ordered even when it makes no sense to be. Or all types which are subranges of integers are considered to be integers. And complete compile time type checking is not possible, in part due to Pascal's treatment of variant records. The lack of dynamic array bounds is a source of unhappiness. But, of course, many new Pascal implementations have corrected many of these faults.

This concludes the section on the 1960s. For far more historical detail on the development of languages in the '50s-'60s, one should consult the "Proceedings of the History of Programming Languages Conference," *ACM SIGPLAN Notices*, ACM, Los Angeles, June 1978. See also its hard cover version in the ACM Monograph Series, Academic Press, edited by Wexelblat.

1.5. Advances in the '70s
The 1970s have seen no abatement in the development of programming languages. But whereas the '50s and '60s witnessed a wide diversity in programming languages, spanning ALGOL60, LISP, APL and SNOBOL, the '70s have seemed to concentrate on improvements to the basic imperative programming language style. Of course, there are exceptions to this statement. Scanning some of the names of the languages of the 70s, we see EL1, CLU, Concurrent-Pascal, MESA, Euclid, MODULA, SMALLTALK, and most recently, Ada.

As any good historian knows, it becomes very hard to analyze objectively the very recent past. Taking this advice to heart, I will shift to a discussion of three major trends in programming language development during this period.

The first trend has been the development of the abstract data type. The concept of procedure was developed early as the appropriate mechanism for abstracting an algorithm. A suitable mechanism for abstracting data was invented more recently. It appeared first in the class concept of the language SIMULA, and it was later incorporated, in various forms, in CLU, Euclid, MODULA, and Ada. This concept is both a way of thinking about software design and a feature of a programming language. Here we will be interested in the latter. We will look at how this feature has been incorporated into these languages, hoping to understand the semantics of the construct and the reasons for any differences between languages. An abstract data type feature in a programming language introduces many issues of semantics, especially issues of scope and type.

The second trend has been the development of exception handling features. These were available in PL/1 which offered essentially an interrupt-branch-and-return facility. Subsequent debate has centered around how normal processing should be continued and how to contain the scope of objects after an exception has been raised. Ada and CLU offer carefully thought-out exception handling facilities, [Ada 79b, Liskov 79b].

The third trend has been the incorporation of features for describing parallel processing. Real-time applications form a very significant part of computing from the development of operating systems, process control systems, airline reservations systems, etc. Languages which intend to support the development of these applications must first permit the programmer to define programs which can be executed simultaneously. These are typically called processes. One of the major issues for the language designer is to provide a means whereby processes can synchronize. One early suggestion for a language feature to control synchronization was made by Edsger Dijkstra who suggested the semaphore concept [Dijkstra 68b]. This idea was followed by the monitor concept of Brinch-Hansen [Brinch-Hansen 73] and Hoare [Hoare 74]. Brinch-Hansen included the idea in his language Concurrent-Pascal. More recently C.A.R. Hoare proposed an approach to synchronization based upon message passing in his paper "Communicating Sequential Processes," *CACM*, 1978. MODULA and Ada are two newer languages with features for describing concurrency which follow the idea of message passing.

The Birth of Ada

The birth of a new programming language is rarely celebrated far beyond the immediate family. But, when the sponsor of the language is the largest consumer of computers in the world, then it becomes a major event. The United States Department of Defense, in the mid-1970s decided to sponsor the development of a new programming language. The goal of the language was to support the programming of *embedded computer systems.* These are applications which are characterized by being large scale, highly complex, containing extraordinary degrees of concurrency, critically dependent upon performance, and continually evolving. As the typical implementation language for such applications was assembly language, it was felt that a better solution could be devised.

An initial draft of the requirements for such a language was formed and called STRAWMAN. These were reviewed and led to revised requirements called WOODENMAN. Subsequent revisions produced the TINMAN and IRONMAN reports. At this stage, a contest was held among four contractors to see who could actually design a language which came closest to the IRONMAN requirements. The competing groups were called red, green, yellow, and blue. Green was the eventual winner, a group from Cii-Honeywell Bull of France headed by Jean Ichbiah. The newest set of requirements, called STEELMAN, and the resulting language, called Ada (after Ada Augusta Byron, Countess of Lovelace), appeared in mid-1980, particularly as publications of the U.S. Department of Defense [Ada 80].

As it is currently constituted, Ada is a language which is Pascal based and additionally contains features for numeric computations, nonstandard input/output, machine dependencies, exception handling, data abstraction, and concurrency. According to its documents, it provides features for program modularity, portability, extensibility, abstraction, development, and maintenance. Though at the time I am writing this it is unclear how popular or influential Ada will become, I have decided to select many examples from Ada as we make our way through this book.

As we enter the decade of the '80s, change and progress in the field of computers and programming languages continues at a rapid pace. The most essential fact with respect to programming languages is the growing number in use. Unfortunately, there has been no extensive survey done that would allow us to create a table similar to Table 1-3, but for programming languages. But we might make some guesses. The top three programming languages, defined by the number of people who have used them to create programs are most likely COBOL, FORTRAN, and BASIC. I would wager that the second group is considerably smaller and contains APL, Pascal and PL/1. Figure 1-6 shows the results of one such survey. As its respondents were all from a business environment, its results are not surprising. Just as Esperanto hoped to unite all people under a single language, some have hoped to do the same with a single programming language. It is now clear that no one programming language can be equally satisfactory for all tasks. ALGOL60 was the *lingua franca* of the 1960s. The 1970s saw ANSI FORTRAN and PL/1 used in addition to ALGOL60. Today it seems as if Pascal has become the *lingua franca* of the 1980s.

I end this chapter with a list of the high level programming languages

Language   Appr. No. of Speakers in Millions

	Language	Appr. No. of Speakers in Millions
1.	Chinese	800
2.	English	400
3.	Hindi	240
4.	Russian	210
5.	Spanish	205
6.	Arabic	130
7.	German	120
8.	Japanese	110
9.	Portuguese	105
10.	Bengali	100
11.	French	85
12.	Indonesian	80
13.	Italian	65

Table 1-3:   Top Thirteen Natural Languages By Usage

which existed during the year 1976-77 as given by Jean Sammet. Two
of her criteria are (i) that it be implemented on at least one general
purpose computer, and (ii) that it be in use by someone other than the
developer. For a complete discussion of the rules, see [Sammet 76].
Though this list will continue to get more and more out-of-date as the
years go by, its interest as a historical curiosity will (hopefully)
increase.

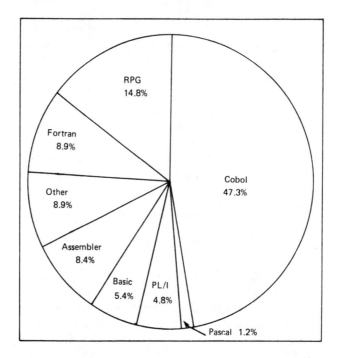

Figure 1-6:   Programming Languages Used by Survey Participants

Scientific	Multipurpose	Engineering
ALGOL60	AED	COGO
ARIEL	ALGOL68	ICES
AUTOGRAF	APL	NASTRAN
AUTOGRP	BALM	STRESS
BASIC	CLU	STRUDL
CESSL	CMS-2	**Hardware design**
FRMT-FTRN	CORAL66	CDL
FORTRAN	CPS	CSL
GLYPNIR	EL1	DCDL
IITRAN	EXT'D-ALGOL	ISPL
JOSS	HAL/S	**Editing**
MAC360	HOS-STPL	CYPHERTEXT
NELIAC	JOVIAL	FILE COMP.
PDEL	LEAP	PAGE
PDELAN	LOGO	**Equipment check**
PROSE	LRLTRAN	ATLAS
SETL	MUMPS	DETOL
SPEAKEASY	NOMAD	DMAD
STIL	OSCAR	RATEL
VECTRAN	PARSEC	**Graphics**
EDP	Pascal	ARTSPEAK
COBOL	PL/1	GRAPHIC-ALGOL
DATABASIC	PLANS	LG
I-D-S/I	PPL	**Machine tool**
UTLTYCODR	REL-ENG.	APT
List processing	RTL/2	
L/6	SAIL	
LAMBIT/L	SIMULA67	
LISP1.5	SPL	
MLISP	SPL/1	
MLISP2	TACPOL	
TREET		

Table 1-4: Roster of Programming Languages for '76-'77

	Accounting	**Social Sciences**
String Proc.	ABLE	CROSSTABS
COMIT-II	**Artificial Intell.**	DATA-TEXT
EOL-3	PLANNER	ESP
SNOBOL4	QLISP	MINITAB-II
TRAC	**Computer Assist. Inst.**	MLAB
VULCAN	CAMIL	OMNITAB-II
Formula manip.	COURSEWRITER-III	PROFILE
ALTRAN	FOIL	SAS
CAMAL	LYRIC	SCEPTRE
FLAP	PILOT	SPSS
FORMAC	PLANIT	TPL
FORMAL	TUTOR	TROLL
MACSYMA	**Circuit design**	**Space planning**
MATHLAB68	ASTAP	SIPLAN
REDUCE	ECAP-II	**Systems prog.**
SCRATCHPAD		B
SETS	**Simulation**	BCPL
Mathematical	CSMP	BLISS
AMBUSH	CSSL	C
GAMMA	DARE	CHILI
MPS-III	DSL	CONVERT
MPSX	DYNAMO-III	IMP
PDS/MAGEN	ECSSL	LITTLE
UHELP	MARSYAS	MAD
Movies	MIMIC	PL/M
BUGSYS	MOBSSL-UAF	PROTEUS
C.A.M.L.	**Simulation disc.**	SDL
Networks	ASPOL	SIMPL-T
FGRAAL	CELLSIM	TMG
GIRL	ECSS-II	ULP
Pharmacology	GPSS	XPL
PL/PROPHET	OSSL	
Real time	PSML	
COMTRAN	SIMSCRIPT-I.5	
	SIMSCRIPT-II.5	

Table 1-5: Roster of Programming Languages for '76-77 (cont'd)

Concepts Discussed in This Chapter

Abstraction

ALGOL-like

Applicative programming language

Concatenation

Data encapsulation

Explicit Typing

General purpose prog. language

Imperative prog. language

Implicit typing

Iteration

Programming language

Selection

Type Checking

Universal prog. language

vonNeumann bottleneck

Exercises

1. Look up the ALGOL60 report, and try to find where it is stated that recursive procedures are admissible.
2. Look up the historical ALGOL60 articles in the SIGPLAN Notices (June 1978), and read over the controversy regarding the use of the period versus the comma. What was the problem, and how was it solved?
3. Investigate the early notations for programming by picking one of the pioneers listed in Table 1-1. Summarize his language in detail, and try to critically analyze it.
4. Look up the FORTRAN II definition of the DO loop, and compare it with the FORTRAN IV version.
5. The text mentions that type checking in ALGOL60 was not sufficient. Can you say why? Look up the ALGOL60 Report, and compare the typing system with Pascal.
6. Get Sammet's list of languages, and see if you can pick out thirteen that you feel were significant in terms of usage and/or concept. For the thirteen that Sammet picked, see her article in the *Encyclopedia of Computer Science*, [Ralston 76], 1169-1174.
7. Everyone knows that FORTRAN stands for FORmula TRANslation, ALGOL for ALGOrithmic Language and LISP for LISt Processor. What are the meanings for the following well-known language names: APL, Pascal, Euclid, SIMULA, CLU?
8. Simulate the program in Table 1-2(a) or Table 1-2(b) on the data $A(i) = i$.

9. Several surveys on the use of higher level programming languages have appeared over the years, especially in the SIGCSE Bulletin, a publication of the Special Interest Group on Computer Science Education of the ACM. Locate one or more of these surveys, and compare their results with the results given in this chapter.

10. Look at Table 1-4 and pick out all the languages you have ever heard of. What percentage of the total is your list?

11. Examine Tables 1-4 and 1-5 and see how many high level programming languages you can name which are not on this list.

Chapter 2

THE CHALLENGE OF PROGRAMMING LANGUAGE DESIGN

"The camel is a horse designed by a committee."
Anonymous

"The most important decisions in language design concern what is to be left out." *Niklaus Wirth*

What makes a programming language successful? If we study the history of this field, we quickly come to the conclusion that success is not based strictly on technical merit. In the early days of computing, FORTRAN was sponsored by a major computer company while the use of COBOL was mandated by the largest user of computers, the U.S. Department of Defense. No doubt these sponsorships helped greatly. But, though LISP has had no major industrial supporters, it has continued to have an enthusiastic group of users, especially in the artificial intelligence community. And Pascal, which was developed as a teaching tool, is fast becoming the standard language available on microprocessors and the major language taught in academic departments of computer science. On the other hand PL/1 did not succeed to the extent it was originally hoped, despite the fact that it had influential backers. So, as it is in many fields, there is no one formula for success. In this chapter, rather than focusing on a formula for success, we will focus on some criteria which can be used to evaluate the quality of any programming language *design.*

A programming language is, by its very nature, a complex tool to design. The main source of this complexity stems from the fact that it must satisfy two diverse needs. On the one hand, there is the need for a notation which is natural for the programmer to use. He must be able to describe real-world problems in an easy manner. As no programming language can hope to anticipate all of the applications one might wish to use it for, it must provide generic facilities. Yet, there cannot be too many of them, because then the language will be too difficult to master. On the other hand, the language must permit the programmer to create efficient programs. That implies that there must be adequate means for translating all possible uses of the language's notation into efficient machine code. These two main criteria are clearly conflicting and lead to many of the difficult issues in programming language design. This makes the design of a programming language an exciting challenge and a field where only a select few succeed.

Before we come to listing and discussing the criteria, we remark that one often hears that *simplicity* is an important goal of programming language design. The reason for this is that programmers who fully understand their tools can tackle more complex jobs and complete them more reliably and efficiently. A quote from C.A.R. Hoare seems most appropriate here.

> "A necessary condition for the achievement of a good language is the utmost simplicity in the design. Without simplicity, even the language designer himself cannot evaluate the consequences of his design decisions. Without simplicity, the compiler writer cannot achieve even reliability, and certainly cannot construct compact, fast, and efficient compilers. But the main beneficiary of simplicity is the user of the language. In all spheres of human intellectual and practical activity, from carpentry to golf, from sculpture to space travel, the true craftsman is the one who thoroughly understands his tools. And this applies to programmers too. A programmer who fully understands his language can tackle more complex tasks and complete them quicker and more satisfactorily than if he did not. In fact, a programmer's need for an understanding of his language is so great that it is almost impossible to persuade him to change to a new one. No matter what the deficiencies of his current language he has learned to live with them; he has learned how to mitigate their effects by discipline and documentation and even to take advantage of them in ways which would be impossible in a new and cleaner language which avoided the deficiency.
>
> It, therefore, seems especially necessary in the design of a new

programming language, intended to attract programmers away from their current high level language, to pursue the goal of simplicity to an extreme, so that a programmer can readily learn and remember all its features, can select the best facility for each of his purposes, can fully understand the effects and consequences of each decision, and can then concentrate the major part of his intellectual effort to understanding his problem and his programs rather than his tool." [Hoare 73]

Though there is a great deal of wisdom in this quotation it should not be accepted uncritically. For example, one might wonder just how complex a language can be before it becomes unmanageable. Certainly many people are capable of mastering programming languages which have a great deal of functionality, such as PL/1. Moreover, languages which provide a wide range of capabilities are necessary for the complex and large software systems which are being built today. At least we can take solace in the fact that the specifications of our programming language do not change at the rate they change for the problems we try to solve with them. I think Hoare's point is that the language designer should avoid *gratuitous* complexity - unnecessarily ornate features or sets of features for providing a specific functionality.

2.1. Criteria for Language Design

In this section I present twelve criteria by which a programming language design can be judged. (This list was originally given by Barbara Liskov of M.I.T.) Programming languages come in many shapes and sizes, but to qualify as a well-designed language, they must all satisfy criterion number one.

1. A well-defined syntactic and semantic description of the programming language is an essential axiom for good programming language design. On the one hand, we shall see in Chapter 3, that supplying a syntactic definition is relatively straightforward, either by the use of BNF or syntax graphs. In 1960, Backus suggested that a means for clearly defining the semantics would also be forthcoming soon. However, in his Turing lecture of 1978, [Backus 78], he suggests that most modern programming languages are so baroque that no simple conceptual model exists. He concludes that a radically new form of programming language is required.

Nevertheless, several methods have been developed for describing semantics. *Interpretive* semantics begins by defining an abstract machine. This machine supports a simple set of operations and data structures. Then the semantics of the language being defined is given by a set of rules which show how programs will be translated onto the abstract machine. The Vienna Definition Language [Wegner 72], which was developed as a means for formally defining PL/1, is the prime example of this approach. *Axiomatic* semantics attempts to provide rules which show the relevant data changes immediately after the execution of some feature of the programming language. The rules are usually written using notation from mathematical logic, and thus, they are independent of any underlying machine, be it abstract or real. Axiomatic semantics are often used to help prove properties of programs [Hoare-Wirth 71]. *Denotational* semantics is a theory originally developed by Scott and Strachey [Scott 70, 71, 72, 76]. It attempts to define programs in terms of mathematical functions and then uses these functions to derive properties of the original programs. Methods are given for taking programs and deriving their associated function, while theorems regarding general classes of functions can be shown.

These three methods do not really compete with each other. Each is designed with a different purpose in mind. Interpretive semantics aims primarily at the implementor of the language. By providing a hierarchy of machines upon which are implemented successive versions of a language, insight can be gained about its eventual implementation. As said before, axiomatic semantics is most often put to use with the verification of programs. Denotational semantics is especially helpful for studying the meaning of a language independent of its implementation and the trade-offs between alternate forms of similar constructs. All three methods for defining semantics may lead to insights about particular features or the interactions between more than one feature.

However, at the time of this writing, the semantics of almost all programming languages is described using natural language. Although these descriptions are worked on for many months and are the subject of extensive review, nevertheless, they are often fraught with errors, ambiguity and incompleteness. A formal approach has the advantage that it provides a mechanism for determining when the language definition is complete and correct. Another advantage of a formal approach to semantics is that it can produce a document which is machine processable. This allows one to develop automatic tools which help to process, verify, and even implement the language [Gordon 79]. Unfortunately, all of the formal approaches to semantic definition require a great deal of sophisticated effort and produce a result which is impossible to read without extensive study. Though I strongly urge all programming language designers to attempt to provide some formal definition of their language, there is still no substitute for a well-written manual; see Table 2-1.

2. Reliability - At the language level this means that features should be designed in such a manner that syntactic and logical errors are both discouraged and easily discovered. To give just one example, consider the fact that programs are read sometimes as often as they are run. This implies that the comment convention of a programming language can play an important role in achieving reliability if it is appropriately designed. In assembly language an instruction such as load accumulator (LDA) would occupy less than half the line while the other half can be used for a comment. E.g.

LDA   X   /LOAD ACC. WITH RATE VALUE

The comment terminates at the end of the line. This encourages one to produce a moderately dense sheet of paper, code on the left, annotated by narrative on the right.

FORTRAN with its convention of 'C' in column one is deficient in that short or in-line comments are illegal. The result is that a fully documented program can occupy many sheets of paper where each sheet is mostly blank.   ALGOL60 introduced two options: either "**comment**.....text.....;" or text placed between an **end** and the next semicolon, **end** or **else**. In both cases, if the semicolon is inadvertently omitted, the compiler will include the next statement into the comment with no warning to the programmer.

For another example of a seemingly innocuous programming language feature which inhibits program reliability, consider the language PL/1 which has the convention that any identifier which appears between an END and its semicolon automatically creates the end of the procedure or block of code which has that identifier as its name, *and of any enclosed program structures if they have no END of their own.*   This feature promotes logical errors, for if an END is inadvertently omitted, its corresponding structure is automatically closed without warning to the programmer.

3. Fast Translation

> "A language that is simple to parse for the compiler is also simple to
> parse for the human programmer and that can only be an asset."
>   Niklaus Wirth

During the 1960s a great deal of research on parsing was done. Versatile methods such as recursive descent, operator precedence, simple precedence, LR(k) and others were devised [Aho-Ullman 72]. Nevertheless, sophisticated parsing techniques are *not* the solution as the quote from Wirth emphasizes. One complicating factor is that the parsing algorithm must be able to handle incorrect programs, and in such a way that the translator can continue in a reasonable manner. But a major obstacle to fast translation may not involve the syntactic structure at all, but rather the semantic definition of the language. At one extreme,a language may be syntactically and semantically designed so that a one-pass compiler is easily built. Though this goal was not explicitly stated for Pascal, it likely influenced its design [Welsh 77]. At the other extreme,some language features cause the translator to use at least two passes. In fact, some translators are known to use more than ten passes over the input.

   4. Efficient Object Code - Though this is not a criterion for an interpreter, it is the *sine qua non* for any compiler. Though many tools and methods have been devised for producing good compilers, the code generation phase remains as more of an art than a science. In addition to the work the compiler writer must do to assure that efficient code is generated, the language designer can help by creating features that can be efficiently translated on current machines. McKeeman has observed that the complexity of the compiler is not linearly related to the complexity of the programming language it compiles, but far worse [McKeeman 75]. Thus, the earlier stated goal of simplicity is manifest here as it is in item 3. One major technique that has been used to help achieve efficient object code is to require the programmer to communicate lots of facts about variables and their potential values. The more information that is supplied, the more efficient can be the code that is produced. But this is done at the expense of the programmer's time.

   Pascal is a language which tries to achieve efficiency by requiring complete detail at compile-time. A language is said to be *strongly typed* if the type of all expressions is known at compile-time. For example,a new type definition in Pascal which is a record may be composed of several fields. All field specifications require the size and type of all components to be communicated by the programmer. This allows the compiler to generate efficient code to access and store the components of this record. If these values were not statically, but dynamically determined, a significant inefficiency would result.

   I observe at this point that a compiler is not the only way to implement a programming language. Another method is to use an interpreter. The distinction between a compiler and an interpreter is discussed in Section 4.2. As we proceed, we shall see which language features favor compilation versus interpretation. For the sake of the discussion here, if a language has features which imply that an interpreter is the proper form of translator, then such a program must be capable of achieving an adequate level of efficiency at run-time.

5. *Orthogonality* - The programming language should have only a few basic features, each of which is separately understandable and free from interactions when they are combined. Orthogonality was a major design goal in the creation of ALGOL68.

6. *Machine Independence* - An original goal for high level languages was the ability to move your programs from machine to machine. We now realize that this goal, though laudable, is terribly difficult to achieve. Machine arithmetic and word size constitute two serious impediments to machine independence. Character codes are another machine dependent feature. It seems as though this goal may never be completely achieved, but it continues to be worth striving for.

The previous six criteria are essential in a good programming language design. Here are some other criteria which have often been mentioned as being desirable.

7. *Provability* - Does there exist a formal definition of all features of the language? This would permit formal verification of programs. But the process of formal verification is very costly, either unaided or aided by machine, and requires a high level of mathematical sophistication.

8. *Generality* - is the idea that all features should be composed of different aspects of a few basic concepts. As an example consider how ALGOL60 introduces the notion of subprogram in two ways, as a declared procedure and as a name parameter to procedures. Since parameter passing is achieved by assignment, a generalization of ALGOL60 would permit procedure texts to be assigned to variables. Now there would exist only one concept of a procedure and variables could assume the value of one or many procedures during execution. This line of thought was followed by ALGOL68. The criteria of generality argues that related concepts should be unified into a single framework.

9. *Consistency with commonly used notations* -One very valuable feature which supports consistency is *overloading*, i.e. the ability to define multiple meanings to the same operator. For example the operator + which is predefined to work on integers, reals, and mixed integer and real arguments, may be extended by the programmer to work on Gaussian integers, complex numbers, matrices, etc.

10. *Subsets* - The idea here is that you don't have to understand the whole language to use a part of it. One successful example of creating subsets, but one which was done after the language was designed, is SP/k. SP/k is a series of increasingly larger subsets of PL/1. SP/1 contains only output and enough statements to run a simple main program. SP/2 adds variables, assignment and input. SP/3 then

includes simple flow of control statements. A primer for these subsets was written by Hume and Holt; see [Hume 72]. The official Ada programming language specifies that no subsets are permitted, but there appears to be support for changing this policy.

11. Uniformity - that similar things should have similar meanings.

12. Extensibility - is the ability to define additional data abstractions and operators. One reason this is considered a desirable feature is that translators are usually forced to choose one representation for all objects of a given type, and this can be very inefficient. For example, APL may represent all arrays by rows (or columns) which is very bad for large sparse arrays. Or LISP, which represents lists using binary trees. This is efficient while the lists can be contained entirely in the store, but it can be inefficient when auxiliary store must be used. It would be preferable in this latter case to be able to use a more compact data representation. The theory behind the extensible language is that the programmer can define his own data representation and code the operations himself. Though many attempts at designing extensible languages have been made, none have proven to be entirely successful. Certainly for any such language, the base language must be efficient. Then, the redefinition of operators should be allowed rather than forcing the programmer to introduce new syntactic forms. Finally, automatic coercions should be avoided so that the programmer can extend the language without concern that the translator will misinterpret the type of a variable. As we shall see in Chapter 7, the language Ada goes far in achieving these goals.

These twelve criteria are only guidelines for creating a successful programming language design. Some languages have doggedly pursued one of these criteria to the exclusion of the others. That has not always proven to be a fruitful path. A successful language design effort will be able to choose a set of criteria and blend them to the right degree. Ultimately, the success of a language will also depend upon whether there exists a clear and concise manual, whether the translator operates well, whether it adequately supports the application domain for which it was intended, and many, many other non-technical issues.

2.2. Some Possible Solutions

In this section I will discuss some methods that have been used to aid in the realization of the goals stated in Section 2.1. Of primary importance is the achievement of those goals within the language design. However, some designers have believed that it is not necessary to achieve these goals within the design, and so they have employed other means. Then, at the end of this section, I conclude with some general advice about achieving a successful language design.

Consider for a moment the design goal of reliability. One mechanism that has been tried to improve a program's reliability is the construction of so-called *diagnostic* or *check-out* compilers. This author first taught students on the PL/C compiler which is Cornell's diagnostic compiler for PL/l. The idea is to build a compiler that accepts PL/l programs and, if correct, executes them properly. However, if the programs are incorrect, and if the error is detected, then the diagnostic compiler can spring into action with an array of auxiliary features not in the PL/l language. In PL/C, spotted syntax errors are given detailed error messages, and an attempt is made to correct the error so compilation can proceed. Many run-time diagnostic features are also included so that the programmer can more easily trace the values of variables as they change and follow the flow of control as it moves from label to label. For students, diagnostic compilers make sense as they spend a great deal of their time getting the program to work and almost no time running the program on real data. However, diagnostic compilers cannot replace building reliability into the language itself. Even diagnostic compilers have limitations. One problem is that they are usually inefficient, especially on large runs. Thus, in a real-world environment, it becomes impossible to use the diagnostic compiler because it will cost too much to try it on significant test cases. Another problem is that the diagnostic compiler and the regular compiler may accept different forms of the language. These forms may be subtly different and result from implementation differences. Thus, a program which runs correctly when compiled on the diagnostic compiler may not run correctly on another compiler and vice-versa.

Now suppose we consider the design goal of fast translation. One suggested way to achieve this goal is to provide the ability to compile separately, different parts of a single program. This facility, for example, exists in FORTRAN. The idea is an attractive one. One person can independently develop part of a software system and produce object code for it in a library. A second person can use this object code while he constructs another part of the system. The lack of separate compilation was a serious concern for ALGOL60. When one made a single change to a program, the entire system had to be re-compiled. For big programs this could mean disastrously long re-compilations. On the negative side, the problem with separate compilation in the form provided by FORTRAN is the fact that once object code is produced, it becomes impossible for the code to check if it is being accessed by a legitimate caller. For example, a FORTRAN procedure with two parameters of type integer and real would have no way to check that a call is supplying type correct values, or that it is even supplying the correct number of values.

With reliability being an overriding factor in the late '60s and '70s, separate compilation was rejected by ALGOL68 and Pascal. However, Ada has reintroduced the concept in a manner which hopes to avoid the problems stated earlier. Ada was influenced by other languages such as SUE [Clark 71] and Mesa [Geschke 77], which attempted to solve the separate compilation problem. The mechanism employed by Ada is the requirement, stated in the langauge document, that every compilation unit must also contain enough information so that any unit which calls this unit can use the data to check that its use of the unit is valid. This information may require a replication of the symbol table which was produced during the compliation of the unit. It remains to be seen if Ada's form of separate compilation will be a success, both from the reliability as well as from the fast translation point of view.

Can one achieve efficient object code by having an optimizing compiler? Yes, but the chief disadvantage is that optimizing compilers are slow and costly to run. Sometimes the optimized version gives different answers than the unoptimized version. Moreover, small source changes may cause optimization to be turned off, causing an unpredictable loss of efficiency. Another aspect of efficient object code is that studies have shown that only a small percentage of the code will often account for the vast majority of the computing time, e.g. see [Knuth 71b]. (Perhaps this is another example of the 80-20 rule?) A consequence is that the optimization as performed by an optimizing compiler can be misplaced and not effective. Moreover, when the conventional compiler produces code which is close to the optimal, then the effort required to improve this code is substantial, and the chance of doing so is negligible.

Finally, with regard to reliability, some language designers believe that it is improved by defining operators as concisely as possible and permitting abbreviations everywhere. When taken to the extreme, we get the famous one-liners of APL. Studies of programming language syntax and its impact on reliability support the notion that redundancy can enforce good discipline on the programmer. Conciseness and abbreviations discourage others from reading through a program.

I conclude this section with some excellent advice for language designers given by C.A.R. Hoare followed by Horowitz's own patented method for producing a successful programming language.

"I have never designed a programming language, only programming language features. It is my belief that these two design activities should be more clearly separated in the future.

1) The designer of a new feature should concentrate on one feature at a time. If necessary, he should design it in the context of some well-known programming language which he likes. He should make sure that his feature mitigates some disadvantage or remedies some incompleteness of the language without compromising any of its existing merits. He should show how the feature can be simply and efficiently implemented. He should write a section of a user manual, explaining clearly with examples how the feature is intended to be used. He should check carefully that there are no traps lurking for the unwary user, which cannot be checked at compile-time. He should write a number of example programs, evaluating all the consequences of using the feature, in comparison with its many alternatives. And finally, if a simple proof rule can be given for the feature, this would be the final accolade.

2) The language designer should be familiar with many alternative features designed by others, and should have excellent judgment in choosing the best, and rejecting any that are mutually inconsistent. He must be capable of reconciling, by good engineering design, any remaining minor inconsistencies or overlaps between separately designed features. He must have a clear idea of the scope and purpose and range of application of his new language, and how far it should go in size and complexity. He should have the resources to implement the language on one or more machines, to write user manuals, introductory texts, advanced texts; he should construct auxiliary programming aids, library programs, and procedures; and finally, he should have the political will and resources to sell and distribute the language to its intended range of customers. One thing he should not do is to include untried ideas of his own. His task is consolidation not innovation." [Hoare 73].

1. Choose a specific application area;

2. Make the design committee as small as possible;

3. Choose some precise design goals;

4. Release version one of the language to a
   small set of interested people;

5. Revise the language definition;

6A. Attempt to build   6B. Attempt to provide a formal
   a prototype compiler;   definition of the language semantics;

7. Revise the language definition again;

8. Produce a clear, concise language
   manual and release it;

9. Provide a production quality compiler
   and distribute it widely;

10. Write marvelously clear primers
    explaining how to use the language.

Table 2-1:   The Ten Step Method to Successful Language Development

Concepts Discussed in This Chapter

Axiomatic semantics   Interpretive semantics
Denotational semantics   Orthogonality
Efficient object code   Portability
Extensibility   Provability
Fast translation   Readability
Generality   Subsets

Exercises

1. Using the scale: poor, adequate, acceptable, or excellent judge the languages you know according to the 12 criteria given in section 2.1.
2. The text mentions the comment convention used in FORTRAN and ALGOL60.   What is the rule for comments in Pascal, PL/1, APL, LISP?
3. Look at the manual of an optimizing compiler, e.g. PL/X or FORTRAN level H, and see if you can determine if it accepts exactly the same language as the regular compiler. Try to give a program example which points up the difference if there is any.
4. Examine the Ada rules about separate compilation. Draw a graph which shows which types of Ada entities must precede others.
5. Some PL/1 implementations try to help the programmer avoid the "all-enclosing END" pitfall discussed under item 2 in this chapter.   Examine some PL/1 implementation, and determine if any special action is taken when this case arises.
6. Try to devise a scheme which would permit separate compilation of ALGOL60 programs. Discuss the problems and what information the compiler would have to produce for your scheme to work.

Chapter 3

DEFINING SYNTAX

"Form follows function."

Dictum of the Bauhaus School of Architecture

3.1. The Character Set

Every language is based upon an alphabet of characters. The English alphabet for example contains 26 letters whose capitals are written

A B C D E F G H I J K L M N O P Q R S T U V W X Y Z

The digits are generally written in Aramaic form

0 1 2 3 4 5 6 7 8 9

The character set for a programming language typically begins with these 36 characters.

The alphabet for the new American National Standards Institute version of FORTRAN, called ANSI FORTRAN 77, includes in addition to the above, 13 special characters

= + - * / ( ) , . $ ' :

You may count only twelve symbols in this list, the thirteenth being a blank which we will denote from now on by "b." These thirteen, when expressed by words are: the blank, equals, plus, minus, asterisk, slash, left parenthesis, right parenthesis, comma, period, dollar sign, apostrophe, and colon. The ALGOL60 alphabet includes *both* upper and lower case for the 26 letters, A-Z and a-z, plus the 28 special characters shown in Figure 3-1.

relational	$<$	$\leqslant$	$=$	$\geqslant$	$>$	$\neq$
Boolean	$\neg$	$\wedge$	$\vee$	$\supset$	$\equiv$	
arithmetic	$\uparrow$	$\times$	$\div$	$+$	$-$	
special	$,$	$\vee$	$_{10}$	$:$	$;$	$'$
special	$"b"$	$($	$)$	$[$	$]$	$'$

Figure 3-1: ALGOL60 Special Symbols

Today there are two main competing character sets, one that was put forth by IBM and another that was proposed by ANSI. The former is called EBCDIC for *E*xtended *B*inary *C*oded *D*ecimal *I*nterchange *C*ode, while the latter is called ASCII, for *A*merican *S*tandard *C*ode for *I*nformation *I*nterchange. The EBCDIC code is an 8-bit code which was first introduced by IBM for its 360 line of computers. The ASCII code is only 7 bits, and so it can represent at most 128 characters. These ASCII characters and their codes can be seen in Table 3-1. There are 95 printable characters including the upper and lower case letters, the ten digits, and 33 special characters. The 33 control characters were originally intended to be used for data transmission between I/O devices. The programming language Ada uses the ASCII character set as its alphabet. The APL character set is among the most novel, which is perhaps due to the fact that its original design focus was a notation to *communicate* algorithms rather than to execute them. The early design of the language proceeded without regard to the characters available on existing keyboards. Only when an implementation was contemplated was a special IBM ball for a selectric typewriter devised. There are the 52 letters A-Z and a-z, the digits 0-9, and the special characters all shown in Table 3-2.

One important issue regarding the alphabet is the ordering between the characters. This ordering is called the *collating sequence.* Naturally

y \ x	0	1	2	3	4	5	6	7
0	nul	dlc		0	@	P	`	p
1	soh	dc1	!	1	A	Q	a	q
2	stx	dc2	"	2	B	R	b	r
3	etc	dc3	=	3	C	S	c	s
4	ect	dc4	$	4	D	T	d	t
5	enq	nak	%	5	E	U	e	u
6	ack	syn	&	6	F	V	f	v
7	bel	etb	'	7	G	W	g	w
8	bs	can	(	8	H	X	h	x
9	ht	eni	)	9	I	Y	i	y
10	lf	sub	*	:	J	Z	j	z
11	vt	csc	+	;	K	[	k	{
12	ff	fs	,	<	L	\	l		
13	cr	gs	−	=	M	]	m	}
14	so	rs	.	>	N	↑	n	~
15	si	us	/	?	O	_	o	dcl

The ordinal number of a character ch is computed from its coordinates in the table as

$$ord(ch) = 16*x + y$$

The characters with ordinal numbers 0 through 31 and 127 are so-called *control characters* used for data transmission and device control. The character with ordinal number 32 is the blank.

Table 3-1: ASCII Character Set

we expect that

$$0 < 1 < 2 < 3 < 4 < 5 < 6 < 7 < 8 < 9$$

and that

$$A < B < C < ... < X < Y < Z$$

if the relational operators are presumed for work on characters or more generally on character strings. But what about the special characters? The ANSI FORTRAN 77 report adds the two assumptions

$$"b" < A , "b" < 0$$

But no other conditions regarding ordering are made. The collating sequence is determined by the implementation, but this sequence usually is influenced by the encoding of the character set. In this regard

Bits

| 0-3 | 4-7 |

	0	1	2	3	4	5	6	7	8	9	A	B	C	D	E	F
0																
1																
2																
3																
4		A	B	C	D	E	F	G	H	I	¢	,	<	(	+	⍓
5	&	J	K	L	M	N	O	P	Q	R	!	$	*	)	;	⌐
6	—	/	S	T	U	V	W	X	Y	Z	:	,	%	·—	>	?
7	&	∧	··	Δ		[ι]			v	`	:	≢	@	'	=	"
8	~	a	b	c	d	e	f	g	h	i	↑	↓	≤	⌈	⌊	→
9	[]	j	k	l	m	n	o	p	q	r	⊃	⊂		○	·	←
A	—	~	s	t	u	v	w	x	y	z	∩	∪	⊥	[	≥	▲
B	α	∈	⍳	ρ	w		x	\	÷		Δ	∇	⊤	]	≠	|
C	<	A	B	C	D	E	F	G	H	I	⍲	⍱	⍀	⌽	Y	⍉
D	>	J	K	L	M	N	O	P	Q	R	I	!	⍶	⍙	[]	A
E	\		S	T	U	V	W	X	Y	Z	≠	⍏	⊓	◊	[+]	⊤
F	0	1	2	3	4	5	6	7	8	9	|	⍒		◊	±

For example, the EBCDIC character 0 has a hex value F0.

Table 3-2:   APL Character Set in EBCDIC
source:IBM 5110 APL Reference Manual

we may commend SNOBOL which provides as the value of the variable name &ALPHABET, its character set in collating order. Also Ada which provides the predefined ordered type CHARACTER which is the full ASCII 128 character set in increasing order.

Every language uses its alphabet to form *words* or *symbols* which make up the vocabulary of the language. Many of the special characters have a well defined meaning in a certain context and are termed a *keyword*. In some programming languages, certain words have a special meaning and their names are set aside as reserved. A *reserved word* has a specific meaning and cannot be used by the programmer to name variables. This is a very reasonable restriction, which helps to create more reliable programs as well as speed up the translation process. In Table 3-3 we see the reserved words for three programming languages. We first observe that the newer languages have increased the size of their reserved word list. While ALGOL60 uses **procedure**, Pascal and Ada have keywords which distinguish between procedures and functions. Reserved words such as **if**, **case**, and **for** have become well accepted. Notice how in ALGOL60 the built-in types are denoted by reserved words such as **boolean**, **integer**, **label**, **real** but neither Pascal nor Ada include these words as part of their reserved word list.

The chief advantage of reserved words are (i) they help to make the program more readable, (ii) they permit the compiler to speed up its symbol table searching, and (iii) they facilitate error recovery. Their disadvantage becomes apparent as the number of reserved words grows large. It becomes harder to remember the set of reserved words. Also, extending the language is complicated as new reserved words may conflict with identifiers in previously correct programs. PL/1 is an example of a language with no reserved words, but many keywords having special significance in a certain context.

3.2. BNF

In a programming language, sequences of words may be combined into *sentences* which form programs. The *syntax* of a language is a set of rules which determines if a sentence is well-formed or not. The ALGOL60 report, released in 1963, contained a notation for describing programming language syntax [Naur 63]. This notation has come to be called Backus-Naur form (or BNF) after the two members of the committee who developed it. Table 3-4 contains an example taken from the ALGOL60 report. There are four rules here (also called productions), which serve to define the syntax of the **for** statement.

array	end	label	switch
begin	false	own	then
boolean	for	procedure	true
comment	goto	real	until
do	if	step	value
else	integer	string	while

A.   ALGOL60 Reserved Words

and	end	nil	set
array	file	not	then
begin	for	of	to
case	function	or	type
const	goto	packed	until
div	if	procedure	var
do	in	program	while
downto	label	record	with
else	mod	repeat	

B.   Pascal Reserved Words

abort	declare	generic	of	select
accept	delay	goto	or	separate
access	delta		others	subtype
all	digits		out	
and	do	if		
array		in		task
at		is	package	terminate
			pragma	then
	else		private	type
	elsif	limited	procedure	
	end	loop		use
begin	entry		raise	
body	exception	mod	range	
	exit		record	when
			rem	while
		new	renames	with
case	for	not	return	
constant	function	null	reverse	xor

C.   Ada Reserved Words

Table 3-3:   Reserved Words in ALGOL60, Pascal and Ada

<for stmt> ::= <for clause> <stmt> | <label> : <for stmt>

<for clause> ::= **for** <variable> := <for list> **do**

<for list> ::= <for list element> | <for list>, <for list element>

<for list element> ::= <arithmetic exp> |
   <arithmetic exp> **step** <arithmetic exp> **until** <arithmetic exp>
   | <arithmetic exp> **while** <Boolean exp>

Table 3-4:   BNF Description of the ALGOL60 **for** Statement

The symbols <, >, | and ::= are not part of the language which is being defined, but are part of the mechanism for describing the language. These characters are called *meta*-symbols. The symbol ::= should be read as "is defined as." The words **for, do, step, until, while** plus the comma, colon-equals, and the colon are required to appear where the productions indicate. These are referred to as *terminal* symbols. The words <for stmt>, <for clause>, <stmt>, <label>, <variable>, <for list>, <for list element>, <arithmetic exp>, <Boolean exp> are meta-variables called *nonterminals* which are used to denote sequences of symbols. The nonterminal <for stmt> is special because these four rules define what a well-formed **for** statement (or <for stmt>) looks like in ALGOL60. Other places in the ALGOL60 report give BNF descriptions for <stmt>, <label>, <variable>, <arithmetic exp> and <Boolean exp>, but their meaning should be clear.

According to the first production a <for stmt> is defined as one of two alternatives. These alternatives are separated by a vertical bar. A <for stmt> is either a <for clause> followed by a <stmt>, or else it is a <for stmt> preceded by a label and colon. This production uses the idea of recursive definition in the second alternative since a <for stmt> is defined in terms of itself. This should present no conceptual problem, as in this case it merely says that a <for stmt> can be preceded by none, one, or several labels and colons. The <for clause> begins with the terminal symbol **for**, which is a reserved word, and is followed by a <variable>, :=, <for list>, and the terminal symbol **do**. The definition of <for list> also uses recursion, so-called *left recursion*. It says that a <for list> can include multiple occurrences of a <for list element> separated by commas. The last production in the example presents a set of three alternatives, each of which is composed of other nonterminals which are defined elsewhere in the ALGOL60 report.

Some examples of syntactically correct ALGOL60 **for** statements are

> **for** i := j **step** 1 **until** n **do** <stmt>
> **for** j := a*b+c **step** h **until** k*m **do** <stmt>
> **for** j := a*b **while** x > y **do** <stmt>
> A:B: **for** k := 1 **step** -1xj **until** n, i+1 **while** j > i **do** <stmt>

Notice that the BNF rules say nothing about how the **for** statement is to be interpreted. This resides in the semantic domain, while BNF deals *solely* with the syntax or form of the statement.

Context-Free Grammars

At about the same time that BNF was being devised, the linguist Noam Chomsky was developing the theory of grammars [Chomsky 59]. One special type of grammar that he identified he called the context-free grammar. This concept, it turned out, is equivalent to languages defined by BNF. I present it here to show how the notion of language can be formalized.

A language L is defined in terms of a quadruple L(T, N, P, S) where T stands for the terminal symbols; N for the nonterminals, P for the productions and S, one of the symbols from N, called the start symbol. Then L(T,N,P,S) is the set of sequences of terminal symbols, say v, which can be generated from S according to a specific set of rules. We write this in mathematical terms as

$$L = \{v : S \rightarrow v \text{ and } v \in T^*\}$$

where T^* is the set of all sequences of elements of T. The rule which describes the generation of sentences of S can be stated in general as follows: v_k can be generated from v_0 if there exist $v_1, v_2, ... v_{k-1}$ such that every v_i can be produced directly from v_{i-1}. Moreover v_i can be directly produced from v_{i-1} if there exist $\alpha, \beta, v'_{i-1}, v'_i$ such that these three rules are valid:

$$v_{i-1} = \alpha \ v'_{i-1} \ \beta$$
$$v_i = \alpha \ v'_i \ \beta$$
$$v'_{i-1} ::= v'_i \quad \text{is a production.}$$

A language is said to be *context-free* if and only if it can be defined in terms of a context-free set of productions. The productions are themselves context-free if and only if each left-hand side consists of a single nonterminal symbol, X, which can be replaced by the right-hand side regardless of the symbols which immediately precede or follow X. As we can see, this restriction is precisely the form of BNF.

The task of a compiler is to recognize well-formed sentences of the language and to generate code which is semantically equivalent. If sentences are not well-formed, then appropriate action must be taken. The process of recognizing sentences is called *parsing*. The theory of syntax analysis, (see e.g. [Aho-Ullman 72]), consists of many parsing algorithms which can handle complex language forms. But a good language designer will employ syntactic forms which both heighten readability and simplify syntactic analysis at the same time.

In order to give a better understanding of BNF, it is helpful to look at how it can be used for parsing. But as our main purpose here is not to cover parsing algorithms (that is generally done in a compiler course), we will make two simplifying assumptions. One, that each reduction (i.e. a replacement of the right-hand side by the left-hand side of a production) depends only upon the present state and on the next symbol being read. Two, that no reduction will have to be changed later on. Collectively these two requirements are termed *one-symbol-lookahead without backtracking*, e.g. see [Wirth 76].

In terms of BNF, the first restriction implies that the initial symbols of alternative right-hand sides of productions are distinct. Let

first(ν) = the set of all terminals that can appear in the first position of sentences derived from ν and ϵ, if ν can produce ϵ.

Then, given a production P ::= $\nu_1 | \ldots | \nu_i | \ldots | \nu_k$, we require that

$$first(\nu_i) \cap first(\nu_j) = \varnothing \text{ for all } i \neq j.$$

(Note, I use $\varnothing$ to stand for the empty set.) The second restriction we must place on the BNF to have one-symbol-lookahead without backtracking is that for every $Q \in N$ which can generate the empty sequence ($Q \rightarrow \epsilon$), the set of its initial symbols must be disjoint from the set of symbols that may follow any sequence generated from Q, i.e.

$$first(Q) \cap follow(Q) = \varnothing$$

where *follow*(Q) is the union of *first*(ν) for all productions of the form X ::= α Q ν.

In the example of the ALGOL60 <for stmt> in Table 3-4, we saw that left recursion was used to express a repeated pattern. This rule is now outlawed because if P ::= Q | P Q then *first*(Q) $\cap$ *first*(PQ) = *first*(Q) $\neq \varnothing$ (as long as Q is not the empty string). But we can get around this restriction by introducing a new meta-symbol for expressing repetition, {x}, which stands for ε or x or xx or xxx, ... where ε is the empty string. One way to view { x } is as a shorthand for the right recursive production x' ::= ε | x x'. { x } satisfies the two equations above. Thus, people have changed the form of BNF to accommodate it to one of its major uses, parsing.

Over the years other notations have been used to describe syntactic structure, and today there is no standard set of symbols. So let's look at the newer programming language Ada and see the conventions its designers used to give a BNF description of its syntax. In addition to the meta-symbols we have seen before, Ada uses square brackets to denote an optional sequence of elements, and they have dropped the angle brackets surrounding nonterminals. Table 3-5 shows the Ada syntax for a block.

```
block ::= [ blockidentifier : ]
          [ declare declarativepart]
            begin   sequenceofstatements
          [ exception { exceptionhandler} ]
            end   [ blockidentifier];

sequenceofstatements ::= statement { statement }

statement ::= {label} simplestmt | {label} compoundstmt

simplestmt ::= assignmentstmt | exitstmt | gotostmt
             | entrycall | raisestmt | codestmt
             | procedurecall | returnstmt
             | delaystmt | abortstmt | null

compoundstmt ::= ifstmt | loopstmt | selectstmt
               | casestmt | acceptstmt | block
```

Table 3-5: Syntax Description of the Ada Block

In Table 3-5 we see that an Ada block is enclosed by the reserved words **begin - end**. Within these reserved words occurs a sequence of statements. A block also may contain a block identifier or a declarative part, but these are optional as indicated. If a declarative part occurs, then it begins with the reserved word **declare** and is followed by a set of declarations. Another optional feature within a block is one or more occurrences of an exception handler. Note the use of repetition within the optional phrase. Also we observe that a blockidentifier may appear immediately following the **end** of the block. The BNF productions which describe sequenceofstatements, statement, simplestmt, and compoundstmt are simpler than the one for block.

Now let's look at another way to describe syntax, one that is equivalent to BNF but far prettier.

3.3. Syntax Graphs

There is another method for describing the syntax of a programming language which is equivalent to BNF, but more pictorial. This scheme is called a syntax graph. We can give rules for taking a BNF description and producing a syntax graph. These rules were first given by Wirth, [Wirth 76], and are shown in Figure 3-2. Terminal symbols are represented by α, nonterminals by either X or ν_i. Note that if in the production $P ::= \nu_1 | \ldots | \nu_k$, $\nu_i = \epsilon$, the null string, then no box will appear for ν_i and only the line will remain.

Since there is such a close association between syntax graphs and BNF, we might ask how the restrictive rules we placed on BNF apply to syntax graphs. One symbol lookahead applied to syntax graphs implies that at every fork the branch to be pursued is determined by the next symbol, and hence, no two connected branches begin with the same symbol. No backtracking implies that if any of the syntax graphs can be traversed without reading an input symbol *at all*, then that graph must be labeled with all symbols that may follow.

Rules for Translating a Syntax Graph Into a Parser

We now show how one can take a syntax graph satisfying the above restrictions and produce a corresponding parsing program. For notation, let "**call N**" (N_i) stand for a procedure call which parses the nonterminal ν (ν_i). In Figure 3-3 we see how each element of a syntax graph can be translated into a set of statements of a program.

We are now ready to try an example, so let's return to the ALGOL60 **for** statement defined in Table 3-4. In Figure 3-4 we see the syntax graph which results from taking the BNF-to-syntax graph translation rules and then merging two of the graphs into two others for simplicity.

The program PARSESTMT in Table 3-6 for parsing a **for** statement was obtained by applying the rules just stated. We assume that the variable *sym* holds the next input symbol (or token). Also, we postulate the existence of a procedure NEXT which causes *sym* to take on the next value in the input stream. A predicate *islabel(sym)* returns true if *sym* is a label and otherwise false. Finally, the term *error* is used

(i) For each production of the form

$$P ::= \mathcal{V}_1 \mid \mathcal{V}_2 \mid \ldots \mid \mathcal{V}_k$$

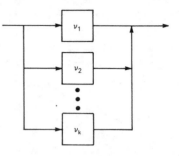

(ii) every occurrence of a terminal symbol
corresponds to the graph

(iii) every occurrence of a nonterminal
symbol X corresponds to

(iv) a production with the form

$$P ::= \mathcal{V}_1 \mathcal{V}_{2'} \ldots \mathcal{V}_k$$

is mapped onto the graph

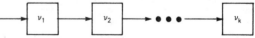

(v) a production with the form

$$P ::= (\alpha)$$

is mapped onto

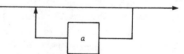

Figure 3-2:   BNF Translated into Syntax Graphs

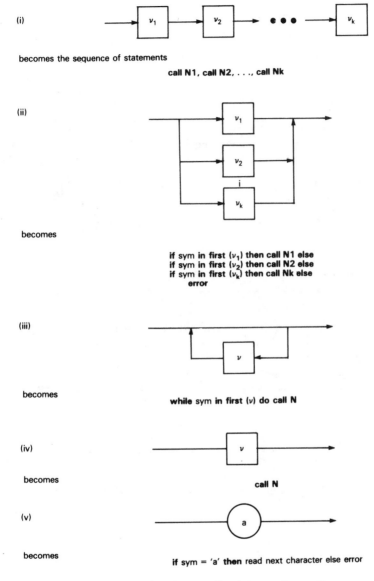

(i)

becomes the sequence of statements

call N1, call N2, . . ., call Nk

(ii)

becomes

if sym **in** first (v_1) **then** call N1 **else**
if sym **in** first (v_2) **then** call N2 **else**
if sym **in** first (v_k) **then** call Nk **else**
error

(iii)

becomes

while sym **in** first (v) **do** call N

(iv)

becomes

call N

(v)

becomes

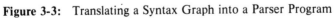

if sym = 'a' **then** read next character **else** error

Figure 3-3: Translating a Syntax Graph into a Parser Program

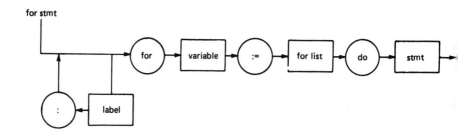

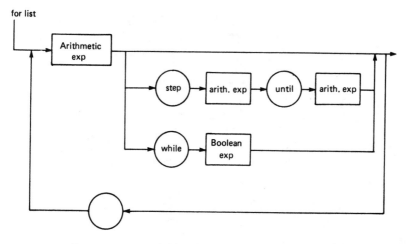

Figure 3-4:   Reduced Syntax Graph for ALGOL60 **for** Statement

generally to denote a failure in correct parsing of the input. We will ignore here the issue of what to do when *error* is encountered.

Another Parsing Method Using Syntax Graphs

Another approach to parsing is to take the syntax graph and produce a data structure. This data structure is used by a general parsing program which is designed to parse any syntax graph when it is expressed in terms of the data structure. This form of table-driven parsing is well-known and more about it can be found in [Aho-Ullman 72], [Cohen 70], [Lewis 76], and [Wirth 76].

For each node in the graph, we create a node in the data structure. Edges of the graph are represented by pointers. As the value in a node can be either a terminal or a nonterminal, we must distinguish those cases, e.g. by using a tag. To differentiate edges which represent other possibilities from edges which indicate the following symbol, we have two different pointer fields, called OTHER and FOLLOW respectively. Thus, a node has four fields and looks like Figure 3-5.

Figure 3-6 gives the rules for translating a syntax graph into its associated data structure. For convenience we assume that all v_i are nonterminals. Also we use the symbol *nil* to denote the end of a list. In Figure 3-7 we see the result when the syntax graph of the **for** statement in Figure 3-4 is translated into its data structure. Table 3-7 contains the procedure which is designed to parse any input string, given that the parsing rules are input in the form of the syntax graph data structure.

Assume that the characters are being read as tokens by the procedure NEXT. The current token is held by *sym*. The variable *t* points to a node. If TAG(t) is true, then the symbol field contains a token or 'empty.' When a terminal symbol is encountered, it is checked against the current input symbol, *sym*, and *flag* is appropriately updated. Otherwise TAG(t) is false, and the symbol field contains a pointer to the graph which represents the nonterminal. If a nonterminal is encountered, then the program immediately tries to parse it by executing a recursive call on itself. When this recursive call terminates with *flag* = true, then the nonterminal was successfully parsed and otherwise *flag* is set to false. Then *flag* is tested and either the FOLLOW or the OTHER direction is taken. A similar program written in Pascal is given in [Wirth 76].

```
procedure PARSESTMT
  var sym : charstring
  //procedure NEXT places the next token as the value of sym//

  procedure FORSTMT
    while islabel (sym) do
          call NEXT
          if sym = ':' then  call NEXT
                        else error
              endif
      repeat
      if sym = 'for' then call NEXT; call VARIABLE
                     if sym = ':=' then call NEXT
                                   else error endif
                     call FORLIST
                     if sym = 'do' then  call NEXT
                                    else error endif
                     call STMT
            else error endif
    end FORSTMT

  procedure FORLIST
    call ARITHEXP
    if sym = 'step' then call NEXT; call ARITHEXP
                    if sym = 'until'
                          then  call NEXT else error
                          endif
                          call ARITHEXP
       else if sym = 'while' then call NEXT; call BOOLEANEXP
            endif
            if sym = ',' then call NEXT; call FORLIST; endif
       endif
    end FORLIST
    call NEXT; call FORSTMT   //the program starts here//
end
```

Table 3-6: Parsing Algorithm Derived From
the Syntax Graph of Figure 3-4

(An informal notation is used.)

TAG	SYMBOL
OTHER	FOLLOW

TAG = $\begin{cases} \text{TRUE, if SYMBOL is terminal} \\ \text{FALSE, if SYMBOL is nonterminal} \end{cases}$

Figure 3-5:   Fields of a Node in a Syntax Graph

3.4. Syntax and Program Reliability

The syntax of a programming language can have a dramatic effect on the reliability of programs. We have already observed in Chapter 2 how a good comment convention can support the writing of well-documented programs. Another key point was the fact that the syntax of a feature should be easily parsable both by man and machine. Several famous examples of violations of this rule come to mind.

Consider the FORTRAN statements

$$\text{DO } 10 \text{ I} = 1.5$$
$$\text{A(I)} = \text{X} + \text{B(I)}$$
$$10 \quad \text{CONTINUE}$$

A brief examination might lead you to conclude that this is a FORTRAN DO loop where the integer variable I will be set to 1, 2, 3, 4 and 5. On closer scrutiny one sees that a period is placed where a comma should be. A well-designed syntax would make this statement illegal. But in FORTRAN this is a legal assignment statement which sets the variable DO10I to the value 1.5. One often hears it cited that an unmanned U.S. spaceship to Venus was lost due to a software error, and the error was eventually traced to this cause.

Another example is the PL/1 statement

$$\text{A} = \text{B} = \text{C};$$

One obvious interpretation would be that B is assigned the value of C, and then A is assigned the value of B. This interpretation would be called a multiple assignment statement. But in PL/1, the multiple assignment statement is written as "A, B = C;" leaving us with the

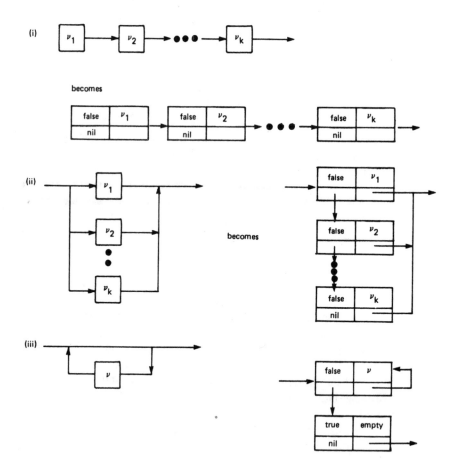

Figure 3-6: Rules for Mapping a Syntax Graph onto a Data Structure

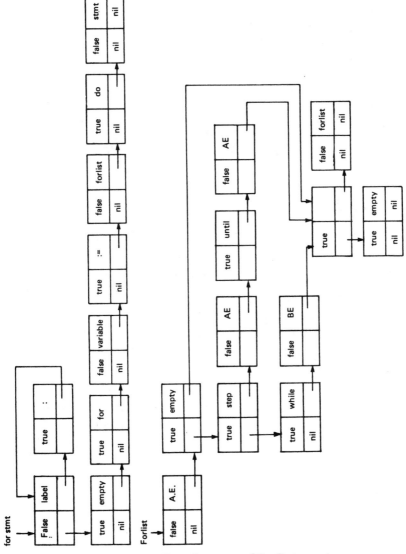

Figure 3-7: Data Structure of **for** Statement

```
procedure PARSEGRAPH (top, flag)
var t, top : pointer; var flag : boolean
//top points initially to the start//
// symbol and later to the current goal//
// flag is a boolean which is set true //
//if parsing is successful //
  t := top
//sym is initialized to contain the first input token//
  loop
      if TAG(t)              //true implies terminal symbol//
        then if SYMBOL(t) = sym
                then flag := true; call NEXT//get next token//
                else flag := (SYMBOL(t) = 'empty')
             endif
    else PARSEGRAPH (SYMBOL(t), flag)//parse nonterminal//
    endif
    if flag then t := FOLLOW(t) else t := OTHER(t)
    endif
  until t = nil repeat
end PARSEGRAPH
```

Table 3-7:   Program to Parse Any Syntax Graph When
              Represented As a Data Structure.(See [Wirth 76])

awkward interpretation of "A = (B = C);" as the assignment of true or false to A depending upon whether or not B and C are equal. The mistake in language design here is the use of the equals sign for two meanings.

Another view of program reliability comes by studying the actual mistakes that people make when they write programs. In a study done by H. Morgan [Morgan 70], he concluded that 80% of the spelling errors in a typical program involve either replacement, insertion or deletion of one character, or the transposition of a pair of characters. In languages which do not require all variables to be explicitly declared, spelling errors are treated as implicit declarations. This makes writing correct programs all the more difficult, and thus contributes to a lack of reliability.

Another famous example of sloppy syntax is the problem of *dangling else*. In FORTRAN the logical conditional encourages the use of GOTOs because of the restriction that only one statement may be executed if the condition is true. ALGOL60 made a significant step forward in clarity by allowing the forms

if cond **then** S
or
if cond **then** S1 **else** S2

where S, S1, and S2 could be arbitrarily complex sequences of statements. One problem with this form of the conditional is when S or S1 is itself a conditional statement. Such a situation leads to an ambiguity about which **if** the **else** should be combined with. Either

(a) **if** cond1 **then** (**if** cond2 **then** S1 **else** S2)
or
(b) **if** cond1 **then** (**if** cond2 **then** S1)
else S2

Thus, the **else** is said to be dangling. In Table 3-8 we see the solutions given by several languages. The solution in ALGOL60 is to disallow the construct of an **if** nested within a **then** clause and to require that the innermost **if** be placed within **begin - end** brackets. If the dangling **else** is to be paired to the innermost **if** then, it is included within the **begin-end**. PL/1 and Pascal offer another solution to this problem. The rule they follow is that if any IF requires an ELSE, then all deeper nested IFs must have corresponding ELSE clauses. If no ELSE clause exists, that is no problem because the ELSE clause can be null. ALGOL68 solved the dangling else problem by requiring each **if** to be

ALGOL60: (to get form (a) write:)
  if cond1 **then begin if** cond2 **then** S1 **end**
          else S2

ALGOL68: (to get form (a) **fi** is required)
  if cond1 **then if** cond2 **then** S1 **fi**
          else S2 **fi**

PL/1: (form (b) requires a null ELSE)
      IF COND1 THEN IF COND2 THEN S1; ELSE S2;
or
      IF COND1 THEN IF COND2 THEN S1; ELSE;
          ELSE S2;

Pascal: (same solution as PL/1)
  if cond1 **then if** cond2 **then** S1 **else** S2
or
      if cond1 **then if** cond2 **then** S1 **else**
          else S2

Table 3-8:   Some Solutions to the Dangling **else** Problem

closed. ALGOL68 uses the word **if** written backwards, **fi**, as the closing
symbol.   And by the way, it uses this rule to close many other
constructs as well. This solution is clean and simple and has the nice
effect of encouraging programmers to consider where their conditionals
end.

We have mentioned that the most difficult part of syntax analysis is
how to act once a syntactically incorrect program has been discovered.
Syntax error recovery schemes abound in the literature, but are often
based on weak or untested assumptions. However, a few studies have
been done with the goal of collecting data about the nature and
frequency of syntactical errors.

In a study of 589 Pascal programs [Ripley 78], Ripley and Druseikis
examined the Pascal compiler for the CDC 6000 series which uses
recursive descent parsing. Their conclusions were

  □ Errors are sparse and in most cases almost all of a statement
    is correct.
  □ 41% of the errors were simply missing a single token.

No. of errors	%	missing token
83	48.5	;
18	10.5	END
13	7.6	BEGIN
8	4.7	identifier
7	4.1	:
7	4.1	=
6	3.5	)
6	3.5	# (string delimiter)
5	2.9	(
5	2.9	DO
<4	7.7	miscel.

Table 3-9:   Missing Token Errors in Pascal

Table 3-9 shows how often a particular token was deleted.

□ The introduction of extra tokens is infrequent, occurring in only 8% of the errors, while wrong tokens made up another 38% of the errors.

□ Spelling errors were also infrequent, though instances of WRTELN, FUNTION, NON, EXRP, UNTIL, WRITLN, INTEGE,and PROGEAM did occur.

The most striking conclusion drawn by Ripley and Druseikis is that people tend to use the semicolon as a *statement terminator* (as in PL/1 and Ada) rather than as a statement separator (ALGOL60, Pascal). Also, programmers view line boundaries as ending a statement, while free format languages ignore end-of-line. Eighty-two of the 83 missing semicolons,or about 20% of all syntax errors,occurred at the end of a line of text.   Other errors in Pascal arose because groups of formal parameters are separated by semicolons, whereas actual parameters are separated by commas.   The requirement in Pascal that the final END be followed by a period caused problems.   Fully 42% of the extra token errors involved the keywords VAR, TYPE and CONST.   For example in the declaration part of Pascal,the second occurrence of VAR is illegal:

VAR A, B : INTEGER;
VAR X, Y : REAL;

This seems to be a result of the fact that people regard the end of a line as the end of a statement.   About 7.5% of the syntax errors were due to missing BEGINs and ENDs. The authors conclude that uniquely bracketed control structures such as IF - ENDIF, FOR - ENDFOR would enable better recovery.

Another interesting and relevant study was done by Gannon and Horning [Gannon 75] in which two languages were compared. TOPPS is an expression-oriented language which looks similar to ALGOL60 as it adopts its scope rules but has right-to-left expression evaluation. A variant of TOPPS, TOPPS II was designed to be statement oriented with left-to-right expression evaluation. In TOPPS the semicolon is used as a separator, while in TOPPS II it is a statement terminator as in PL/1. Table 3-10 summarizes the differences in these two languages.

TOPPS	TOPPS II
1. Expression evaluation right-to-left with equal precedence.	Expression evaluation left-to-right with traditional precedence.
2. Assignment operator	Assignment statement
3. Logical operator &, |	Logical functions **all any**
4. Semicolon as separator	Semicolon as terminator
5. Selection statement **if**	Selection statements **if, case**
6. Repetition statement **repeat**	Repetition statements **repeat, for each**
7. Brackets used to close compound expressions	Brackets used to close compound statements
8. Automatic inheritance of environment	Inheritance only by specific request
9. Constants: literals	Constants: literals and named constants

Table 3-10:   Differences Between TOPPS and TOPPS II

One observation they made was that TOPPS II had far less semicolon errors, thereby supporting Ada's decision to use the semicolon as a statement terminator. There were more errors in TOPPS with respect to statement brackets. There were four classes of errors with high persistence: assignment, inheritance, expression evaluation, relation connector. All of these were worse in TOPPS than in TOPPS II. Thus, they conclude that assignment (:=) should not be treated as just another operator but recognized as having special significance.

Concepts Discussed in This Chapter

ANSI	Nonterminal symbols
ASCII	One symbol lookahead
BNF	Parsing
Character set	Reserved words
Collating sequence	Syntax
Context free grammar	Syntax graphs
Dangling else	Terminal symbols
EBCDIC	

Exercises

1. Take the following BNF description of the Pascal **if** statement and (i) produce the corresponding syntax graph, and (ii) program the parser which results by application of the rules.

```
<if stmt>        ::=  if <expression> then <stmt>  |
                     if <expr> then <stmt> else <stmt>
<expression>  ::=  <simple expr>  |
                     <simple expr> <relop> <simple expr>
<relop>          ::=  =  |  =  |  <  |
                     < =  |  > =  |  >  |  in
<simple expr> ::=  <term> | <sign><term> |
                     <simple expr><addop><term>
<addop>          ::=  +  |  -  |  or
<term>           ::= <factor>|<term><mulop><factor>
<mulop>          ::=  *  |  /  |  div  |  mod  |  and
<factor>          ::=  <vble>  |  <unsigned constant>  |
                     (<expression>)
                     | <function desig> | <set> |not <factor>
```

2. ALGOL60, Ada and Pascal do have reserved words. What about FORTRAN and ALGOL68? Make a list of their reserved words, if any.

3. The text defines the function *first* (v_i) for a production $Q = v_1 \mid v_2 \mid ... \mid v_i \mid ... \mid v_k$. Make some reasonable assumptions about the BNF and give an algorithm which

computes this function.

4. Show why a production of the form P ::= ε | P Q violates
   the rule that *first(P)* ∩ *follow(P)* = ∅. What restrictions
   on P or Q must be assumed?

5. Figure 3-3 does not give an explicit translation rule for the
   syntax graph in Figure 3-8. What should the translation
   be?

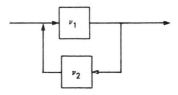

Figure 3-8:   Another Syntax Graph Fragment

6. Is this a syntactically legal ALGOL60 **for** statement?

$$\textbf{for } x := 5 \textbf{ do } y := x+2$$

7. Ada defines an **if** statement in the following way

> if-statement ::=   **if** condition **then**
> sequence of statements
>
> {**elsif** condition **then**
> sequence of statements}
>
> [**else**
> sequence of statements]
>
> **endif**

The { } denote repetition and [ ] denote an optional phrase.
Rewrite this BNF description as a syntax graph. How is the
dangling else problem solved in Ada?

8. When using BNF one must always be aware of the
   semantics of the construct one is defining. Below are two

grammars describing a language with variables and subtraction, but notice how differently they parse a - b - c.

$$P ::= Q \mid P - Q \quad P ::= Q \mid Q - P$$
$$Q ::= a \mid b \mid c \quad Q ::= a \mid b \mid c$$

Write a BNF description for arithmetic expressions which implements the operator hierarchy of any imperative language you choose. See section 4.4 for a discussion of operator hierarchies.

9. Choose any reasonable subset of the syntax graphs of Pascal; see pp. 116-118 of the book [Jensen-Wirth 74], and produce a recognizer. Limit the problem so variables are only one character and no symbol table is needed.

10. Some compilers distinguish between identifiers which are written in upper case from those written in lower case while others do not. This can lead to problems such as the one shown here.

> **begin integer** *NEWITEM;*
> *NEWITEM := 100;*
> **begin integer** *Newitem;*
> *NEWITEM := 200;*
> **end**
> *write(NEWITEM);*
> **end**

Compilers which *do* distinguish cases will associate the second assignment with the outer declaration. The program prints 200. Compilers that *do not* distinguish will print 100. A similar problem occurs with long identifiers as some compilers truncate names while others do not. Examine your own local Pascal or PL/1 compiler and see how it treats both of these issues.

11. (For courageous APL fans) Some of the APL symbols as shown in Table 3-2 have funny names. Match the appropriate symbol with the correct name.

open bracket	not equal	quote quad
close bracket	alpha	log
open paren	epsilon	nand
close paren	iota	nor

semicolon	rho	lamp
slash	omega	delta stile
slope	comma	del stile
left arrow	exclamation	circle bar
right arrow	circle stile	slash bar
dieresis	base	slope bar
plus	top	domino
bar	circle	top nul
times	query	base nul
divide	tilde	ampersand
star	up arrow	at
upstile	down arrow	pound
downstile	open shoe	dollar
stile	close shoe	delta
and	cap	dot
or	cup	overbar
less than	underscore	quote
not greater	circle shoe	colon
equal	I-beam	del
not less	null	del tilde
greater than	quad	not
left brace	fork	dble quote
right brace	chair	percent
hook	long vertical	cent
logical or	vertical bar	gr. accent

Chapter 4

VARIABLES, EXPRESSIONS AND STATEMENTS

"Once a person has understood the way in which variables are used

in programming he has understood the quintessence of programming."

Dijkstra 1972

4.1. Variables and the Assignment Statement

The central characteristic of imperative programming languages is that they allow the creation of variables. An identifier (or name) is usually some combination of alphabetic and numeric characters of restricted length. But what is a variable and how is it distinguished from a name? As we will see a name is merely one component of a variable.

Suppose we have the assignment statement

$$X := 1.4142135$$

We often hear it said that "X is a variable whose value is now 1.4142135." Actually this phrase blurs the complete story. We could say, giving more detail, that "X names a place where 1.4142135 is now stored." But even this phrase is incomplete. Therefore, it is important that we distinguish between several aspects which collectively make up the concept we call a variable. In the case of this assignment statement we have:

(i)   the name of the box: X;
(ii) the name or description of its current contents, the square root of 2.
(iii) the box or storage location(s) which hold(s) the value;
(iv) the contents of the box or 1.4142135.

Note that the name of the box and its storage location are fixed, but the contents and its name may vary over time. Though we might wish to regard the string "1.4142135" as both the value and the name of that value, in general this point of view is too narrow. These considerations lead us to the following definition.

Definition: A *variable* is a quadruple which is composed of a name, a set of attributes, a reference, and a value.

It should be understood that the value may change, but at all times a value exists within the box (as *undefined* is considered a value). The attributes of a variable usually mean the *kind* of values it may hold. The attributes may be fixed once and for all at compile-time, or they may vary during the course of the program. Communicating these attributes may be done by using a declaration, or the attributes may be implicitly defined by setting the variable to a new value. The reference part of a variable identifies an area of storage where the value will be kept. This area may be larger or smaller than a single memory location according to how many locations the value will require. Following D. W. Barron, [Barron 68b], we will draw the variable X with value 1.4142135 as shown in the diagram in Figure 4.1. The current contents of the box is a value drawn as a circle.

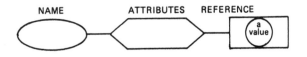

NAME   ATTRIBUTES   REFERENCE

Figure 4-1:   The Four Components of a Variable

Viewing a variable as a quadruple now lets us make explicit many facets of variables which people often assume but don't mention. For example, consider the simple assignment statement

$$X := X + 1$$

We understand that the X on the right-hand side of the colon-equals refers to the current value component, while the X on the left-hand side refers to the reference component. Another way to look at this distinction is as follows. First the value of X is retrieved in order that the expression X + 1 can be evaluated. The assignment operator, in this case denoted by colon-equals, now has two arguments: a value and a reference. It assigns the value to the storage location pointed at by the reference component of X. Thus, in this simple assignment statement the variable X is used in two ways, as the name of a reference and as the name of a value. In the literature one encounters the terms *l-value* and *r-value* to refer to the reference and value components of a variable, respectively. These terms come from the different way a variable, like X, is used on the *left* and *right* sides of the assignment operator.

We assume that an operator, *contents ( )*, exists for the purpose of retrieving values from variables. Given a variable, the *contents* operator uses the reference and attribute information to return its current value. As we see in Figure 4-2, the mapping implemented by *contents* from a variable's reference field to its value is unique, but not necessarily in the other direction.

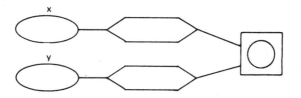

Figure 4-2:   Aliasing

We see in Figure 4-2 that X and Y both refer to the same storage location. Thus X is called an *alias* of Y and vice versa. A programming language which allows one variable to alias another is said to permit aliasing. Most programming languages permit aliasing and some even provide a mechanism which helps to accomplish it. I'm thinking of the EQUIVALENCE statement in FORTRAN, whose purpose is precisely this, to let the programmer define names which act as aliases for the same location. But recently aliasing has come to be regarded as affecting reliability in a negative way. A change in value made to one name causes all aliases to have a value change. There is a belief that all changes of values should be explicit in the program text and not permitted to be implicit as through aliasing. At least one modern programming language, Euclid, took the removal of aliasing as a major design goal, but it was unable to remove it entirely; see [Euclid, Popek 77]. There will be more on aliasing later.

The term *dereferencing* is used to refer to the act of taking a reference and returning its associated value. In most languages you have used, dereferencing is applied implicitly. However, in BLISS, [Wulf 71], a language designed for systems programming, all names stand for their references. To get dereferencing in an expression, one must write it explicitly by prefacing the variable with a period. For example, the previous assignment would be written in BLISS as

$$X := .X + 1$$

The distinction between the box containing a value and the reference component of a variable makes clear what goes on when one writes an array name. The denotation A(i) actually contains an implied operation. This operation takes two arguments, a variable A(i) and an expression (i). The result is a reference, in this case a pointer to the location holding the value named A(i). When A(i) appears on the right-hand side of assignment, a subsequent dereferencing takes place and the *contents* operator will be applied to retrieve the value.

These two examples point out that assignment and array reference can both be viewed as binary operators, one of whose arguments is a reference and whose result is a reference. This naturally leads one to consider a generalization of this idea, namely a programming language which allows variables to be assigned references as their values. This leads to the pointer data type discussed in Chapter 5.

Another generalization would permit an if-then-else expression (as opposed to a statement) which returns a reference. This could be used to write

$$(\textbf{if } cond \textbf{ then } r \textbf{ else } s) := a*b+c$$

or even the more complicated

$$(\textbf{if } cond1 \textbf{ then } r \textbf{ else } s) := \textbf{if } cond2 \textbf{ then } t \textbf{ else } u$$

This last assignment seems clearer than its ALGOL60 or Pascal alternative

$$\textbf{if } \text{cond2 } \textbf{then } z := t \textbf{ else } z := u,$$
$$\textbf{if } \text{cond1 } \textbf{then } r := z \textbf{ else } s := z$$

We will elaborate more on this idea in later sections, first when we discuss expression languages and then when we present the pointer data type. Expressions returning references, as just shown, was discussed early by Barron in [Barron 68b].

Another issue concerning the assignment operator is the order in which its two arguments are evaluated. For example, in APL does the statement $a[b \leftarrow 1] \leftarrow b$ assign $a[1]$ the value 1 or the prior value of b? Or, consider the invocation of the function named P whose result is assigned to an element of the array A, $A[x] \leftarrow P(x)$. If $P(x)$ is a function which alters the value of x, then we immediately see that the order of evaluation will determine the computation. Both Pascal and ALGOL60 evaluate the left-hand side first.

This issue of order of evaluation becomes even more pronounced when we consider a generalization of the assignment statement called the *multiple assignment statement.* In its most general form it looks like:

$$N1, N2, \ldots , Nk := Exp1, Exp2, \ldots , Expk$$

where Ni denotes the ith name and $Expi$ the ith expression. Being imprecise, the meaning of this statement is that the values on the right-hand side are stored into the corresponding names on the left-hand side of the assignment statement. This could be very useful, say, if we wished to interchange two elements, we could write

$$p, q := q, p$$

Now to be more precise, we must answer several questions. Will all *Expi* be evaluated before the locations on the left-hand side are computed? And in what order will they be evaluated? And in what order will these values be assigned to the left-hand sides? In the presence of side effects as seen in the previous paragraph, the answers to these questions are essential for understanding what this statement will do. Typically, the l-values of the elements on the left-hand side are evaluated first followed by the r-values on the right-hand side. Then the updates are done, in some order. This order could well be significant, for example if $i = j$ in the statement

$$b[i], b[j] := p, q$$

and p, q are distinct. See [Gries 80] for a formalization of multiple assignment.

Before leaving this section on the assignment statement, I would like to say something about defining its semantics in a formal manner. So far I have merely pointed to some of the issues which arise in the evaluation of the assignment statement. It would be nice if there existed a mechanism which completely captured, in a succinct manner, all of the semantic consequences of this statement. Following the axiomatic approach first introduced by Hoare in [Hoare 69], let P stand for an assertion, x := e an assignment statement, and P[e → x] the result of textually substituting the value of e for every occurrence of x in P. Then, the definition of the assignment statement can be written as

$$\{ P[e \rightarrow x] \} \ x := e \ \{P\}$$

We read such a formula by saying "if P[e → x] is true before executing the assignment, then P is true afterwards." This rule is valid only if distinct names refer to distinct variables. This statement is so obvious that it is surely not surprising. But the definition says nothing about how the assignment statement is to be evaluated. It is, in effect, implementation independent. Instead it asserts that certain relations must exist between certain variables both before and after execution of the statement. The virtue of being implementation independent is that it permits one to focus on static relationships rather than on the dynamic process of execution.

4.2. Binding Time and Storage Allocation

One often hears about compiled versus interpreted programming languages. A language is *compiled* if the source code is translated primarily into machine code instructions. A language is *interpreted* if the source code is translated only into an intermediate form, which cannot be executed directly but must be interpreted at run-time. In general a language which is compiled can achieve greater efficiency than one which is interpreted. But an interpreted language can offer a degree of flexibility far in excess of compiled languages. Typically, imperative programming languages are compiled, e.g. FORTRAN, ALGOL60, Pascal and Ada. Typically applicative languages are interpreted, e.g. (pure)-LISP and (though not applicative) APL and SNOBOL. But LISP has been successfully compiled.

Figure 4-3 shows the logical components of a hypothetical compiler. One sees four distinct phases. The lexical scanner looks at the program text and breaks it into its constituent tokens, namely special characters and identifiers. The syntactic analysis phase uses these tokens and the symbol table to check for well-formedness. The output of this phase is a computationally equivalent program, which is "closer" to the machine's instruction set, but not necessarily executable. This intermediate form is processed further until all of the outputs as shown in Figure 4-3 are produced. For a more complete discussion of compilers the reader can consult [Aho-Ullman 77], [Gries 72], and [Lewis 76].

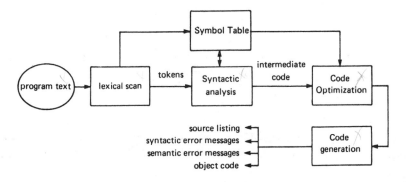

Figure 4-3:   Hypothetical Structure of a Compiler

The distinction between compiled and interpreted languages has become blurred with some of the modern languages. If a language design requires that certain things can only be determined at run-time, then only calls to special software routines are generated at compile-time. Dynamic storage allocation for arrays and strings, recursive procedures and pointers require so much execution time processing that the compiled code looks more like an intermediate form than machine code.

It is crucial to understand the time at which certain decisions are made relative to a language. The key times are: (i) language design time, (ii) language implementation time, (iii) compile-time of a program, (iv) load-time, and (v) run-time. For example, given the ALGOL60 statement, x := y, we say that x receives the value of y at run-time, the attributes of x and y are determined at compile-time, the programmer chose attributes for x out of a set which was defined at language design time and the code which is generated to assign the value of y to x is decided upon at language implementation time. For languages which permit separate compilation, such as Ada, there are some extra steps. At load-time the separate modules are combined, various interface checks done, and then the resulting program is stored in memory ready for execution.

The decision about whether a compiler or an interpreter is the logical kind of translator to build is largely a result of the language design. The degree to which the properties of a variable are defined at translation time is one factor which dictates the extent to which the language can be successfully compiled. Thus, because (pure)-LISP allows names to hold values of any type (e.g. integers, reals, atoms or lists) during the course of execution, it becomes less worthwhile to compile machine code directly. This argues for an interpretive system. But there are other factors which influence the decision of compiler versus interpreter. In the case of LISP, the fact that data can be treated as programs and the interactive, accessible programming environment, also cause implementors to choose an interpreter as the logical vehicle for the implementation.

When it is decided to require the programmer to communicate attributes of a variable at compile time, a mechanism called a declaration is used. A *variable declaration* is a program statement which gives the translator information about a variable and its attributes. These attributes may include the type of data it can reference, whether it names composite data such as an array or a record, the manner in which it should be passed to a procedure, and whether in the procedure its value may be changed or not.

Variable declarations in a program might typically look like this:

integer x; **char** a(80); **real array** w[1 : 10];

These declarations might create the picture at compile-time shown in Figure 4-4. Each identifier name is bound to its attributes when the declaration is encountered. Each identifier name will be bound to its storage at run-time.

Note how the reference fields are not present in Figure 4-4. One issue of language design is precisely when storage is bound to a variable name. A related question is the time during which storage is associated with the variable name. For example in FORTRAN, it is common to implement storage in such a way that all variables and their storage are allocated at the beginning of the program and the same storage remains bound to the same variables throughout the duration of the program's

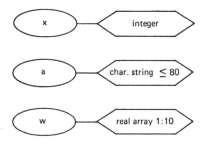

Figure 4-4:   The Effect of Declarations

execution.   This is shown in Figure 4-5.   Note, however, that the
FORTRAN language does not require storage to be allocated in this way,
and any programs which depend upon the old value of a location to be
present on a subsequent execution are relying on a feature which is not
part of the language definition.

Figure 4-5:   Effect of FORTRAN Declaration INTEGER X

However, in ALGOL60 or any language with dynamic storage
allocation, the storage is produced and bound to its variable when its
defining block is entered. Thus at run-time, encountering a declaration
causes several actions to be taken.   This is probably why FORTRAN
declarations are called non-executable statements, because they produce
no action at run-time.   In some languages, such as SIMULA, when
storage is allocated, it is assigned a default value.   Thus declarations
serve several purposes.   At compile time they introduce a new name,
and they may associate some attributes with this name.   At run-time
they cause storage to be allocated, possibly once for the entire duration
of the program or possibly many times.
     For another example consider this simple Ada block,

```
declare I : INTEGER := 0;
   begin
      while I < N loop
         I := I + 1;
         A(I) := B(I) - 1
      end loop
   end
```

When the declaration of I is encountered at compile-time the name I is associated with the attribute INTEGER and placed in the symbol table. At run-time when the declaration is reached, it has the effect of allocating some new storage and binding it to I. Then, that storage is assigned the value zero. In Ada these two steps are called *declaration elaboration.* Suppose the storage is at location m in memory. The storage at m is now in use and is bound to the identifier I. Assignments to I may alter the contents of m, but it will not disturb the binding of m to I. In languages with dynamic storage allocation, the allocation of new storage occurs each time the block is entered, and storage is released when a block is exited. Thus, the reference field of a variable may change many times during the process of execution.

4.3. Constants and Initialization

It has been recognized by language designers that one major use of variables is to give a common or mnemonic name to a value which is never changed. For example, a programmer may naturally write "$pi :=$ 3.1415926" and then use the name pi throughout the program to denote this value. But the programmer would not likely want to change this value during the execution of the program. At a later time if more accuracy is desired, e.g. "$pi := 3.14159265359$," then the programmer need only change one assignment statement, the one which defines pi. To support this use of variables, some programming languages have introduced the concept of a *constant.* (Ada and Pascal are two such languages.) A constant is a name and an associated value such that the value may never be altered by the program during execution. By providing this feature in a language, the compiler is easily capable of determining if the programmer mistakenly tries to re-assign the identifier denoting the constant, thus increasing the reliability of programs.

Some design issues surrounding the feature of a constant in a programming language are :

□Can only simple variable names be used for constants or can structured names,such as arrays and records,also be used;

□What expressions may be used to assign the constant a value; must they be only constants or are arbitrary expressions allowed, implying translation time or perhaps run-time evaluation;

□ When is the value assigned, e.g. once before the program begins execution or each time the block defining the constant is entered;

□ Does the language specify any predefined constants?

A constant definition in Pascal introduces an identifier as a synonym for the constant value. The constant value can only be a number, string or another identifier which denotes a constant including the values of enumerated types. Pascal uses the reserved word **const** to begin a constant declaration. When a block is entered,the expression defining the constant is assigned to the name. In Pascal, only *false*, *true*, and *maxint* are predefined constants. If one examines the BNF description of Pascal, Table 4-1, then one sees that constant definitions are required to appear before all other declarations other than labels.

> block ::= declaration-part statement-part
>
> declaration-part ::= [label-declaration-part]
>   [constant-defn-part]
>   [type-definition-part]
>   [variable-declaration-part]
>   [procedure-and-function-declaration-part]
>
> constant-defn-part ::= **const** constant-defn { ; constant-defn}
>
> constant-defn ::= identifier = constant
>
> constant   ::= integer-number | real-number |
>   string | [sign] constant-identifier

Table 4-1: A Partial Syntax for a Pascal Block

In ALGOL68 one can define a constant by writing

real root2 = 1.4142135.

This causes every occurrence of root2 to be replaced by the token 1.4142135. Thus the assignment to the constant is prohibited because placing root2 on the left-hand side of the assignment operator causes the constant value to be placed there, which causes a compile-time error.

In Ada a constant declaration is denoted by the reserved word **constant**. In contrast to Pascal, Ada allows expressions to be used when defining a constant. Moreover, it is not necessary that the value of the constant be determinable at translation time. It is possible to use functions in defining a constant's initial value. These functions may be evaluated at run-time, but once a named constant has been set to its initial value, its value may not be subsequently altered. Constant arrays and constant records are permitted.

The use of constants must be distinguished from the initialization of variables in declarations. Some languages provide such a facility. In ALGOL68 one can say

$$\textbf{real } root2 := 1.4142135$$

This first declares root2 as referencing a real and then initializes root2 to the value 1.4142135.

The FORTRAN DATA statement places values into variables at compile-time and is thus a form of initialization. Pascal essentially has no initialization features, while in Ada initializations are repeated each time they are encountered in the flow of control of the program. Ada also permits once-only initializations with packages. See Chapter 8 for more details.

Ada provides a uniform notation for setting constants to initial values and for initializing variables. For example the Ada declaration

$$X : \textbf{constant } INTEGER := 17;$$

defines X as a constant of type integer with initial value 17. But the declaration

$$Y : INTEGER := 17;$$

declares Y not as a constant but as a variable, with initial value 17. In both cases a colon-equals appearing in a declaration denotes that an initial value is to be assigned. And as for constants, the elements of their assigning expressions may include functions. Initialization can get complex when structured variables are involved. For example, given the declaration

> **type** NATURAL **is** 1 .. N;
> **type** ROSTER **is array** (NATURAL) **of** INTEGER;

LINEUP : ROSTER(1 .. 100);

one can write in Ada

LINEUP := (1 .. 50 => 1, 51 .. 100 => -1);

which initializes the first fifty elements of LINEUP to 1 and the remaining elements to -1.

4.4. Expressions

The purpose of an expression is to specify a value to be computed. Expressions are composed of operands such as constants and variables, operators, and possibly function calls. The process of evaluation is to substitute values for the operands and perform the operations. The values which are associated with the variables of a program form the *state space* or *environment* of the program. Evaluation of an expression should only produce a value and not change the environment. This idea is called by the grandiose name *referential transparency.* Since a function may be present in an expression, the possibility of the function changing the environment exists. Some language designs have initially tried to forbid this form of side effect, e.g. Ada and LISP, but have eventually provided mechanisms for side-effects in functions.

One major issue is how to associate operands and operators in an expression. One way would require programmers to fully parenthesize their expressions. So A/B*C+D must be written either as

$$((A/B)*(C+D)), (((A/B)*C)+D), ((A/(B*C))+D),$$

$$(A/((B*C)+D)), \text{ or } (A/(B*(C+D)))$$

Any one of these seems too tedious. So instead programming languages define a priority for the operators such that the higher the priority the sooner the operation is performed. And to override this priority, one can use parentheses. Table 4-2 shows the priority for operators in some programming languages. The relative priority for some operators has become standard; e.g. multiplication and division are higher than addition and subtraction. When included, exponentiation is higher than multiplication. The relational operators are typically placed on the same level. And for such situations there must be a rule which determines how operators which are assigned the same priority are to be treated. The typical rule when confronted with an expression with two adjacent operators of the same priority is to associate the operations and operands left-to-right. This is followed, with only a few exceptions, in Pascal, Ada, FORTRAN, PL/1 and ALGOL60.

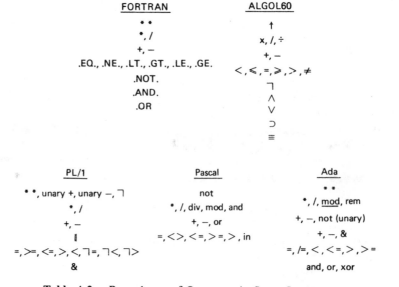

Table 4-2:   Precedence of Operators in Some Languages
(in decreasing order)

Note that associating operators and operands by priorities still leaves the precise order of evaluation of an expression undefined.   For example in the expression A + B + C * D, * may have higher priority than +, which implies that A + (B + C) * D is not a correct way of evaluating the expression. However, A + B could be evaluated before C * D or vice-versa and the priority scheme is not violated. Moreover (A + (B + (C * D))) may also be the order in which evaluation is made.

It is important to observe how the priority of operators can be implied by the BNF description of expressions. In Table 4-3 we see a BNF for expressions in Ada. This can be compared with the priority of the operators for Ada shown in Table 4-2. Given the Ada expression

not A ** B * C / D > -E + F **and** G **mod** H > = I

the parse tree which results is shown in Figure 4-6. Notice that the order of evaluation is still not completely implied by the BNF, as it is not clear which order to take -E+F or (A ** B) * C / D.

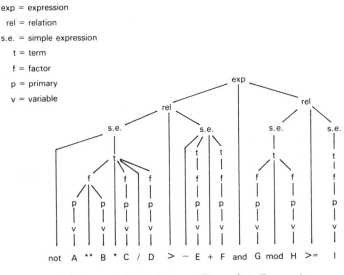

exp = expression
rel = relation
s.e. = simple expression
t = term
f = factor
p = primary
v = variable

not   A   **   B   *   C   /   D   >   −   E   +   F   and   G   mod   H   >=   I

Figure 4-6:   Ada Parse Tree of an Expression

Boolean Conditions

In general, evaluation of an expression such as *operand1* **op** *operand2* involves evaluating the two operands and then applying the operator **op** to the results. This is called *applicative order* of evaluation. Certain properties of the boolean operators, however, often make it possible and desirable to have a different order of evaluation. In particular the operators **and** and **or** have the property that it is sometimes possible to know the value of the expression knowing the value of only one operand. For example in

$$x \neq 0 \text{ or } y/x < 1$$

if $x \neq 0$, then the result of the expression is true, regardless of the value of the second operand. On the other hand, if the condition was

expression   ::=   relation {**and** relation} | relation {**or** relation}
                   | relation {**xor** relation}
relation   ::=   simpleexpression [relationalop simpleexpression]
simpleexpression ::=   [unaryop] term {addop term}
term   ::=   factor {mulop factor}
factor   ::=   primary [exponenop primary]
primary   ::=   literal | aggregate | name | allocator | functioncall
                | qualifiedexpression | (expression)
relationalop   ::=   = | /= | < | <= | > | >=
addop   ::=   + | - | &
unaryop   ::=   + | - | **not**
mulop   ::=   * | / | **mod** | **rem**
exponenop   ::=   **

Table 4-3:   A Slightly Abbreviated BNF for Ada Expressions

$x \neq 0$ **and** $y/x < 1$

then if $x = 0$, the condition is undefined, but we may not wish the
second part of the condition to be evaluated. If $x \neq 0$, then the result
depends upon whether $y/x < 1$. Some compilers, such as the ICL 1900
Pascal compiler, take advantage of this property of Boolean operators to
avoid evaluation of parts of a Boolean expression. Others, such as the
CDC 6000's Pascal compiler, [Pascal6000 74], do not. This
inconsistency is unfortunate, because the difference is visible to the
programmer. The simplest example is the expression above with
the **and** operator where if x = 0, then one does not want to evaluate
the second part of the **and** clause. In an attempt to remove this
inconsistency between compilers, some language designers have
introduced new Boolean operators into their language. The term *short
circuit* evaluation is applied to the process of Boolean expression
evaluation in the following cases: given "x **and** y" where x is false, then
y is not evaluated; and given "x **or** y" where x is true, then y is not
evaluated. Some languages such as Ada now provide distinct Boolean
operators for cases where short circuit evaluation is desired. Assuming
complete evaluation, one can simulate short circuit evaluation, but it gets
rather clumsy. For example

if x $\neq$ 0 **and** y/x < 1 **then** S1 **else** S2 **endif**

might be written as

if x ≠ 0
    then if y/x < 1 **then** S1
               else S2 **endif**
    else S2
endif

This is quite clumsy if S2 is long and the solution of introducing special short circuit operators is far more elegant. A typical approach would include the operators **cand** and **cor** whose definitions are

x **cand** y = **if** x **then** y **else false**
x **cor** y = **if** x **then true else** y

In Ada these are called **and then** and **or else**. Both of these operators have the same precedence as the logical operators. The rule they follow is that the operand on their right-hand side is evaluated if and only if the operand on the left-hand side evaluates to a certain value. In the case of **and then**, that value is true; and in the case of **or else**, that value is false. See [Gries 81] for a further discussion on short circuit evaluation operators.

4.5. Conditional Statements

In Chapter 1 we saw that FORTRAN version 0, [Backus 57], introduced two forms of the conditional statement,

IF(BCOND) L1, L2 and IF(ACOND) L1, L2, L3

where if BCOND is true, a branch to L1 is made, else a branch to L2 is made; and if ACOND is negative, a branch to L1 is made; if ACOND is zero, then a branch to L2 is made, or else a branch to L3 is made. Subsequent versions dropped this form of the logical conditional and replaced it by IF(BCOND) <stmt> where <stmt> is a *single* FORTRAN statement. Unfortunately this form of the Boolean conditional statement encourages the use of a GO TO and a corresponding label when more than one statement is involved in the truth clause. As this forces the programmer to scatter related segments of code, the feature inhibits readability. ALGOL60 corrected this deficiency with the form **if** cond **then** S1 **else** S2 where S1 and S2 can be compound statements and the **else** clause is optional. This form is now widely accepted, except some solution to the dangling **else** problem must be supplied. Some popular solutions were already discussed in Chapter 3. The new ANSI FORTRAN 77, [FORTRAN 77], now includes this form of the IF-THEN-ELSE and requires an ENDIF to solve the dangling-else problem.

Another recent improvement to the if-then-else statement is a form which improves the syntax when testing for a set of conditions. The problem arises when we have a series of conditions to test for, producing a statement of the form shown in Table 4-4,

> **if** C1 **then** S1
>   **else if** C2 **then** S2
>   **else if** C3 **then** S3
>
>   . . . . . .
>   **else if** Cn **then** Sn
>   **else** S(n+1)
> **endif endif endif . . . endif**

Table 4-4:   Nested IF Statements

where the n conditions C1, C2, . . . Cn are to be tested, with the first one evaluating to true causing the corresponding Si to be executed. To avoid the writing of all of the **endif**s, a new form is provided, Table 4-5, shown in Ada.

> **if** C1 **then** S1
> **elsif** C2 **then** S2
> **elsif** C3 **then** S3
>
> . . . . . .
> **elsif** Cn **then** Sn
> **else** S(n+1)
> **endif**;

Table 4-5:   The ELSIF Construct

Actually ALGOL68 was the first language to introduce this syntactic form, called **elif**, see [ALGOL68].

Another conditional statement which has gained great popularity is the so-called **case**, originally proposed by Hoare and included by Hoare and Wirth in the language ALGOL-W [Wirth 66]. The case statement is a construct which permits the programmer to choose one alternative out of a set of choices which are mutually exclusive. Though the case statement can be simulated by a set of nested if-then-else statements, the case construct more clearly reflects the computation. In ALGOL-W the case statement has the following form:

```
case <integer expression> of
   begin
         S1; S2; ... ; Sn
   end
```

The integer expression must evaluate within the range one to n or else the result of this statement is undefined. If the result of the expression evaluation is i, then the statement Si is selected for execution.

In Pascal the case statement has the form

```
case <expr> of
      <case label list>: <stmt>

               .
               .
               .

      <case label list>: <stmt>
   end
```

Whatever the type of the <expr>, the <case label list> may contain only constants of that type. If <expr> does not match any entry in any of the case label lists, then the result is undefined. Most importantly, case labels cannot be branched to by a **goto** statement. Also, the labels must be unique.

It is interesting to observe how Pascal has generalized the case statement over the earlier ALGOL-W form. Rather than using the expression to index the alternatives, one can now list a variety of alternatives within a single choice. Also, note that the values of enumerated types can be included within the case label list.

Finally we examine the case statement in Ada. There we have a somewhat different syntax:

```
case stmt ::=
      case expression is
         {when choice { | choice } => sequence of stmts}
   end case;
```

choice ::= simpleexpression | discreterange | others

The type of the expression can be either an integer or an enumerated type. Once again the alternatives must be mutually exclusive. The major difference is that the cases must be exhaustive for whatever the type of the expression. If *expression* is a variable of type *days-of-the-week*, then there must be cases for all seven days. Of course if the expression is of type integer, one is not required to list all of the integers. This is handled by the **others** clause. One can write

         when others => null;

to indicate that for all other choices only a null statement need be executed. Of course,the **null** may be replaced by any statement.

     In summary, the case statement is a programming language construct which allows the clear expression of a set of alternatives. In examining different forms of the case statement in different languages,we observe that several design issues arise:

    □ What is the type of the selector expression;
    □ What is the type of the case labels;
    □ Can labels be branched to, either from inside the case or from the outside;
    □ Need the labels be mutually exclusive;
    □ Must the labels handle all possible cases of the type of the expression?

    As a final example suppose we have the following definitions:

        type *months* = *(Jan, Feb, March, April, May, June,*
                       July, August, Sept, Oct, Nov, Dec);
       var *thismonth : months;*

The following **case** statement in Pascal, Table 4-6, may be used to determine the number of birthdays of *thismonth.*

      case *thismonth* **of**
        Feb , April , June , July , August :
           birthdays := 4;
        Sept : birthdays := 1;
        Jan , March , May , Oct ,Nov , Dec :
          birthdays := 0
     end

Table 4-6:   Example of Pascal CASE statement

Clearly this program segment would be improved if there existed an **else** clause. Another improvement would be to permit case labels to be ranges of values. All of these features are included in Ada's form of the **case** statement:

      case *thismonth* **is**
        when *Feb | April | June . . August* => *birthdays := 4;*
        when *Sept* => *birthdays := 1;*
        when others => *birthdays := 0;*
      end case;

4.6. Iterative Statements

The concept of looping has been essential to programming, first at the machine language level and then at the programming language level. The simplest syntactic form of looping is to enclose a set of statements within parentheses. But to aid readability, one usually makes those delimiters more informative by calling them, say, **loop** instead of the left parenthesis, and **repeat** instead of the right parenthesis. The meaning of the **loop-repeat** statement is that all statements within its range will be executed in the order in which they are encountered, and upon reaching the keyword **repeat**, a transfer of control is made to the corresponding **loop**, and the process is repeated. Of course, we need some way of terminating such a loop. That can be accomplished by the use of a **go to** statement, or if that seems too dangerous to include in your language, one can supply restricted forms of the **go to**. One typical example is the **exit** statement. Upon reaching this statement, a transfer of control is made to the first statement immediately following the range of the **loop-repeat** which contains the **exit**.

One language which specifically removed the **go to** statement (and labels) from its repertoire is BLISS, [Wulf 71]. In its place BLISS-10 provided seven forms of an exit statement: exitblock, exitcase, exitcommand, exitselect, exitloop, exitset, and exit. The first six cause a transfer of control to the first statement immediately following the block (or case, command, select, loop, or set) in which the statement occurs. However, one should not assume that removing the **go to** causes so much complexity. Later versions of BLISS, including BLISS-11, BLISS-360, and Common-BLISS (for VAX, DEC-10 and DEC-20 computers) have used an "**exit** <label>" construct only. The <label> labels a scope, such as a loop body or a compound statement or a case body, etc. The statement causes transfer to the first statement beyond the labelled scope. Thus, removal of the **go to** is not intrinsically difficult. However, for some the removal of the **goto** seems like an extreme act and is argued against by Knuth in [Knuth 74]. Though the **go to** is a statement which is easily misused, banishing it from the language repertoire seems like too severe a form of surgery.

There are several instances which arise quite often when we examine how loops are typically terminated. Perhaps the most common is the situation where initially a test is made, and if the result is true, then the loop is entered, and all statements within the loop are executed once.

Then the test is tried again. When the test returns false, then the loop is skipped, and control goes to the first statement following the range of the loop. This type of looping is so common that many languages provide a specific construct for it, such as in Pascal:

> **while** *bcond* **do**
>   statement
> **end**

This form of statement is typically called a while loop.

Another typical kind of loop is where the test is done at the end of the loop's range rather than at the beginning. In Pascal we write

> **repeat**
>   statement
> **until** *bcond*

The essential distinction between the **repeat** and the **while** is that in the **repeat** statement the body of the loop is executed at least once. Using a **loop-repeat** and an **exit**, one can simulate the effect of a Pascal **while** and a **repeat**, namely

> **loop**   **loop**
>   **if not** *bcond* **then exit**   compound statement
>   compound statement   **if** *bcond* **then exit**
> **repeat**   **repeat**

In addition, one can also branch from anywhere within a **loop-repeat** statement to the first statement out of the range of the loop. Thus, the **loop-repeat** coupled with **exit** offers a simple way to describe several common forms of iteration. (These statements were used by this author in the design of SPARKS, see *Fundamentals of Data Structures*, Computer Science Press.) The language designer must decide, not only on a set of looping constructs which are sufficient, but on a collection which is not too large, yet capable of easily describing most commonly occurring computations. A further analysis of looping statements appeared earlier and can be found in [Wulf 81], pp. 68-70 and in [Knuth 74].

One of the looping statements which has a most fascinating history is the **for** statement. In contrast to the **loop-repeat** or **while** statements, the **for** statement is used to express an iteration whose length is fixed by certain parameters. We have already seen the syntax for the ALGOL60 **for** statement in Chapter 3. A typical form of this statement is as follows:

for <vble> := <init> **step** <incr> **until** <final> **do** <statement>

There are several issues which must be resolved before we can fully understand the way the **for** statement works in any language. These are

☐ What type of values may <variable> assume;
☐ How complex can the expressions <init>, <final>, and <incr> be and what type must their result be;
☐ How often are the <final value> and <increment value> evaluated as the looping continues;
☐ When is the <variable> checked against the <final value>;
☐ Can <variable> be changed by assignment within the loop;
☐ What is the value of <variable> after the loop is terminated;
☐ Is transfer into or out of the loop permitted;
☐ What is the scope of the looping variable?

Some language designers have chosen "conservative" answers to these questions while others have been more liberal. Let's begin with ALGOL60, [ALGOL60]. The ALGOL60 report says that the test of the control variable with the final value is made first, implying that the <statement> may be executed zero or more times. The <initial value>, <final value>, and <increment> may be arbitrary arithmetic expressions. Thus, their type may be integer or real and may contain mixed mode arithmetic. The <final value> and <increment value> are re-evaluated each time the test is made. For the "*a* **step** *b* **until** *c*" element, the report gives a translation in terms of other ALGOL60 constructs, namely

$$v := a$$
$L1:$ **if** $(v - c)$ x $sign(b) > 0$ **then go to** *elementexhausted;*
$\qquad$ < *statement*> ;
$\qquad v := v + b$
$\qquad$ **go to** $L1;$
elementexhausted:

Thus, we see clearly that *b* and *c* are re-evaluated each time. In addition to the **step-until** clause, there is also the **while** clause, *e* **while** *f*, whose meaning is given in the ALGOL60 report as:

$$v := e$$
$L3:$ **if** *not f* **then go to** *elementexhausted;*
$\qquad$ < *statement*> ;
$\qquad$ **go to** $L3;$
elementexhausted:

The report goes on to state that the value of the control variable is undefined if the loop is exited normally, but if it is exited because of a **go to**, then it retains the value it had immediately before the transfer. Finally a transfer into a **for** statement from outside produces an undefined result.

In contrast we can look at the FORTRAN II DO loop which is a predecessor of the ALGOL60 **for** statement. First of all the DO loop was always executed at least once. Second, the initial, final, and increment values could only be integer constants or simple integer variables. Nothing was said about the value of the control variable after the loop was exited.

A more modern, but conservative approach to the **for** statement was selected by N. Wirth for Pascal. There he allows two forms:

> **for** <variable> := <initial value> **to** <final value> **do** <stmt>

or

> **for** <variable> := <initial value> **downto** <final value> **do** <stmt>

The <variable>, <initial value>, and <final value> must all be the same scalar type except **real** and must not be altered by <stmt>. The <initial value> and <final value> are only evaluated once at the beginning, and the loop body may be entered zero or more times. The final value of the variable is left undefined upon exit. Most importantly we see that no step clause exists, and it is taken to be +1 for the first version and -1 for the second. One of the nice aspects of the Pascal **for** is the way it interfaces with enumerated types. If *months-of-the-year* is an enumerated type then one can write

> **for** *i* := *january* **to** *december* do <stmt>

and the iteration will be performed twelve times, each time with the variable *i* assuming one of the months as its value.

ALGOL68 has retained the rather complex form introduced by the ALGOL60 **for** statement. Again it looks like

> **for** *vble* **from** *Exp1* **by** *Exp2* **to** *Exp3* **while** *Exp4* **do** *S* **od**

The differences between the ALGOL68 and the ALGOL60 version are that *Exp1, Exp2*, and *Exp3* must be integer-valued, and they are evaluated only once. The scope of *vble* now extends only from the beginning to the end of the statement. Many of the statement's constituent parts may be omitted including the "**for** *vble*," "**from** *Exp1*," "**by** *Exp2*," "**to** *Exp3*," and "**while** *Exp4*." Only the phrase "**do** *S* **od**" must be present.

Before closing this section on iterative statements, let's return once more to the axiomatic method for defining programming language semantics. In section 4.1 I presented the definition of the assignment statement. Suppose we now consider the definition of the **while** statement. Assuming { P **and** B } S { P } we have

$$\{P\} \text{ while B do S } \{P \text{ and (not B)}\}$$

This definition is read as "suppose that the execution of the loop body S under the precondition B leaves a specific assertion P invariantly true. If the **while** statement is executed with P true initially, then upon termination of the loop, P will still be true, and in additon, B will be false". Once again we see that the definition does not discuss how the **while** loop is executed but how it preserves or changes certain relationships between the associated variables. If we were going to use this definition of the **while** loop to help us prove that a particular program (which uses the **while** loop) is correct, then the definition shows us that we must determine P and show it is true before executing the loop; determine the relation between the variables after the loop is terminated, and show that this relation is implied by P **and not** B; show that P is preserved over each execution of the body of the loop; and show that the loop halts.

The use of axiomatic theory in the definition of programming languages can be useful. When devising programming language features, one should consider the proof rule which would define it. A complex proof rule implies that use of the statement may cause proofs to be harder, and thus may need refining. In short, providing the proof rule can be used as a guide to cleaner and simpler semantics. For more examples of this type of proof, the reader should consult [Hoare 69] and [Hoare-Wirth 71].

4.7. The GOTO Statement and Labels

The **goto** statement has had a long and bumpy history in programming languages. In this section I intend to trace some of this history so that the reader may appreciate why this statement has caused so much controversy.

The form of the statement is generally

GO TO <statement-label>

where the <statement-label> represents a legal label in the language.

In a language such as FORTRAN, which lacks block structure, recursive procedures, and where all labels are local, the semantics of the GOTO are easily understood. At run-time each statement label is associated with a machine location, and upon encountering the GOTO statement, execution shifts to the instruction occupying that location. In short the GOTO statement is nothing more than a machine language branch instruction. Perhaps the only additional level of complication of the GOTO in FORTRAN is that one is not allowed to branch into a DO-loop. Clearly this is necessary as it would prevent the required initializations of variables that take place upon a normal entrance.

FORTRAN introduced two additional forms of the GOTO statement. One is called the *computed* GOTO. In FORTRAN all statement labels are numeric values. The computed GOTO is a multiway branching statement which looks like

GO TO (L1, L2, . . . , Ln), INDEX

where the Li are FORTRAN labels and INDEX is a FORTRAN integer variable. At run-time if the value of INDEX is i, then a "GO TO Li" is executed. If INDEX is out of range, then the result is undefined. The second additional form of the GOTO introduced in FORTRAN is called the *assigned* GOTO. Its syntax is similar to the computed GOTO:

GO TO LABEL, (L1, L2, . . . , Ln)

Now LABEL is a FORTRAN variable whose value must be a label, either L1 or L2 or . . . Ln. Upon reaching this statement at run-time, a branch to the appropriate label is taken. Note that the entire list of labels is not apparently needed as the branch depends only upon LABEL. Nevertheless, it is included for the convenience of the compiler. The variable LABEL can be assigned a label value by using the statement

ASSIGN Li TO LABEL

In the case of languages such as ALGOL60, Pascal and Ada the semantics of the **goto** can get complex. One of the complications arises from the more complex scope rules in these languages. For example if one says "**go to** L," then L must be known. If L is not defined in the existing block, it must be in a containing block. And if it is in a containing block, then the execution of the **go to** will require the deallocation of variables. Thus, in this case, the **go to** must be treated as a block exit instruction. Similar complications arise when a multi-level exit is defined by a **go to** in a recursive procedure. More about this in

Chapter 6 where a complete discussion of the semantics of static scoping is presented.

One early language which extended the concept of labels and the GOTO was PL/1. In addition to labels (or so-called label constants) PL/1 introduced *label variables.* Such variables are treated in the same way as all other variables in PL/1, namely they can be assigned to, tested for equality, passed as arguments to a procedure and returned as the value of a function. This power to create complex sequencing instructions is counterbalanced by the logical problems which arise. For example, a label value may be legitimately assigned to a label variable, but when the time comes to execute the branch, the scope of the label value may have been exited. This is called a *dangling label reference.* Clearly the readability of a program is decreased when one cannot determine to which section of code a branch is pointing.

In Pascal, labels are denoted by numerals followed by a colon. There are quite a few rules which govern where a label may be placed. One constraint on a label is that one cannot jump into the middle of a block or a procedure. These must be entered normally because the declarations have an active effect at run-time. In FORTRAN, ALGOL60 and Pascal this restriction is enforced by letting the scope of a label binding be the innermost block or procedure body that contains the binding itself. In Pascal, a label may not be placed at any arbitrary point in its scope. It may only be attached to statements within the scope, but not placed within these statements. If the statement is compound, then the label may be used in the nested block or in any nested procedure. This allows jumps to be made within a sequence of statements at the same level and out of the sequence, as we see in the examples of Tables 4-7 and 4-8. In Table 4-7 we see two jumps to label 100. One jump is to a statement in the same block while the other is to a statement in a containing block. A consequence of this rule is that jumps from procedures to statements in a containing block are allowed. In Table 4-8 the **go to** statement causes a branch out of procedure *A* to a statement in the block containing *A*.

The real controversy concerning the GOTO was started by Professor E. Dijkstra, when he wrote a letter to the *Communications of the ACM* which was published in March of 1968. In this letter he argued that this statement was being misused by many to create less readable and less reliable programs. Coupled to this misuse was the fact that, on theoretical grounds, the GOTO statement was difficult to model. This started a long series of discussions about the usefulness of the GOTO. [Van Wijngaarden 66] and [Bohm-Jacopini 66] had discussed conditions under which the GOTO could be eliminated. [Knuth 71a] presented

begin

  . . .

  go to 100;

  . . .

  .

100: ....

  . . .

  .

  begin

    . . .

    go to 100;

    . . .

  end

  . . .

  .

end

Table 4-7:   Example 1 of Labels and Jumps

label 100;
procedure *A(x : integer)*;
  begin

    .

    .

    .

    go to 100;

    .

    .

    .

    end;
  begin

    .

    .

    .

100: ......

    .

    .

    .

  end

Table 4-8:   Example 2 of Labels and Jumps

examples of where the GOTO could be avoided. [Ashcroft-Manna 71] showed how programs with the GOTO could be translated into GOTO-less programs containing only the while-statement as its means for control. In [Knuth 74], he strongly advocates the retention of the GOTO on the basis of algorithm efficiency. Over the years the controversy has died down, and the GOTO remains in modern programming languages. Additional constructs (such as the **exit** statement) have been added so that the wise programmer can structure his program for readability. But all of the discussion was not in vain, as this work led to a greater understanding of our programming languages.

4.8. A First Look at Ada

Now that we have had a look at variables, statements and expressions in general, it seems like an appropriate time to see where Ada fits into this picture. To get a quick overview without much detail, let's look at a simple Ada program. This is a very simple program whose purpose is explained in the commentary part of the program. Nevertheless,we can already see a lot of the structure of Ada in this simple example. First of all we see a procedure with a name. This procedure consists of two parts, a declarative part and a statement part. The former includes declarations of variables, while the latter contains the body of the procedure. One sees that comments in Ada are begun with a double hyphen and conclude at the end of the line. We see that the assignment operator is the colon-equals. The two control structures used in this example are the **if-then-else** and the **while-loop**. Note for the former the use of **elsif** to delineate a set of alternatives. Also note how both of these statements are terminated by a unique delimiter, **end if** or **end loop**, and even **end** BINSRCH. Therefore ,we see that reading (at least simple) Ada programs will not be hard as they are very similar in form to Pascal or ALGOL60.

In addition to the assignment, **if-then-else**, and **while** statements, Ada offers a **case** statement and several more forms for looping. We have already seen an example of the **case** statement in this chapter. The looping statements are described by the BNF:

> *loop-statement* ::=
> *[loop-identifier:] [iteration-clause] basic-loop [loop-identifier];*

> *basic-loop* ::= **loop**
>   *sequence-of-statements*
>   **end loop**

```
procedure BINSRCH( A : TABLE, N : INTEGER, X : ITEM,
              out J : INTEGER) is
-- This program takes an array A of size 1 to N of ITEM
-- and an item X and it searches A for an occurrence of X.
-- It is assumed that the elements of A are in increasing order.
-- If X is present in A then the index J is returned
-- such that A(J) = X. Otherwise J is returned as zero.
LOWER, MID, UPPER : INTEGER;
begin
   LOWER := 1; UPPER := N;
   while LOWER <= UPPER loop
     MID := (LOWER + UPPER)/2;
     if X > A(MID)
         then LOWER := MID + 1;
     elsif X < A(MID)
         then UPPER := MID - 1;
     else J := MID;
         RETURN;
     end if;
   end loop;
   J := 0;
end BINSRCH;
```

Table 4-9:   Binary Search in Ada

> *iteration-clause* ::=
> > **for** *loop-parameter* **in** [**reverse**] *discrete-range*
> > | **while** *condition*
>
> *loop-parameter* ::= *identifier*

From this BNF we see that the loop-identifier is optional, but when it occurs, it must be supplied at both ends. The simplest form of looping is given by the *basic-loop*. Because this specifies an infinite iteration, it can be aborted by using an **exit** or **return** statement. If the **for** statement is used, the *loop-parameter* is implicitly declared at the time the statement is first reached. It can be referenced only within the loop body, and it is treated as a constant. Increasing order for the discrete range is assumed unless the **reverse** option is specified. In Table 4-10 we see three examples of Ada iteration statements.

> CYCLE:
> **loop**
> > -- a sequence of statements
> > **exit** CYCLE **when** CONDITIONFOUND;
> > -- another sequence of statements
> **end loop** CYCLE;
>
> **while** MORELEFT **loop**
> > -- a sequence of statements
> **end loop**;
>
> **for** I **in** LIST'RANGE **loop**
> > **if** LIST(I) = ITEM **then**
> > > PUT(LIST(I));
> > **end if**;
> **end loop**;

Table 4-10:   Three Looping Statements in Ada

The first statement in Table 4-10 is the simplest form of iteration, an infinite loop with an **exit** statement in the middle. The second is the conventional **while** statement which was already seen in **procedure** BINSRCH. The last example in the table shows the **for** statement. The variable I is the loop-parameter. Notice that it will assume the appropriate index values for the array LIST.

Concepts Discussed in This Chapter

Assignment

Binding time

Conditional statement

Constants

Declarations

Dereferencing

Expression language

for statement

Initialization

Iteration

l-value

Referential transparency

r-value

Variable

Short circuit evaluation

while loop

Exercises

1. In the text the question was raised of how evaluation of the two sides of an assignment statement is done. Test the assignment $A(X) = P(X)$ in FORTRAN and PL/1 where $P(X)$ is a function which alters X.
2. Some languages actually limit the length of identifiers while others say nothing. Make up a two column list of those which prescribe a limit and those which don't. Which languages require the first character of a name to be alphabetic and why?
3. Choose a language for which an interpreter is available. Try to determine a description of the intermediate code which is generated from the source. The instructions of the intermediate code define an abstract machine, and if it is carefully defined, it will permit easy transference of the interpreter from one machine to another. Judge the quality of this code with respect to transferability.
4. Study the ALGOL60 report, and determine all features of the language which require run-time analysis before machine instructions can be executed. This chapter mentions two such features.
5. In Table 4-2 what operations are symbolized by ↑, **div** in ALGOL60; &, | in PL/1; **div**, **in** in Pascal; and / =, xor in Ada?
6. Which language treats all operators as having the same priority? In what order are the operations performed?
7. PL/1 violates the left-to-right rule for equal priority

operators. Determine if this statement is true, and if it isn't, state the rule it follows.

8. ANSI FORTRAN 77 still has some restrictions on the type of statement allowed in a LOGICAL IF. What are the rules?

9. PL/1 has introduced complex factoring rules for simplifying declarations. See if you can succinctly summarize these rules.

10. Examine the Ada Language Reference Manual and determine all the rules pertaining to the **for** statement.

11. The programming language Euclid distinguishes between constants and so-called *manifest constants*. How do these concepts differ?

12. Consider the following Pascal program fragment:

```
label 1, 2, 101, 102;
var i;
begin i := 1
    case i of
        1: 101: begin
                go to 202;
            end
        2: 202: writeln ('success');
    end
end
```

Is this a legal Pascal program? Should it be permitted and why?

13. Here is another fun Pascal program to consider:

```
program T;
    var true : Boolean
    begin
        true := 1 = 2;
        if true = false then writeln ('success')
                        else writeln ('failure');
end.
```

Is this a legal Pascal program and if so what does it print?

14. A *static expression* is an expression which is so restricted that it can be evaluated before run-time. Mention three places where static expressions are required in Pascal.

15. Consider the numbered **case** statement of ALGOL-W and

the idea of adding a clause such that if the integer selector is out of range the clause is executed. Is this clause a good idea? Should it be required for all **case** statements?

16. How can one achieve in Pascal the effect of an **others** clause in a **case** statement? Consider surrounding the **case** by an **if-then-else** statement.

17. Consider the two program segments

> **for** $i := 1$ **to** $A(x)$ **by** 1 **do**
> $\quad S$
> **end**

> $i := 1$
> **while** $i < = A(x)$ **do**
> $\quad S$
> $\quad i := i + 1$
> **end**

Under what conditions are these two programs equivalent? Treat S as any sequence of statements.

18. In terms of power, a programming language which includes recursive procedures does not need to supply statements for iteration. Show how one could write recursive procedures to get the same effect as the **while** and **for** statements of Pascal.

19. Consider the following program which computes the nth power of an integer p. See if you can derive formulae which describe the relationships between the variables at the beginning, end and middle of the program.

> **var** p, r, x, y : *integer;*
> $r := 1; x := p; y := n;$
> **while** $y \neq 0$ **do**
> $\quad$ **begin**
> $\quad\quad$ **while** *even*(y) **do** $y := y/2; x := x*x;$ **end**
> $\quad\quad y := y - 1; r := r*x;$
> $\quad$ **end**

20. In FORTRAN, ALGOL60 and Pascal an assignment such as x := e causes a copy of the object referred to by e to be copied into the location given by the reference field of x. This contrasts sharply with the assignment statement of

(impure)-LISP, "SETQ(x e)," which causes x to be bound to the object e, rather than bound to a memory location which contains a copy of e. The LISP form of assignment is called *assignment by sharing*. The notion called *assignment by copying* is the one we are usually familiar with. Discuss the difficulties of implementing a language which only provides assignment by sharing and compare it with a language based on assignment by copying, both from the implementation point of view as well as from the semantic point of view.

21. The **case** statement was supposedly introduced as a replacement for the ALGOL60 switch designator. Below is an outline of the latter statement. Look up the ALGOL60 report and then make a comparison of the switch designator with the **case** in Pascal.

> **switch** *oneof* := *L1, L2, L3, . . ., Ln;*
> .
> .
> .
> **go to** *oneof[e]*
> *L1: S1;* **go to** *done;*
> *L2: S2;* **go to** *done;*
> .
> .
> .
> *Ln: Sn;* **go to** *done;*
> *done:*

22. A control structure which permits multiple exits from a loop but still satisfying the one-entrance one-exit criteria was proposed by Zahn.

> **loop until** <event1> **or** . . . **or** <eventn> **in**
>   <loop body>
> **repeat**
> **then** <event1>: <termination action1>
>   . . .
>   <eventn>: <termination action n>
> **end loop**

All events are evaluated immediately preceding the execution of the loop body. The loop body is repeatedly executed until one of the events becomes true at which point the loop is terminated and the associated termination action executed. Discuss Zahn's construct and how it can be used to simulate the **while** and **repeat** statements. Would you prefer it in a language and why?

23. With the advent of *structured programming* came the idea that a programming language which lacks the "structured" control constructs (if-then-else and while-do) was lacking. One solution is to write a preprocessor which permits such statements to be added without changing the compiler or interpreter for the language. For example, to accomplish this in APL we could define

IF (BOOLEXP1) THEN	$\rightarrow$ *(NOT BOOLEXP1)/L2*
S1	*S1*
ELSE	$\rightarrow$ *L1*
S2	*L2:*
ENDIF	*S2*
	L1:

WHILE (BOOLEX1) DO	*L1:*$\rightarrow$ *(NOT BOOLEX1)/L2*
S1	*S1*
ENDWHILE	$\rightarrow$ *L1*
	L2:

First see if you can define a repeat-until and a for-do statement in APL. Then make some general comments about the positive and negative features of an APL preprocessor.

24. FORTRAN preprocessors were very popular a few years ago as a means to add to the language the "proper" structured control constructs. But now, with the advent of FORTRAN77, the need for a FORTRAN preprocessor is severely diminished. Look up the new FORTRAN77 standard, and list those new language features which would have typically been provided by such a preprocessor. For a discussion of preprocessors to FORTRAN77, see the articles by Wagner in *ACM Sigplan Notices*, December 1980 and by Sakoda in *ACM Sigplan Notices*, January 1979.

25. One very interesting exercise is to study the use of a programming language to see which features are used how

often and in what way. Such a study was done several
years ago by D. Knuth entitled *An Empirical Study of
FORTRAN Programs.* To give you a flavor of what he
uncovered, the chart below shows the results of examining
250,000 cards representing 440 programs. The distribution
of statement types gives the compiler-writer an insight into
how often various sections of his compiler will be used.
You should attempt to run a similar experiment for
another language.

Assignment	51%
IF	8.5%
GOTO	8%
CALL	4%
CONTINUE	3%
WRITE	5%
FORMAT	4%
DO	5%
DATA	.3%
RETURN	2%
DIMENSION	1.5%
COMMON	3%
END	1%
BUFFER	0%
SUBROUTINE	1%
REWIND	0%
EQUIVALENCE	1%
ENDFILE	0%
INTEGER	.3%
READ	1%
ENCODE	0%
DECODE	0%
PRINT	0%
ENTRY	.2%
STOP	.1%
LOGICAL	.1%
REAL	0%
IDENT	0%
DOUBLE	1%
OVERLAY	0%
PAUSE	.1%
ASSIGN	0%

PUNCH	.1%
EXTERNAL	0%
IMPLICIT	1.5%
COMPLEX	0%
NAMELIST	0%
BLOCKDATA	0%
INPUT	0%
OUTPUT	0%
COMMENT	(11)
CONTINUATION	(7)

Note that the percent of the total number of statements excludes comments and continuation cards. Also the IF ( ) *statement* counts as an IF and a *statement* so the total exceeds 100%.

Chapter 5

TYPES

5.1. Data Types and Typing

A *data type* is a set of objects and a set of operations on those objects which create, build-up, destroy, modify and pick apart instances of the objects. Every programming language begins by supplying a set of data types. In LISP, the major data type is the binary tree (called an S-expression), and the basic operations are called CAR, CDR and CONS. More on this in Chapter 12. In modern imperative programming languages, the usual built-in data types include **integer**, **real**, **character** and **Boolean**. Table 5-1 lists the built-in types for some of these languages.

There are two main issues we will be concerned with here. One is an investigation of the usual built-in data types, their representation, and the available operations. The second is the features which permit the definition of new data types by the programmer. But before we begin our discussion we should first consider the question: What is a typing mechanism, and is it necessary or desirable in a programming language? We would all agree that some types must be provided by the language. But a typing system is much more. By a *typing system* I mean a facility for defining new types and for declaring variables whose values are restricted to elements of a specific type with the expectation that type

FORTRAN 77	ALGOL60	Pascal	Ada
INTEGER	integer	integer	INTEGER
REAL	real	real	FLOAT
LOGICAL	Boolean	Boolean	BOOLEAN
CHARACTER		char	CHARACTER
DOUBLE PRECISION			
COMPLEX			

Table 5-1:   Built-in Data Types of Some Languages

checking will be performed.   Thus even FORTRAN has a typing system, though it is restrictive compared to the facilities offered in more modern programming languages.

When a programming language allows the declarations of types, then common properties of variables are collected together in a declaration. The type name declared refers to these common properties.   If one desires to change the properties, then one need only change the type declaration, which aids in maintainability of the program.   Another useful feature of typing is that it supports the separation of specification from implementation.   For example, when a variable is declared to be of type stack, this communicates a specification to the reader.   The reader need not know precisely how the stack data type is implemented, but only its properties.   Thus we say that the declaration of the variable with its type gives an abstract description of its values, while the actual implementation details are reserved for the type definition.   With a typing system, objects with distinct properties are clearly separated, and this allows the compiler to enforce these restrictions.   Thus the typing facility increases not only the reliability, but the readability of the program.

Though many language designers subscribe to the concept of typing, there are several issues upon which people differ.   A major one is whether or not type information should be conveyed at compile-time or at run-time.   Recall that a programming language is strongly typed if all attributes are determinable at compile-time.   Though it is a burden when one is required to list all variables and their types, the return is increased reliability, maintainability, and readability.   Another issue which arises is what, if any, mechanism should be provided which determines if two types are compatible or equivalent.   Though we don't usually want to mix apples and oranges, we might want to mix variables whose type is Macintosh apples with variables of type red apples.

Another typing issue is the question of parameterization. Should there be a way to parameterize types and when should the evaluation of those parameters take place? All of these topics will be discussed in the upcoming sections, and we will see how some languages have resolved these issues.

To understand a data type, we must begin with its members (sometimes called objects, elements or values). These constitute the *domain* of the data type. When these members are written in a program, they are called *literals* because a literal is a constant whose value is given by its sequence of symbols. Thus {true, false} are the literals of the data type Boolean. We say that a data type is *scalar* if its domain consists only of constant values. Examples of scalar types are integer, real, boolean, and char as in Pascal. In contrast to the scalar data types, there are the structured types. These are types whose domain consists of members which are themselves composed of a set of types. This implies that the elements of a structured type have fields, and these fields have types of their own. The two chief examples of structured data types are arrays and records, and we will discuss them in a later section. We now begin our discussion of types with the simplest type of all.

The subject of data types and typing systems was first discussed this way by Wulf, Shaw, Hilfinger, and Flon in [Wulf 81]. Another good reference on types is the discussion provided by *The Rationale for the Design of Ada*, [Ada 79b].

5.2. Enumerated Data Types

An *enumerated* data type is a data type whose domain values are given in a list and whose only operations are equality and assignment. Pascal was one of the first languages to offer a facility for programmers to define their own enumerated data types. Before facilities for enumerated types were included in programming languages, programmers would represent these literals as numbers, possibly 1,2,...,n. This tended to obscure the program. A facility for defining enumerated types is a simple and efficient way to raise the expressive power of a programming language. To make this facility useful, a programming language must provide a mechanism for declaring and defining the new data type and for declaring variables whose values will come from the elements of the type. It is assumed that these literals are distinct and thus equality can be directly defined.

In Pascal we can write

> **type** *months* = *(Jan, Feb, Mar, Apr, May, Jun,*
> *Jul, Aug, Sep, Oct, Nov, Dec);*

This defines the type called *months* which has 12 literals making up its domain. To define variables of type *months* we need to write

> **var** *x, y, z* : *months*;

and then we can perform assignment and equality tests on these variables. For example

> *x* := *Jan*
> *y* := *Jun;*
> **if** *x* = *y* **then** *z* := *Nov* **else** *z* := *Dec*

We can extend the usefulness of this data type definition facility by permitting data type elements to be ordered. The order in which the programmer lists the literals determines the order of the elements of the type. This allows the translator to define the relational operators such as >, <, > =, < = as well as ≠ which is defined as a corollary of equality. Two other operations which are useful for working with ordered enumerated types are successor (*succ*) and predecessor (*pred*). Treating the data type *months* as ordered we have for example that

> *pred(Jun)* = *May*
> *pred(Jan)* = *Undefined*
> *succ(Jun)* = *Jul*
> *succ(Dec)* = *Undefined*

Note that "*Undefined*" is not a legal member of the type, but merely designates that the result of the operation is not known.

Unfortunately, problems may arise even with a feature as simple as an enumerated type. One issue occurs when two different enumerations contain the same constant. How can one check the type correctness of statements which involve this constant? Pascal makes multiple definitions of the same enumeration literal illegal. The designers of Ada have taken a different approach to this issue. Their solution is to declare that all occurrences of enumeration constant identifiers in type and variable declarations are binding. The same identifier may be used in different enumerations in the same scope, or in a nested scope. Then the correct interpretation of multiply defined literals is either made by the context of its use or the name must be fully disambiguated or qualified. For example, given the Ada type definitions

type MONTHS **is** (JAN,FEB,MAR,APR,MAY,JUN,
            JUL,AUG,SEP,OCT,NOV,DEC);
type SUMMERMONTHS **is** (JUN,JUL,AUG);
X : MONTHS; Y : SUMMERMONTHS;

to determine the ordinal position of the month JUL one must write either MONTHS'ORD(JUL) or SUMMERMONTHS'ORD(JUL).

Pascal introduced the concept of the *subrange type*, whereby a new type is created from a subset of an existing enumerated or integer type. The range of this new type is constrained by writing the lower and upper bounds. The new type includes all values of the original type which satisfy the range constraint. Also, all of the operations of the old type are inherited by the new type. For example in Pascal we might have "**type** *months*" as before,followed by the new range type definition

type *summermonths* = *Jun . . Aug*

Now the type *summermonths* includes the values *Jun, Jul,* and *Aug.* Variables of type *summermonths* can be compared with other variables of the same type,and assignments of values of *summermonths* can be made. Whether or not variables of type *months* can be intermixed with variables of type *summermonths* varies from language to language. Note that we cannot define type *winter* as the range *Dec .. Mar,* because in the ordering of *months* the literal *Dec* ends the sequence. One important result of using variables whose type is a subrange is that at run-time, checks must be made to assure that only values from the range are assigned to these variables.

5.3. Elementary Data Types

Numbers

The main advantage and disadvantage of the built-in data types integer and real is that they rely upon the machine implementation of arithmetic. The advantage is the speed which results when integer and real operations described in a higher level programming language are translated into code which uses the machine's built-in arithmetic capabilities. On the other hand,this use causes a lot of difficulties when one tries to move a program in a high level language from one machine to another. The fact that precision and number representation vary from machine to machine implies that the same computation can yield different results on different computers. To help overcome the propensity towards machine dependence, Ada has made an attempt to make some of the implementation dependent features of arithmetic explicit. In addition to the predefined constants MAX_INT and MIN_INT, allowance is made for short or long integers and their specification in a declaration. For real numbers one can define the number of digits and the minimum width of numbers. For example in Ada

type COEF **is digits** 10 **range** - 1.0 .. 1.0;

defines COEF to range between -1 and 1 and have 10 digits of accuracy.

type HUNDRETHS **is delta** 0.01 **range** 0.0 .. 1.0;

defines HUNDRETHS to contain 101 numbers: 0, 0.01, 0.02, 0.03, ... , 0.99, 1.00. This form of definition also allows Ada to automatically define such quantities as the number of digits (T'DIGITS), the smallest (T'SMALL) and largest (T'LARGE) possible values expressible for an ordered numeric type T.

The term *polymorphic* is used to describe an operator which has multiple meanings depending upon the types of its arguments. The symbol + is a binary operator which is defined when its arguments are both of type integer or both of type real. How are we to interpret + when one argument is integer and the other is real ? One solution is to provide a table where the rows and columns are the different data types accepted by the operator and the items in the table show the type of the result. Table 5-2 gives an example for handling + with integer and real arguments.

+	integer	real	double
integer	integer	real**	double***
real	real**	real	double*
double	double***	double*	double

Table 5-2:   Rules for Handling Integer-Real Expressions

In Table 5-2, * implies that the single length argument is extended; ** implies that the integer is converted to real and *** implies that both * and ** occur.

A second approach is to scan the expression and determine a resultant type. Then the operations are performed, but when an argument of a type other than the resultant is encountered, the argument is converted (or coerced) to the resultant type. These two approaches are semantically distinct. For example, given the FORTRAN statement P = Q + I/J, the first method would compute P as Q + REAL (I/J) whereas the second would compute it as Q + REAL(I)/REAL(J).

ALGOL68 actually provides a syntactic mechanism for representation changing called a *cast*. If an expression is prefixed by a type declaration such as **real val**, then the expression is converted to a real value. When a value is converted from integer to real or real to double precision, there is no loss of information. That is called *widening* in ALGOL68. On the other hand, transformations of type which may lose information such as a real to an integer conversion, or e.g. I = P in FORTRAN, are not carried out automatically, but are provided for in ALGOL68 by the use of functions.

In PL/1 another level of complication for arithmetic operations is introduced since numerical values can be either BINARY or DECIMAL and can have attributes such as FIXED, FLOAT, and various precisions. The introduction of precision forces the language to supply rules for the precision of the result of an operation. These rules are very complex, and their occasionally unexpected results have become legendary. For example, if all variables are defined by default, then the expression 1/3 + 25 produces the result 5.33333333333333. This happens because the division rules give (15, 14) as the precision of the result of dividing one by three. This means 15 digits of which 14 are to the right of the decimal place. The addition must have a precision as large as the precision of its operands, so the final result can only have one place to the left of the decimal place. This causes the leading digit, 2, to be truncated. In defense of PL/1, this truncation will cause a SIZE error which the programmer can sense and take action. But the default is to ignore SIZE errors. In the early '70s my students often encountered arithmetic problems while programming in PL/1. This story first appeared in print in [Barron 68b]. There he states a folk law of language design which is violated by this example. It says that languages should not perform in a totally unexpected manner to a reasonably knowledgeable user. This is called the *law of least astonishment.*

Boolean

The domain of the Boolean data type consists of only two objects, true and false. One can expect to find five operations defined on this type: **and, or, not** , implies **(imp)**, and equivalence **(equiv)**.

Axiomatically, these five operations can be elegantly defined, assuming the existence of an if-then-else expression and where x, y are either true or false.

x **and** y = **if** x **then** y **else** false
x **or** y = **if** x **then** true **else** y
not x   = **if** x **then** false **else** true
x **imp** y = **if** x **then** y **else** true
x **equiv** y = **if** x **then** y **else not** y

One interesting issue is the representation of the constants. ALGOL60 represents them by literals **true** and **false** and disallows mixing them with numeric values. In Pascal and Ada, Boolean is viewed as a predefined enumerated type ordered so that FALSE < TRUE. However, they are not literals as they may be redefined by the programmer. PL/1 says that false is any bit string that contains all zeros or the empty string, while true must contain at least one nonzero bit. Since comparison operators yield bit strings of length one, one could write

cond * A + NOT *cond* * B

where *cond* stands for any relational expression yielding a Boolean value, to simulate the statement

IF *cond* THEN A ELSE B

The PL/1 scheme of Boolean representation is similar to APL and makes "187 + TRUE" meaningful. In PL/1 if one writes A < B < C, it gets parsed as (A < B) < C. Since the expression in parentheses evaluates to either one or zero, this whole expression is true for any value of C > 1 given any values of A and B. For example 9 < 8 < 7 evaluates to true.

Characters

In the mid-1960s there was a realization that facilities for processing character string data were needed. FORTRAN and ALGOL60 had emphasized numeric computation and had included only very weak forms of character string manipulation. In FORTRAN the Hollerith string (named after the person who introduced punched card equipment into the U.S. Bureau of the Census, Herman Hollerith) could be used to denote a field of characters, for example,

17H THIS IS A STRING

Hollerith strings could be used in FORMAT statements for output, and they could be used as arguments to subroutines. However, they could not be arguments to functions, [Backus 78b]! The A-format was included so that character data could be input and output, but no facility for character string variables was provided. Character input is typically stored in integer variables, thereby avoiding unwanted conversions which could occur if the machine believed a conversion was needed from a floating point number to an integer or vice-versa. ALGOL60 was not an improvement. It did allow for character string constants enclosed by quotes, but string variables were not allowed nor were any operations on strings provided.

So, by the mid-1960s, it became clear that general purpose programming languages had to have better features for character string manipulation. First, this implied a data type *character string* so that variables could hold character strings as their value. Second, the relational operators could be generalized so that they worked on character strings, assuming a collating sequence (see section 3.1) for the character set is well-defined. A more difficult problem for the language designer and implementor was to provide a set of operations which allows strings to be pulled apart or combined together. Allowing full generality, these operations could produce strings whose length cannot be determined at compile-time, and thus their implementation requires dynamic allocation and deallocation of storage. PL/1 was one of the first general purpose programming languages to provide such a comprehensive facility, and so it is worth looking at it in some detail.

In PL/1 there are three ways that character string variables may be declared. The declaration

$$\text{DCL A CHAR(10);}$$

declares A to be a character string variable of length *exactly* 10 characters. If A is assigned a value which is too long, it is truncated; or if it is less than 10 characters, it is padded with blanks. The declaration

$$\text{DCL B CHAR(80) VARYING;}$$

declares B to be a character string variable of length *at most* 80 characters. B can be assigned the empty string, or any string up to length 80. Strings longer than 80 characters are truncated. The third form of character string declaration is called a PICTURE and is borrowed from COBOL. A variable defined by a PICTURE is given a form which it must satisfy, for example,

$$\text{DCL C PIC 'AAXX99';}$$

declares C to hold character strings of length 6 where the first two
characters must be alphabetic or blank, the next two characters can be
any character, and the last two must be digits.

Once string variables are declared they can be used with relational
operators to yield Boolean values, and they can appear on the left and
right-hand side of assignment. In order to form expressions involving
strings and to manipulate them in a meaningful way, PL/1 provides six
operators: |, INDEX, LENGTH, SUBSTR, TRANSLATE, and VERIFY.
The concatenation operator, |, is an infix operator (that is, it appears in-
between its two arguments). The other five are prefix operators and
appear like built-in functions.

Suppose we are given the declarations

DCL A CHAR (15), B, C, D, CHAR (20) VARYING;

then we could write

A = 'WHAT,' | '?' | 'ME' | '?' | 'WORRY?'

which assigns to A the string

'WHAT,?ME?WORRY?'

Then LENGTH(A) would return the value 15 or in general the length
of its character string argument. The empty string, denoted by two
consecutive quotes, has length zero.

A very powerful operator is SUBSTR(A, I, J) which returns as its
value the part of the character string of A which is J characters long and
begins at character numbered I. Thus SUBSTR(A, 7, 2) returns the
string 'ME'. Interestingly, SUBSTR can also be used on the *left-hand
side* of assignment where the section of string it identifies is replaced by
the value of the right-hand side. For example

SUBSTR(A, 7, 2) = 'US'

produces the string

'WHAT,?US?WORRY'

The function INDEX(A, B) has two string arguments. If B is a
substring of A, then INDEX returns an integer which is the position in
A where the first occurrence of B begins. Otherwise the result is zero.
VERIFY(A, B) also has two string arguments and returns an integer
value. If every character in A appears someplace in B, then the result is
zero. Otherwise, the position of the first character in A which is not in

B is returned. For example

VERIFY(GSTRING, 'ABCDEFGHIJKLMNOPQRSTUVWXYZ')

tests if GSTRING contains only alphabetic characters. Finally, the function TRANSLATE(A, B, C) scans A for any character in C, and if it finds such a character, it replaces it by the corresponding character in B. Thus the statement TRANSLATE(A, '-', '?')   replaces every occurrence of a question mark in A by a minus sign, giving for the previous example 'WHAT,-ME-WORRY-'.

In Table 5-3 we see a complete PL/1 program which makes use of just a few of the string processing facilities. If you have not used PL/1 before, it would be worthwhile to examine it closely. Its purpose is to read a line of text and output a table of the number of times each letter of the alphabet occurs. Note the use of both a fixed size string variable, ALPHABET, and a varying size string variable, SENTENCE. The main loop selects each of the 26 letters and counts its number of appearances.

The power of the string processing facility in PL/1 comes at a large cost, particularly in the difficulty of implementation, and also in terms of run-time efficiency. Pascal moved away from providing such a general set of capabilities, but it has been criticized for doing so. In Pascal, a data type *char* exists which declares variables to hold a single character. Character strings are formed by declaring one-dimensional arrays of type *char*, with the penalty being that a maximum size array must be declared. There are no built-in operators on character strings though for single characters equality testing is permitted and there are two operators:

ord(c) returns the ordinal number for the character *c* as it occurs in the collating sequence (see Figure 3-1).

chr(x) for *x* an integer returns the character whose ordinal number is *x*.

See [Sale 79ab] and the exercises for extending Pascal to contain a strings data type.

SNOBOL and String Processing

One group which took the call to provide string processing capabilities to heart was Farber, Griswold and Polonsky at Bell Laboratories, [SNOBOL 64], who in 1964 developed the language SNOBOL. In a leap of imagination they created a language with very powerful features tailored to string processing. They also provided an implementation which was largely machine independent and eventually an exceedingly well-written primer [SNOBOL4 71]. All this guaranteed a large

```
    COUNT:  PROCEDURE OPTIONS(MAIN);
/*THIS PROGRAM READS A SENTENCE AND PREPARES A
TABLE WHICH CONTAINS A COUNT OF THE LETTERS USED*/
    DECLARE ALPHABET CHARACTER (26) INITIAL
           ('ABCDEFGHIJKLMNOPQRSTUVWXYZ'),
           SENTENCE CHARACTER(100) VARYING,
           SEEK     CHARACTER(1),
           NUMBER   FIXED,
           (I,J,K)  FIXED;
    ON ENDFILE (SYSIN) STOP;
    DO WHILE ('1'B);
     GET LIST (SENTENCE);
     PUT SKIP LIST  (SENTENCE);
     DO K = 1 BY 1 TO 26; /*GO THROUGH THE ALPHABET*/
      SEEK = SUBSTR(ALPHABET,K,1) /*GET NEXT LETTER*/
      I,J = INDEX(SENTENCE, SEEK);
      DO NUMBER = 0 BY 1 WHILE (I ≠ 0);
       I = INDEX(SUBSTR(SENTENCE,J+1),SEEK);
       J = J + I;
      END;
      PUT SKIP LIST(SEEK, 'OCCURS', NUMBER, 'TIMES');
     END;
    END;
END COUNT;
```

Table 5-3:   A Sample PL/1 Program
Using Character String Manipulation.

following and SNOBOL has many adherents.

In SNOBOL the concatenation operator is implicit. It is represented by juxtaposing two quantities together. For example

Y = 'UP'
X = 'HURRY'
Z = X Y

Here we see three SNOBOL statements. The first two assign strings to the string-valued variables X and Y. The third causes Z to be assigned the concatenated value 'HURRYUP'. Thus, the blank between the X and the Y is significant. Compare this with FORTRAN where blanks are not significant.

All variables in SNOBOL are initialized to the null string. To assign the null string to a variable X one writes

X =

and the act of leaving the right-hand side empty causes X to be assigned to the null string.

The simplest form of statement in SNOBOL is called the pattern matching statement. It has the general form

[label] subject pattern   [: goto]

The label and the goto clauses are optional. Labels must begin in column one, which is how SNOBOL distinguishes between a label and a subject. The functioning of this statement is that the pattern is searched for in the subject. If it is found then the statement succeeds and otherwise it fails. To make use of success or failure the optional goto clause can specify either or both of these cases, e.g.

AXIOM = 'SNOBOL IS A NIFTY LANGUAGE'
AXIOM 'NIFTY'   :S(FOUND) F(NOTFOUND)

The variable AXIOM is set to a string and the pattern is 'NIFTY'. Since NIFTY does occur in AXIOM, the success branch will be taken to the statement labeled FOUND.

A more sophisticated form of pattern matching is done with the replacement statement. This has the form

[label] subject pattern   =   object   [: goto]

If the pattern is found in the subject then the value of the object is used to replace the pattern in the subject and the statement succeeds.

Otherwise the statement fails. An APL fan might prefer to write

    AXIOM 'SNOBOL' = 'APL'   :S(LOOP)

If 'SNOBOL' were not found in AXIOM then the next statement to be executed would be the one following this one rather than taking the branch to the statement labeled LOOP.

A one line SNOBOL statement which removes all of the blanks in a string can be written as

    LOOP AXIOM ' ' =   :S(LOOP)

In addition to the data types integer, real, and string SNOBOL also permits variables to hold pattern values. For example we can write

    PAT = 'RED' | 'GREEN'

which assigns the pattern matching 'RED' or 'GREEN' to the variable PAT. We can then use this variable as

    SAMPLE = 'ONE SHOULD NOT EAT GREEN APPLES'
    SAMPLE PAT   :S(LABEL)

In the pattern matching statement, the first occurrence of a substring matching one of the alternatives in PAT is selected. In this example "GREEN" does occur and the statement terminates successfully. Actually, in SNOBOL there are two different forms of pattern matching, called unanchored and anchored mode. The latter description was for unanchored mode. In anchored mode the pattern succeeds only if an *initial* substring matches one of the alternatives in the pattern. Patterns can become very complex as they can be created using not only alternation but using concatenation as well. For example

    FANCY = ('R' | 'B') ('EDS' | 'ED')

This pattern is formed using a combination of alternation (|) and concatenation (represented by the implicit operator the blank between the right and left parentheses). If FANCY is used as the pattern then it will check for the following strings:

                    REDS, RED, BEDS, BED

in that order.

Another very useful feature that SNOBOL provides is called conditional assignment. One is allowed to associate a variable name with a pattern. If that pattern contains a set of choices, then whichever one is successful, the string it matches is assigned to the associated variable. For example if we write

SAMPLE FANCY . ITEM   :S(FOUND) F(NOTFOUND)

then if the statement is successful, ITEM will be assigned either the value REDS, RED, BEDS or BED.

There are many built-in functions in SNOBOL for developing sophisticated patterns. For example,

- [ ] LEN(N) -- matches any N consecutive characters;
- [ ] SPAN(string) -- matches a consecutive group of characters each of which occurs in string;
- [ ] BREAK(string) -- matches a consecutive group of characters none of which occur in string;
- [ ] ANY(string) -- matches any character that occurs in string;
- [ ] NOTANY(string) -- matches any character that does not occur in string.

To give an example of the power of pattern formation in SNOBOL , recall the BNF description of the ALGOL60 **for** statement (section 3.2). We might consider writing a pattern in SNOBOL which would parse an input string and determine if it contains a legal ALGOL60 **for** statement. Such a pattern might be written as follows:

FOR-STMT = (*FOR-CLAUSE STMT) | (LABEL ':' *FOR-STMT)

FOR-CLAUSE = 'FOR' VARIABLE ':=' *FOR-LIST 'DO'

FOR-LIST = *FOR-LIST-ELEM | (*FOR-LIST-ELEM ',' *FOR-LIST)

FOR-LIST-ELEM = ARITH-EXP |
+   (ARITH-EXP 'STEP' ARITH-EXP 'UNTIL' ARITH-EXP) |
+   (ARITH-EXP 'WHILE' BOOLEAN-EXP)

The + indicates that the statement is continued on the next line. The asterisk (*) which precedes *FOR-CLAUSE, *FOR-STMT, *FOR-LIST, and *FOR-LIST-ELEM tells the SNOBOL interpreter to delay evaluation of the name which appears after the asterisk until it is actually needed during the pattern match. This permits recursive definition of patterns as well as forward referencing. Using this pattern, we could now test that a variable INPUTSTRING contains a valid **for** statement by writing:

INPUTSTRING FOR-STMT :S(PARSE) F(NOPARSE)

We end this subsection on SNOBOL by supplying a complete program which does the same as the PL/1 character counting program.

```
        ALPHA = 'ABCDEFGHIJKLMNOPQRSTUVWXYZ'
        T = TABLE()
NEXTSTR STRING = INPUT                     :F(END)
        OUTPUT = STRING
NEXTCHAR STRING ANY(ALPHA) . CHAR = '*'   :F(PRINT)
        T<CHAR> = T<CHAR> + 1              :(NEXTCHAR)

PRINT   INDEXLIST = ALPHA
NEXTIND INDEXLIST LEN(1) . INDEX =         :F(NEXTSTR)
        T<INDEX> LEN(1)                    :F(NEXTIND)
        OUTPUT = INDEX ' OCCURS ' T<INDEX> ' TIMES.'
        T<INDEX> =                         :(NEXTIND)
END
```

Table 5-4: The Character Counting Program in SNOBOL.

T is a variable whose value is a one-dimensional array which is indexed by strings. The SNOBOL interpreter uses hashing to implement the table. INPUT and OUTPUT are keywords which cause those operations to be performed. INPUT is a function which returns the next card image as its value. Assigning a string to OUTPUT causes the corresponding value to be printed as a side-effect. ANY(ALPHA) matches the first alphabetic character, assigns it to CHAR and replaces it by *. Then T<CHAR> is increased by 1 (the null string is treated as zero). When the statement labeled NEXTCHAR fails, INDEXLIST is assigned to the alphabet. LEN(1) matches its leading character, places it in INDEX and deletes it. The next line checks to see if T<INDEX> is non-null. If so, a line of output is produced giving the number of times the character appears in the sentence. T<INDEX> is then reset to zero and an unconditional branch to NEXTIND is taken.

There is a lot more to SNOBOL. The interested reader should consult [SNOBOL 64] and [SNOBOL4 71] for more information.

5.4. Pointer Data Type

A *pointer* is a reference to some object. A *pointer variable* is an identifier whose value is a reference to some object. Pointers and pointer variables were not included in many of the earlier high level languages, but are present in the newer languages such as Pascal and Ada. There is more than one reason for providing pointers. There are certain problems which arise often in computing which call for an undetermined number of items to be produced. One way to handle this situation is to declare an array with some unusually high upper bound. Then the elements of the array can be used to refer to however many objects get produced during a certain run. Clearly this is an inefficient way to proceed. Pointers address this problem by providing a way that many data items can be connected together without providing explicitly, names for all of the objects. Another problem in programming is the need to define multiple relationships between data items. Pointers permit data to be placed on many lists simultaneously. During the course of computation, we imagine that objects will be dynamically produced, will be attached to other objects, and then processed in some fashion. When some object is no longer needed, then its storage may be returned and anything which points to it should realize that it no longer refers to an existing object. By declaring only a few pointer variables, one can write a program which produces widely varying numbers of objects, connected in a myriad of ways, and they can all be accessed in a uniform manner.

As a consequence of our desire to offer pointers as a data type, the following problems can arise. First, several pointer variables may be pointing to the same object. They may all be pointing to the same spot of the object or to different spots. This sharing of objects by more than one pointer variable can lead to programming difficulties, namely if the programmer forgets that two pointer variables are really pointing to the same thing. A second problem which may arise is when some objects are no longer pointed at by any pointer variables. Since these objects do not have an explicit name in the program, there will be no way for the programmer to access this object. In some systems, if this occurs there will be no way for the system to reclaim the storage and it will remain inaccessible for the duration of the program. A third problem arises from the fact that whereas other variables denote either a location or a value (l-value and r-value) depending upon the context in which they are used, a pointer variable must somehow additionally denote the value of the object it is pointing to. Thus, the language must provide some notation for distinguishing between these three different meanings.

Let us begin by reviewing Pascal's use of pointers as I assume most of my readers will be familiar with it. In an attempt to offer the pointer data type in a controlled way, Pascal introduced the idea of declaring pointer types so that they are restricted to point only to objects of a single type. For example, in Pascal one may write

type *nextnode* = ↑ *node*,
  node = **record**
      number : *integer*,
      next : *nextnode*
end

This defines two types called *node* and *nextnode*. Together they permit us to form singly linked lists where each node in the list has two fields called *number* and *next*. The type *nextnode* is a pointer data type, as indicated by the uparrow which precedes the name *node*. Note that in Pascal the occurrence of *node* in the definition of *nextnode* appears before *node* is defined. This is one of the few places in Pascal where a forward reference is permitted. The inclusion of *nextnode* as an element of node allows a linear chain of nodes to be formed. Now, to declare pointer-valued variables which would traverse this linear list we would write

  var *x, y* : *nextnode*

This declares *x* and *y* to be pointer variables, but it does not assign them any values. To create an object for these variables to point to, Pascal provides the special procedure *new*, so if we write *new(x)* the effect is to create a new variable of type *node* and to set the pointer variable *x* to point to it. Since this new node has no name of its own, we call it an *anonymous* variable. If we wish to denote this variable we can write *x*↑. Summarizing we have that

  □ *x* -- denotes a pointer variable of type *nextnode* whose value is a variable of type *node*;
  □ *x*↑ -- denotes the variable of type *node* which was just created by *new(x)*;
  □ *x*↑.*number* -- denotes the integer component of this new node;
  □ *x*↑.*next* -- denotes the pointer component of this new node.

What are the operations one can perform on pointer variables? In Pascal for example, the only operations which are defined are assignment, equality and dereferencing. Also, there is the special constant *nil* which belongs to every pointer type and points to no element at all.

Once storage is created by *new(x)* its lifetime is not related to the block in which *new* occurs nor to the block in which *x* is declared. In fact, if the program exits the block in which *x* is declared, then the pointer variable *x* disappears but the storage which was allocated has not been reclaimed. If there is no longer any other pointer to this object, there is no way that the programmer can access it, and it will be wasted for the duration of the program. In order to allow such storage to be reclaimed and perhaps reused, some Pascal implementations provide a function called *dispose(x)*. The purpose of this function is to cause the system to reclaim dynamically allocated storage which is no longer needed. However, this puts the burden of storage management on the programmer. An alternative to this approach is the method followed by LISP, called garbage collection. If a programmer uses *dispose(x)* it must be remembered that x no longer points to anything meaningful. If the programmer tries to reference the storage pointed at by x, he or she will get an undefined result. Some implementations of *dispose(x)* automatically set x to *nil*. The term *dangling reference* refers to a pointer variable whose value points to something which is no longer meaningful. In PL/1 it is also possible for a pointer to reference storage which no longer exists. However, in ALGOL68 this is not possible. That is because ALGOL68 enforces the rule that pointer variables can never be assigned values which point to a location whose lifetime is potentially shorter than that of the pointer variable.

As a contrast to Pascal's implementation of pointers as a data type, let's consider Ada's implementation.

type NODE;
type NEXTNODE **is access** NODE;

type NODE **is**
    record
        NUMBER : INTEGER;
        NEXT : NEXTNODE;
    end record;

    P, Q : NEXTNODE := **new** NODE(175, **null**);

Here we see the same data types as before, NODE and NEXTNODE. Note how an incomplete definition of NODE is provided first, so that NEXTNODE can be fully defined. Objects of type NODE are records with two fields as shown. The variables P and Q are declared to be of type NEXTNODE and at execution time, when the declaration is encountered both P and Q will have storage set aside for themselves and in addition storage for two records will be allocated. The NUMBER field of both records will be assigned the value 175, and the NEXT fields will contain the special pointer value **null**. The **new** operator is called an *allocator.* To access these fields, we can write P.NUMBER or P.NEXTNODE,and to assign to these fields,we write the same thing but on the left-hand side of assignment, e.g.

> P.NEXTNODE := Q.NEXTNODE;
> Q.NUMBER := P.NUMBER;

Thus dereferencing is automatic. Another feature in Ada which is not present in Pascal is the use of the **all** designator. If we write

> P.**all** := Q.**all**;

then the entire contents of the record pointed at by Q is assigned to the record pointed at by P. In an attempt to rid the language of the dangling reference problem, Ada views the life of all dynamically created objects as the scope of the pointer variable which points to them. When a scoping unit is exited and if the storage for all pointer variables pointing to this storage is deallocated, then any objects pointed to by those variables will be deallocated as well. A final feature contained in Ada is the ability to assign default values to fields as the storage is created by the allocator operation. For example

type STOCKPTR;
type STOCK **is**
   record
      NAME : STRING;
      PRICE : **array** (1 .. 365) **of** REAL;
      TYPE : (INDUSTRIAL, UTILITY, TRANSPORTATION);
      NEXTSTOCK : STOCKPTR;
   end record;
type STOCKPTR **is access** STOCK;

> P : STOCKPTR := **new** STOCK(IBM, 1 .. 365 => 0,
>   INDUSTRIAL, **null**);

Figure 5-1:   A Linked List of Stocks in Ada

Here we see P being declared as a variable of type STOCKPTR. At the same time a new record of type STOCK is allocated and its various fields are set. Note how the PRICE array is succinctly initialized.

In closing, I observe that the pointer data type is generally regarded as an essential feature in modern programming languages. It has been pointed out by some that the undisciplined use of pointers can lead to unmanageable programs. This is no doubt true as anyone who has tried to debug a program using pointers can easily attest. One final observation is that the notation for pointers remains unsettled. When designing a notation for pointers, one must adopt a form that makes it clear during assignment whether the assignment refers to the value of the pointer variable or to the value of the dynamic variable which is being pointed at. No consistent notation has yet been agreed upon. Table 5-5 portrays examples of this.

language	pointer assign.	value assign.	compont. sel.
ALGOL68	p := q	T(p) := q	field **of** p
Pascal	p := q	p↑ := q↑	p↑.field
Ada	p := q	p.**all** := q.**all**	p.field

Table 5-5:   Examples of Pointer Notation

In that table, p and q are pointer variables and field is a component of a dynamically allocated record. For ALGOL68, T is assumed to be the mode (or type) of the record values.

5.5. Structured Data Types

There exists in modern programming languages two ways of joining (aggregating) data so that it can be treated as a unit. These are called the *array* and the *record* (or structure). An array is an aggregate of homogeneous data elements which are identified by their position within the aggregate. A record is an aggregate of (possibly) heterogeneous data elements which are identified by name. We begin our investigation with arrays.

An array is characterized by a name, a list of dimensions, a type for its elements and a type and range for its index set. Typically the index set of an array is a consecutive set of integers, but as we shall see this need not necessarily be so. If the index set is the integers, then each dimension is defined by stating an integer lower (lb) and upper (ub) bound which implies that lb $\leq$ ub and that ub - lb + 1 is the size along that dimension. This list of lower and upper bounds is bracketed in some way, typically by square brackets or by parentheses. In FORTRAN, PL/1 or Ada we might write A(5,3,7) to denote the "5,3,7" element of the three dimensional array whose name is A. In ALGOL60, ALGOL68, and Pascal square brackets are used for array dimensions, e.g. A[5,3,7]. This has the advantage that there is no confusion between an array name and a function call in an expression.

One important language design issue is whether the bounds of each dimension must be constants or can be expressions. In a language such as FORTRAN where storage is allocated at compile-time, these bounds must be constants. FORTRAN77 has loosened up on its predecessor's constraints allowing, for example, arbitrary integer lower bounds (whereas before, the bound was always required to be one). However, 7 is still the maximum number of dimensions. In ALGOL60, where storage is allocated dynamically, it was natural to allow the bounds of arrays to be determined at run-time. Thus the lower and upper bound of a dimension can be any arithmetic expression which evaluates to an integer. The Pascal report [Wirth 71b] only allows constant values for specifying array bounds. This was a carefully reasoned decision for Wirth who felt that the loss of efficiency of dynamic array bounds was not worth the gain in flexibility. But the real problem is not the constant array bounds, but the fact that procedures *cannot* accept arrays of arbitrary size. The difficulty is that in Pascal, the size of an array is considered to be part of its type definition. If we say

type *asize10* = array *[1 .. 10]* **of** *integer;*
asize20 = **array** *[1 .. 20]* **of** *integer;*

then *asize10* and *asize20* are arrays of different types. And as we cannot write, say a sorting procedure which will accept arrays of more than one type,we are forced to think of ways around this limitation. One solution is to use a maximum size array for all possible inputs. This solution works, but is neither elegant nor efficient. But of greater consequence is the fact that this limitation inhibits the development of libraries of procedures. This restriction has generated sufficient controversy that some Pascal implementations do allow dynamic array bounds.

In FORTRAN we must write

DIMENSION A(100), B(10,10)

to declare a one-dimensional array of 100 elements and a two-dimensional array of 100 elements. For A the elements are A(1), . . . , A(100) and for B they are B(1,1), B(1,2), . . . , B(1,10), B(2,1), . . . , B(2, 10), . . . , B(10, 10). The only time we can replace a constant in the definition of the bounds of an array is when it is a parameter of a subroutine. Then we can write

SUBROUTINE SORT(A, N)
DIMENSION A(N)

But one should not be mislead into thinking that changing the value of N will alter the size of the array. On the contrary, in FORTRAN only a pointer to the starting address of the array is passed to the subroutine. The actual value of N is ignored. It denotes A as an array and must be either a parameter or COMMON variable. The actual array which corresponds to A must have been defined using constant bounds.

In Pascal there is a bit more freedom in the sense that one can write

> **const** *numberofdays* = *30;*
> **var** *day : array [1 . . numberofdays]* **of** *real;*

which defines the size of array *day* in terms of the constant *numberofdays*. However, the Pascal Report [Wirth 71b] does not permit array sizes to vary during the execution of a program. Some languages that do permit this are Ada, PL/1, ALGOL60, and SIMULA. (Note that what actually happens is an entirely new array with possibly different bounds is assigned to an array pointer.)

For example, in Ada one can write

> **type** SEQUENCE **is array** (INTEGER **range** < >) **of** FLOAT;
> **type** SEQREF **is access** SEQUENCE;
> P : SEQREF;
>
> . . .
>
> P := **new** SEQUENCE(1 . . 1000);

Here SEQUENCE is a type whose variables are arrays of floating point numbers whose indices are of type INTEGER but whose bounds are not specified. The second line defines SEQREF to be a pointer (type **access**) to an array of type SEQUENCE. Then P is a variable of type SEQREF. In the last line P is assigned a pointer to a new array which is allocated at run-time and has the dimension bounds of 1 to 1000. In place of 1 and 1000 it is legal to put arbitrary integer expressions.

Since the store of a computer is generally a one-dimensional array, it is common to store all or large parts of arrays in consecutive locations in memory. Given a multi-dimensional array reference such as $A(5,3,7)$ a mapping is made to the proper location in the store. To implement this mapping one associates with each array a descriptor of information. This *array descriptor* contains the array name, the type of its elements, the length of each element, say s, the starting address of the array *stad*, the number of dimensions followed by the lower and upper bounds of each dimension lb_i, ub_i, $1 \leqslant i \leqslant n$. The elements themselves are generally stored in row major order. For $A(1:3, 1:3)$ row major order is

$A(1,1)\ A(1,2)\ A(1,3)\ A(2,1)\ A(2,2)\ A(2,3)\ A(3,1)\ A(3,2)\ A(3,3)$

The major alternative is to store the elements in column major order. Then they would be stored as

$A(1,1)\ A(2,1)\ A(3,1)\ A(1,2)\ A(2,2)\ A(3,2)\ A(1,3)\ A(2,3)\ A(3,3)$

For an array of n dimensions, *row major order* implies that the elements are so ordered that the *last* index varies the fastest, while *column major order* implies that the *first* index varies the fastest. In Figure 5-2 we see pictures of a one and two-dimensional array of reals with their descriptors.

Given an array reference $A(i)$ or $B(j, k)$, where row major order is used, how is the proper location determined? Consider the one-dimensional case first, where the elements are stored in row major order. By inspection we see that the location of $A(i)$ is given by the formula

$$loc(A(i)) = stad + (i\text{-}lb_1)\ s$$

where *stad* is the starting address, lb_1 is the lower bound of the first dimension and *s* is the element size. Rearranging terms we get

$$loc(A(i)) = stad - lb_1\ s + i\ s$$

where only the last term needs to be computed at run-time and added to the precomputed sum of the first two terms to get the correct position.

For the two-dimensional case we get

$$loc(B(i, j)) = stad + (i\text{-}lb_1)(ub_2\text{-}lb_2+1)\ s + (j\text{-}lb_2)\ s$$

The term $(ub_2\text{-}lb_2 + 1)$ is the number of elements in the second dimension. Again, rearranging terms one gets

$$loc(B(i, j)) = stad - s\ lb_1\ (ub_2\text{-}lb_2+1) - slb_2 + js + is(ub_2\text{-}lb_2+1)$$

Only the last two terms depend on *i* or *j* so only two multiplications and two additions are needed to compute the address of $B(i, j)$. For a generalization of this formula to more dimensions see [Horowitz 76].

In some languages an array need not be indexed only by integers. For example in Pascal one can use an ordered enumerated type as the index set of an array. Using the enumerated type *months* which we previously defined we could write:

temperature : **array** [*months*] **of** real;

integer A (−2:5)

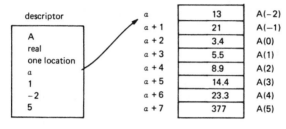

descriptor			
A	a	13	A(−2)
real	$a + 1$	21	A(−1)
one location	$a + 2$	3.4	A(0)
a	$a + 3$	5.5	A(1)
1	$a + 4$	8.9	A(2)
−2	$a + 5$	14.4	A(3)
5	$a + 6$	23.3	A(4)
	$a + 7$	377	A(5)

real B (0:3, −2:1)

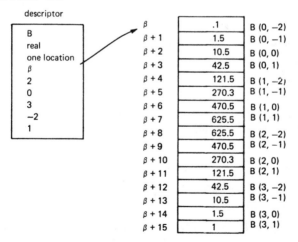

descriptor			
B	β	.1	B (0, −2)
real	$\beta + 1$	1.5	B (0, −1)
one location	$\beta + 2$	10.5	B (0, 0)
β	$\beta + 3$	42.5	B (0, 1)
2	$\beta + 4$	121.5	B (1, −2)
0	$\beta + 5$	270.3	B (1, −1)
3	$\beta + 6$	470.5	B (1, 0)
−2	$\beta + 7$	625.5	B (1, 1)
1	$\beta + 8$	625.5	B (2, −2)
	$\beta + 9$	470.5	B (2, −1)
	$\beta + 10$	270.3	B (2, 0)
	$\beta + 11$	121.5	B (2, 1)
	$\beta + 12$	42.5	B (3, −2)
	$\beta + 13$	10.5	B (3, −1)
	$\beta + 14$	1.5	B (3, 0)
	$\beta + 15$	1	B (3, 1)

Figure 5-2: Two Arrays Stored in Row Major Order

rainfall : **array** [*months*] **of** real;

Assuming the arrays are initialized as shown:

temperature := (15.5, 12, 10.4, 29, 45, 65.5, 78, 84, 82,61, 42, 22.5);
rainfall := (10.6, 15.5, 22.5, 30, 15, 5.4, 0.5, 0.1, 0.6, 1.8, 6.6, 10.5);

we can retrieve element values by writing *temperature[May]* or *rainfall[Jun]*. We could even write a **for** loop such as

for *i* := *Jan* **to** *Dec* **do** *x* := *x* + *temperature[i]*;

However, if integers are used as the index set of an array in Pascal, then they must belong to a specified subrange of the integers. No *real* subranges are permitted, and thus we cannot declare an 11 element array as A[1.0 : 2.0 **by** 0.1].

In ALGOL68 one can define nonrectangular arrays by writing, for example "[1:3] **ref** [ ] **real** w" which declares w as an array of three items, where each item references an array of reals. Thus if we also have

[1:a] **real** x
[1:b] **real** y
[1:c] **real** z

we can then write

w[1] := x
w[2] := y
w[3] := z

which gives a two-dimensional array whose rows are of length a, b and c respectively. We can refer to the 2,3 element of w as either w[2] [3] or y[3].

Selecting a portion of an array is nicely done in PL/1 where an asterisk (*) in any position implies all possible indices of that dimension are included. Given W(1:3, 1:5), then W(3, *) denotes the third row and W(*,5) denotes the fifth column. In ALGOL68 one would write w[3,] and w[,5] or in APL w[3;] and w[;5]. ALGOL68 adds the simplification that if the omitted subscript is the last one, then the comma can be deleted. Finally, in ALGOL68 a subarray can itself be indexed, so one can write further w[,5][4] to stand for w[4,5]. PL/1 does not allow subarrays to be indexed. In essence PL/1 yields an array "slice" as a value and hence it cannot be indexed. An ALGOL68 slice is an array reference which can either be dereferenced to give a value or subscripted. Another ALGOL68 feature for identifying segments of an array is called *trimming*. For example, assuming the declaration for w above, w[3,2:4] stands for the three elements w[3,2], w[3,3], w[3,4]. In ALGOL68 user defined enumeration types are not permitted, and hence one final disadvantage of arrays is that the index must always be an integer.

Neither FORTRAN nor ALGOL60 provide array operations, other than allowing an array element to act as a scalar. But APL, PL/1, and ALGOL68 allow us to write A ← B, A = B, or A := B respectively as long as A and B are arrays or subarrays of the same size. The operation copies every element of B into A. In PL/1 we could have

$$\text{DCL A}(10,10) \text{ , B}(10)$$

and then write

$$B = A(I,{}^*)$$

which causes no problem as the right-hand side is treated as a one-dimensional array of the same size as B. But trying this in APL is likely to cause grief.

Ada provides a nice way of initializing arrays. One may write

type MATRIX **is array** (INTEGER **range** 1 .. 2,
                        INTEGER **range** 1 .. 2) **of** REAL;
A : MATRIX : = ((10, 20), (30, 40));

This assigns 10, . . , 40 in row major order to A. One may also write

A : MATRIX : = (1 = > (1 = > 10, 2 = > 20),
                2 = > (1 = > 30, 2 = > 40));   or

A : MATRIX : = (1 = > (1 = > 1, **others** => 0),
                2 = > (2 = > 1, **others** => 0));

creating the 2 x 2 identity matrix.

In summary, although arrays are standard parts of programming languages, there are many ways in which they differ from language to language including:

- ☐ syntax for naming arrays and array elements;
- ☐ what types can be assumed by the value components;
- ☐ what types can be used as index components;
- ☐ whether array bounds must be determinable at compile or run-time;
- ☐ how complex the addressing of array names can become;

☐ what form of array slicing is provided;
☐ what kind of array initialization statements are allowed;
☐ what built-in operations on compatible arrays are provided?

The distinction between scalar and structured data types has been explored by Wulf, Shaw, Hilfinger and Flon including the analysis of arrays as they are implemented in various languages; see [Wulf 81].

Records

A record type is a structured type which is composed of heterogeneous data. A declaration of a record type describes the various fields and the type of their values. For example,

> **type** *stock* =
>   **record**
>   *name* : **array** *[1 .. 30]* **of** *char;*
>   *price* : **array** *[1 .. 365]* **of** *real;*
>   *dividend* : *real;*
>   *volume* : **array** *[1 .. 365]* **of** *integer;*
>   *exchange* : *(nyse, amex, nasdaq)*
>   **end**
>   **var** *newstock : stock*

This declaration defines *stock* as a type whose values have five components. The first component is an array of characters which is the name of the stock. The fields *price* and *volume* are numeric fields which are arrays of numbers. *Dividend* is a real number. Notice that the field called *exchange* is defined by an enumerated type which is composed of three literals. The variable *newstock* is declared to be of type *stock*.

The issue of how to reference the components of a record has not been resolved in the same way by all languages. There continue to be a variety of forms. One method advocated by Knuth [Knuth 68], is the so-called functional notation. If *ibm* is a variable of type *stock*, then he suggests we access its fields by writing *name(ibm)*, *price(ibm)[25]*, *dividend(ibm)*, *volume(ibm)[25]*, *exchange(ibm)*. This notation uses the field names as function selectors. An alternative to this syntax is the so-called qualified name form, obtained by appending a dot and the field name to the variable name. Thus we would write *ibm.name[20]*, *ibm.price[25]*, *ibm.dividend*, *ibm.volume[25]*, and *ibm.exchange*. Both Pascal and Ada use the dot notation for accessing fields of a record. ALGOL68 is close to the functional notation. For example, a record definition using ALGOL68 syntax would be

mode stock = **struct**(**string** name, **int** dividend, **int** exchange)

and one could then write "*name* **of** *ibm*," or "*exchange* **of** *ibm.*"

The history of the record goes back to COBOL which introduced it and called it a *structure.* PL/1 followed in the COBOL tradition. More recent languages such as Pascal use the term **record** and prefer a syntax such as

record-type ::= **record** field-list **end**
field-list ::= fixed part [";" variant part] | variant part
fixed-part ::= record-section { ";" record-section }
record-section ::= { identifier-list ":" type }

Ignoring the variant part for the moment, a Pascal record consists of the symbols **record** and **end** enclosing a fixed-part, which is a list of one or more record-sections separated by semicolons. Each record-section is described by a list of one or more identifiers followed by their type. These identifiers are called field designators. It is important to note that the scope of the field identifiers is the record itself and so they must be distinct from each other, but not necessarily distinct from identifiers declared outside of the record.

It would be nice if a language offered a mechanism to initialize a record. Such a facility can be thought of as an extension to the array initialization facility which we have already seen. For example, we might write

var *ibm, csc* : *stock*;

and then initialize these variables by writing

ibm := *make-stock('IBM', 0 .. 0, 5.25, 0 .. 0, nyse);*
csc := *make-stock('Computer Science Corp.', 0 .. 0, 0, 0 .. 0, nyse);*

ALGOL-W, ALGOL68, and Ada provide these constructors as part of the built-in language features.

Once a record type is defined, variables may be declared to be of that type. In Pascal to refer to one of the component fields of a record one must qualify a record variable by adding a period after its name followed by the component field. When working with record variables it may become tedious to have to continually refer to the record name qualified by all of its fields. To avoid this Pascal provides the *with* statement. Instead of having to write

newstock.name := "*dec*"
newstock.dividend := 36;

newstock.exchange := amex;

one need only write

> **with** *newstock* **do**
>   **begin**
>   *name := "dec"*
>   *dividend := 36;*
>   *exchange := amex;*
>   **end**

In Ada the components of a record can be of any type. If we have

> **type** FLIGHT;
> **type** LISTOFFLIGHTS **is access** FLIGHT;
> **type** FLIGHT **is**
>   **record**
>   FLIGHTNO   : INTEGER **range** 0 .. 100;
>   SOURCE : STRING;
>   DESTINATION : STRING;
>   RETURNFLIGHT : LISTOFFLIGHTS;
>   **end record**;

If X,Y are variables of type LISTOFFLIGHTS, then the variable X.RETURNFLIGHT can be assigned to point to another FLIGHT, e.g. X.RETURNFLIGHT := Y;. This allows for extended qualification of names, such as X.RETURNFLIGHT.FLIGHTNO or X.RETURNFLIGHT.SOURCE, etc.

A record type with a variant part specifies several alternative variants of the type. Thus the set of possible record values consists of the union of the set of values which make up all of the alternatives. A variant part depends on a special component of the record, called its *discriminant*. Each variant defines the components that are legitimate for a specific value of the discriminant. The form for expressing the variant is often taken as the **case** statement of the language. In Pascal the syntax for a variant is

> variant-part = **case** tag-field type-identifier **of** variant { ; variant}
> tag-field = [identifier :]
> variant = [case-label-list : (field-list)]

or in Ada the syntax is

> variant-part ::=

```
case discriminant-name is
  { when choice { | choice } => component-list }
  end case
choice ::= simple-expression | discrete-range | others
```

In Pascal if we had the type definition

type *option* = *(sixmonths, ninemonths)*

then we could consider adding a field to the record *stock* by adding this variant part

```
case x : option of
    sixmonths : (exprice : real)
    ninemonths : (nuprice : integer)
end
```

When the value of *x* is *sixmonths* then one can legally access the *exprice* field of *stock*. When *x* has the value *ninemonths*,then one can legally use the field *nuprice* of *stock*.

The variant record is essentially a mechanism for creating a union of types. Looking at a second example in Pascal,we see the definition of a generalized list, i.e a list whose elements may be either atoms or sublists. The record definition contains a variant field.

```
type listpointer = ↑ listnode;
type listnode =
    record
      link : listpointer;
      case tag : boolean of
          false : ( data : char);
          true : ( downlink : listpointer)
    end;
var p, q: listpointer;
```

If we are writing a program which has the above type definition, then $p\uparrow.data$ may exist and be of type *char* only if $p\uparrow.tag$ = *false*. Unfortunately this correspondence cannot be checked at compile-time for several reasons. First,the *tag* field of a variant record is optional. Secondly,when it is present, it may be assigned to, permitting a trap door for programmers who can now legitimately write:

```
p↑ .tag := true;
p↑ .downlink := q;
p↑ .tag := false;
```

writeln(p↑ .data);

Here we see the *tag* is first set to *true* and the variant field *downlink* assigned the value of *q*. However, the *tag* field is next altered to *false* and the current value printed. Therefore,the integer with the same bit representation as the value of *q* may be output. In fact, the programmer has little choice about avoiding this illegality, as Pascal does not supply array or record constants. The programmer must, therefore, resort to element-by-element assignment, thus guaranteeing that the record must pass through an inconsistent state.

In ALGOL68 the discriminated union is not part of the record mechanism, but is treated as a separate type. This approach was advocated by Hoare in [Dahl-Dijkstra-Hoare 72]. For example, we might have

> **mode** *hamster* = **struct** (**int** *height, weight);*
> **mode** *mouse* = **struct** (*[1 : 3]* **int** *size);*
> **mode** *pets* = **union** (*hamster, mouse);*
> **mode** *menagerie* = **struct** (**string** *names, pets s);*

The first line defines a record called *hamster* which has two fields. The second line defines a record called *mouse* which is composed of an array of integers. The record called *pets* is the union of two modes, *hamster* and *mouse*. Finally the mode *menagerie* can be viewed as a record which contains the names, and depending upon whether it represents a hamster or a mouse either the height-weight or the sizes of the menagerie. In contrast to Pascal, we see that there is no variant tag field which can be accessed. ALGOL68 gets around this by providing a so-called "case conformity clause" which allows one to write

> **case** *s* **of** *x* **in**
>   *(hamster)* : . . .
>   *(mouse)* : . . .
> **esac**

where *x* is a variable of mode *menagerie*.

The language designers of Euclid were aware of the problem of nonsafe variant records in Pascal and corrected it. Euclid permits parameterized types and so the tag can be treated as a formal parameter to the declaration. This means that when a variable is declared to be of record type (or a pointer to a record type) one also states the allowable value of the tag. Returning to our earlier example one could now write

> **var** *x* : *listnode (true)*

var *y : listnode (false)*
var *z : listnode* (**any***)*

In Euclid no assignments to the tag field are possible once they have been initialized. The **any** permits *z* to hold a value of either *listnode(true)* or *listnode(false)*. One can say *z := y* because the type of the right-hand side can be coerced to the type of the variable on the left-hand side. But the coercion in the other direction is not permitted, so *y := z* is illegal. The only way to retrieve a value of the original type is to use a discriminant in a **case** statement such as

case discriminating *w = z* **on** *tag* **of**
    true => *x := w;* **end**
    false => *y := w;* **end**
end case

This discriminating case statement permits a fully successful run-time check of which variant of a record is currently being used. We will see in Chapter 8 that SIMULA also provides a feature similar to discriminated unions, the concatenated class. An example is given there.

5.6. Type Coercion

To review, if the decision is made to have typing, then several questions arise. Can the type of all variables be determined at compile-time, *static type checking*, or will run-time routines be needed, *dynamic type checking*? Static type checking allows the compiler to do a great deal of consistency checking, and in addition, it can produce more efficient object code. But if the type is not known until run-time, all that the compiler can do is generate a call to a subroutine that will check the types and perform the correct operation. With dynamic type checking variable names may be declared, but their type is not stated. The gain here is greater flexibility at run-time and increased simplicity in the writing of programs. LISP and APL are two languages which follow this approach. This flexibility seems especially desirable for interactive languages. The penalty is that each variable must carry with it a property list which is queried at run-time to determine its type.

Coercion is the term that is used to describe the process whereby a value of one type is converted into a value of another type. This conversion process may take place implicitly, perhaps during the evaluation of an expression or in the process of performing an assignment. The idea of implicit conversions appeared in several early programming languages, such as FORTRAN, which permits mixed mode arithmetic. The FORTRAN statement R = I causes an integer to real conversion. The language PL/1 took the concept of coercion to the extreme by providing implicit default conversions between all built-in types, e.g. character to real, real to integer, bit to character, etc. One can conveniently classify some of these type conversions into the general classes called widening and narrowing. The term *widening* refers to those coercions for which every value in the domain has a corresponding value in the range type. One example of widening is converting an integer to a real. Conversely, the term *narrowing* refers to those mappings where not every domain type has a value in the range. Conversion from real to integer is an example of narrowing. In the case of narrowing some languages will provide messages saying that a loss of information has occurred, while others will not. In PL/1, the narrowing of a real to an integer may cause truncation. Some languages, however, may use rounding. Some coercions are just illegal, as when someone attempts to convert a character string such as 'abc' to a real in which case a run-time error condition is raised.

Typically a language will provide for type conversion between scalar types, but not for structured or user defined types. For the latter, there is no obvious way to generate the conversion procedures so it is left to the programmer's discretion. In Pascal, for example, the only built-in conversions are the widening of integers to real and the widening and narrowing of subranges. Pascal's restrictions on narrowing arise presumably because Wirth wanted to maintain the semantics of assignment, i.e. that the left and right sides be of the same type. Thus an assignment such as "$i := 3.1415$" where i is an integer is not permitted even though the right-hand side could be narrowed. But some narrowing has crept in as in the case of subranges. This is allowed because of the fact that subranges require run-time checks in any case. A definition such as $i : 1 .. 10;$ followed by $i := 4;$ would be an illegal assignment of an element of type integer to a variable of type subrange unless narrowing is permitted. The assignment

> **var** r : *real*;
> i : *integer*;
> $i := r;$

is not allowed in Pascal. It must be replaced either by "$i := trunc(r)$" which truncates any fractional part of r or by "$i := round(r)$" which rounds r to the nearest integer. Finally we note that there may still be some problems with widening, in particular for large integers as the width of the typical real mantissa can be shorter than the maximum length of the integer type.

The language ALGOL68 has approached the issue of coercion in a complete and formal manner. The language defines six kinds of coercions: widening, dereferencing, deproceduring, rowing, uniting and voiding. It does not allow narrowing. Since variables are allowed to hold values which are procedures, then for a procedure called *random* a statement such as

$$x := random;$$

needs to have the procedure name dereferenced so that the value can be assigned to *x*. The coercion called rowing is used to extend a single length argument into a row of that argument. A declaration such as

$$[\,] \text{ real } P = 100;$$

causes P to be coerced into a one-dimensional array of one element. The uniting coercion refers to the meta-conversion of a mode (type) into a union of which that mode is a member. For example,

> **mode** *realbool* = **union** (**real, bool**);
> *realbool p;*
> *p* := **true**;

Besides implicit conversions, ALGOL68 introduces a mechanism for explicit conversions. Called the *cast*, it is a construct which forces a coercion in a context in which it would not normally take place. See [Tanenbaum 76] or [ALGOL68] for details.

5.7. Type Equivalence

One of the major contributions of ALGOL68, ALGOL-W, and Pascal was their data type facilities. The attempt at a strongly typed language coupled with a nice mechanism for user-defined types was a significant step forward in language design. However, its definition also had some inadequacies which have led to further understanding of typing. Many of the language definition problems of Pascal, including type equivalence, have been detailed in the paper by Welsh, Sneeringer and Hoare [Welsh 77] and the paper by Berry and Schwartz [Berry 79] discusses type equivalence in general terms.

The Pascal report declares that both sides of an assignment statement "must be of identical type," though some minor exceptions exist.

Nowhere is the notion of identical type formalized, which has led to misunderstanding. The term *type compatibility* refers to the semantic rules that determine whether an object's type is valid in a particular context. By the term *context* we might mean type compatibility in conjunction with assignment or array indexing or procedure calls or with the application of any of the operators. By objects we mean variables, elements of variables, constants, expressions, functions or formal parameters. Consider the following example first given by [Welsh 77].

> **type** T = **array** *[1 .. 100]* **of** *integer;*
> **var** x, y : array *[1 .. 100]* **of** *integer;*
> z : **array** *[1 .. 100]* **of** *integer;*
> w : T;

Type T is defined over the subrange of integers from 1 to 100. Variables x and y are declared together to have a type which looks the same as T. Similarly z is declared, but on a separate line and w is of type T. Are w, x, y, z to be interpreted as names of the same type? Or, shall we interpret w differently from x (and y), or differently from z? The Pascal report gives no answer to these questions and it has been criticized for this, see [Habermann 73].

There are at least two ways of stating a rule which solves the problem;

Rule 1: Two variables will be recognized as being of the same type if and only if they are declared together or declared using the same type identifier name:

Rule 2: Two variables will be recognized as being of the same type if and only if the components of their type are the same in all respects.

Rule 1 is called *name equivalence* while rule 2 is called *structural equivalence*. According to name equivalence x and y are equivalent, but w is distinct from x and z . This scheme extends naturally to the elementary types, so that if p and q are declared to be **real**, then p and q are type equivalent. According to rule 2, $w, x, y,$ and z are all names of the same type.

Now suppose one tries to write in Pascal

> **type** T1 = T2

where T2 is previously defined. Rule 1 does *not* imply that T1 is just another name for T2. Rather it implies they will be treated differently. Rule 2 however implies that they are equivalent. So these two rules clearly give different results in different instances.

Note that for structural equivalence the example

array [1 . . 100] **of** *real*;
array [1 . . 10, 1 . . 10] **of** *real*;

has component types which are the same, but not in all respects as they differ structurally.

The merits of these rules vary. Name equivalence is simple to determine, but forces the programmer to define extra type names. Structural equivalence has its own problems. For example, how does one treat two enumerated type definitions which are alike except for ordering? Or suppose we write

type *dice* = *1 .. 12*
         dozen = *1 .. 12;*

Structurally these types are the same but conceptually we might want them to be different. Another problem of structural equivalence is shown by the two record definitions

var *A :* **record** *x,y : real* **end***;*
         B : **record** *u,v : real* **end***;*

Here the structures are the same, but the field names are different.

Determining structural equivalence can get very complex for a compiler. In this example from ALGOL68 all three types, *p*, *q*, and *r* are equivalent using the structural equivalence rule.

mode *p* = **struct** (**int** *x*, **ref** *p z*)
mode *q* = **struct** (**int** *x*, **ref** *r z*)
mode *r* = **struct** (**int** *x*, **ref** *q z*)

The determination of structural equivalence necessitates expansion of the recursive type definitions into potentially infinite trees where edges are marked by selectors and leaves by basic types. Identical trees imply equivalent types.

Another problem with the typing system in Pascal is that all subranges are treated as new types since all bounds are known at compile-time. For example *1 .. 100* and *2 .. 99* both define different subrange types. This may seem natural, but how then do we interpret the type of *2,3 , . . . , 99* which are elements of both and hence any value is legally assignable to a variable of either type.

The Pascal 6000 compiler release 1 [Pascal6000 79] used the name equivalence rule for type compatibility. Release 2 used structural equivalence and release 3 (plus the new ISO Pascal standard) uses a third possibility called declaration compatibility. Two types are compatible using *declaration equivalence* if their structures were described by the same actual type specification. This means that either the type names are equal or they lead back to the same actual **array**, **record**, or **file** specification. For example, here we see two records defining three **var**'s: *industrial, utility,* and *transportation.*

> **var** *industrial, utility* : **record**
>> *name* : **array** *[1 .. 30]* **of** *char;*
>> *dividend* : *real;*
>> *price* : **array** *[1 .. 365]* **of** *real;*
> **end**

>> *transportation* : **record**
>>> *name* : **array** *[1 .. 30]* **of** *char;*
>>> *dividend* : *real;*
>>> *price* : **array** *[1 .. 365]* **of** *real;*
>> **end**

In this example *industrial* and *utility* are declaration equivalent because their structures are described by the same declaration. But *industrial* or *utility* are not compatible with *transportation* despite the fact that they are structurally identical. If instead we declared *industrial, utility,* and *transportation* as shown:

> **type** *stock* = **record**
>> *name* : **array** *[1 .. 30]* **of** *char;*
>> *dividend* : *real;*
>> *price* : **array** *[1 .. 365]* **of** *real;*
> **end**

> **var** *industrial, utility* : *stock;*
>> *transportation* : *stock;*

then under declaration equivalence *industrial* and *utility* are type compatible, but not *transportation.* However under name and structural equivalence all three are compatible.

5.8. A Look at Ada and Types

In this section we review many of the salient features of Ada's types and typing system.

In Ada there are essentially four groups of types called: scalar types, composite types, access (or pointer) types, and private types. The scalar types include the conventional numeric types plus user-defined enumerated types. The composite types are arrays and records. The access type provides objects which are pointers to other objects. Finally private types create objects whose precise structure is not known to the user. A private type is defined and enclosed in a so-called package. The only aspects of the private type that are known are the operations on the type.

As with other languages we have studied, Ada requires that all objects be declared as to their type in a declaration. Thus, Ada is said to be a strongly typed language. Elements of enumeration types can be tested for equality, inequality, can be assigned to, and tested for order using the relational operators. Also there are so-called attributes of enumerated types such as 'FIRST, 'LAST, and 'SUCC, so for example

```
MONTHS'FIRST = JAN
MONTHS'LAST = DEC
MONTHS'SUCC(JUL) = AUG
```

The declaration of objects proceeds in the conventional manner, e.g.

```
THISMONTH : MONTHS;    --declares a variable
LASTMONTH : MONTHS  := NOV;
     --declares and initializes a variable
FIRSTMONTH : constant MONTHS := JAN;
     --declares, initializes constant
```

In Ada one may get confused with terminology. A type definition defines a type, whereas a type declaration defines both a type and declares a name with that type. An object declaration declares either a constant or a variable of a certain type.

Ada offers the Boolean type

```
type BOOLEAN is (FALSE, TRUE);
```

with the conventional operations: **and, or, not, xor**. There is a type CHARACTER which includes the entire ASCII character set, (see Chapter 3 for more details). As for the other enumerated types the attributes 'FIRST, 'LAST, and 'SUCC are available. Also available are 'POS (for position in the sequence) and 'VAL (for value, given its index in the sequence).

It is possible to define a restricted set of values of a type by using a *range constraint.* This constraint does not alter the allowable operations, but merely restricts the legitimate values at run-time. For example,

SUMMERMONTHS : MONTHS **range** JUN . . AUG;

Here SUMMERMONTHS is a variable of type MONTHS whose values are constrained to be either JUN, JUL or AUG.

One important typing concept introduced by Ada is the notion of subtypes. A subtype is essentially an abbreviation for a type whose range has been constrained. For example,

subtype AUTUMN **is** MONTHS **range** SEP . . DEC;

AUTUMN is a subtype indicator for the type whose values are SEP, OCT, NOV, DEC. When a subtype declaration is encountered the constraints are evaluated, as we can have constant expressions delineating a range constraint as well as constants.

Now let's look for a while at array types in Ada. We can define a two-dimensional table by writing:

type ROSTER **is**
array(INTEGER **range** < >, INTEGER **range** < >) **of** REAL;

ROSTER is a two-dimensional array whose index values are integers, but whose bounds have yet to be specified. The range values of the array are real numbers. To create an array with specific bounds we might write "LINEUP : ROSTER(1 .. 100, 1 .. 100);" which will create a two-dimensional array of 1000 elements.

For another example, suppose we wished to define a type which consisted of strings of characters. We might write

subtype POSITIVE **is** INTEGER **range** 1 . . INTEGER'LAST;

type STRINGS **is array**(POSITIVE **range** < >) **of** CHARACTER;

An *index constraint* in Ada is designed to specify the bounds of an array type declaration. We could then define a subtype by saying

subtype OUT **is** STRINGS(1 . . 120);

which produces a type that consists of strings of 120 characters.

The operations on arrays include equality, inequality, and assignment as long as the number of components of both arrays are equal. Indexing arrays (e.g. A(I)) and slicing are also possible. Another new and nice feature of Ada is array initialization using aggregates. For example one can write

X : NUMBERS(1 .. 6) := (1 .. 6 = > 0);

X := (1 .. 3 = > 50, 4 .. 5 = > 100, 6 = > 200);

X(2 .. 4) := (25, 50, 75);

The first line declares X to be a one-dimensional array of type NUMBERS and also initializes the array to zero. The second line assigns the integer 50 to X(1), X(2), and X(3) and assigns 100 to X(4) and X(5) and assigns 200 to X(6). In the last line we see that X(2), X(3), and X(4) are assigned 25, 50 and 75 respectively.

The record type in Ada is very similar in form to Pascal. The operations include equality, inequality, and component selection using the dot notation. As for arrays there is a similar notation for aggregate initialization. Variants in records are permitted.

```
type FLIGHT is
  record
     FLIGHTNO : INTEGER range 0 .. 100;
     SOURCE : STRINGS;
     DESTINATION : STRINGS;
     RETURNFLIGHTNO : INTEGER range 0 .. 100;
     case SUPERSAVER is
          when TRUE = > CHEAPSEATS : INTEGER;
          when FALSE  = > FULLFARE : REAL;
     end case;
  end record;
```

Here we see a record declaration named FLIGHT which has a variant part whose discriminator is SUPERSAVER. When SUPERSAVER has the value TRUE, then the CHEAPSEATS field applies, whereas if the value is FALSE the FULLFARE field applies. To initialize a record of type FLIGHT we might write, using aggregate notation, (TRUE, 65, 'LAX', 'KEN', 66, 50) or (FALSE, 66, 'KEN', 'LAX', 65, 420.50). In contrast to Pascal, discriminants in Ada may only be altered by changing an entire record, rather than by selective updating. We can define record subtypes by writing for example

```
subtype SUPERSAVERFLIGHTS is
     FLIGHT(SUPERSAVER = > TRUE);
```

Ada uses the name equivalence rule. Every type definition is viewed as introducing a distinct type. Thus, two names refer to the same type only if they are declared using the same type name. Ada has rejected structural equivalence on the grounds that the substitution algorithm is too complex and may by chance result in type equality. Values of subtypes of T are considered to be compatible with objects of type T. They may be assigned to variables as long as they are subtypes of T. As regards coercions, Ada allows conversion between array types by the use of explicit functions. Each type name becomes the name of a function which will convert an object of one type into an object of the named type.

The final notion of types in Ada that I wish to discuss in this section is called derived types. A derived type is defined from an existing type and hence it has the same set of values, same attributes, and the same operations as the existing type. However, it is a *distinct* type. So for example if SUMMERMONTHS is an enumeration type

type SUMMERMONTHS **is** (JUN, JUL, AUG);

and we write

type NEWSUMMERMONTHS **is new** SUMMERMONTHS;

then NEWSUMMERMONTHS is also an enumeration type which has the same values, JUN, JUL, AUG and the same attributes such as 'FIRST. If we declare "A : SUMMERMONTHS; B : NEWSUMMERMONTHS;" then we can write

A := SUMMERMONTHS(B); --this is OK

B := NEWSUMMERMONTHS(A); --this is also OK

A := B --this is illegal as A and B are of different types

We will have more to say about Ada types in Chapter 8.

Concepts Discussed in This Chapter

Array
Coercion
Data type,
  built-in
  Boolean
  enumerated
  pointer
  ordered
Derived type

Mixed mode arithmetic
Record
Scalar
Strings
Subtype
Type equivalence
Variant records

Exercises

1. Find two languages other than Pascal which allow pointer variables. What operations are provided for these variables? Compare them with Pascal.

2. Choose two high level programming languages and contrast their definitions of the array data type.

3. Can you determine where the array values came from in Figure 5-2? From where?

4. In PL/1 what happens if A, B are character string variables of different lengths and they are compared? Define the rule completely.

5. In PL/1 if A = 'WHAT?ME?WORRY', what is the value of A after the statement "SUBSTR(A, 7, 2) = 'YOU';" is executed?

6. Investigate how type equivalence is handled by your local Pascal compiler. Check if record types are equivalent if their fields are the same. Check if identical packed and unpacked structured types are equivalent.

7. Augment Table 5-1 by listing the built-in data types for as many other languages as you can.

8. For Algorithm 5-1, PROCEDURE COUNT, supply a trace for the input sentence, 'HE WHO LAUGHS LAST, LAUGHS BEST'.

9. Look up the PL/1 rules for determining the attributes of a variable when its attributes are not completely given by the programmer.

10. PL/1 has a function called ADDR which returns the l-value of its actual parameter as a pointer value. This value may be stored in a pointer variable. Discuss the advisability of having such a function in a programming language.
11. Look up and summarize the meaning of the predefined Ada attributes T'MANTISSA, T'EMAX, and T'EPSILON for real numbers.
12. The Pascal 6000 compiler release 3 uses declaration equivalence for types, but there are special rules for dealing with parameters. Why are more restrictive rules required? If possible locate the manual and discuss these rules or else postulate some of your own.
13. Pascal does not permit the definition of non-enumeration scalar types, i.e. user defined scalar types whose values are not necessarily listed. One possibility would be to permit new types of infinite size such as

    type oddint=**integer** n **such that** n **mod** 2 < > 0;

    Discuss the merits of adding this kind of definition facility into Pascal.
14. What does the ALGOL68 statement **flex** [1 : 0] **integer** A; mean?
15. Pascal provides the types **file** and **set**. Describe the data objects of these two types and the operations that are available.
16. In Pascal the subrange is a type which consists of a consecutive subset of previously defined primitive types. Subranges of all scalar types except *real* are permitted. Mention two problems which this leads to in Pascal.
17. ALGOL68 has two statements which can be used to generate storage. One of these is **loc** and the other is **heap**. Explain the difference between the two.
18. In Ada type coercion is accomplished by requiring the programmer to explicitly use the type name as a function. Compare Ada's treatment of coercion to Pascal. What happens if the programmer uses another function of the same name as the type? How are they distinguished?
19. The array is the major data object in APL and, therefore, APL should be studied carefully for its use of arrays. Write a short report on the definition of arrays in APL. Discuss such topics as the syntax (use of square brackets),

the number and size of dimensions, array constructor operations, ravel, rho, and the built-in operators.

20. APL also provides very comprehensive string manipulation features. Write the APL functions which are equivalent to concatenation, SUBSTR, LENGTH, INDEX, and VERIFY.

21. In contrast to PL/1, APL does permit subarray indexing. For example, if A is a 5 x 5 array of zeros then one can assign a three element vector to a subarray of A by writing A[1; 3 4 5] ← 1 2 3. How does one index an array slice in APL?

22. In the text we saw PL/1 and SNOBOL programs for counting the number of letters in a sentence. Here is an APL program for doing the same thing.

$$+ / \text{ text } o . = \text{'abcdefghijklmnopqrstuvwxyz'}$$

Show how this program works on the input sentence "hello there APL".

23. One problem often encountered in programming is the use of an uninitialized variable. One way to "eliminate" such errors is to provide each new variable with a default initial value. Discuss the values you would use for the types offered in Pascal. How would you handle enumerated types and elements of variant records?

24. In [Sale 79ab] Sale proposes that a string in Pascal be defined as

type *string* = **file of** *char,*

The six primitive operations available on a string are therefore

rewrite - ready for writing;
reset - ready for reading;
↑ - look at the character in the window;
get - move the window forward one position when reading;
put - deposit a character in the window moving
        it ahead one position;
eof - examine if the window is past the end of the string.

Like a file, a string can only be in a reading or writing state and errors should be signalled for inconsistent operations such as *rewrite; get;*. Discuss how Pascal will treat the following issues assuming this scheme is fully implemented:

string assignment, string comparison, reading and writing strings, string value parameters, pointers to strings, and files with strings.

Chapter 6

SCOPE AND EXTENT

6.1. The Basics

Scope refers to the way in which named entities such as variables, labels, types, and procedures are controlled in their ability to have an effect in a program. To be more specific, the *scope* of a name is that part of the program text where all uses of the name are the same. This concept should not be confused with the related but distinct concept called *extent* which is the time during execution that the storage used to hold a value is bound to its name. In this chapter we study both of these notions. As scope and extent have long been recognized as essential issues of programming languages, they have been discussed in many texts before. Other treatments of this subject can be found in [Wulf 81 and Tennent 81].

Why incorporate the idea of scope into programming languages at all? The simplest notion of scope would be that a given identifier X always denotes the same variable and all names of variables are known in all program units. Though the sharing of variables between program units is clearly desirable, so too is the ability to name objects such as variables and have them known *only* within a restricted range of program text. This frees a programmer from remembering all of the previous names which have been used and permits several programmers to contribute pieces of the final program.

ALGOL60 introduced the idea of scope in a very elegant way by tying it to the notion of a compound statement. It is exceedingly useful to be able to treat a group of statements as a single statement. The lack of such a facility in FORTRAN causes one to create for the IF statement extra jumps and labels. To denote a set of statements that would be treated as one, ALGOL60 introduced the reserved words **begin-end**. Then it allowed declarations of variables, procedures, and labels as well as statements within any **begin-end** pair. The scope of these declared items are the bracketing symbols **begin-end**. They called the **begin-end** a block and the term *block structure* is often used to denote this method for defining scope. Names of entities declared in a **begin-end** block are said to be *local* to the block.

In ALGOL60 at compile-time, when a declaration such as "**integer** x" is encountered, a variable name and its attributes are produced as shown in Figure 6-1(a). This information is stored in the compiler's symbol table during the compilation process. At run-time when this block is entered and the same declaration is found, storage is allocated producing the diagram of Figure 6-1(b).

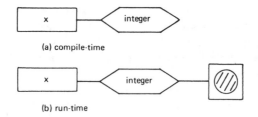

(a) compile-time

(b) run-time

Figure 6-1:   The Effect of Declarations

Since no initialization facility exists in ALGOL60, the storage area contains an undefined value. During execution within the block, values may be assigned to the variable. On block exit, this storage is reclaimed.

An entire ALGOL60 program is composed of a single block, but one or several blocks may be nested inside another block *as long as no overlapping occurs*. This requirement guarantees that storage which is allocated on entry to a block will not have to be given up until storage is reclaimed for all variables declared in blocks nested inside this block.

This permits the run-time mechanism for storage allocation to behave in a last-in-first-out manner as a stack.

```
 1  a: begin integer i, j;  real x, y;
 2      b: procedure test(integer a, b)
 3              begin boolean i;
 4                  . . .
 5              x := i*j+y;
 6                  . . .
 7          end b;
 8      . . .
 9  c: begin integer x, y; real i, j;
10          . . .
11      d: begin boolean j;
12              . . .
13          call test(x, y);
14              . . .
15      end d;
16          . . .
17      end c;
18      . . .
19 end a;
```

Table 6-1:   A Program Shell Containing Four Blocks

Consider the ALGOL60 program fragment in Table 6-1. There we see a program fragment which contains four blocks named a, b, c, d. Each block contains some declarations of variables. For example, in block a we see that i and j are declared to be of type integer and x and y of type real. Declared in block a is a procedure called *test* which has two parameters and one local variable i of type boolean. Within *test* we see an assignment statement on line 5 involving the variables x, i, j, y. Since i is declared locally in procedure *test*, the i of the assignment statement refers to this local variable and is of type boolean. However, neither x, j nor y are defined in *test*. In this case these names are referred to as *free variables*. A programming language must answer the question: what declarations of x, j and y will be used. For compiled languages the answer is usually the following: for all free variables, search in the next textually containing block to see if the name is declared. If not, then search in the next containing block and continue in this way until you either find the name for the first time or you arrive at the outermost level of the program, and the name has not been declared. In the latter case the variable is undefined. In the former case we have found its definition using the so-called *static scoping* rule. This rule is called static because one can determine a variable's definition by looking at the program text alone. In our example, the static scoping rule applied to the variables *i, j, x, y* yield the following type definitions shown by the line numbers:

	i		*j*
integer	1, 2, 8, 18, 19		1 - 8, 18, 19
boolean	3 - 7		11 - 15
real	9 - 17		9 - 10, 16, 17

	x		*y*
integer	9 - 17		9 - 17
real	1 - 8, 18, 19		1 - 8, 18, 19

Table 6-2: Types of Variables from Table 6-1 by Line Numbers

Therefore, under the static scoping rule the types of *x, i, j, y* on line 5 are real, boolean, integer and real respectively.

There is another way to resolve the definition of free variables. Rather than involving the program text, this rule is dynamic in nature. To determine the declaration of a name, look at those procedures and blocks which have not yet terminated, and try to find the first occurrence of the name. Examine these procedures and blocks in the reverse order of their invocation. In agreement with the previous rule, if the identifier is not found, then the identifier is undefined. Otherwise the first appearance of the identifier causes those attributes to be associated with the name. This mechanism is called the *dynamic scoping* rule. For example, suppose the assignment statement of line 5 was reached because the procedure call on line 13 was executed. Using the dynamic scoping rule the type of *x* is integer from block *c*, the type of *i* is real from block *c*, the type of *j* is boolean from block *d*, and the type of *y* is integer also from block *c*. Languages such as LISP, APL and SNOBOL use the dynamic scoping rule.

One of the anomalies that results from the static scoping rule can clearly be seen from Table 6-1. When block *c* re-introduces the names *i, j, x, y*, they effectively wipe-out the previous declarations until block *c* is exited. Thus, throughout block *c* the name *x* is associated with the attribute integer, and nowhere within block *c* can the real variable named *x* defined in block *a* be accessed. This is referred to as a *hole-in-scope.* Later we will see how Ada has removed the hole-in-scope problem, while still retaining the static scoping rule.

As I said before, the alternative to static scoping is dynamic scoping or sometimes called *fluid binding.* Here the association of a name to a variable depends exclusively on the run-time environment. The meaning of a variable is taken as the most recently occurring and still active definition of the name during execution. This rule is followed by LISP and APL, so we will see more of it in Chapter 12. In the meantime, here is a simple example which points up the difference.

> **begin boolean** *b* := **true***;*
> **procedure** *P; print(b)* **end***;*
> **begin boolean** *b* := **false***;*
> *P*
> **end**
> **end**

Table 6-3: Difference Between Static and Dynamic Scope

A Boolean variable *b* is assigned **true** in the outer block. Following that comes the definition of a procedure *P* which contains only a print statement. In an inner block, a new Boolean variable *b* is declared and initialized to **false**. Then procedure *P* is invoked. The question is: which value of *b* is printed? Using static scoping, the *b* in *P* refers to the *b* in the outer block so that *P* prints **true**, but using dynamic scoping it refers to the other *b* so that P prints **false**.

A brief look at FORTRAN in relation to scope shows that every variable is either explicitly or implicitly declared as local to the procedure (SUBROUTINE or FUNCTION) in which it is used. The effect of global variables is achieved by the COMMON feature. Variables which are named in a COMMON statement may be shared among other procedures which also contain COMMON statements. However, it is not required that the variables in COMMON be referred to in the same way in different subroutines, and there is no checking to see if the COMMON declarations are consistent. Though this probably has its uses, it is more likely to have an adverse impact on program reliability. The option of naming a COMMON block, called *labeled* COMMON (or *named* COMMON), and shown in Table 6-4, also exists and this permits a set of procedures to share a named set of variables exclusively. This feature can be used to encourage program modularity and information hiding. The named COMMON block A contains variables X, Y, and Z(1), . . . , Z(10) which it shares with

```
C THIS IS THE MAIN PROGRAM
  COMMON/A/X,Y,Z(10)
  COMMON GO, IRED, TEMP
  .
  .
  .

  END
  SUBROUTINE A1(P, Q)
  COMMON GO, IRED, TEMP
  .
  .
  .

  END
  SUBROUTINE A2(P, Q)
  COMMON/A/X,Y,Z(10)
  .
  .
  .

  END
```

Table 6-4:   An Example of the Use of Global Variables in FORTRAN

SUBROUTINE A2, but not with SUBROUTINE A1.

Another language of interest is JOVIAL (Jules' Own Version of the International Algorithmic Language), which has been used chiefly by the U.S. Department of Defense. The language is rooted in ALGOL58, a predecessor of ALGOL60. With respect to scope, JOVIAL follows the static scoping rule. But in contrast to ALGOL60,it permits separate compilation of modules. Its so-called COMPOOL (COMmunications POOL) facility permits data, procedures and definitions to be shared among modules. The COMPOOL is considered to be a module and is separately compilable. Each module which desires to share the data and procedures which are declared in the COMPOOL do so by issuing a COMPOOL directive. At run-time the consistency of actual and formal parameters is monitored. As this is done even for procedures which are separately compiled, but which use the COMPOOL, it substantially eliminates the major criticism of separate compilation, i.e. the lack of checks between actual and formal parameters of procedures or between the definition of variables and their global use. For more information read [JOVIAL].

PL/1 followed the ALGOL60 lead by introducing the BEGIN-END group analogous to the **begin-end** block. But PL/1 runs into trouble by not insisting on explicit declarations of all variables. If a variable appears without a corresponding declaration, it is assumed to be declared, with default attributes, immediately following the PROCEDURE statement of the external procedure in which the variable is used. This can cause difficulty, as the following situation shows.

```
PEC: PROCEDURE;
  A : BEGIN;
      . . .
    B : BEGIN;
        J =  X;
        . . .
      C : BEGIN;
          J = Y;
          . . .
      END C;
      D :  /* J AT LABEL D */
    END B;
  END A;
END PEC;
```

Table 6-5:   Scope Issues in PL/1.

In Table 6-5 when J appears in block B, PL/1 will assume it is declared immediately after label PEC. The programmer who uses J in block B and then in block C might have mistakenly assumed it was local to each block. But any statement which uses J at label D will find that J contains not X but Y as its value. In this example, J is global to blocks A, B and C. This PL/1 design decision runs opposite to the expectation that most variables of a block are local and produces an unexpected (from an ALGOL60 frame of reference) result, thus violating again the law of least astonishment.

ALGOL68 has generalized the ALGOL60 idea of a **begin-end** as the only syntactic means for delimiting scope. In ALGOL68 declarations may appear after any so-called *opening context symbol* and extend in scope to the corresponding *closing context symbol.* Statements such as **if-fi, then-else, else-fi** and **begin-end** are just four such pairs.

Pascal took another point of view than ALGOL68. It retained the **begin-end** as a bracketing symbol for compound statements, but removed the **begin-end** as a scope delimiter. In Pascal only procedures or functions can delimit scope. This was likely done because it was felt that following good programming practice, procedures should be small. Nesting of procedures is allowed, and inheritance of globals as in ALGOL60 was adopted.

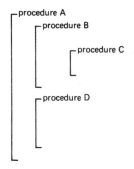

Figure 6-2:   Nested Procedures

Consider the nested program structure in Figure 6-2 as it might occur in a Pascal program.   Procedure A is global to B, C and D, and hence they can all invoke A. As B and D are defined within A, A may call them, but not C as it is shielded from view by B. B is global to C so C can invoke B and vice versa.   But in contrast to ALGOL60, in Pascal B cannot invoke D because its name is not known to B. Since each procedure can call itself recursively, we conclude that

A can invoke A, B, D
B can invoke A, B, C
C can invoke A, B, C
D can invoke A, B, D.

If a variable is declared in procedure B, then it is unknown to A and D and global to C, following the usual ALGOL60 scope rules.

Euclid's approach to scoping is that there is *no* automatic inheritance of names unless explicitly indicated by the programmer on an import list; see [Euclid]. A consequence of this decision is that programmers must write excessively long import lists. Those who try to use over and over a single, long import list defeat the original purpose of importing. Since the nesting of program text already implies a dependency between the names, the requirement of import lists doesn't add much to reliability and has its disadvantages.

In conclusion, the concept of scope via block structure is good for several reasons. First of all it encourages programmers to declare variables near the program text where they will be used. Thus programs exhibit an added measure of locality. Second, locality of program text and variables implies that under an operating system which uses paging, only a small working set of pages will be required. Third, a standard package of routines may be included with a user's program by combining the two into a single outer block. None of the names in the user's program will conflict with names in the standard package. Last, but not least, it encourages the stepwise refinement method of program construction.

Now let's turn to a discussion of extent. In ALGOL60 we observe that all local variables are lost on block exit. Thus ALGOL60 introduced a new type of variable it called **own**. An **own** variable is not deallocated on block exit, and it retains its value so that on subsequent entries to its defining block it can be assumed to have the value it had on the previous block exit. But one difficulty with **own** variables is that the programmer is forced to introduce code which tests if this is the first time through the block or not. This is cumbersome and time consuming. A second problem arises in connection with **own** arrays, which in ALGOL60 can have dynamic bounds. If a procedure containing such an array is initially invoked, producing array bounds of say 1 : 100, can the array change its bounds on subsequent block entries while still retaining the original values? This problem in the language definition has caused many ALGOL60 implementations to drop dynamic **own** arrays from their compiler.

Whereas in FORTRAN all storage is allocated at compile-time (static) and ALGOL60 allocates all storage at run-time (dynamic, except for **own**), PL/1 allows the programmer to specify the type of storage allocation as an attribute of a variable. The types they offer are STATIC as in FORTRAN, AUTOMATIC as in ALGOL60, and a third called CONTROLLED. A variable whose attribute is CONTROLLED is not allocated any storage until an ALLOCATE command is encountered in the program at run-time. Storage is then assigned and remains assigned until a FREE command is encountered. A variation on CONTROLLED storage in PL/1 is called BASED.

A statement such as

```
DECLARE 1 STUDENT BASED( P )
    2 NAME CHARACTER(25) VARYING,
    2 SSNUMBER FIXED,
```

```
        2 AGE  FIXED,
        2 MAJOR CHARACTER(10),
        2 LINK  POINTER;
```

declares a structure (or record) called STUDENT and a variable P which is a pointer. Storage for P is allocated using the AUTOMATIC attribute, but no storage for STUDENT is allocated until an "ALLOCATE STUDENT;" statement is reached. Then enough storage is produced to hold one STUDENT structure and P is set to point to that storage. Table 6-6 summarizes the different types of storage in PL/1 and their extent rules.

Storage Type	Time of stor. creat'n	Time, stor. delt'n
STATIC	Start of main proc.	End of main proc.
AUTOMATIC	Enter proc/block	Exit proc/block
CONTROL'D	Exec ALLOCATE	Exec FREE stmt or exit task,free AREA
BASED	Exec ALLOCATE stmt sys. stor., named AREA	Exec. FREE stmt or exit task,free AREA

Table 6-6:   Summary of PL/1 Storage Classes

In the section on the pointer data type we have already been introduced to the idea that some objects have an extent which exceeds the scope of their name. In particular the run-time allocation of records in Pascal have this property when the *new* operator is used. (Reread section 5.4 for more details). One implication of this fact, is that not all storage management can be done using a stack. Storage which is not allocated and freed on a last-in-first-out basis such as PL/1's CONTROLLED or Pascal's allocation of dynamic records, requires other than stack allocation for its implementation. A *heap* is the term which is used to describe the pool of available storage for created objects whose extent does not obey the last-in-first-out discipline. The implementation of stack and heap storage may share the same block of consecutive memory locations. The stack grows from one end, and the heap occupies the other end. Storage from the heap is allocated on an as needed basis as long as sufficient locations are available. If collectively the stack and heap exhaust the storage pool, then the program must be terminated. The topic of implementing the heap is beyond the subject matter of this book, but more can be found in [Horowitz 76].

In the original definition of Pascal, no mechanism was provided to return dynamically allocated storage to the free list. Thus, once all pointers to the storage from named variables is lost, the storage becomes irretrievable for the duration of the program. Newer versions of Pascal have added a *dispose(x)* command which returns the storage pointed at by x to the heap. But this puts the responsibility of returning storage no longer needed in the hands of the programmer. In some languages such as LISP or ALGOL68 no explicit freeing statement is necessary. But instead of storage being lost for the duration of the program, a technique known as *garbage collection* is used to reclaim storage which is no longer being used. This mechanism has the advantage that it frees the programmer from having to worry about storage allocation. Its disadvantage is that garbage collection occurs at unpredictable times and may severely slow down the program. This slow-down is especially burdensome when the program is interacting in real-time with a user.

6.2. Run-time Implementation

As all storage in FORTRAN is static, all data can be allocated at compile-time. At run-time when a subroutine is invoked, all of its storage will have been set aside in some fixed region, including space for parameters and for the return address of any subroutines. On subsequent calls a subroutine will find all of its storage in the same place. This simple allocation scheme works because of the restrictions in FORTRAN which prevent recursive procedures and preserve the value of data across successive subroutine invocations.

But when we examine a language such as ALGOL60, with its ability to define recursive procedures and to declare local variables in nested scopes, then the allocation scheme must become more complex. Since more than one activation of a procedure may exist, each having its own local variables, we can only allocate space at run-time. In this section we look at how these language design features can be implemented.

We have seen how in ALGOL60 scope is delimited by **begin-end** pairs denoting blocks. Using the static scoping rule, the meaning of a global name is determined by finding the innermost declaration of the name in a block which contains the block where the name is being referenced. At run-time each block has an *environment* which includes entries for all local variables and pointers to all global variables. Also included in the environment are labels and procedures defined in the block. The representation of the environment is called the *activation record*. A similar treatment of run-time implementation of block structured languages appears in [Wulf 81].

A : **begin real** x, y;
    procedure $P(...)$
        begin integer i;
          . . .
        $x := x + i$;
          . . .
    end P
     . . .
  B: **begin boolean** x, y;
    C : $P(...)$
     . . .
    D : **begin integer** x, y;
      . . .
      E : $P(...)$
    end D
    . . .
  end B
 . . .
end A

Table 6-7:   An Example of Nested Blocks and Procedures.

In Table 6-7 one sees a main block named A containing three blocks: P a procedure and blocks B and D. The procedure P is called at labels C and E. In procedure P we see the statement $x := x+i$. The variable i is local and of type integer. The variable x is global, and by the static scoping rule, it is of type real defined immediately following label A.

In Figure 6-3 we see the run-time stack as it grows and shrinks during the execution of the program in Table 6-7. As each new block is entered, its activation record is placed on top of the stack. It is easy to see that local variables, local labels and procedures can all be addressed by using the starting address of the activation record followed by an offset which is defined at compile-time. Note that when P is invoked at labels C and E, the value of the global variable x needs to be determined. But it is *not* sufficient to move through the stack until the first occurrence of x is encountered. If we did this, then at label C we

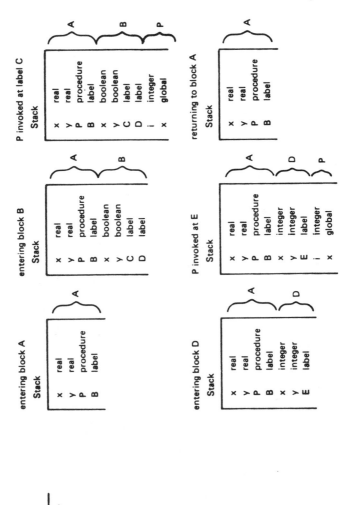

Figure 6-3: Runtime Stack for Table 6-7

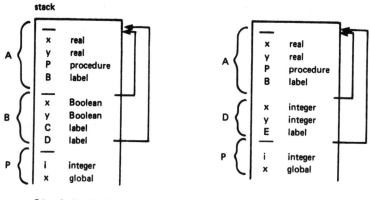

Figure 6-4: Activation Records With Static Pointer

would first find x as Boolean and at label E we would find x as integer. (See Figure 6-3.) Both of these are incorrect as the program text shows us that the x of type real defined at label A is the correct definition. The problem is that the stack contains the activation records in the order of their dynamic invocation in the program. The solution is to add a pointer with each activation record, called the *static pointer* which points to the activation record of the nearest lexically enclosing block which is currently on the stack.

Using this solution gives us the modified stacks as seen in Figure 6-4. Now the static pointer for P in both cases is seen to point to the activation record for A which gives the correct definition for the variable x. But this scheme of using the static pointer would seem to be inefficient as it implies searching back through the list of containing blocks and for each block looking at all variables, until a recurrence of x is discovered. Actually, this is not necessary.

For any block which is nested i levels deep in a program, the linked list of static pointers can only be i long. Secondly, for any global variable in a block, its definition occurs at k levels back along the static pointer list *every* time execution occurs. Moreover, we can determine the *offset* this global variable has in its defining block. Thus, for any global variable the compiler can determine at compile-time that at run-time its definition will be found k positions down the static pointer list and at position *offset*. Thus the modified method for finding the correct definition of a global is to move down the static pointer list exactly k positions, and then look at this base address plus *offset* to find the variable's definition. The problem of having to address global variables is called *up-level addressing* because these variables are declared in a block which is at a lower level number than the block in which the variable is referenced.

Now the only question which remains is how the static pointer is initially set when a new activation record is placed on the top of the stack. If a new block is entered that is nested in the previously active block, then the pointer is merely set to point to the previous activation record on the stack. But if instead procedure B is invoked from the block named C, as shown in Figure 6-5, while procedure B is contained in block A, what should be done then? The solution is contained in the activation record for C which is now on the top of the stack. Since the program text of block C has a reference to procedure B in the call statement, the compiler can generate code so that at run-time C will follow its own static links back a pre-determined number of levels to get the appropriate value for B. Then when placing B's activation record on top of the stack at run-time, the program retrieves this value and sets

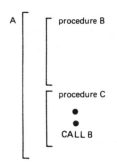

Figure 6-5: Handling Nested Blocks

the static pointer appropriately.

The Display

The previous scheme for implementing the run-time environment would be improved if we could avoid having to walk down the static pointer list to the correct enclosing block. An alternative solution exists and is called the *display.* As with everything, the display doesn't come for free. The cost is an increase of time required on each entry to and exit from a block.

The idea is to remove the static pointer list in each activation record and replace it by a small stack called the display. This small stack contains all of the pointers to activation records that would have previously been kept in the static pointer list, but are now kept in the display. The display can be thought of as a stack of pointers to activation records. A global variable in the current top activation record is still represented by a 2-tuple, say (k, j). But, now the k is used to access the kth location in the display, whose value is a pointer to what would have been the kth activation record on the static pointer list for this block. The offset j is then used as before. Using indirect addressing this calculation is very fast and is independent of the nesting of blocks.

When a new subprogram P is invoked at run-time, the display must be updated. Assume that procedure P is called by procedure Q and that the level of P is the same as the level of Q. Then the only difference between their displays is in the last element of the stack. Instead of having a pointer to the activation record for Q, it must be replaced by the activation record for P. However, if P is up-level (i.e. at a lower level number) from Q, then the displays for P and Q are the same only for the first *level(P)* entries. These entries should be preserved and a pointer to the activation record for P placed on top to form the new display. Then by taking that portion of the display which points to the activation records of blocks which do not enclose subprogram P and saving it somewhere, we guarantee that we will be able to restore the display properly when P terminates. As for where the elements of the display are to be saved, the natural place is in the activation record of P itself, so when P is exited the display can be restored.

Table 6-8 shows the block structure outline of an ALGOL60 program with two calls to a procedure P. Figure 6-6 shows four views of the run-time stack containing the activation records plus the display stack. When P is invoked the first time, two pointers are removed from the display and placed in the activation record for P. When P is exited, these pointers are restored. On the second call of P, only the activation record for A is on the stack and as A encloses P, nothing need be removed from the display.

        A : **begin**

         . . .

          procedure P(...)

            begin . . . **end** P;

           . . .

        B : **begin**

          . . .

           C : **begin**

             . . .

              D : **call** P(...)

             . . .

           end C

          . . .

         end B

         E : **call** P(...)

        end A

Table 6-8:   An ALGOL60 Fragment with Nested Blocks

Two issues remain to be discussed before we have a complete implementation of static scoping. The first is the issue of arrays. Since FORTRAN and Pascal both require array sizes to be fixed at compile-

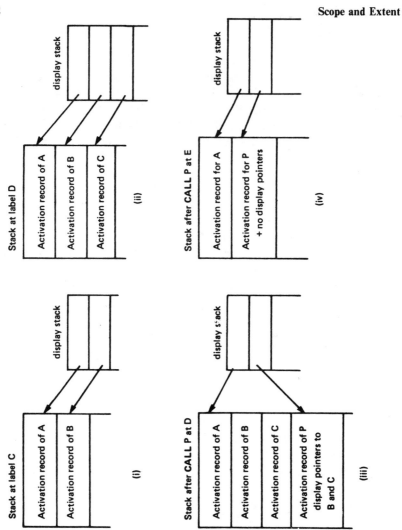

Figure 6-6:   Example of the Use of a Display

time, the activation record can contain space for local arrays. However, for languages in which dynamic array bounds are possible, a different scheme is needed. The typical solution is to include a *descriptor* for the array in the activation record. The descriptor contains all the information necessary to compute the sizes of each dimension. Since the size of the descriptor (the number of array dimensions) can be determined at compile-time it can easily be included in the activation record. After the activation record has been placed on the stack, but before the body of the procedure (or block) executes, the bounds are evaluated and storage for the array is allocated. This storage is also placed in the run-time stack.

The second issue is the question of procedure parameters. For a solution to this part of the problem and for more discussion of this topic the reader is advised to consult [Wulf 81], chapter 16.

6.3. An Extended Example

Now that we have discussed static scoping and its implementation, suppose we look at a fairly complex problem. This problem was originally given by J. Johnston in an excellent paper where he introduces a pictorial method for understanding static scoping, called the contour model [Johnston 71]. The example appears in Table 6-9. This program includes a main block labeled A containing two procedures, P and Q. Procedure P contains a procedure also called Q. We will differentiate between these two procedures called Q by subscripting them with the line number where they are defined, Q_3 and Q_{12}. The algorithm begins on line 16 by setting i to 3 and then invoking P. The question is, what gets printed in line 18, but the more important issue is to see how this computation proceeds.

In Table 6-10 we see the activation records for A, P, Q_3 and Q_{12}. For example, A contains four entries; an integer, two procedures and a label L. In P we see seven entries including i and L which are not local to P but are defined in the enclosing block A. Now in Figures 6-7 and 6-8 we see the run-time stack as the computation progresses. At line 15 block A begins execution and its activation record is placed on the stack. The variable i has value 3 while the values of P, Q_{12} and L are pointers to the code for P, Q_{12} and label L respectively. We denote pointers by the right arrow. The symbol nil denotes the end of a list in this case the end of the static pointer list. P is invoked at line 17 and at line 2 its activation record is placed on the stack. The parameters X and j have values Q_{12} and 4. The global names i and L are defined by following

```
1      A : begin integer i;
2          procedure P(x,j); value j; procedure X; integer j;begin
3              procedure Q(t); label t; begin  //call Q, Q₃//
4                  i := i + j
5                  X(K)
6                  go to t
7              end Q
8          J : if j > i then X(J) else P(Q, j+1)  //refers to Q₃//
9          K : i := i+j
10            go to L
11         end P;
12         procedure Q(L); label L; begin  //call Q, Q₁₂//
13             i := i+1
14             go to L  //refers to parameter//
15         end Q
16      i := 3
17      P(Q,4)  //refers to Q₁₂//
18      L : print(i)
19      end A.
```

Table 6-9:   Sample ALGOL60 Program

the static pointer list to block A further down the stack. At line 8, j is greater than i and $Q_{12}(J)$ is invoked. At line 12, Q_{12}'s activation record is placed on the stack with its parameter L assigned to J and i gets its meaning from block A via the static pointer. An exit is made to line 8 where j is not less than i, so P(Q,5) is invoked recursively. Two activation records for P are now on the stack. Since $j > i$ (5 > 4), $Q_3(J)$ is activated and i is increased by j at line 4. Note how the static pointer for Q_3 points to the first activation record of P in the stack rather than to the second. This is a consequence of the static scoping rule. Now, the value that is used for j is not the value in the recursive invocation of P, namely 5, but in the version of P which is on the static pointer list, which is $j = 4$. Therefore, $Q_{12}(K)$ is invoked, (see the stack at line 12), i becomes 9 and the **go to** L in line 14 causes Q_{12}, Q_3 and the recursive activation of P to be terminated yielding the stack at line 9. Then i is increased to 13 and a branch to line 18 prints 13 and ends. By tracing through this example carefully, one will appreciate fully the intricacies of implementing the static scoping rule.

A	P
i, integer	X, procedure parameter
P, procedure	j, integer value parameter
Q_{12}, procedure	Q_3, procedure
L, label	J, label
	K, label
	i, global in A
	L, global in A

Q_3	Q_{12}
t, label parameter	L, label parameter
i, global in A	i, global in A
j, global in P	
X, global in P	
k, global in P	

Table 6-10: Activation Records for Blocks of Table 6-9

6.4. Binding, Scope and Extent Together

By now one should understand the difference between the binding of a name to a storage location and the updating of that storage. The term *environment* is used to refer to the association of identifiers with the locations they are bound to, and the term *store* is used to refer to the association of locations with the values they hold. Thus, a declaration yields a new environment and a command yields a new store.

One important thing to notice in a programming language is where bindings take place. For example in the Pascal program fragment in Table 6-11, the occurrence of *i* in the declaration is a binding, while the use of *i* in the two assignment statements are not bindings but are so-called *applied occurrences*. An example of an identifier appearing in a programming language which causes both a binding to happen and an applied occurrence is found in PL/1. The statement

DECLARE X EXTERNAL FIXED;

names X as an applied occurrence whose attributes come from the external environment, but at the same time this statement causes X to be bound in the current program.

In Pascal, identifiers are bound in many places including immediately

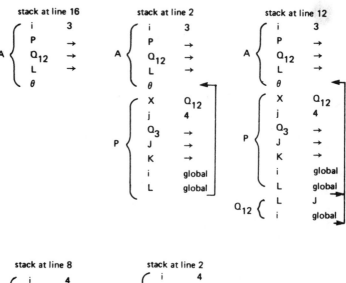

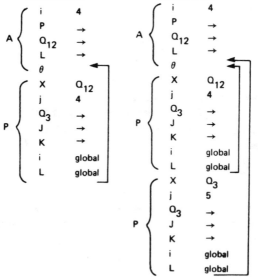

Figure 6-7: Run-time Stack for Table 6-9

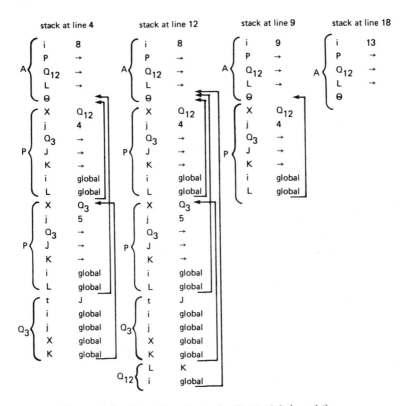

Figure 6-8: Run-time Stack for Table 6-9 (cont'd)

var *i* : *integer;*
begin
　i := *0;*
　.
　.
　.
　i := *i* + *1;*
　.
　.
　.
end

Table 6-11:   Pascal Program Fragment

after the keywords: **program, procedure, function, const, type**, and **var**.
They also are bound in records including in the **case** part of variant
records. Unfortunately not all bindings in Pascal are explicit.

var *gaussian* : **record** *realpt* : *integer; imagpt* : *integer* **end**;
begin
　.
　.
　.
　with *gaussian* **do**
　　. . .
　　realpt := *realpt* + *1;*
　　. . .
end

Table 6-12:   Example of Binding in Pascal

The execution of the statements in Table 6-12. makes use of an applied
occurrence of *realpt* in the **with** statement denoting a field of the record
gaussian.   However , the binding of *realpt* takes place in the record
definition which may be far removed from the appearance of the **with**
statement. This potential obscurity in language design is similar to the
use of default declarations in languages such as FORTRAN. Though
these default bindings are meant to be a convenience, they contain less
information for readers of the program text who may wish to locate the
binding, but are not sure if it is explicit. Thus ,they are susceptible to
errors.

Recall that the extent of a block of storage is defined as the time
during execution of the program that the storage is allocated. Though

for local variables in ALGOL-like languages there is an intimate connection between scope and extent, one must be careful to understand the differences. The notion of scope is tied to the program text, while extent is tied to program execution. Though FORTRAN, ALGOL60, and Pascal all use static scoping, they have different kinds of extent. For example, in most FORTRAN implementations, the extent of all storage is the entire time the program is executing.

In ALGOL60 there are two different types of extent. The first and usual one is local extent, namely on entry to a new block or procedure, storage is allocated for all local variables. This storage remains until the scoping unit in which it was defined is exited. The second type of extent is called **own**. Variables in ALGOL60 which are declared to have extent of type **own** are just like the variables in many implementations of FORTRAN. The storage for **own** variables lasts for the life of the program. These variables were thought to be useful for writing functions such as random number generators where the seed value needs to be retained over successive calls.

With respect to non-**own** variables in ALGOL60, the fact that extent is tied to scope permits the run-time allocation to be handled with a stack. An advantage of this type of allocation is that a decision about the amount of storage to be used can be postponed until execution time. However, this is at the expense of a more complicated mechanism for handling storage than the FORTRAN situation.

Another form of extent is found in PL/1 and Pascal. This form gives control over the life of the storage to the programmer. This is usually called dynamic extent and is often implemented by the mechanism called a heap. We have already seen how in Pascal records may be dynamically created by the *new* operation. This storage will exist even after the block in which it was created is exited by the program.

When dynamic extent is used in a programming language, then there are different possible ways to terminate the life of storage. One way is to simply assume that the storage lasts forever as in FORTRAN. Another way is to provide in the language an explicit mechanism for "freeing" the storage, i.e. for telling the program that it can be reused. A third way is to permit the storage to exist until there are no more references to it in the program. Then an automatic mechanism reclaims the storage for further use. The second possibility has become very popular, and in many Pascal implementations one typically finds a procedure called *dispose* for returning storage to the free list. However, this can create a problem if the programmer forgets that he or she has another pointer to the storage and mistakenly frees it using *dispose*. The third alternative, often called garbage collection, is an elegant solution in that the programmer is freed from worrying about the management of storage. Storage is allocated as needed and is automatically reclaimed when the pool of available storage becomes small. The major problem with this method is that reclamation can be time consuming and can occur unpredictably.

This chapter has dealt with a variety of subjects involving scope and extent and it will be useful to summarize the main points with respect to some key languages. I do this here.

☐ FORTRAN: The scope unit is the SUBROUTINE or FUNCTION. All variables defined therein are local. The sharing of variables is achieved by the COMMON statement. The extent of all storage is the duration of the entire program.

☐ ALGOL60: The scope units are the block and the procedure. All non-**own** variables defined therein are local. Blocks and procedures may be nested. The sharing of variables is achieved by nesting scope units with the lexical scope rule applying. The extent of all storage extends from the time the scope unit is entered to the time it is exited. The one exception to this is the **own** variable which has the same extent as variables in FORTRAN. A stack of activation records plus a statically allocated region for **own** variables is all that is required to implement this strategy.

☐ Pascal: The scope unit is the procedure. All variables defined therein are local. Procedures may be nested. The sharing of variables is achieved by nesting procedures. The extent of such storage is as in ALGOL60. Also, there exists the dynamic allocation of records referenced by pointer variables. The Pascal function *new* is used to accomplish this allocation. The scope and extent of pointer variables is the same as the scope and extent of any other variables. However the extent of dynamically allocated records may be the life of the entire program. (Some Pascal implementations do provide a *dispose* function which permits the programmer to return storage to a free list during program execution.) A heap is used to implement the dynamic storage allocation which is required.

☐ Ada: The scope units are the procedure, block, package and task. All variables defined therein are local. Procedures and blocks behave as in ALGOL60. There exists dynamic allocation of all types. Ada also has explicit deallocation and may have garbage collection. It can also achieve the effect of **own**. The scope and extent rules for packages are presented in Chapter 8 and for tasks in Chapter 10. A closer look at Ada and scope follows.

The reader should consult [Wulf 81] chapter 15, for further discussion of scope and extent.

6.5. A Look at Ada and Scope

Though it is true that Ada has adopted the ALGOL60 scoping rule, that is only one part of the story. In Ada there are really three different scoping units called subprograms, packages and tasks, and these make the explanation of scope more complicated. Subprograms follow the conventional ALGOL60 mold. In particular they consist of two types, either procedures or functions. Both of these entities are made up of two parts: a declarative part and a sequence-of-statements part. The declarative part contains declarations of objects such as types, labels, variables and other subprograms, while the sequence-of-statements part contains the body of the subprogram. See Figure 6-9.

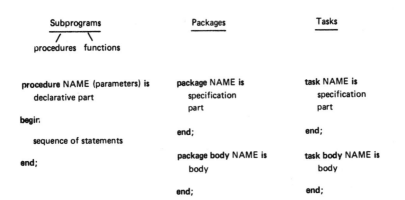

Figure 6-9:   The Three Scoping Units in Ada

When nesting of subprograms is used, identifiers from an outer enclosing context are visible in the inner context. Also, an identifier declared in an inner context having the same name as an identifier in an outer context, may hide that identifier. This is the hole-in-scope issue discussed earlier. But in contrast to ALGOL60 or Pascal, the identifier in the outer scope with the same name can be seen in the inner context by using *qualification*. To qualify a name in Ada, one prefixes it with the scope name in which it was defined. For example in Table 6-13 we see three subprograms, HERE, THEN, and NOW, each one nested inside the next. In **procedure** NOW there are two assignment statements with comments which explain their meaning. Note how qualification is used in the second assignment statement to override the fact that the identifier in the outer context is hidden.

```
procedure HERE is
    procedure THEN is
        A : REAL;
        B : REAL;
        procedure NOW is
            B : REAL;          --this declaration hides THEN.B
            C : REAL;
        begin
            B := A;            --NOW.B := THEN.A
            C := THEN.B;       --NOW.C := THEN.B
        end NOW;
    begin
        . . .
    end THEN;
begin
    . . .
end HERE;
```

Table 6-13:   An Example of Nested Subprograms
and Qualification in Ada

In addition to local and global variables which are visible in a block, there may in Ada also be visible another set of identifiers. These identifiers are declared in a package, say named X, and their use is mandated by the programmer when employing the "**use** X;" statement in the declarative part of the subprogram. For example, Table 6-14 contains an Ada program fragment. This fragment contains a package LOGICS with three Boolean variables and a procedure MAIN which contains a package NUMBERS and a procedure DOSOMETHING nested inside it. Within procedure DOSOMETHING, we see some declarations and a **use** clause naming packages LOGICS and NUMBERS. The general rule for determining name visibility in an Ada

```
package LOGICS is
  A, B, C : BOOLEAN;
end LOGICS
procedure MAIN is
  package NUMBERS is
    C, D, E : INTEGER;
  end NUMBERS
  procedure DOSOMETHING is
    A, F : REAL;
    use LOGICS, NUMBERS;
  begin
    the name A means DOSOMETHING.A, not LOGICS.A
    the name B means LOGICS.B
    the name D means NUMBERS.D
    the name E means NUMBERS.E
    the name F means DOSOMETHING.F
    the name C is illegal. Either LOGICS.C or NUMBERS.C.
  end
  end DOSOMETHING
begin
  . . .
end MAIN
```

Table 6-14:   Ada Example of Name Qualification

scope is that after locals, then globals are inherited followed by the application of any **use** clauses to the names which remain undefined. Thus the meanings of the variables A, B, C, D, E, F are as shown in the program text.   Both packages and tasks inherit global variables. Packages can be nested.   Only library units, such as packages and subprograms, do not implicitly inherit external declarations.   However, one can use the **with** clause to import these declarations into library units.   Note that since tasks cannot be library units, they always have an open scope.   We will discuss packages and tasks at greater lengths in Chapters 8 and 10.

One of the major program structuring features of Ada is that it permits separate compilation.   Thus there is the concept of a program library which contains Ada compilation units.   But in contrast to FORTRAN, these compilation units are separate, but not independent. In particular some units may depend upon others and may need to be recompiled when others are altered.   A library of information is kept, allowing interface checks to be performed, thus aiding program reliability. When programmers submit a new or revised unit to be compiled in Ada, they may assume that a program library of existing compilation units will be available to the compiler. The output will be an updated program library plus the usual program listings, object code and/or diagnostic reports.

If a package definition plans to make use of other subprograms or packages, then it must state so by using a **with** statement. The **with** statement names the packages upon which this package depends. Thus a partial ordering is created among the compilation units and the Ada program library keeps track of it. At the start of compilation of a unit, the identifiers which are visible are those which exist in the pre-defined environment (such as TRUE, FALSE), all the names mentioned in **with** clauses which preceded this unit and the name of the unit itself. As the unit begins to be compiled, its local variables become defined as their declarations are reached. For a complete discussion of scope in Ada,one should consult the Ada reference manual [Ada 80].

We have now finished this chapter, but not our discussion of scope and extent. Scope questions will arise again when we consider abstract data types in Chapter 8, exception handling facilities in Chapter 9 and concurrency in Chapter 10.

Concepts Discussed in This Chapter

Activation record
Block
Common
Dangling reference
Display
Dynamic scoping
Extent

Global variables
Heap storage
Hole-in scope
Local variable
own variables
Qualification
Scope

Exercises

A : **begin**

  . . .

  B : **b egin**
  procedure P(...)

  . . .

  end P
  C : **begin**

    . . .

    D : **call** P(...)

    . . .

    end C

  . . .

  E: **call** P(...)

  . . .

  end B
  end A

1. For the program above show the run-time stack and the display immediately before and after the two calls to P at labels D and E.

2. Direct recursion (when the call of procedure X occurs in the definition of procedure X) is easy for a compiler to detect. but indirect recursion is not. Map out an algorithm which a compiler could use to determine if recursion were possible. Discuss how efficient your method is in terms of the number of passes it must make over the source text and the amount of information it must retain.

3. If a language has features in it which require heap allocation, then perhaps there is no need for a stack at all. Is a stack truly necessary · and if not provide an implementation of run-time storage allocation which uses only a heap.

4. Devise a function f that alters the value of a global variable x as well as returning a value. This makes programs which use f and x sensitive to the order of evaluation of . expressions. Discuss the different possible values which might be printed by your function.

5. What is the scope of a loop parameter in Ada? Compare this with the rule in Pascal.

6. Boom and DeJong in [Boom 80] report finding many machine and compiler dependent features on some compilers they studied. For example, in the Pascal compiler they found that

Power sets may have only 59 elements;
These 59 elements must be such that *ord(element)*
is between 0 - 58;
Strings may be compared only if their length
is less than 10 or a multiple of 10;
Only the first 10 characters of an identifier are significant.

In the FORTRAN compiler they found

DO loop indices had to be less than 131072;
DO loop indices may be nested at most 50 deep;
At most 63 parameters to a subprogram are permitted;
At most 125 labelled COMMON blocks are allowed.

Examine your local Pascal and FORTRAN compilers to see what machine or compiler dependent features you can discover.

Chapter 7

PROCEDURES

"Men have become the tools of their tools."

Henry David Thoreau

7.1. General Features

In Chapter 2 we mentioned the importance of supplying a means for abstraction in a programming language. The procedure was the earliest major form of abstraction and continues to be a central concept, so it certainly deserves a chapter of its own. A *procedural abstraction* is a mapping from a set of inputs to a set of outputs that can be described by a specification. The specification must show how the outputs relate to the inputs, but it need not reveal or even imply the way the outputs are to be computed. We can view the procedure concept in a programming language as an abstraction because it allows a user to focus only on what is done (at the point of call) and not on how it is accomplished.

A procedure is comprised of four elements; its name, a list of names called *parameters*, a body, and an environment. A typical order would be:

procedure NAME (parameter list)

      declarations
      body
end NAME

A procedure is usually begun by writing a keyword which designates the following program text to be a procedure. This is followed by its name. Afterwards there is a list of identifiers called the *formal parameters*. These are not variables but merely names which act the role that the real arguments will play when the procedure is called. The variables and expressions which are supplied to the procedure to replace the formal parameters are called the *actual parameters*. There is a direct correspondence between the actual and formal parameters usually based upon the order in which they appear in the parameter list. However, Ada also permits one to ignore the order and instead to associate actual and formal arguments by name, as seen by the following procedure definition.

     procedure MASH(A, B : **in** REAL; C : **in** INTEGER);

which can be invoked as

             MASH(0.0, 100.0, 50);

or as

         MASH(A => 0.0, B => 100.0, C => 50);

or as

         MASH(B => 100.0, C => 50, A => 0.0);

or even as

         MASH(0.0, 100.0, C => 50);

The trend today is to supply lots of information in the parameter list in addition to the names of the formal parameters. Thus, some people now call this list the *parameter specification*. The parameter specification may contain, in addition to the names of the formals, their associated type and the manner in which they will be used at run-time.

The procedure is often used to delimit scope. The declarations within a procedure describe the attributes of variables, constants, labels and may possibly contain other procedures all of which are local to the procedure in which they are defined. The body of a procedure consists of a statement, simple or compound, which directs the computation. In addition to the local variables and the formal parameters, a procedure may refer to global variables inherited from an outer block. The procedure's *environment* consists of those variables which are defined outside of the body of the procedure, but which may be used or altered at run-time by the procedure's statements.

There are essentially two different kinds of procedures which we shall call subroutines and functions. A *subroutine* is a procedure which accomplishes its task either by assigning its results to one or more of its parameters or by changing its environment or both. A *function* is a procedure which is characterized by the fact that it returns a value. This allows an invocation of it to be a component of an expression. In many programming languages a function may also change the value of a parameter or the value of a variable in the environment. Many programming languages provide a syntactic mechanism for differentiating between a function and a subroutine. Some languages require that one precede the name of the latter by either the keyword **procedure** (or SUBROUTINE) and the former by **function**. One way that the value of the function can be set is by assigning it to the name of the function which is treated as a local variable. This is the scheme adopted by FORTRAN, ALGOL60 and Pascal. Alternatively, PL/1 and Ada require one to place the result immediately following the RETURN statement.

```
function gcd(m,n : integer) : integer;
  begin if n = 0 then gcd := m
    else gcd := gcd(n,m mod n);
  end;
```

Pascal

```
GCD : RECURSIVE PROCEDURE(M,N)RETURNS(INTEGER);
    IF N = 0 THEN RETURN(M);
       ELSE RETURN( GCD( N, MOD( M, N));
    END;
    PL/1
```

Table 7-1: Two Examples of the Greatest Common Divisor Method

What sort of value can a function return? FORTRAN and ALGOL60 restrict this value to be a single scalar: **real**, **integer**, or **Boolean**. PL/1 also permits a character string or a pointer to be returned. Pascal, in addition to scalars also permits a pointer to be returned. Ada is far more general, permitting a function to return a value of any type.

When we examine a procedure, we can distinguish three classes of names. First, there are the names which denote formal parameters. Second, there are the names of local variables. Third, there are the names of global variables. There are three key issues we must understand about procedures. One, what is the environment which is used to bind global variables to values? Two, how are actual parameters evaluated? Three, how are formal parameters bound to actual parameters?

7.2. Parameter Evaluation and Passing

By *parameter evaluation* we mean the process whereby each actual parameter is identified as being associated to its corresponding formal parameter and is subsequently evaluated. By *parameter passing* we mean the manner in which the evaluated actual is transferred (or bound) to the procedure. In this section I present three popular methods for parameter passing.

In *call-by-value*, the actual parameter is dereferenced giving an r-value which is copied to a new location. This location is bound to the formal. This is the default for parameter evaluation and passing in Pascal. It is possible to use it in ALGOL60 by writing **value** followed by the desired formal parameter. In PL/1, actual parameters which are expressions are evaluated in this way, but not variables. To force call-by-value in PL/1 for single variable arguments, one can surround the variable name by parentheses. It will then be treated as an expression.

The virtue of call-by-value is that the actual parameter is a read-only value of the procedure, and no assignments can be made to it which will influence the program outside the procedure. The disadvantage is that a *copy* of the argument is stored in the new location. For structured objects such as arrays, producing the copy can be both time consuming and space inefficient.

In *call-by-reference* if the actual parameter is a location such as a variable name, then its location is bound directly to the formal parameter. This is the mechanism usually employed in FORTRAN and PL/1. (Occasionally one finds call-by-value-result instead.) In Pascal it is used when one declares a parameter in the parameter list as being **var**. Its chief advantage is that it is very efficient in comparison with copying the actual. It allows one to alter the value of an actual parameter as a result of the procedure.

However, there can be some subtle problems. One implementation

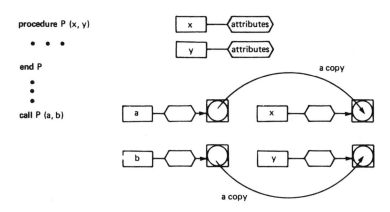

Figure 7-1:   Call-by-value

problem that has happened in the past occurs when the formal parameters of P are declared **var**, as in *P(***var** *x,y : integer)*, and the call has an expression as an actual parameter, like **call** *P(10,z)*. Then the value 10 will be stored in a location which is then bound to the formal *x*. If in P, *x* is assigned another value, then that internally generated location, called an *anonymous variable* contains a possibly different value. If the constant 10 is used anywhere else in the program, a "smart" compiler may unwittingly use the same location assuming it still holds a 10.

Call-by-value-result is a method designed to incorporate the good features of call-by-value and call-by-reference. When the actual parameter is a location, it is dereferenced and copied into a new location as in call-by-value. Throughout the body of the procedure this new location is used. On exit the address of the actual parameter is computed again and the value of the formal parameter is copied into the location of the actual. ALGOL-W, a dialect of ALGOL60 incorporated this scheme into its language. One variation of this rule is to avoid the second calculation of the address of the actual and to use the original reference. However, as discussed in section 7.5 (on aliasing), this modified rule can give different results than the call-by-value-result rule and one should be careful to differentiate between the two.

In summary we have the following rules:

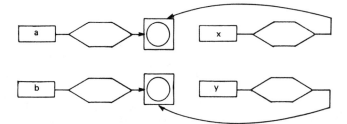

Figure 7-2:   Call-by-reference

	call-by-value	call-by-reference
FORTRAN	no	yes or val-result
ALGOL60	**value** declaration	no, call-by-name
Pascal	**const** declaration	**var** declaration
PL/1	expressions	default

These three methods are not the only ways for handling parameter evaluation and passing. For example, in INTERLISP one can use the A-list facility to specify different binding schemes for different parameters, (see [Teitelman 75]), and in the next section we study call-by-name.

7.3. Call-By-Name

The term call-by-name was introduced in ALGOL60 as the default method for handling parameters. Though it is usually referred to as a method for parameter passing, this is actually misleading, as it is really concerned with the evaluation of parameters. In order to better understand why this is so, we first define the notion of closure. A *closure* is a binding of a procedure body to an environment. By this we mean that the text of the procedure is combined with the environment that exists at the time of the call. The actual execution of the procedure body may take place at a later time. But when it does, this associated environment will be used. When the call-by-name strategy is used, the actual parameters are each treated as self-contained procedures with no parameters but with an environment. The environment which is used is the one which exists at the time of closure, namely the environment which existed at the time of the call. When the corresponding formal parameter is encountered at run-time, the actual parameter is evaluated using the environment obtained at the time of closure. The implementation of call-by-name is discussed by Ingerman who introduces the term *thunk* to refer to this form of closure [Ingerman 61]. (The term thunk was presumably a reference to the "noise" that a static chain pointer makes as it moves within activation records.)

Using the concept of a closure we see that there are alternatives to call-by-name. One alternative would be to postpone taking the closure of the actual parameter at the time of the call and instead wait until the formal is encountered. Then the actual would be evaluated using as the closure the environment of the called procedure. This parameter evaluation mechanism is referred to as *call-by-text.* It requires that the actual parameter must be denotable in the environment of the called procedure. This mechanism is used in LISP in connection with FEXPRs. More about this subject in Chapter 12.

```
begin integer x;  x := 1
    procedure p(y)
        integer x; x := 2; print(y);
    end p;
    p(x)
end
```

Table 7-2: Algol60-like program fragment

In Table 7-2 we see a main block which contains a procedure definiton p and a call on p. Call-by-name will cause the value 1 to be printed while call-by-text will cause the value 2 to be printed.

Call-by-name has been discredited as a useful mechanism chiefly because of its relative inefficiency in places where call-by-reference or call-by-value-result was intended. We observe that if the actual parameter is a simple scalar variable. then call-by-name is the same as call-by-reference. If the actual parameter is a scalar expression, then call-by-name is equivalent to call-by-value except the expression is evaluated every time the formal is encountered. If the actual parameter is an array, the subscript will be re-evaluated each time. Though call-by-name is very powerful. it fails at simple tasks. The classical example is the inability to write a swapping procedure as in Table 7-3.

> **procedure** *SWAP(a, b);*
> **real** *a,b;*
> **begin real** *t;*
>   *t := a; a := b; b := t;*
> **end;**

Table 7-3:   A swapping procedure

When the statement **call** *SWAP(i,A[i])* is encountered, assuming call-by-name, then the resulting sequence of statements is produced:

$$t := i; i := A[i]; A[i] := t$$

which is not what is wanted.

To show the usefulness of call-by-name, there is a famous example called *Jensen's device* shown in Table 7-4, [Knuth 67]. Its ALGOL60 realization follows.

The first call of SIGMA will return the sum of $A(1)+A(2)+...+A(10)$ as x is replaced by $A(i)$. The second call returns the sum $A(1)*B(1)+A(2)*B(2)+...+A(10)*B(10)$. This example shows how one can parameterize a procedure to handle a diverse range of applications.

Another use of call-by-name is to allow programmers to avoid the evaluation of one or more of their actual parameters. For example

> **procedure** *cand(p, q)*
> **boolean** *p, q;*
> **if** *p* **then** *cand := q* **else** *cand := false;*

Here procedure *cand* (for conditional **and**, see section 5.3) first evaluates p and if it is true. then the evaluation of q is done, but otherwise the evaluation of q is suppressed.

> **real procedure** *SIGMA* (x, j, n);
> **value** n, **real** x, **integer** j, n,
> **begin real** s,
>   s := 0;
>   **for** j := 1 **step** 1 **until** n **do** s := s + x;
>   SIGMA := s
> **end**
>
> .
> .
>
> .
> SIGMA(A(i), i, 10)
> SIGMA(A(i)*B(i), i, 10)

Table 7-4: Jensen's Device

Very few languages have chosen to use call-by-name since its introduction in ALGOL60 and its subsequent use in ALGOL-W. One that has is Smalltalk76. In ALGOL68 it is possible to obtain the same effect as call-by-name. See the exercises for details.

7.4. Specification of Objects in a Procedure

The trend in modern programming languages is to require programmers to tell the translator (and the reader) more facts about their formal parameters. In Pascal for example, one must list the types of all parameters, and if the procedure is a function, the type of the result as well (but no types of arguments of procedure parameters). This allows an increased measure of type checking between the actual and formal parameters. Another level of specification has to do with how the parameter will be used. This enables the compiler some freedom to choose the method of parameter evaluation and passing. In ALGOL60 one could write "**value** x" to indicate that the actual parameter corresponding to the formal parameter x was read only and hence should be passed using call-by-value. Otherwise call-by-name was assumed. In Pascal call-by-value is assumed, but one can override the default by writing "**var** y" to indicate that y should be treated using call-by-reference.

When we consider parameters of a procedure in a general sense, then each will behave in only one of three ways. Either a parameter brings a value *into* the procedure and is read but never written, or it carries a value *out* of the procedure and is never read, or it carries a value *into* and *out of* the procedure. In Ada one can specify each of these alternatives by writing the keywords **in**, **out** or **in out**. (Actually the use of this terminology is not new with Ada and appeared earlier in the language SPARKS by Horowitz and Sahni, see [Horowitz 78].) Ada does not specify the parameter evaluation mechanism that the translator will use for structured types, but it does specify call-by-value-result for scalars and access types. For those scalar and access types declared as **in**, only call-by-value will be employed. If they are declared **out**, then an address computation and a copy at the end of the procedure are performed. For **in out**, call-by-value-result is used. However, it appears that the address computation is only done once rather than twice, see section 6.2 of [Ada 80]. Finally any program which relies on the parameter mechanism for a structured or private type is considered to be in error. Though it is expected that call-by-reference will be used, this is not guaranteed by the language definition.

Another trend in modern programming languages, which is followed in Ada, has been to constrain the way a function may have an effect. In FORTRAN, ALGOL60 and PL/1, functions may change one or more of their parameters and change the values of global variables in addition to returning a value. Assignments of these sorts are called *side-effects.* This permits a "Pandora's Box" of problems. For example, in the evaluation of an expression where such a function is present, it would be unclear what values the other variables in the expression might contain both during and after the function is evaluated.

The Ada language initially insisted that all parameters to a function had to be read-only, that is, having attribute **in**. Also, a function could not assign values to global variables or invoke procedures which update globals, or update components of records, or allocate heap storage. These restrictions implied that no input or output could be performed as that too is viewed as a form of side-effect. The attempt was being made to define a function in a modern imperative programming language as it is in mathematics, an object that produces a value and nothing else. Nevertheless, some of the language designers considered these restrictions as too extreme and subsequently included a concept called "a value returning procedure". After much discussion, the value returning procedure has been dropped. Now functions in Ada may not alter their actual parameters (only **in** permitted), and they may have side-effects, either by changing global variables or invoking other functions which somehow change the state. Compare the [Ada 79] and the [Ada 80] language reference manuals to see all the changes that were made.

Now we shift our attention from the specification of parameters to the specification of other objects in a procedure. These may include constants, variables, new types and other procedures. As the syntax for describing these new entities has already been discussed in Chapter 5, the question here is the order in which these statements may appear. This may, at first, seem to be an issue of syntax, but actually it is not. A BNF description captures the syntax, but programming languages are not context-free. We are about to see one instance where BNF is insufficient and additional rules are required.

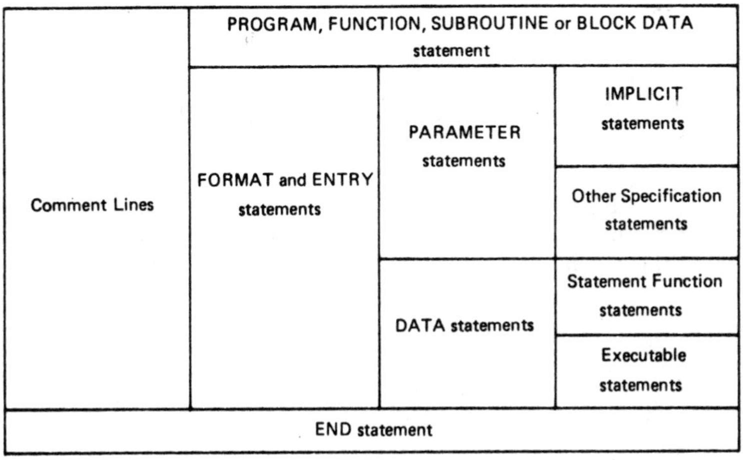

Comment Lines	PROGRAM, FUNCTION, SUBROUTINE or BLOCK DATA statement		
	FORMAT and ENTRY statements	PARAMETER statements	IMPLICIT statements
			Other Specification statements
		DATA statements	Statement Function statements
			Executable statements
	END statement		

Figure 7-3: Required Order of Statements in a FORTRAN77 Program

Figure 7-3 shows the order in which these statements must appear in FORTRAN77. Items appearing in a rectangle must be placed before any items which appear in a rectangle which is below it. Comments may appear anywhere except for the END which must be the last statement. We see that FORMAT statements may be interspersed with IMPLICIT statements, statement functions or executable statements. Unfortunately this diagram doesn't include all of the restrictions. For example ENTRY statements may not appear in the range of a DO-loop and a PARAMETER statement must precede all other statements which contain the symbolic names of constants that appear in that PARAMETER statement.

In Table 7-5 we see how ALGOL60 orders statements using BNF. A procedure name may be prefaced by a type (**integer**, **real**, or **Boolean**),

```
<procedure declaration>   ::=  procedure <heading><body>|
                 <type> procedure <heading> <body>
<heading>        ::=  <procedure identifier> <formal parameter part>;
                 <value part> <specification part>
<body>           ::=  <statement>
<formal parameter part>  ::=  (formal parameter {,formal parameter}) |
                 empty
<value part>     ::=  value <identifier list>; | <empty>
<specification part >  ::= <empty>|<specification> <identifier list>; |
                 <specification part> <specifier> <identifier list>;
<specifier>      ::=  string | <type> | array |
                 <type> array | label
                 | switch | procedure | <type> procedure
<type>           ::=  real | integer | Boolean
```

Table 7-5: Syntax for ALGOL60 Procedure Heading

the word **procedure**, and then followed by a heading and a body. This heading is composed of a name and a formal parameter part, value part and specification part in that order. The specification part allows for the use of **string, array, label, switch,** and **procedure** declarations in any order. But ALGOL60 runs into trouble if there are mutually recursive procedures and one-pass compilation is being attempted.

> **procedure** $A(x,y)$
>   **value** x; **integer array** $y[1:x]$;
>   . . .
> $B(x,y)$
>   . . .
>   **end**
>   **procedure** $B(u,v)$
>   **value** u; **integer array** $v[1:u]$
>   . . .
> $A(u, v)$
>   . . .
>   **end**

Table 7-6: Example of Mutually Recursive Procedures

For example, in Table 7-6 the call of B in A will be encountered before the definition of B is reached. Some versions of ALGOL60 have solved this problem by requiring a heading for B to appear before A, saying in effect that the definition of B will follow, [EXTENDEDALGOL].

In Figure 7-4 we see the Pascal syntax diagram for a block. It is clear from the diagram that certain statements must appear in a fixed order. In particular label declarations must precede constant declarations which precede the definitions of procedures and functions. The level of specificity would normally be sufficient, except when one considers building a one-pass compiler for Pascal. Pascal was designed for easy compilation as well as for efficient object code. Though one-pass compilation is not mentioned in the Pascal report, many such compilers have been attempted.

It would seem as if Pascal should have a rule which states that all identifiers must be defined before they are used. However, that would likely be too restrictive in some cases. For example,

$$\textbf{type} \quad A = \textbf{record} \; c1 : integer;$$
$$c2 : \uparrow \; B$$
$$\textbf{end};$$

$$B = \textbf{record} \; c3 : \uparrow \; A;$$
$$c4 : real$$
$$\textbf{end};$$

Here we have two records each of which references the other in its definition. We would not want to rule out this possibility. A similar circumstance arises in the case of mutually recursive procedures. The Pascal report says nothing about how to handle this, but the *Pascal User Manual and Report* [Jensen-Wirth 74] mentions the existence of a **forward** declaration. A procedure, its name, formal parameters and their type, followed by the word **forward**, can be placed before a procedure which uses it.

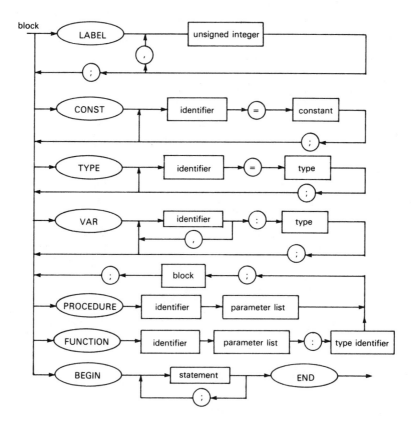

Figure 7-4: Pascal Syntax Graph for a Block

7.5. Aliasing

We have defined aliasing in Chapter 4 and noted that it generally is considered a dangerous feature of programming languages. Here we look at how aliasing can arise in connection with procedures. The simplest form of aliasing occurs when a procedure is called with an actual parameter which is the same as a global variable, that appears in the procedure's body. For example,

> **procedure** $p(x)$;
> $\quad x := x+1$;
> $\quad x := x + y$;
> **end** p

Here procedure p contains a global variable y. If p is invoked using the call $p(y)$, then x and y are now aliases as there are two paths to the same location. This is assuming that call-by-reference is used. If y is initially 2, then on exit y contains 6. However, if x is handled using call-by-value-result, then the final value of y is 5.

If this example seems contrived, consider the following program in Table 7-7 which finds the greatest common divisor of two integers and divides both numbers by this quantity. The example is due to Bob Schwanke.

> **procedure** *simpleratio* (a, b);
> $\quad$ **begin integer** c, d;
> $\qquad c := a; \quad d := b$;
> $\qquad$ **while** $c \neq d$ **do**
> $\qquad\quad$ **if** $c > d$ **then** $c := c - d$
> $\qquad\qquad\qquad$ **else** $d := d - c$;
> $\qquad b := b/c$;
> $\qquad a := a/c$;
> $\quad$ **end**

Table 7-7:   An Example Where Call-by-Value-Result Pays Off

If $a = 10$ and $b = 5$ then the result is to set $a = 2$ and $b = 1$. One would hope that *simpleratio* (x,x) would set x to one but actually this does not happen. Instead x is set to zero because a and b are aliases for x. The assignment to b sets b to one and a/c (or one divided by c) sets a and b to zero. The call-by-value-result scheme was devised so that assignments to the actual parameters during computation would be suppressed until the end. Assuming call-by-value-result in the procedure, *simpleratio* now gives the correct answer for *simpleratio* (x,x).

The assignment to *b* does not alter *a* as they are both representing local copies of the actuals. When the **end** is reached, the correct values are copied to the actuals.

A possible problem with call-by-value-result is that the address of the actual parameter is computed two times, once on entry and a second time on exit. If an actual parameter is an element of an array then it is possible that its subscript expression has been altered through side-effects. If so, then the swap routine will not work properly. Also, if more than one parameter carries out a value, then the order of the recopying is undefined making different results possible. The solution seems not to lie in more clever schemes for parameter evaluation and passing but in outlawing the possibility of aliasing.

The language Euclid makes the bold statement "This language guarantees that two identifiers in the same scope can never refer to the same or overlapping variables" [Euclid]. To accomplish this, Euclid has not allowed automatic inheritance of globals within a nested scope. Instead an **imports** clause is provided through which the programmer must list all names which are known in the enclosed scope. Euclid views these names as denoting objects which may be altered. The second way in which aliasing may occur is through the use of pointers. For this Euclid introduces *collection variables* which denote receivers of variables of a given type. A pointer variable may only point to a member of a collection variable and its value is viewed as an index into the collection. Unfortunately, it is impossible to check at compile-time whether or not two pointer variables in the same collection denote the same index. The solution is to rely either on verification to prove that this is not the case or to insert run-time checks which verify the condition.

7.6. Overloading

A construct in a typed language is said to be *overloaded* if there are several distinct meanings of the construct and the appropriate meaning is selected based upon the type information of its arguments. Perhaps the oldest example of overloading of operators is in connection with +. In languages such as FORTRAN, ALGOL60, PL/1, and others.the + is used to denote both integer and real addition as well as addition involving both integers and reals. It makes sense to use this symbol to also denote addition of complex numbers, rational numbers, Gaussian numbers, and others. Thus. a language which offers overloading is supporting the use of natural and conventional notations. Another advantage of overloading is that the same name or operator can be used by several programmers in different contexts and combined into a single system without confusion in the language.

In some languages it is possible to define several procedures which all have the same name and all are visible within the same scope. This is in contrast to the hole-in-scope phenomenon described in section 6.1 such that when a name is redeclared it wipes out the visibility of the earlier declaration. This common procedure name is said to be *overloaded* because it serves to denote more than one procedure. Overloading can be permitted as long as it is possible to distinguish the proper instance of the different procedures.

In Ada there are six types of operators: logical, relational, adding, unary, multiplying, and exponentiating. Any one of the operators in any of these six categories may be overloaded. Neither the short circuit operators nor the membership operators may be overloaded. When overloading an operator such as *, a function is declared such as

function "*" (X,Y : MATRIX) **return** MATRIX;

This declares that * can take two matrices as its arguments and it will return a matrix as its result. The programmer must appropriately define the body of this function. But Ada itself will define the equality operator for the new type MATRIX unless the programmer supplies one. This equality operator will return a Boolean value, and must necessarily take as its arguments two variables of the same type. Two matrices will be equal if all of their corresponding components are equal.

When an overloaded operator or subprogram name appears, the essential problem for the translator is how to determine which one of several possible meanings applies. The type information which is included with the arguments of the operator or the parameters of a subprogram provide the only clues. One obvious rule to adopt involves a check on the types of the arguments. If they uniquely determine one operator or subprogram then the decision is made. This is the rule that ALGOL68 has adopted, namely that the types of the parameters must be sufficient to identify the correct procedure. For example.here we see the operator *abs* overloaded with three definitions:

op *abs* = (**real** x) **real**: **if** x < 0 **then** -x **else** x **fi**
   abs = (**int** i) **int**: **if** i < 0 **then** -i **else** i **fi**
   abs = (**long real** x) **long real**: **if** x < 0 **then** -x **else** x **fi**

The operator called *abs* is defined to work on three sets of distinct arguments: **real, int,** and **long real**, so there is no difficulty for the

ALGOL68 compiler to determine the correct version to use.

One way to think of this rule being implemented is to imagine the parse tree which is produced as an expression is parsed and assume that we associate the type information with the appropriate nodes in the tree. In languages such as FORTRAN or ALGOL60. each leaf of the parse tree for an expression has a unique type, and all overloadings can then be resolved by a single pass which moves up the tree in postorder fashion, [Horowitz 76]. For example, Figure 7-5 shows the parse tree for an arithmetic expression with the type information for each node in parentheses. Given the types of the leaf node elements, the types of the inner nodes are easily determined.

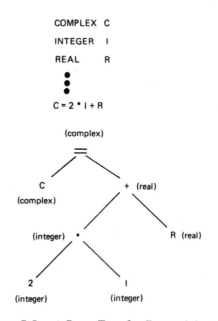

Figure 7-5: A Parse Tree for Determining the
Type Of Overloaded Operators

In Ada the resolution of overloaded names is more complicated for two reasons: (i) constructs which may appear as leaf nodes in the parse tree can be overloaded such as literals and parameterless functions; (ii) the programmer can insert explicit constraints on the resolution of overloaded constructs. This implies that it is necessary to propagate information up and down the parse tree in order to resolve overloadings. In fact the rule in Ada is

The types and the order of the actual parameters, the names of the formal parameters (if named associations are used), and the result type (for functions) must be sufficient to identify exactly one overloaded subprogram specification [Ada 80].

Table 7-8 portrays an example of overload resolution in Ada. This rule essentially says that all possible information will be used to resolve the overloaded name. In [Wallis 80] an algorithm is given for resolving overloaded constructs in Ada which requires only one pass up and one pass down the tree. The following example selected from the Ada manual shows how the resolution of overloading works. In Table 7-8 we see a procedure which contains a package P, three function definitions F, G, and K, a use clause and a body. The package P also contains definitions of functions F, G, and K. Thus, the names F, G, and K are overloaded. The fully qualified name of each function follows the definition in a comment. In the first assignment statement, F(V) returns a REAL and so P.F(V) is the appropriate choice. In the second statement the type of U is BOOLEAN so the function definition of F in MAIN is the proper choice. The third assignment statement is ambiguous as the use of K can be taken from either MAIN or P and the rest of the statement does not resolve the ambiguity. Similarly for the fourth assignment. Any use clauses have the same status as other declarations with the added assumption that they are declared in a scope enclosing the STANDARD package; see [Ada 80].

7.7. Generic Functions

Many of us have written subprograms for sorting. They may have been for sorting integers or reals or character strings or some other objects, but we might have realized that the sorting procedure would essentially work just as well for any ordered objects. The difficulty we have in a language that follows the strong typing principle is that we must specify at compile-time the types of the objects to be sorted. Therefore we must have separate routines for sorting integers, reals, etc. even though these routines are identical in every respect except for the type declarations. The generic facility is intended to correct this problem.

Generic procedures are procedure *templates*, one or more of whose

procedure MAIN **is**
. . .
package P **is**
  function F(X : REAL) **return** RANGE;   -- P.F
  function G(X : DOMAIN) **return** REAL;   -- P.G
  function K(X : DOMAIN) **return** BOOLEAN; -- P.K
end P;

  function F(X : BOOLEAN) **return** RANGE;   -- MAIN.F
  function G(X : DOMAIN) **return** BOOLEAN; -- MAIN.G
  function K(X : DOMAIN) **return** REAL;   -- MAIN.K
  S : DOMAIN;
  T : RANGE;
  U : BOOLEAN; V : REAL;
use P;
. . .
begin
  T := F(V); -- means P.F(V)
  T := F(U); -- means MAIN.F(U)
  T := F(K(S)) --this is ambiguous
-- it could mean either MAIN.F(P.K(S)) or P.F(MAIN.K(S))
  T := F(G(S)); --this is ambiguous
-- it could mean either MAIN.F(MAIN.G(S)) or P.F(P.G(S))
end

Table 7-8: An Example of Overload Resolution in Ada

elements have been parameterized. These parameters are instantiated at compile-time yielding an actual procedure. The generic facility, therefore, causes a decrease in the size of the program text with a subsequent reduction in coding errors and provides another level of abstraction.

One typical use of generic procedures is to factor out the dependency of procedures on types. Several languages have introduced mechanisms of this sort including EL1, SIMULA and CLU. Though EL1 has by far the most powerful feature, it requires run-time checking of types for its implementation adding substantially to the overhead of the language. SIMULA and CLU have a simpler form than EL1, which arises chiefly from the restriction that all objects of a parameterized type must be handled by reference. In this chapter we will examine the generic facility offered in Ada.

The generic facility in Ada for subprograms or packages is akin to a macro expansion feature. Generic programs are templates, and they cannot be invoked. Instead, they must be instantiated in the program text at compile-time and actual procedures must result.

```
generic type ITEM is private;
procedure SWAP(X, Y : in out ITEM) is
      TEMP : ITEM;
   begin
      TEMP := Y;
      Y   := X;
      X   := TEMP;
   end;
```

Table 7-9:   A Generic Procedure for Swapping in Ada

For example in Table 7-9 we see a generic procedure which swaps the values of X and Y. X and Y are the formal parameters and are used to bring a value into the procedure and to carry out a potentially different value. The type of X and Y, namely ITEM, is the parameter of this generic procedure. This parameter must be substituted for at translation time. Notice how the parameter ITEM is used in the declaration of the local variable TEMP. Also note that the operation of assignment $(:=)$ is assumed to exist for operands of type ITEM.

To instantiate such a generic procedure one might write

```
procedure SWAPINTEGER is new SWAP(INTEGER);
procedure SWAPREAL  is new  SWAP(REAL);
```

Each statement will produce a distinct procedure which differs only in the type of its arguments.

One language design issue involved with generic procedures is what operations one can use on a parameterized type. In Ada the answer is that operations on generic types must be specified by generic operators. For example, in Table 7-10 we have a generic procedure which adds the elements of type VECTOR. Since the type of the elements contained in the VECTOR is parameterized, called VALUE, we must include a parameterized specification for the operation of + which is used within the function. This generic function has four parameters which must be supplied for a proper instantiation. These include actual values for VALUE, VECTOR, ZERO, and +. One example of an instantiation is

```
function SUMVECT is new SUM(INTEGER, VECTOR, 0, "+");
```

generic
type VALUE **is private**;
type VECTOR **is array**(INTEGER **range** < >) **of** VALUE;
ZERO : VALUE;
with function "+"(U, V : VALUE) **return** VALUE;
   function SUM(X : VECTOR, N : INTEGER) **return** VALUE **is**
     SUMX : VALUE := ZERO;
   begin
     for I **in** 1 .. N **loop** SUMX := SUMX + X(I); **end loop**;
     return SUMX;
   end;

Table 7-10:   Example of Ada Generic Function

This defines the operation + as having arguments of type INTEGER and thus the conventional integer operator will be used.

Other Issues Involving Procedures

Some programming languages have elevated functions to first-class status by making them storable data objects. In ALGOL60 and Pascal, procedures are denotable and expressible but not storable. In ALGOL68, functions defined by **proc** can be assigned to variables and generally manipulated as objects. For example, if *random* is a function of no arguments which produces a real result, then one may write

     real *a* ; **proc real** q;
     q := random;
     a := q;

In the first assignment statement *q* is assigned a copy of the procedure body of *random* and the last line causes the function to be executed and the result assigned to *a*. ALGOL68 introduced the term *deproceduring* to refer to the act of invoking a delayed procedure variable.

Can functions be parameters to procedures? Yes, for in FORTRAN one can use the EXTERNAL statement, ALGOL60 allows procedure parameters and PL/1 denotes them using the ENTRY attribute. The classic example of when a procedure as a parameter is desirable is a routine which uses some rule to integrate an arbitrary function. Then the function to be integrated is a natural parameter. Pascal allows procedures as parameters, but requires no specification of the arguments of the parameters. This creates a hole in the typing system. However, Pascal does insist that all of the arguments are passed using call-by-value.

7.8. Coroutines

The dynamic relationship between procedures is very constrained. A procedure P invokes Q and waits for its termination before it resumes. Mutually recursive procedures make this relationship more complex, but for any pair of consecutive invocations, the master-slave relationship exists. In this section, we discuss a different type of relationship between procedures developed fairly early in the history of programming languages. The *coroutine* relationship between two procedures is one of mutual control. Procedure P may invoke procedure Q while suspending its processing. At some later point, Q continues P at precisely the point where P invoked Q. Now Q is suspended, but it remembers its state. P and Q may call each other alternately, and each time the procedure begins at the place it last was suspended. Only the original task, in this case P, can delete Q and reallocate its resources. A more general situation permits the original procedure to generate many coroutines. The coroutines may all continue each other and the original procedure as well.

In Table 7-11 we see procedure A which activates procedure B as a coroutine at statement label L0. B executes past label M1, until it resumes A. A resumes at label L1 and continues to execute until it resumes B just prior to label L2. B starts executing at label M2 until it resumes A a second time. A begins at label L2 and eventually resumes B which continues executing at label M3. When B terminates, control is returned to A at label L3, and it eventually terminates.

procedure A(..)	procedureB(..)
L0: *coroutine* B	. . .
L1: . . .	M1: . . .
resume B(..)	resume A(..)
L2: . . .	M2: . . .
resume B(..)	resume A(..)
L3: . . .	M3: . . .
end A	end B

Table 7-11: Two Coroutines Which Execute the Labeled Sequence:
A starts, L0, B starts, M1, L1, M2, L2, M3, B ends, L3, A ends.

Some languages have built-in coroutines features. These include Burroughs extended version of ALGOL60 [EXTENDEDALGOL], SIMULA [Dahl-Nygaard 66], SL5 [Hanson 78], BLISS [Wulf 71], and INTERLISP [Teitelman 75]. Other people have extended existing languages with coroutines such as coroutine-FORTRAN [Gentleman 71], concurrent-Pascal [Brinch-Hansen 75], and coroutine-Pascal [Lemon 76]. One of the first people to exhibit an important application of coroutines was Conway in [Conway 63].

There are several issues which must be resolved in a programming language which includes coroutines. How should a coroutine be referenced, what is its scope and its extent and what happens when a coroutine is suspended or resumed? What rules shall exist for parameters to coroutines? We will see that these issues have been resolved in different ways by different languages.

When a coroutine instance is created, its activation record is placed on the stack. In SIMULA for example, coroutines (or class objects) are executed immediately as they are created, while in SL5 the user must first create the coroutine and later on provide a command which begins its execution. Another issue is the relationship between coroutines. In some languages communication between coroutines is *symmetric*, meaning that each one can resume the other. *Semi-symmetric* communication refers to the situation in which a set of coroutines exists, but the coroutines do not pass control between each other. Instead they all pass control between themselves and a "controller" program. Another issue is what happens when a coroutine is suspended. Naturally its current instruction pointer must be saved and it is tagged as temporarily suspended. But how does suspension occur? In BLISS there is no explicit suspension command. When the flow of control of the program moves out of the coroutine, the coroutine is suspended. Another alternative is to have a command which causes the active coroutine to suspend. Finally, we must consider who gets control when a coroutine terminates. In SL5, coroutine termination is not permitted. In other languages termination may return control to the activating coroutine or to the main program or to the coroutine's creator.

A popular way to implement coroutines was suggested by Bobrow and Wegbreit in [Bobrow 73]. There they generalize the notion of the run-time stack so that activation records retain the information needed for coroutine reactivation. This includes storage for pointers to the coroutine's creator, its activator, its continuation point, a pointer to the start of the activation record, and some room for temporaries. During execution it is necessary to keep track of the number of references to an activation record, and when no more references exist, it may be removed.

In the usual case, a coroutine contains only one pointer to its body which indicates where it will resume execution when reactivated. This is called a *moving* activation point. An alternative is to save a pointer to its body for each coroutine which activates this coroutine. This is referred to as *static activation points*. The coroutine may resume in different places depending upon who reactivates it. This type of mechanism is found in INTERLISP and is useful for applications which are state driven such as backtracking. However, in [Pauli 80] their investigation of several coroutine applications indicated no use or need of static activation pointers.

When a procedure ends, its activation record must be removed from the stack. But in the case of coroutines the basic activation record must be retained. But by retaining the activation record in the stack, it may block another coroutine or procedure if there is not enough room in the stack to grow. Therefore.the part of the activation record which is used for coroutine information is copied to another part of the stack where there is enough space. This copying leaves a gap in the stack and is presumably the reason why this implementation mechanism is referred to as a *spaghetti* stack. Bobrow and Wegbreit used dynamic scoping in their presentation of the spaghetti stack. Its modification to static scoping was undertaken by Pauli and Soffa in [Pauli 80].

A coroutine in SIMULA is represented by an object of a class. This coroutine interacts with others by using the statement *resume(p)* where *p* is the name of a coroutine to be resumed. Data of coroutines can be accessed by means of reference variables and can either be global to all coroutines or reside in one of them. For an object to be generated one writes "**new** class-name." This produces an instance of the class which can be assigned to a reference variable. In order for this new object to return control to its generator.the statement *detach* is provided. The generator may, at a later time resume this detached object by using the statement **call**(p). The object will resume execution at the place immediately following the last *detach* it executed. If an **end** is encountered, control returns to the generator. Thus SIMULA really offers two mechanisms for establishing coroutines, the resume/resume mechanism and the call/detach mechanism.

Let's consider an example of coroutines in SIMULA, this one first given by Grune in [Grune 77]. The problem to be solved calls for a process A which copies characters from input to output. However, wherever it finds a string "aa" it converts it to "b". Meanwhile there is a second process B which converts "bb" to "c". One way to solve this problem is to let B act as the main procedure using A as a subroutine. But since A contains several calls to the output routine, these will all have to be moved to the end where the final output character is determined. This is a clumsy solution as it requires us to chop up

A. Instead we consider having A and B act as coroutines. Table 7-12 contains this example of SIMULA coroutines.

Table 7-12 contains two SIMULA classes called *double-a-to-b* and *double-b-to-c*. The statements beginning with *ref* declare objects of the class. The call on *proc A* starts the entire computation. The *detach* statements within each class cause the procedures to simply be activated, and to suspend their execution until they are resumed later via the call of *proc A*. The call of *proc A* gets the coroutines interacting. In *double-a-to-b* there is an infinite loop controlling the main computation. A character is read into *ch*. If it is an 'a' then a second character is read. If it is also an 'a', then *ch* is assigned 'b' and coroutine B is resumed. Similarly if the first character to be input is not an 'a', then B is resumed. If an 'a' is not followed by a second 'a', then first *ch* is set to 'a' and B is resumed followed by *ch* set to the following input character and B resumed. Class *double-b-to-c* is similarly easily to follow. Both coroutines are able to clearly reflect the logic required by the problem statement.

```
begin character ch;
  class double-a-to-b;
    begin detach;
      while true do
        begin ch := inchar;
          if ch = 'a' then
            begin ch := inchar;
              if ch = 'a' then
                begin ch := 'b'; resume(proc B) end
                else begin character ch1; ch1 := ch;
                  ch := 'a'; resume(proc B);
                  ch := ch1; resume (proc B)
                end
            end else resume (proc B)
        end infinite loop
    end double-a-to-b;

  class double-b-to-c;
    begin detach;
      while true do
        begin
          if ch = 'b' then
            begin resume(proc A);
              if ch = 'b' then outchar('c') else
                begin outchar('b'); outchar(ch) end
            end else outchar(ch);
            resume(proc A)
        end infinite loop
    end double-b-to-c;

  ref (double-a-to-b) proc A;
  ref (double-b-to-c) proc B;
  proc A :- new double-a-to-b;
  proc B :- new double-b-to-c;
  call (proc A)
end
```

Table 7-12: An Example of SIMULA Coroutines

Concepts Discussed in This Chapter

Abstract syntax
Actual parameter
Aliasing
Anonymous function
Anonymous variable
Call-by-name
Call-by-reference
Call-by-text
Call-by-value
Call-by-value-result
Classes
Closure
Collection variables
Coroutines

Concrete syntax
Deproceduring
Formal parameters
Function
Generic function
Imports list
Jensen's device
Overloaded operator
Procedure
Procedural abstraction
Subroutine

Exercises

1. Investigate the ways FORTRAN, ALGOL60, PL/1 and Pascal treat parameterless procedures.

2. In ALGOL60 we can say

   real procedure *root2;*
   root2 := 1.4142135

   Compare the use of *root2* in an ALGOL60 program to the constant definition "root2 = 1.4142135;" in ALGOL68.

3. On page 12, Section 4.7.3 of the revised ALGOL60 Report, is the definition of evaluation of actuals call-by-text or call-by-name?

4. On page 9, Section 3.5.3 of the revised ALGOL60 Report the word recursive occurs in reference to switches. Can you find where procedures are allowed to be recursive?

5. Show the values printed by this program when parameters are passed by value, reference and value-result.

   begin integer *a*
   procedure *P(b)* ; **integer** *b*
   begin *b := b+1* ; *print (b,a)* **end**

```
    a := 1;
    P(a);
    print(a);
end
```

6. What does the following ALGOL60 program do when invoked by the calls *P(a[i], i, 1, 100)* and *P(b[i,i], i, 1, 100)*?

```
procedure P(x, ind, j, h);
  value j,h ;
  begin for ind := j step 1 until h do
    x : = 0
  end
```

7. [Fleck] The text points out that call-by-name prevents a simple swapping procedure from being written. Consider this ALGOL60 procedure for swapping integers.

```
procedure SWAP(x,y)
  begin
  integer procedure SWAP1(p,q)
    begin
    SWAP1 := p;
    p := q;
  end SWAP1
  x := SWAP1(y,x);
  end SWAP
```

Now the address of *x* is computed first, SWAP1 saves *y* and stores *x* in *y* and returns *y* which is stored in *x*. Does the procedure work correctly on *SWAP(i,A[i])*? Does the procedure work if *i* is a procedure which evaluates to a different address each time it is invoked?

8. Does procedure *simpleratio(a[i],i)* work properly when the parameter evaluation and passing method is call-by-value-result? What about call-by-name?

9. If a language provides ALGOL60 procedures but functions with no side-effects, how can a random number generator function be written, as that must alter its environment as well as returning a value?

10. Some languages permit a procedure to have multiple entry points. Discover one such language and present its rules. Why is such a facility useful?

11. Show how to write Jensen's device in ALGOL68 using the idea outlined in section 7.3.

12. What is the value of y at label L?

```
begin real x,y;
 x := 41;
 begin real procedure p(a)
  real a ; p := a + x;
     . . .
  x := 3 ;
 end
 L : y := p(4);
end
```

13. Assume that a Pascal program is written for multiplying two 10 x 10 matrices of integers, MATMULT(**var** x, y : matrix). Write the procedure and then show what happens when the procedure is called by MATMULT(A, A), trying to compute the 10 x 10 matrix A^2. Then do the same for ADDMULT(A, A).

14. Suppose one wants to write a function which concatenates two strings.and it calls the storage allocator to get space for the new string. Should this be considered a side-effect? Justify your answer.

15. In some programming languages, e.g. POP-2, it is possible to bind a procedure to its actual parameters, but not execute the body. This brings up the question of when should the actuals be dereferenced and when should storage be allocated for locals. Discuss the merits of doing these things at the time the procedure is bound to its arguments versus the time the procedure is executed.

16. Though Pascal and FORTRAN both use call-by-reference, they work differently in certain special cases. Discuss the differences.

17. Consider the example

```
procedure fact(n, ans : integer);
 ans := 1;
 while n < > 1 do
  ans := n * ans;
  n := n - 1
 end
end
```

Is there an error in this program? If so, explain what it is.

18. For coroutines what would you expect to happen if one coroutine executes a **return** statement. What does happen in extended-ALGOL or SIMULA?

19. Suppose you have designed a programming language which permits procedures and coroutines to be intermixed. If procedure P calls procedure Q, then Q may either return to P via **return** or it may **resume** P. Also Q may recursively call P which may then resume Q. Show how the **return** and **resume** statements work together.

20. Following the discussion in section 7.4, use your Pascal compiler to see if it allows one to define the base type of an array in an enclosing block. Then see if it will permit the re-definition of this base type following its use in the array definition.

21. Consider the procedure declaration **procedure** $P(i : integer)$ where the parameter passing mechanism is call-by-value-result. Is it correct if the call $P(A[i])$ is implemented as

    ☐ create a new local variable, say z;
    ☐ assign to z the value of $A[i]$;
    ☐ execute the body of P using z for $A[i]$;
    ☐ set $A[i]$ to z.

22. Imagine a programming language where one cannot choose to name your formal parameters. Instead the variable names A1, A2, . . . are reserved and all procedures must assign their arguments to these variables before invocation. Is this a good or a bad idea and why?

23. Imagine that you are trying to include a coroutine capability in FORTRAN. You have postulated four commands: COROUTINE, ENTER, RESUME and DETACH. The translation of "COROUTINE name" is to create a subroutine called NAME with labels on all statements where this coroutine may resume. For this problem you are to supply the ANSI FORTRAN translations for the operations: COROUTINE, ENTER, RESUME and DETACH.

24. It would be nice if in Pascal we could write

        type color = (red, white, blue);
            const stop = red;

Why is this illegal?

25. Here is a Pascal program which is legal but violates the law of least astonishment.

function *i;*

   . . .

   i := i + 1;

   . . .

end

The three dots indicate, as usual, any segment of code that does not involve *i*. Explain the meaning of the assignment statement and what it does.

26. Here is another interesting Pascal program.

```
program fun
   function outer : integer;
      procedure inner;
         begin
            outer := 1;
         end
      begin
         inner;
      end;
   begin
      writln(outer);
   end.
```

Notice the use of the global variable *outer* in the *inner* procedure and the use of *inner* in function *outer*. What should be printed out by this program?

27. Show how to get the effect of call-by-name in ALGOL68. The idea is to make the compiler regard the parameters of a procedure as procedures themselves which are invoked at each procedure call.

Chapter 8

DATA ABSTRACTION

8.1. An Introduction

An abstraction is a way of representing a group of related things by a single thing which expresses their similarities and suppresses their differences. The procedure is the time honored method for abstracting out how something is done leaving only a description of what is done. Only comparatively recently has the need for a mechanism which abstracts a data type been recognized, and now several languages have developed methods for describing a data abstraction. A *data type* is a set of objects and operations on those objects. The operations create, build-up, destroy and pick apart instances of the set of objects. A *data abstraction* in a programming language is a mechanism which collects together (or encapsulates) the representation and the operations of a data type. This encapsulation forms a wall which is intended to shield the data type from improper uses. But it also provides a "window" which allows the user a well-defined means for accessing the data type. Thus a data abstraction facility is more than just a new way of defining a data type, like a record, array, set or file would be in Pascal. In addition to defining a new type and usually allowing variables to be declared as only holding values of that type, it also shields the representation of the type, allows implementors to provide some operations to the user of the type, but possibly retain others for themselves. It usually does all this by introducing new scope rules into a programming language. In this section we will examine how all or some of these features have been combined into an abstract data type facility in the latest programming languages.

Historically, the types of Pascal and the modes of ALGOL68 were an important step forward. But the first occurrence of a data abstraction facility in a programming language appeared in SIMULA67. Quoting Professor Bill Wulf

> "The so-called data abstraction languages,..., all derive from the methodological considerations of modular decomposition and employ the language device originally called "classes" in SIMULA67." [Wulf 76]

Thus, one of the languages we will investigate in this chapter is SIMULA67.

Before we begin to discuss how data abstraction actually appears in a real programming language, let's discuss an imaginary form of it. Following tradition, I will introduce a new name for the concept, **structure**, and use it as a keyword and as a scope delimiter. I note that MODULA and Euclid use the term **module**, Ada uses **package**, SIMULA uses **class**, CLU uses **cluster**, and ALPHARD uses **form**. Perhaps there are some others.

Within a **structure** we will find the name of the data type, declarations, a representation of the data type in terms of other data types and a set of procedures. For example, the abstract data type *queue* could have the following outline in Table 8-1: The keywords **structure** *queue* ... **end** *queue* denote the beginning and end of a new data type definition. In addition, it defines a *closed scope* which means that names defined within this structure are not known outside of it, except for those we explicitly export and names from the outside are not inherited. This **structure** definition has four components: a list of the operations of the data type, the representation of the data type, the implementation of the operations in terms of the representation and a section of code for initialization. There are three operations listed in the **operations** statement, but there are four procedures that are contained within the structure. All operations listed in the **operations** statement are to be known, or exported out of the structure. *NEXT* is not exported and is hence termed a *local function*. The keywords **representation** ... **end rep** denote that part of the **structure** in which the representation of queues is defined. This section may include constants, variables, arrays, other structures or any structuring elements of the language. Given this

     structure *queue* =
      operations *ADDQ, DELETEQ, ISEMPTYQ*
      representation ... **end rep**
      procedure *ADDQ(...)*

        . . .

      end *ADDQ*

      procedure *DELETEQ(...)*

        . . .

      end *DELETEQ*

      procedure *ISEMPTYQ(...)*

        . . .

      end *ISEMPTYQ*

      procedure *NEXT(...)*

        . . .

      end *NEXT*

      begin *initialization code*
      end
    end *queue*

Table 8-1:   A Queue Structure

queue structure, when we wish to declare variables of type *queue*, then we need merely write

    var *x : queue*;

When this declaration is encountered at run-time, storage is allocated for *x* as described in the **representation** ... **end rep** and the initialization code at the end of the structure is executed. As this structure cannot contain any global variables, so it cannot be affected by or affect the outside environment. The user may only access a structure of type *queue* by using those operations which are exported via the **operations** statement.

In Table 8-2 we see a completely specified *queue*. The representation is a one-dimensional array indexed from 0 to 99. Variables, *front* and *rear* are used to point to the opposite ends of the queue and have the obvious interpretation. The procedures QUEUEFULL and QUEUEEMPTY are left unspecified. These may be viewed either as error handling procedures or as exception conditions, the latter we

structure *queue* =
   operations *ADDQ, DELETEQ, ISEMPTYQ;*
   representation
      integer array *q(0 : 99);*
      integer *front, rear;*
   end rep

   procedure *NEXT(i : integer);*
      $i := (i+1)$ **mod** *100*
   end *NEXT;*

   procedure *ADDQ(q : queue, item : integer);*
      NEXT(rear)
      if *front* = *rear* **then** *QUEUEFULL*
            else *q(rear)* := *item*
      endif
   end *ADDQ;*

   procedure *DELETEQ (q : queue)* **returns** *item* : **integer;**
      if *ISEMPTYQ(q)* **then** *QUEUEEMPTY*
            else *NEXT(front)*
                item := *q(front)*
      endif
   end *DELETEQ;*

   procedure *ISEMPTYQ (q : queue)* **returns** *flag* : **boolean;**
      flag := *front* = *rear*
   end *ISEMPTYQ;*

   begin
      front := *rear* := *1*
   end;
end *queue*

Table 8-2: Complete Definition of a Queue

discuss in the next chapter.

In the following sections we will examine the variations that several programming languages have taken when they implemented this basic concept. But before we do, let's summarize the questions we should ask about an abstract data type facility.

□ What is the syntactic form of the construct?
□ What are its scope rules, and what is the lifetime of the objects which are created?
□ Does it allow for initial and final code segments?
□ Can one get one or more instances of the data type, i.e., is the facility a type constructor?
□ Is it possible to parameterize an abstract data type definition?
□ Can one share data between instances?

8.2. MODULA

The data abstraction facility in MODULA is called a module. A MODULA program is a module which is a collection of declarations (of constants, variables, types and procedures) and a sequence of statements which constitute the initialization code. A module forms a closed scope and any identifiers brought in from the outside (imported) must be listed in a **use**-list. Any identifiers which are to be available outside must be listed in a **define list** (exported). If a type is defined in a module and named in a define list, then only the type's identity is known outside, but not its structure. Thus, the only way the type can be used is by procedures which are exported. If a variable is exported, it may only be read and not written. The statement sequence at the end of a module is executed when the procedure to which the module is local is called. Modules may be nested. The major difference between a module in MODULA and the data abstraction facility discussed before is that the module *is not a type constructor.* One cannot instantiate variables of the type defined by the module. Its purpose is primarily as a mechanism for restricting scope. But though the module establishes a scope, it does *not* determine the life of its local objects. Objects local to a module are local to the procedure which contains the module and hence the objects appear when the procedure is called and disappear when the procedure is exited. In this rather simple example of a queue expressed as a MODULA module in Table 8-3, we see most of the essential parts. The **define** operation indicates that the procedure names which are listed will be exported. The representation of the queue will consist of a 100 element array and two integer pointers *front* and *rear*.

```
module queue;
  define addq, deleteq, isemptyq;
  var front, rear : integer;
  q : array 0 .. 99 of integer;
  procedure addq(item : integer);
    begin
      next (rear);
      if front = rear then QUEUEFULL
                      else q[rear] := item end
    end addq;

  procedure deleteq() : integer;
    begin          •
      if isemptyq then QUEUEEMPTY
                  else next(front);
                       deleteq := q[front]   end
    end deleteq;

  procedure isemptyq () : boolean;
    begin
      isemptyq := front = rear
    end isemptyq;

  procedure next (var i : integer);
    begin
      i := (i+1) mod 100
    end next;

  begin
    front := rear := 1
  end queue
```

Table 8-3:   A Queue in MODULA

The procedure *next* is known internally, but as it is not named on the **define** statement, it is not exported. The section of code at the end of the module is the initialization sequence.

A more substantial example from MODULA would show that it accomplishes data type instantiation by permitting new type definitions to be exported out of the module. This is precisely the approach taken by Ada and is also permitted in Euclid. In order to see an example of how this is done. I present a second example from MODULA. This module creates the data type binary search tree and provides two operations, an *insert* and a *find*. The second line in Table 8-4 defines the type *bstree*, *maxsize* the maximum number of nodes in the tree, two procedures for operating on the set and finally a procedure *init* for initialization. The type *bstree* is represented by the record shown on the fifth through eighth lines of the module. Looking at procedure *insert* we see that it has two parameters, a character c which is the element being inserted and a variable p whose type is *bstree*. When an *insert* command is issued the local variable j is set to one and then a loop is begun over the nodes currently in *bstree*. Note the use of the representation of *bstree*, namely *p.data[j]*, *p.rightlink[j]* and *p.leftlink[j]*. The *insert* procedure will move along the tree, going either left or right depending upon the value of c and its relation to the value in *p.data[j]*. If the item is not already in the tree a new node at location *avail* will be assigned and attached to the tree in the appropriate place.

For someone to make use of this module he could declare a variable such as

var q : *bstree*

Then to insert the integer k he would write

insert(k, q)

Similarly one can test whether k is in the *bstree* by writing *find(k, q)*. Note that the initialization procedure creates the empty available nodes and would be called immediately after the declaration of a variable to be of type *bstree*. In MODULA, the initialization procedure can refer to parameters as well as global variables that have been imported. However, it can only modify variables which are local to the module and the instance of the type which is being initialized. One of the important features of the module in MODULA is that one can define many abstract types and when instances of those types are created, they may share the local memory (variables) of the module.

Recently Wirth has modified his language and has produced a new

```
module bstreemodule;
  define bstree, maxsize, insert, find, init;
  const maxsize = 1000;
  var avail : integer;
  type bstree = record data : array 1 : maxsize of char;
                       rightlink : array 1 : maxsize of integer;
                       leftlink : array 1 : maxsize of integer;
                end;
  procedure insert( const c : char; var p : bstree);
    var j : integer
    begin j := 1;
      if avail = 1 then p.data[j] := c; avail := avail + 1;
      else loop
            when c > p.data[j] do
                    if p.rightlink[j] <> 0
                       then j := p.rightlink[j];
                       else p.rightlink[j] := avail;
                            p.data[avail] := c;
                            avail := avail + 1;
                    end
            when c < p.data[j] do
                    if p.leftlink[j] <> 0
                       then j := p.leftlink[j];
                       else p.leftlink[j] := avail;
                            p.data[avail] := c;
                            avail := avail + 1;
                    end
            when c = p.data[j] do exit end
      end
    end insert;
```

Table 8-4:   First Part of Binary Search Tree Module

```
procedure find (const c : char; const p : bstree) : Boolean
   var j : integer
   begin j := 1; find := false;
      if avail <> 1 then
         loop
            when c > p.data[j] do
               if p.rightlink[j] <> 0
                  then j := p.rightlink[j]
                  else exit
            end
            when c < p.data[j] do
               if p.leftlink[j] <> 0
                  then j := p.leftlink[j]
                  else exit
            when c = p.data[j] do
               find := true; exit;
            end
         end
   end find;

procedure init( var p : bstree);
   begin avail := 1;
      loop
         p.rightlink[avail] := 0;
         p.leftlink[avail] := 0;
         avail := avail + 1;
         if avail > maxsize then exit
      end
      avail := 1
   end init;
end bstreemodule
```

Table 8-5:   Second Part of Binary Search Tree Module

version MODULA-2, [Wirth 80]. One addition is the ability to qualify identifier names with the name of the module they come from. The need for this can be seen by the following example in Table 8-6:

module *P;*
   module *Q;*
     export *x;*
     var *x : integer;*

     . . . . .
   end *Q*

   module *R;*
     export *x;*
     var *x : boolean;*

     . . . . .
   end *R;*
   L1:
end *P;*

Table 8-6:   Dual Modules in MODULA

Here we see a module *P* which contains two modules *Q* and *R*. Both *Q* and *R* export the variable *x*. Therefore at label *L1* the name *x* denotes two different variables. In MODULA-2 one may write *Q.x* or *R.x* to specify one of the proper interpretations. Another change has to do with the exportation of types. If a type defined in a module contains several fields, and if the type is exported, are the field names also accessible outside of the module? In MODULA only *obscure export* of types is permitted meaning that the field names are not known. In MODULA-2 a change to *transparent export* has been made the default, with obscure export permitted only in certain special cases.

In MODULA-2 one now distinguishes between three different species of modules. The "normal" module which we have been discussing so far can be nested and can export variables and types as described. A *definition module* specifies all of the exported objects of a module. An *implementation module* belongs to the definition module of the same name and forms a pair. The implementation module contains the bodies of the procedures whose specifications are listed in the definition module. Definition and implementation modules may be compiled separately. The implementation module imports all objects defined in its associated definition module. By using these coupled modules, Wirth treats obscure versus transparent types in a manner similar to

Ada. If a type is fully specified in the definition module, then transparent export is followed. If only the type name is listed in the definition module, and the complete declaration is given in the implementation module, then obscure export is followed.

8.3. Euclid

The programming language Euclid [Lampson 77, Popek 77] was designed with the dual goals of supporting the writing of formally provable system software, and to differ from Pascal as little as possible. Thus, this language represents an interesting transition between a language totally lacking an abstract data type facility, such as Pascal, with one where the designers specifically tried to design such a facility, as in Ada.

The Euclid report views a module as a generalization of the record type. A module is denoted by **module**---end **module**, and has components which may include constants, variables, types and procedures. All names are local to the module unless they are explicitly exported. Exported names (on an export list) are known in all places where the module is known. Generalizing on MODULA, exported variables can be either **read only** or **var**. In general Euclid has been thorough about defining type equivalence, and the rule for modules is that two modules which define types are necessarily distinct. The exporting of operations must be complete; for example, if x and y are defined as instances of a type T, then x cannot be assigned to y or tested for equality unless the assignment and equals operators are exported. As a module is a closed scope, (as a general rule Euclid does not allow automatic inheritance of variables), any names to be used inside a module from the outside must be imported via an **imports** list. But variables which are **pervasive** needn't be imported. As with MODULA, an initial code segment may be included. It is executed whenever a new variable of the module type is created. A final action may also be included and executed whenever a variable of the type *type* is destroyed.

Euclid modules are not true abstract data types, because access to identifiers within a module is allowed. It is up to the programmers to enforce the discipline necessary to ensure that only the objects accessible to routines outside will be used. To further add to the complications there are actually two distinct methods of defining objects and their associated operations. One way is to define a module type and then to declare instances in the enclosing scope. A second way consists of exporting a type definition from a module so that objects of the type can be declared in the enclosing scope. To show an example of these two methods, we present two implementations of the type stack as originally presented in [Chang 78].

    type *Stack(Stacksize : unsignedInt)* = **module**
        exports *(Pop, Push)*
        var *IntStack :* **array** *1 . . StackSize* **of** *signedInt*
        var *StackPtr : 0 . . StackSize := 0*

        procedure *Push(X : signedInt)* =
          imports *(***var** *IntStack, StackPtr, StackSize)*
          begin
          procedure *Overflow* = . . . **end** *Overflow*
           if *StackPtr = StackSize* **then** *Overflow*
            else *StackPtr := StackPtr + 1; IntStack(StackPtr) := X*
          endif
        end *Push*

        procedure *Pop(***var** *X : signedInt)* =
          imports *(***var** *IntStack, StackPtr)*
          begin
           procedure *Underflow* = . . . **end** *Underflow*
           if *StackPtr = 0* **then** *Underflow*
            else *X := IntStack(StackPtr); StackPtr := StackPtr - 1*
           end if
          end *Pop*

    end *Stack*

Table 8-7:   Definition of a Stack Module in Euclid

In Table 8-7 we see the type *Stack* defined as a module type with its size being a parameter of the type definition. The only operations exported out of the module are *Push* and *Pop*. The representation consists of an array whose limit is the parameter *StackSize* and a stack pointer, *Stackptr*. The implementations of *Push* and *Pop* are straightforward. The definitions of *Overflow* and *Underflow* are not provided. To make use of this type definition one could say:

    var *P, Q : Stack(100)*
    var *item : signedInt*
     . . . . .

P.Push(20);
Q.Push(35);
P.Pop(item);

The alternative method for defining a stack module consists of defining a module *Stack* which exports a type definition, say *Stk.* The type *Stk* is equivalent to the stack data type. An example of this follows in Table 8-8.

type *Stack* = **module**
  exports *(Stk, Pop, Push)*
  type *Stk(Stacksize : unsignedInt)* = **record**
    var *StackPtr : 0 . . StackSize* := 0
    var *Body :* **array** *1 . . StackSize* **of** *signedInt*
  end *Stk*

  procedure *Push (***var** *IStk : Stk(* **parameter** *), X : signedInt)* =
  begin
    procedure *Overflow* = . . . **end** *Overflow*
    if *IStk.StackPtr* = *IStk.StackSize* **then** *Overflow*
    else *IStk.StackPtr* := *IStk.StackPtr* + *1*
        IStk.Body(IStk.StackPtr) := *X*
    end if
  end *Push*

  procedure *Pop (***var** *IStk : Stk (***parameter***),* **var** *X : signedInt)* =
  begin
    procedure *Underflow* = . . . **end** *Underflow*
    if *IStk.StackPtr* = *0* **then** *Underflow*
    else *X* := *IStk.Body(IStk.StackPtr)*
        IStk.StackPtr := *IStk.StackPtr - 1*
    end if
  end *Pop*
end *Stack*

Table 8-8:   A Second Euclid Stack Module

In Table 8-8 we see a module definition which contains a record type named *Stk.* This type is contained in the **exports** list and is thus known to the outside. The implementations of *Push* and *Pop* are similar except for the use of the dot notation to access fields of the record, e.g. *IStk.StackPtr.* The only other difference is the need to include the proper stack parameter as an argument to the procedures. For example to use this type one could write:

> **var** *S1 : Stack*
> **var** *P : S1.Stk(100)*
> **var** *Q : S1.Stk(200)*
> **var** *item : signedInt*
> . . . . . .
> *S1.Push(P, 29)*
> *S1.Pop(P, item)*

The first line declares *S1* to be an instance of the module *Stack*. The *P* and *Q* are declared to be stacks of integers of size 100 and 200 respectively. To access either *Push* or *Pop* we must either employ a **use** clause for *Stack* or resort to dot notation as shown.

One of the interesting uses of a module in Euclid is in connection with a **for** statement. Observe the syntax for the Euclid **for** statement below.

for stmt :: = **for** parameter generator ["; "] **loop** executable scope **end loop**
   generator :: = **in** module type | [**decreasing**] **in** index type | **in** set type

The parameter generator of a module type defines a sequence for the values of the type defined by the module. A module which acts as a generator must have three components called *value, stop* and *NEXT*, the latter being a procedure. Their names must be exported. When a **for** statement has the form

> **for** *i* **in** *module type generator* **loop** *body* **end loop**

it is equivalent to the block (using Euclid syntax)

> **begin var** *j : module type generator*
>   **loop exit when** *j.stop*
>   **begin** *const i : = j.value ; body* **end**
>   *j . NEXT*
>   **end loop**
> **end**

First the variable *j* is declared to be of type *module type generator*. This causes the initial statements to be executed. The **loop** is entered and if *j.stop* is true, then the loop is exited. Otherwise *i* is assigned the next value *j.value,* and the loop body is executed. Then the procedure *j.NEXT* is executed. When control leaves the block of the **for** statement, any final action of the module will be taken. The main virtue for the Euclid scheme is that as long as the generator imports no variables, the loop body and the generator are guaranteed to be independent. Therefore, termination can be shown (or proved) solely by considering the procedures of the generator.

8.4. Ada

In Ada a program unit is either a subprogram, package or task. The last two are special cases of a module. The task is concerned with concurrency so we defer its discussion until Chapter 10. A package (or a module) may contain simply a group of declarations of variables, and may in addition contain a set of related subprograms and type declarations which describe an encapsulated data type. A package is split into two parts, a specification and a body. In turn, the specification part is made up of two parts, a visible part and a private part. Types declared in the visible part of a package specification can be made known to other program units by means of a **use** clause. Entities declared in the private part cannot be exported, nor can any entities defined in the package body. A variable which is declared in either the package specification or body retains its value between calls to subprograms in the visible part of the package. Ada calls these **own** variables. Note that from a philosophical standpoint one might well argue that the private part does not belong in the specification of an abstract data type. However, in Ada it needs to be there to support separate compilation.

If one has to define an abstract data type in Ada, one uses a package module, lists any exported operations and types in the visible part of the module specification, but defines the representation in the private part. The actual subprograms are defined in the package body.

In Table 8-9 we see a definition of the abstract data type binary search tree. It is a package with three operations: HAS, INSERT, and EQUAL. Note how a record defines the representation of BSTREE as containing DATA, LEFTCHILD and RIGHTCHILD fields where the latter two are of type pointer (or access). In Table 8-10 we see the package body of BSTREES. HAS is a function which determines if I is present in BSTREE P, returning TRUE or FALSE. INSERT will determine if I is present in P and if not, it inserts a new node containing I in the proper position. EQUAL tests if two binary search trees have the same shape and data values at each node. A user might access this package by writing

```
package BSTREES is
   type BSTREE is private;
   function HAS (I:ITEM, P:BSTREEPTR) return BOOLEAN;
   procedure INSERT (I ; ITEM, in out P : BSTREEPTR);
   function EQUAL(P, Q : BSTREEPTR) return BOOLEAN;
   private
      type BSTREEPTR;
      type BSTREE is
         record
            DATA : ITEM
            LEFTCHILD : BSTREEPTR;
            RIGHTCHILD : BSTREEPTR;
         end record;
      type BSTREEPTR is access BSTREE;
end;
```

Table 8-9:   Ada Package Specification of BSTREE

```
   declare
   use BSTREES;
   P, Q : BSTREEPTR;
    begin
      P := new('A', null, null)
      INSERT('B', P);
      INSERT('Z', P);
      INSERT('H', P);
    end;
```

In Table 8-11. we see a second abstract data type defined in Ada, the familiar structure STACK. Here is an example of a generic package where the parameters are the stack size and the type of the stack's elements. Notice how there are two parts, the specification and the body which make up this package. PUSH and POP are the two operations and two exception conditions may be raised. To create a specific instance of a stack, say an integer stack of size 100 we would write

```
package INTEGERSTACK
    is new STACKS(SIZE => 100, ELEM => INTEGER);
```

Then to declare variables whose type is INTEGERSTACK of size less than or equal to 100 we would write

```
   declare
      use INTEGERSTACK;
```

```
package body BSTREES is
  function HAS(I : ITEM,P : BSTREEPTR) return BOOLEAN is
    Q : BSTREEPTR;
    begin
      Q := P;
      loop
        if Q = null then return FALSE;
        elsif I < Q.DATA then Q := Q.LEFTCHILD;
        elsif I > Q.DATA then Q := Q.RIGHTCHILD;
        else return TRUE;
        end if;
      end loop;
    end HAS;
  procedure INSERT(I : ITEM, in out P : BSTREEEPTR);
    -- SUPPLY DEFINITION HERE;
  function EQUAL(P, Q : BSTREEPTR) return BOOLEAN;
    if P = null and Q = null then return TRUE;
    elsif P = null or Q = null then return FALSE;
    elsif P.DATA = Q.DATA
      then if EQUAL(P.LEFTCHILD, Q.LEFTCHILD)
      then return EQUAL(P.RIGHTCHILD, Q.RIGHTCHILD);
        else return FALSE;
        end if;
    else return FALSE;
    end if;
end BSTREES;
```

Table 8-10:   Binary Search Tree Package Body in Ada

```
generic SIZE : INTEGER; type ELEM is private;
package STACKS is
      type STACK is limited private;
      procedure PUSH(S : in out STACK;  E : in ELEM);
      procedure POP(S : in out STACK;  E : out ELEM);
      OVERFLOW, UNDERFLOW : exception;
      private
      type STACK is
         record
            SPACE : array (1 .. SIZE) of ELEM;
            INDEX : INTEGER range 0 .. SIZE := 0;
         end record;
end;

package body STACKS is
    procedure PUSH(S : in out STACK;  E : in ELEM) is
    begin
      if  S . INDEX = SIZE then raise OVERFLOW;
      endif;
      S . INDEX := S . INDEX + 1;
      S . SPACE (S . INDEX) := E;
    end PUSH;
    procedure POP(S : in out STACK ;  E : out ELEM) is
    begin
      if S . INDEX = 0 then raise UNDERFLOW;
      endif;
       E := S . SPACE(S . INDEX);
       S . INDEX := S . INDEX - 1;
    end POP;
  end STACKS;
```

Table 8-11:   A Stack Package in Ada

X,Y : STACK;
. . .
begin
  PUSH(X, 175);
  PUSH(Y, 82);
  POP(X, I);
  POP(Y, J);
end;

In Table 8-11 the record which defines the representation of the stack is termed **limited**. In addition to being shielded from the outside, the phrase **limited** means that assignment, equality, and inequality are *not* automatically available for stack objects. In some cases it makes sense to automatically generate algorithms for these operations. But one doesn't usually compare stacks or assign them to variables. In any case, declaring the stack to be **limited private** then requires programmers to provide procedures for implementing these three operations, if they intend to use them. Also note the initialization of INDEX to zero, creating the empty stack. This initialization takes place only once when the package is elaborated and not for each instantiation. See [Schwartz 81] for a discussion of the deficiencies of Ada packages.

8.5. SIMULA67

As SIMULA was the first language to introduce a data encapsulation feature, it is an instructive language to examine. SIMULA is an ALGOL60 derivative which tried to incorporate useful primitives for simulation, [Dahl 68], [Dahl-Nygaard 66], and [Birtwistle 73]. Recall that the scope rules in ALGOL60 are intentionally constructed to guarantee that the most recently activated block is terminated first. This fact allows ALGOL60 to use a stack to implement its dynamic storage allocation. However, from the simulation point of view this fact can be interpreted in a negative manner, as no activating block can ever interact with a block it invokes, as that block is terminated when control is returned. Only the results of the nested block can be seen. In simulation one deals with entities -processes and objects- whose lifetimes are largely independent of each other. For example, one process may start another and then vanish, leaving the other to continue. Thus, ALGOL60 block structure does not offer a sufficiently nice way to model such interactions. In SIMULA67, entities whose lifetimes are independent and who can interact are called *class instances*. A **class** declaration has the format

```
[ prefix class ] class name [ ( parameters ) ];
   parameter specifications
   begin
      declarations
      statements
   end
```

where the **begin - end** is an ALGOL60 kind of block which among other things can contain **class** declarations. The **class** declaration can appear in the program wherever a procedure declaration is permitted.

A simple example of a **class** which creates a structure similar to a Pascal record is

```
class vehicle;
   begin
      integer licenseno;
      real weight, load, maxload;
   end
```

Meaningful operations on the objects may be implemented as procedure attributes within the **class**. Variable attributes may be initialized as parameters or by initial statements such as

```
class vehicle2(weight, maxload);
   real weight, maxload;
begin
   integer licenseno;
   real load;
   Boolean procedure tooheavy;
      tooheavy := weight + load > maxload;
   load := 0;
end
```

To create new objects of a class one writes

   new class name

or for our example

   new vehicle;

There is no dispose function as the designers of SIMULA chose to include a garbage collector as an automatic means for returning storage that is no longer usable.

Pointers, called reference variables, are introduced to name and reference class objects and to construct arbitrary structures. Reference variables are *qualified*, meaning a pointer is declared to point to objects of a certain class only. For example, one might write

ref *(vehicle) rv1, rv2;*

Note that SIMULA pointers may only reference class objects and not objects of arbitrary data types of the language such as integers or reals. SIMULA67 introduces special operators to work with reference variables

:-   denotes reference assignment
= =   denotes reference equality
=/=   denotes reference inequality

Every reference variable is initially assigned the special value **none** which refers to no object. If we write

rv1 :- **new** *vehicle;*
rv2 :- *rv1;*

Then *rv1* and *rv2* both point to the same object, in this case the class *vehicle* with four fields *licenseno, weight, load,* and *maxload.* Now both statements

rv1 = = *rv2;*
rv2 =/= **none**

are true.

Attributes of class objects are accessible from outside through the dot notation, such as

rv1.licenseno := *3987;*
rv2.load := *rv2.load* + *150;*

When class objects contain procedure attributes, these are invoked from outside of the object by means of the same dot notation, e.g.

ref *(vehicle2) pickup;*
pickup :- **new** *vehicle2(3000,   1500);*
    . . .
    if *pickup.tooheavy* **then** . . .

Cleverly, SIMULA has designed this qualification of names so that type checking can be done at compile-time. However, there is no enforced protection of names within a class and the user is free to access any part of the representation. Later versions of SIMULA have introduced scoping rules that ensure greater protection.

```
class bstree (item); integer item;
  begin ref (bstree) left, right;
    procedure insert(x); integer x;
      if x < item
        then begin if left == none then left :- new bstree(x)
                                     else left.insert(x)
             end
        else if right == none then right :- new bstree(x)
                                 else right.insert(x);
    end
    ref (bstree)
    procedure inorder(t); bstree t;
      if not t == none then
                  left.inorder;
                  print(t.data);
                  right.inorder;
    end
  end bstree
```

Table 8-12:   A Binary Search Tree in SIMULA67, see [Dahl 72]

Table 8-12 contains the data type binary search tree expressed as a class. It contains two procedures, one for inserting a new element into the tree and one for performing an inorder traversal of the tree, see [Horowitz 76]. The representation of a node of a *bstree* is composed of an integer *item* and two references to *bstrees* called *left* and *right*. If we write

```
ref (bstree) root;
root :- new bstree(150);
root.insert(100);  root.insert(200);
```

This produces a tree with three nodes whose values are 100, 150 and 200. The variable *root* points to the root of the tree while fields without explicit pointers are set to **none**.

In addition to being ahead of its time in introducing the notion of an abstract data type, SIMULA extended the way a class can be used. This extension greatly facilitates the programmer's ability to combine different abstractions into new ones. The operation for accomplishing this is called *concatenation*, and it is defined between two classes or between a class and a block. The result is either a new class or a new block. Essentially, when two classes X and Y are concatenated, their constituent parts are merged, and the actions they describe are combined. Any formal parameters in X are adjoined with any in Y as are the declarations and program statements of X and Y. If X is defined as

    class X(a,b,c);
        declarations for X
    begin
        statements of X
    end

Then we concatenate X with Y by writing

    X class Y(d,e)
        declarations for Y
    begin
        statements of Y
    end

This is then equivalent to having written

    class Z(a,b,c,d,e)
        declarations for X
        declarations for Y
    begin
        statements of X
        statements of Y
    end

If there is a conflict of local names in X and Y, then the compiler will systematically change those conflicting names in Y. If Y is a block instead of a class, the result is similar except the resulting object is a block and not a class. Concatenation can be viewed as being similar to variant records in Pascal or to the union of types in ALGOL68. But this is only a similarity and is not equivalence. For example *bstree* can be defined without knowledge of the types that will be concatenated to it. Also, one does not define the individual members of the union in isolation from the union type itself. They all have access to and knowledge of the common operations and structure of the union type.

To see an example of the usefulness of concatenation, we return to the binary search tree class. Suppose that the value of a node is more than an integer item but a separate class. For example, it might be a person's bank account number, together with their name, address and balance. We could define the concatenated class

```
bstree class account;
    begin integer accntno,bal;
        integer array nameaddr[1:100];
        procedure checkbal;
            begin
                if bal < 0
                    then print('overdrawn');
            end
    end
```

Now it is possible to operate on *account* as if it was part of *bstree*.

SIMULA has had an important impact on modern programming languages by virtue of its introduction of the class and concatenation features. Though good implementations still exist, especially on DEC machines, it may be the case that newer languages have surpassed it in refining these kinds of features.

8.6. Abstract Data Types

In the previous section we have examined how several languages have attempted to incorporate features which support data type abstraction. In this section I want to step back from a particular programming language and talk about the *abstract specification* of data types. Though the mechanism to be presented here is not presently incorporated into an existing programming language, and is perhaps more useful for the design rather than the implementation of a data type, it may inspire future programming language development.

When one considers the definition of a data type in its most general form, one sees that there are several classes of attributes that may be distinguished. One class consists of those attributes which describe the representation of the objects of the data type in terms of other objects. Another describes the implementation of the operations in terms of other operations. For example a data type *Stack* may be represented in terms of an array, and the operations of *Push* and *Pop* are described in terms of array accessing and storing operations. Another class consists of those attributes which specify the properties of the objects with respect to the operations. For example a stack being a type whose objects obey a last-in-first-out discipline, this property must somehow be capable of being expressed. Moreover, if we desire a data *abstraction* mechanism, then our formalism should permit us to specify properties of the objects *independent* of their implementation. In fact the term *abstract type* is often used in the literature to refer to a class of objects which are defined by a *representation independent* specification. Finally, if we are to have a means for data type abstraction, then it should allow us to distinguish these classes.

All of the examples of data abstraction features which we have seen in the previous sections have incorporated the use of strong typing into their abstract data type mechanism. This serves to support at least two goals. First, it permits authentication by checking that operations to be performed on certain objects are in fact legal. The second goal one might call security or even secrecy. Its purpose is to prevent users of the data type from writing programs which somehow depend upon the type's representation, rather than upon its abstract properties. The ability to define a *Stack* allows a translator to check that the user only accesses the *Stack* objects by using legitimate operations. This prevents him from destroying the integrity of the data structure and from writing programs which depend upon the representation of the type.

The *algebraic specification* of an abstract data type is a formalism which supports the goals I have just outlined in the previous paragraphs. The method was introduced by Guttag and is expounded upon in [Guttag 77a,b 78a,b 80]. An algebraic specification consists of three parts: a syntactic specification, a semantic specification, and a restriction specification. The syntactic specification lists the names of the type, its operations and the type of the arguments of the operations. If an operation is a function, then the type of the range value is given. The semantic specification consists of a set of algebraic equations which describe in a representation independent manner the properties of the operations. The restriction specification states various conditions which must be satisfied either before the operations can be applied or after they are completed.   One of the powerful aspects of algebraic specifications is that the language which is used is very sparse when compared to conventional programming languages. This makes the language easy to read and to learn to use. The language consists of five primitives: functional composition, an equality relation, two distinct constants named *true* and *false* and an unbounded number of free variables. Given these ingredients we can extend the specification language by defining new types. For example we can define a function called *ifthenelse* by stating the following rules (called axioms)

ifthenelse(true, q, r) = q
ifthenelse(false, q, r) = r

This function is so important that we shall assume its use and moreover rename it as the infix operator **if** *p* **then** *q* **else** *r*. We shall also assume that Boolean and integer values and expressions have been defined and may be used to form other specifications of data types. Now that we have defined the language, let's look at a simple example.

structure *Stack;*
newstack() → stack
push(stack, item) → stack
pop(stack) → stack
top(stack) → item
isnew(stack) → Boolean

declare *stk : stack, i : item*

pop(push(stk, i)) = stk
top(push(stk, i)) = i
isnew(newstack) = true
isnew(push(stk, i)) = false

restrictions
pop(newstack) = error
top(newstack) = error

Table 8-13: An Abstract Specification of a Stack.

First we see the five functions of the *Stack* data type declared as to the type of their inputs and outputs. Notice that all of the operations are expressed as functions. Though this is not necessary, we shall continue to do this as it does offer advantages of clarity. Following the syntactic definitions are declarations of two variables, one of type *stack* and one of type *item* which will be the values contained in the stack. Following that there appear the axioms which define the meaning of the operations. The first axiom states that if some stack, *stk*, has had the item *i* placed into it and then that stack is popped, the result is *stk*. Equivalently this says that the last element inserted will be the first removed. The second axiom shows that the function *top* will return the first element as its value. The latter two axioms define *isnew*. This function will only return *true* if its argument is *newstack*,and otherwise it returns *false*. Finally the restrictions list shows us when it is illegal to apply *top* or *pop* and the result is the special undefined element I shall call *error*.

Now that you have a seen a simple example let's get a bit more complicated by defining the data type queue using algebraic axioms.

structure *Queue*
newq () → queue
addq (queue, item) → queue
deleteq (queue) → queue
frontq (queue) → item
isnewq (queue) → Boolean

declare *q, r : queue; i : item;*

isnewq (newq) = true
isnewq (addq (q,i)) = false
deleteq (newq) = newq
deleteq (addq (q, i)) = **if** *isnewq (q)* **then** *newq* **else** *addq (deleteq (q),i)*
frontq (addq (q,i)) = **if** *isnewq (q)* **then** *i* **else** *frontq (q)*

restrictions
frontq (newq) = error

Table 8-14:   An Abstract Specification of a Queue.

Here we see five functions making up the definition of a queue. The syntactic specification should be clear, so let's look more closely at the axioms. The definition of *isnewq* is essentially identical to the definition of *isnew* for stacks. The function *addq (q, i)* represents a queue to which has been adjoined a new value *i*. It's the definitions of *deleteq* and *frontq* which are the most interesting as here we see for the first time the use of the **if-then-else** function on the right-hand side of an axiom. When we apply *deleteq* to *addq (q, i)* then if *q* is the new or empty queue, then it is returned as the result. Otherwise we know that the queue we should return must contain the element *i*. Therefore, we adjoin *i* to the queue which is produced by applying *deleteq* to *q*. This adjoining is done by using *addq*. If this is still not clear, the axiom for *frontq* is a bit easier. In *frontq (addq (q, i))* if *q* is the new queue then the result is *i*. Otherwise we apply *frontq* recursively to *q*. This recursive application must eventually terminate when it reaches the front of the queue. Note that *dele teq (newq)* is taken to be the new queue rather than *error*. This is a matter of choice and is left to the specifier of the data type.

As a final example of this form of specification. I present the data type *binary search tree* in Table 8-15. This is a binary tree which contains data items at each node such that for any node, its item is alphabetically greater than any item in its left subtree and alphabetically less than any item in its right subtree, see [Horowitz 76]. In this example of a binary search tree, let's look at the axioms for *isin*. *make(l, d, r)* represents a binary search tree whose left subtree is named *l*, right subtree is named *r* and whose data item is named *d*. If we are trying to determine if the item *e* is in such a binary search tree then the axiom states the following: if d = e then *true* can be returned. Otherwise *e* may only be in either the left or right subtrees. If $d < e$ then we apply *isin* to the right subtree and otherwise to the left subtree. This axiom is similar to *insert*.

There is not enough space here to review all of the data types which have been specified algebraically. The reader is advised to consult the references [Guttag 77a,b 78a,b 80]. Some concluding comments are in order. First this method of specification may seem unnatural. But to those of you who have had experience with LISP, it should present no problem. For others, the most one can say is that with practice, specification becomes very easy using this formalism. Recall from our previous discussion that one of the chief advantages of this method is that it gives a representation independent definition of the data type. Also, I observe that no specification technique can be substantially "simpler" than the data type it purports to define. Thus, the definition of the *bstree* must contain a set of axioms which are sufficient to completely define the data type. In general the determination of whether one has supplied a sufficiently complete set of axioms is undecidable, see [Guttag 80]. Another interesting question is whether or not a set of axioms are inconsistent. The same reference discusses methods for making such a determination. One advantage of following any completely formal mechanism is that it usually can be automated in some way. A system for accepting a set of axioms and for automatically producing an implementation is discussed in [Guttag 78b].

structure *BinarySearchTree;*
newtree() → bstree
make(bstree, item, bstree) → bstree
isnewtree(bstree) → Boolean
left(bstree) → bstree
data(bstree) → item
right(bstree) → bstree
isin(bstree, item) → Boolean
insert(bstree, item) → bstree

declare *l, r : bstree; d, e : item;*

isnewtree(newtree) = true
isnewtree(make(l, d, r)) = false
left(make(l, d, r)) = l
data(make(l, d, r)) = d
right(make(l, d, r)) = r
isin(newtree, e) = false
isin(make(l, d, r), e) = **if** *d=e* **then** *true*
$\quad\quad$ **else if** *d < e* **then** *isin(r,e)* **else** *isin(e)*
insert(newtree, e) = make(newtree, e, newtree)
insert(make(l, d, r),) = **if** *d=e* **then** *make(l, d, r)*
$\quad\quad$ **else if** *d < e* **then** *make(l,d, insert(r, e))*
$\quad\quad$ **else** *make(insert(l, e), d r)*

restrictions
left(newtree) = error
data(newtree) = error
right(newtree) = error

Table 8-15:   An Abstract Specification of a Binary Search Tree.

Concepts Discussed in This Chapter

Class	Form
Concatenation	Import list
Data Abstraction	Module
Define-list	Package
Export list	Parameter generator
	Use list

Exercises

1. Tables 8-4 and 8-5 containing the MODULA form of a binary search tree did not handle the case of deletions. Rewrite this module so that it handles deletions in a reasonable manner.

2. Consider the following SIMULA program which computes a frequency histogram from [Dahl 72].

   class *histogram(X,n);* **array** *X;* **integer** *n;*
     begin integer *n;* **integer array** *T[0 : n];*
     procedure *tabulate(Y);* **real** *Y;*
       begin integer *i; i := 0;*
       while (**if** *i < n* **then** *Y < X[i+1]* **else false**) **do** *i:=i+1;*
         T[i] := T[i] + 1; n := n + 1;
       end *tabulate;*
       real procedure *frequency(i);* **integer** *(i);*
         frequency := T[i] / n;
     end *of class histogram;*

   Suppose you have three files called *heightfile, weightfile,* and *lengthfile.* Show what to write in SIMULA to create histograms for each of these three files and then to compute the frequency of the *i*th interval.

3. SIMULA allows one to concatenate a class and a block to yield a new block. What happens when the class has parameters?

4. It was pointed out in the text that one very important feature of an abstract data type which is lacking in SIMULA is scope protection of the representation of the

type. Discuss what would have to be done to add such a feature to the SIMULA **class** while preserving the current forms of access.

5. Neither FORTRAN nor PL/1 offer an abstract data type facility. Choose one of these languages and explain how you would program so as to simulate as closely as possible such a facility.

6. Try to use algebraic axioms to specify the data type *graph*. Basic operations would include *addnode, addedge, neighbors, deletenode* and *deleteedge*.

Chapter 9

EXCEPTION HANDLING

"It is human to err; it is devilish to remain willfully in error."

-St. Augustine, Sermons No. 164, sec. 14

9.1. Design Issues

A procedure may terminate in many ways. We may have an intentional termination caused by encountering either a **return** or a **go to** which branches out of the procedure. Or, an error may occur, such as division-by-zero or subscript-out-of-range, which causes a system interrupt which terminates execution. Or, an anticipated but rare condition may arise such as end_of_file. The **return** or **goto** mechanisms of a programming language do not allow us to handle these last two occurrences very well. On the one hand, they provide no real means for the programmer to make use of the interrupt capability of the underlying machine. On the other hand, it encourages awkward and inefficient programming, in the following sense. To handle anticipated errors, one typically adds a parameter to a procedure, which is appropriately set if the *anticipated* error is encountered. Then, a **return** is taken and the error flag must be queried to see if an abnormal event has occurred. An alternate approach once the error is encountered is to jump out of the procedure to an error routine, thereby disrupting the normal flow of control. Neither of these alternatives offers a powerful way to structure exception handling.

In this section we will examine the features of programming languages which have been expressly designed for the purpose of giving the programmer control over exceptional conditions. PL/1 was the first language to offer such a facility. Several more recently developed languages such as MESA, CLU and Ada have provided exception handling capabilities. But before we examine them in detail, let's consider the problem in general terms.

An *exception handling* feature is a linguistic mechanism which allows both communication of certain information among procedures which are at different levels and permits a special kind of transfer of control different from the conventional procedure invocation and termination. The term *exception* is chosen to emphasize that the condition which arises needn't be an error, but merely some event whose possibility requires versatility of action.

In its early form, the exception handling feature was focused on the interrupt capability of the underlying machine. But this is too narow a conceptual view. Exception handling must be viewed not only as emanating from the computer, but from the problem description as well. It is an often occurring process in the real world and therefore its description should be supported by a programming language in some way. The interrupts on a computer may be used to detect specific conditions, such as overflow, but that merely implies that a partial facility exists for raising an exception, but not for handling it. One of the goals of such a facility in a higher level language is to isolate the machine dependencies to as great a degree as is possible while retaining control for the programmer.

To speak about exception handling, we need to introduce some terminology. The procedure A *invokes* another procedure B which causes B to be *activated*. An activation may either terminate normally or *signal* an exception. The signal causes the exception to be *raised*. In considering the design of an exception handling facility there are two fundamental issues: one must determine which procedure activations may handle the signaled exceptions, and if the activation which raised the exception continues to exist after signaling. Other issues can be found listed at the end of this section.

In considering which procedure may handle the raised exception, the obvious candidates are those procedures which are already active. Should one permit the signal to be sent to any one of these procedures or should the signal be restricted in some manner? Let's consider the case of three procedures: P which calls Q which in turn calls R. When an exception is raised in R, can R signal only Q (Figure 9-1(a)) or may it signal either Q or P (Figure 9-1(b))? Suppose we consider the first possibility. While Q is handling the exception raised in R, it may raise its own exception and hence signal P. P may handle it and then resume Q which eventually resumes R. This is seen schematically in Figure 9-1(a). Viewing the second possibility, if R can signal P or Q which in turn can signal either of the other two procedures, we get the situation of Figure 9-1(b). (This figure appears in [Liskov 79b]). One can see from these two figures that the constraint that an exception may only be handled by the caller greatly simplifies the semantics of exception handling. Another simplification of this figure would be to not allow the procedure where the exception arose to be resumed. Viewed another way, in conventional programming the relationship between procedures is as a master-slave, Q calls R which returns control to Q. An exception handling facility which allows R to resume after Q handles the exception changes this relationship and makes them mutually dependent.

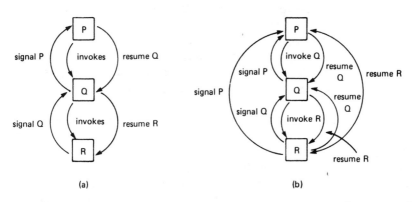

Figure 9-1: Two Possible Semantics for Exception Handling, [Liskov 79b]

On the other hand if the exception handling facility requires termination of R, then Q clearly must be capable of treating both normal and exceptional termination. The specification of all of these cases must appear in the specification of Q. In [Goodenough 75] Goodenough proposes a facility which includes *both* termination and resumption. As is so often the case, this approach of offering combined features only further complicates matters. He introduces three types of signals which allow the raising of exceptions where termination of the raiser is required, resumption is required, or either may occur. Additional semantics must then be defined to support these options. Though this appears to make a flexible exception handling scheme a messy affair, in a more recent work by Shaula Yemini, [Yemini 81], she develops a model of exception handling which is quite powerful yet conceptually simple. The model supports: resumption after handling of an exception, aborting an operation and replacing it by another, retrying a failed operation, and terminating the current activation record and propogating an exception one level up the dynamic chain. Despite all these facilities, the mechanism requires only three new keywords and two new type constructors to implement. Strong typing is maintained and she shows that verification rules can easily be defined. Though this scheme has yet to be included in an actual programming language, it provides encouragement that a clean yet powerful scheme exists.

In the following sections we will look at how exception handling has been included in PL/1, CLU, MESA and Ada. But before we do, let me summarize the important design issues we should be watching for as we learn about how these languages have implemented their exception handling facility. The following issues are apparent.

☐ Is there a way to access the interrupt capabilities of the underlying computer?

☐ Can the system action be overridden?

☐ Are user defined exceptions possible? How are they raised?

☐ What are the scope rules for an enabled exception? Can they be attached to statements, blocks, procedures and/or expressions?

☐ What are the scope and extent rules for an exception handler?

☐ Is a resumption or a termination model followed?

☐ Can multiple exceptions be propagated?

☐ Can signaled exceptions have parameters?

☐ Is a mechanism provided for automatically catching all unexpectedly raised exceptions?

☐ Can exceptions be raised in an exception handler, and what are the consequences?

9.2. PL/1 ON-Conditions

In Table 9-1 we see the names of the exceptional conditions available in PL/1. A condition that is being monitored such that its occurrence will raise an exception is said to be *enabled*. The first five in this list are always enabled unless explicitly disabled. The next five are always disabled unless explicitly enabled. To enable or disable an ON-condition, one may prefix a scope by writing a list of one or more condition names, for example

(NOUNDERFLOW, STRINGSIZE)

disables UNDERFLOW and enables STRINGSIZE in the scope. All other conditions in Table 9-1 are always enabled throughout the execution of the program. This prefix can be attached to a single statement, in which case that statement is the scope of the prefix. If attached to an IF statement, the scope is only the conditional part and does not include the THEN or ELSE portions. But when a prefix is attached to the PROCEDURE or BEGIN statement, then the listed conditions are enabled for all statements contained up to and including the corresponding END. Thus, any nested procedures will inherit the enabled/disabled conditions of the prefix, but called procedures which are outside the PROCEDURE...END or BEGIN...END scope do not inherit the prefix.

1	CONVERSION	12	CONDITION
2	FIXEDOVERFLOW	13	ENDFILE
3	OVERFLOW	14	ENDPAGE
4	UNDERFLOW	15	ERROR
5	ZERODIVIDE	16	FINISH
6	SIZE	17	KEY
7	SUBSCRIPTRANGE	18	NAME
8	STRINGRANGE	19	PENDING
9	CHECK	20	RECORD
10	AREA	21	TRANSMIT
11	ATTENTION	22	UNDEFINEDFILE

Table 9-1:   PL/1 ON-Conditions, [PL/1 76]

When a condition is raised, a standard system action exists, but it can be overridden by the programmer. To do this one writes

ON condition ON-unit

where the condition is selected from Table 9-1 and the ON-unit is a single statement or begin block composed by the programmer. When *condition* is raised, the associated ON-unit is executed as if it were a parameterless procedure that was called when the interrupt occurred. When the ON-unit completes execution, it returns either to the statement in which the ON-condition was raised or to the next statement. This varies depending upon the type of interrupt. But to avoid this return, a branch out of the ON-unit can be used.

It is possible to simulate the occurrence of an ON-condition by means of the SIGNAL statement, "SIGNAL *condition*". An interrupt will occur unless *condition* is disabled. The ON-condition

CONDITION (identifier)

permits the programmer to define an ON-unit and then raise it by using the SIGNAL statement,

SIGNAL CONDITION (identifier)

An especially useful ON-condition is called CHECK. It is raised whenever the value of a listed variable is changed or whenever control is transferred to a listed label or entry point. This allows easy checking of variables during the debugging process. By listing labels and entry points in a CHECK prefix, one can get a flowtrace of the program.

The execution of an ON statement associates this ON-unit with the named condition. Once this association is established, it remains until it is overridden or until the block in which the ON statement is executed is then exited. Thus PL/1 ON-conditions are executable statements and in contrast to other declarations they may not be in effect for some instantiations of the containing block.

In Table 9-2 we see a PL/1 program containing three ON-conditions. The purpose of this program is to read a set of student numbers, called PERSON, and their grade on an exam, called GRADE. The values are stored in a table (SUMMARY) which is printed at the end. If any of the input data are improper, appropriate ON-conditions are raised. The array SUMMARY is set to zero and the loop in lines 22-25 is entered. Values for PERSON and GRADE are input and the appropriate position in SUMMARY is incremented. However, if an index is out of bounds, then SUBSCRIPTRANGE is raised and the corresponding ON-unit in lines 7-13 is executed. If this is the first time this interrupt has occurred, ENDPAGE is signaled and a heading for input errors is printed. In line 24, SUBSCRIPTRANGE will be raised twice. Therefore, line 10 of the ON-unit checks if a new occurrence of an error has been found, and if so, a line of output is printed, I, PERSON and GRADE, followed by the updating of LAST. Finally, when the end_of_file is encountered, the associated ON-unit prints some heading information followed by the correct values in array SUMMARY, and followed by a warning message indicating there were some errors, if in fact there were some.

The PL/1 capabilities for exception handling are extensive and remarkable when viewed in the light as the first programming language to offer such a facility. But there are useful lessons that can be learned by examining some of the problems which exist. One difficulty is that when an exception is raised corresponding to some condition C, the ON-unit which is invoked is determined by the run-time order in which an ON-statement with condition C was encountered. This deviation from PL/1's normal static scoping rule was likely unwise. A new block activation will inherit a potentially complex environment of established ON-units. In fact, some of these may have been set in separately compiled external procedures. This is not consistent with structured programming methodology. Another aspect of this problem is that some activated block may inherit ON-units which are totally inappropriate. An occurrence of such a condition may invoke an unexpected ON-unit instead of producing an error. The only solution is to supply for each block ON-units for all conceivable conditions which might arise, and this is particularly onerous.

Another difficulty with the PL/1 ON-condition is the fact that the ON-unit may act like the use of a nonlocal goto. This causes difficulties for the compiler which cannot simply release all of the local storage for the terminated blocks. Of course, it could be argued that this difficulty has nothing to do with the exception handling mechanism, since one can also leave a block via a nonlocal goto. For an example of this nonlocal branching, consider the ON-unit:

```
ON OVERFLOW GO TO L;
  . . .
BEGIN;
  OPEN FILE(F);
  . . .
  CALL P;
  . . .
  CLOSE FILE(F);
END;
```

If OVERFLOW occurs during the execution of procedure P and the

```
1    TEST: PROCEDURE OPTIONS (MAIN);
2    DECLARE (PERSON,GRADE) FIXED;
3    DECLARE LAST FIXED INIT (0);
4    DECLARE SUMMARY (1:50,0:100) FIXED;
5    ON ENDPAGE(SYSPRINT)   /* prints heading for error listing*/
6 BEGIN PUTPAGE; PUT LIST(' ', 'LIST ERROR DATA'); END;
7    ON SUBSCRIPTRANGE BEGIN
8      IF LAST = 0 THEN SIGNAL ENDPAGE (SYSPRINT);
9 /*THE FIRST TIME AN ERROR IS FOUND
  THE HEADING IS PRINTED*/
10     IF I NOT= LAST THEN    /*CHECK FOR A NEW CASE*/
11       PUT SKIP DATA (I, PERSON, GRADE);
12       LAST = I
13     END;
14     ON ENDFILE(SYSIN) BEGIN;
15       PUT PAGE LIST (' ', ' ', 'OUTPUT FOR CLASS');
16       PUT SKIP LIST (' ', ' ', 'SUMMARY');
17       PUT SKIP(3) LIST(SUMMARY);
18       IF LAST NOT= 0 THEN PUT SKIP(4) LIST
19         ('SOME DATA IS INCOMPLETE, SEE OUTPUT');
20       STOP; END;
21       SUMMARY = 0;
22       A: DO I = 1 BY 1 ;
23         GET LIST (PERSON,GRADE);
24         SUMMARY(PERSON,GRADE)=
             SUMMARY(PERSON, GRADE)+GRADE;
25       END A;
26     END TEST;
```

Table 9-2:   Sample PL/1 Program with ON-Conditions

above ON-unit is invoked, then the BEGIN block is terminated. But this will cause the file F to remain open whereas a clean-up facility would allow the programmer to catch this and close the file. The Multics system [Organick 72] includes such a facility. Along this same line of reasoning, a call such as P(A | B) (where A | B stands for concatenation of two string-valued variables) would cause extra local storage to be allocated to the activation record for P to hold the concatenated string. If P is now terminated as a result of an ON-unit becoming effective, this storage should be released.

PL/1 has treated computational conditions in a somewhat inconsistent manner. Conditions such as OVERFLOW and SUBSCRIPTRANGE do not permit a return from an ON-unit, whereas others such as UNDERFLOW and STRINGSIZE do. A more dangerous situation arises in connection with the possibility of disabling conditions. Programmers may forget that disabling a condition only implies that it will not check for it. If the disabled condition arises, it may be an error and the rest of the program's actions are undefined. More examples of problems with PL/1 ON-conditions can be found in [MacLaren 77].

9.3. Exception Handling in CLU

Now we consider the mechanism as it is introduced in CLU. The first major distinction between CLU and PL/1 is that when an exception is raised in some procedure B, its signal may *only* be sent to the procedure which invoked B. The CLU designers argue persuasively, [Liskov 79b] that this constraining of the possibilities supports the goals of good program structuring with only a minor loss in expressive power. The second difference of CLU from PL/1 is that the signaling procedure is terminated rather than resumed. The resulting simplicity in semantics does,however, create an added burden on the procedure for handling varied returns.

A CLU procedure is allowed to terminate by executing either a **return** or a **signal** statement. Each signal statement may be associated with a different exception. These are specified in the procedure heading, e.g.

    for_fun = **proc**(a : int, b:real) **returns** (int)
        signals (zero(int), overflow, bad_format(string))

declares the procedure *for_fun* with two parameters. *for_fun* is a function which returns an integer,or else it may terminate by signaling one of the three listed exceptions. Note how exceptions can have parameters and the types of the parameters are listed. This allows the

CLU compiler to check consistency between the exception names in the procedure body and the names in the procedure heading. Also it may check the type of the arguments of the exceptions. Even more, it permits the compiler to check that any exceptions which occur in a called procedure are handled in the calling procedure.

As for the code which treats a raised exception, this is called a *handler* and in CLU, handlers may be attached to any statement. They may not be attached to expressions, thereby eliminating the need to determine what value the handler should return. The form of a handler is

statement **except** *handler list* **end**

The statement may raise one or many or all of the exceptions in CLU. The effect of the handler list is to override the system responses to those exceptions and instead to provide a programmer defined action. Each item in the handler list names one or more exceptions followed by a handler body which describes the action to be taken. When it is desired to communicate some objects along with the signaled exception, these objects are listed as actual parameters in a procedure heading, e.g.

when *overflow, bad_format (i:int, s:string):body*

The conditions *overflow* or *bad_format* are associated with this handler *body*. Also two objects, *i* of type integer and *s* of type string are communicated. The handler body may contain any legal CLU statements and if either a **return** or **signal** is executed, the procedure enclosing the handler body is terminated. Otherwise, after the body is executed the next statement in the enclosed procedure is executed.

It may occur that an exception is raised for which a handler body is not supplied. In such a case CLU provides a special exception called **failure** which returns a string as its result. Every procedure may signal **failure**, and failure needn't be listed in the procedure heading. For example

nonzero = **proc** *(x : int)* **returns** *(int)*
            return *(sign(x))*
          end nonzero

Procedure *nonzero* returns the sign of *x* except when *x* is zero. Then the exception zero will be raised and the string "unhandled exception: zero" will be passed with the failure exception and *nonzero* will be terminated.

In Table 9-3 we see two CLU procedures, *sum_stream* and *get_number* as described by Liskov and Snyder in [Liskov 79]. The main procedure *sum_stream* reads a sequence of signed decimal integers from a character stream and returns their sum. The input is composed of fields which are separated either by blanks or a new line. Each field must contain at least one digit with a possible minus sign preceding. Looking at *sum_stream* we see that it may signal three exceptions: *overflow* if *sum* exceeds the range of integers, *unrepresentable_integer* if a field contains an integer which is too large, and *bad_format* if the above definition of field is violated in any way.

Procedure *sum_stream* uses *get_number* to return the next integer. It does this by first calling *get_field* which returns the next sequence of characters representing a field. Then it passes the field to procedure *s2i* which converts it from a string to an integer. In the meantime, *get_number* will signal end_of_file if no more fields exist, in which case *sum_stream* will return the result, *sum*. If either an unrepresentable integer or bad format is encountered by *get_number*, it will signal these to *sum_stream* and pass it the value of *field*. Procedure *sum_stream* defines *f : string* as the formal parameter corresponding to the field. The **resignal** statement propogates an exception up one level and is legal if both the caller and the called program have an exception of the same name and number and types of results.

Note how in *get_number* the exceptions are attached to the assignment and **return** statements. *get_number* handles the exceptions raised by either *s2i* or *get_field*. Note that if either of these routines signals *bad_format* or *invalid_character*, then *get_number* does not bother to make use of the arguments of the raised exceptions. This is indicated in Table 9-3 by writing (*) after the exception name. This program and a more complete discussion of exception handling in CLU can be found in [Liskov 79a, 79b].

9.4. Exception Handling in MESA

The exception handling facility in MESA is part of their more general programming facility, and a complete description can be found in [Mitchell 79]. MESA introduces some new terminology: *signals* and *catches.* Exceptions are caught by "catch-phrases," which contain a list of exceptional conditions or the reserved word ANY. The latter term covers any exception which might arise and is not specifically listed. A catch phrase may appear in several places: at the end of a list of parameters, following the symbol !, or in an ENABLE clause appended to the beginning of a block, loop, or following the reserved word ENABLE.

```
sum_stream = proc (s: stream) returns (int)
          signals (overflow, unrepresentable_integer (string)
                   bad_format (string))
     sum : int := 0
     while true do
          sum := sum + get_number (s)
                    resignal unrepresentable_integer,
                             bad_format, overflow;
     end
     except
          when end_of_file : return (sum)
     end
  end sum_stream
  get_number = proc (s:stream) returns (int)
  signals (end_of_file, unrepresentable_integer (string), bad_format (string))
     field:string := get_field (s)
                    resignal end_of_file;
     return (s2i (field))
       except
          when unrepresentable_integer (field)
          when bad_format, invalid_character (*):
          signal bad_format (field)
       end
  end get_number
```

Table 9-3: CLU Program Using Exceptions

As in PL/1, the association of exceptions with handlers is dynamic. Thus, once an exception is raised, potentially all activation records are searched for the first occurrence of a handler which names the raised exception. An exception may be raised by executing either SIGNAL, ERROR or RETURN WITH ERROR. Each of these commands differs somewhat in the action which is taken.

If an exception is declared as a SIGNAL, then it can be raised by any one of the three commands above. But, if an exception is declared as an ERROR, then it must be generated by one of the latter two commands. A handler may not resume an exception which is generated by an ERROR command. However, it is not known at compile-time whether a handler will catch a SIGNAL or an ERROR command, so this must be checked at run-time. A distinction between ERROR and RETURN WITH ERROR is that whereas a handler for ERROR searches the dynamic activation records for the first occurrence, the latter first causes the procedure which generates the exception to be terminated.

So much of the MESA exception handling facility requires run-time monitoring that an elaborate run-time monitor called the *signaller* is used. It is the *signaller's* responsibility to pass exception signals and their arguments from one enabled catch-phrase to another. If a signal is produced by the command **Errorcall**, and the catch-phrase requests a RESUME, then the *signaller* will automatically generate the system exception **Resumeerror**. The *signaller* essentially responds in one of three possible ways. It may **Reject** if the raised exception was not handled, or it may raise the **Unwind** exception, or resume the *signaller*. The **Unwind** is an especially interesting feature. It is used to allow a programmer to execute some code after an exception has been raised, but before any GOTO, EXIT, LOOP, RETRY, or CONTINUE is executed in a catch-phrase. The action it takes is to return to *Signaller* with result **Unwind**. This will cause the *Signaller* to pass the signal **Unwind** to each activation record on the dynamic chain. If any handlers for **Unwind** are present, then these may perform cleanup operations. Then the *Signaller* deallocates the activation record and continues until it arrives at the activation record for the catch-phrase which originally raised **Unwind**. *Signaller* then returns control to this phrase. If a catch-phrase is being processed because of **Unwind**, and it implicitly raises **Unwind** itself, then the new raising overrides the first. This will cause the *Signaller* to stop processing the original **Unwind**.

There are several commands which permit a catch-phrase to alter the flow of control after the handler is done. CONTINUE causes the statement immediately following the one to which the catch-phrase is attached to be resumed. RETRY causes the statement to which the catch-phrase is attached to be retried. RESUME returns control to the procedure which generated the signal. This last command may cause an activation record to be resumed which is far from the processing catch-phrase. In [Mitchell 79] an example is shown where this can lead to trouble, and no general solution is offered.

As MESA incorporated such a general exception handling facility, it was a useful experiment in language design. But some critical comments are in order. One issue is that signals can be generated throughout the dynamic chain of active procedures. This implies that the programmer must anticipate unexpected signals and provide for them. Programmers can code a "catch-all" handler or decide that they cannot handle unexpected exceptions and allow them to propagate to the caller. This violates the principle of modularity. Related to this criticism is the fact that catch-phrases may also generate exceptions, thus further compounding the range of possibilities which the programmer must consider. Another major concern is the complexity which arises with such a general facility. For example, there are ten reserved words required to support the exception handling mechanism, many of which have similar but not identical semantics. There are three commands for raising exceptions, three for specifying flow of control after the catch-phrase is completed, two for attaching catch-phrases to program units and two distinct classes of exceptions. Finally the run-time support mechanism by *Signaller* is expensive.

9.5. Exception Handling in Ada

The Steelman requirement [Steelman 79], is the document which defines the specifications to be met by the new U.S. Department of Defense programming language, Ada. In those requirements an exception handling facility is explicitly mentioned. Moreover, it was stated there that a raised exception should cause a transfer of control to a handler without resuming the elaboration of the declaration or the execution of the statement where the exception occurred. Thus, one of the major design issues for exception handling was built into the requirements and Ada has followed these guidelines.

Predefined exceptions are provided in the predefined environment and hence needn't be declared by the programmer. See Table 9-4 for a list of these exceptions.

CONSTRAINT_ERROR	Raised when a range, index or discriminant constraint is violated; or raised when access to **null** value is made
NUMERIC_ERROR	Raised when a result lies out of range
SELECT_ERROR	Raised when all alternatives of a select that has no else part are closed
STORAGE_ERROR	Raised when the storage allocator cannot function
TASKING_ERROR	Raised during intertask communication

Table 9-4:   Ada Predefined Exceptions, [Ada 80]

An exception declaration defines one or more exception names.

These names may be used in a **raise** statement or in an exception handler which is contained in the scope of the declaration. So, in addition to the predefined exceptions one may write

BAD_FORMAT, SINGULAR : **exception**

to declare two user-defined exceptions. The handler associated with an exception has the form

exception-handler ::= **when** exception-choice { | exception-choice} =>
                                              sequence-of-statements

where

        exception-choice ::= exception-name | **others**

A handler processes just those exceptions listed, unless the name **others** is used, which means that this handler will also take care of those exceptions not listed in other alternatives or not visible within the scope of the handler's scope unit.

An exception may be raised either because a given statement has resulted in the exception or because a **raise** statement naming the exception has been executed. When an exception is raised, the current subprogram either does or does not have a handler for it. In the former case, control is given to the handler, and the termination of the handler terminates the subprogram. In the latter case, the current subprogram, say R, is terminated and the exception is raised in the procedure Q, which called R, at the point of Q's invocation. If no handler exists, Q is terminated and the procedure which called Q has the exception raised. This is called *propagation* of the raised exception.

An exception may occur either during the execution of a statement or during the elaboration of a declaration. The existence of an exception may terminate either a block, a subprogram, a task body or the elaboration of a package body. Exception handlers may be placed at the end of any sequence of statements enclosed by **begin-end**. For example:

```
begin
  --this is a sequence of statments
exception
  when NUMERIC_ERROR => --do something
  when BAD_FORMAT =>    --do something else
  when others  =>     --this code must handle all other cases
end;
```

To raise an exception one writes "**raise** EXCEPTION_NAME;" or simply "**raise**", which will cause the same exception, which is currently being processed, to be raised again, i.e., in the calling subprogram.

In Ada, when an exception is raised the current block is searched for a handler. If one exists, then control is given to it and when it completes, then the block is terminated. If not, then execution of the block is terminated and the blocks on the dynamic chain are examined, in most recent invocation order, looking for a handler. Consider this example from Ada in Table 9-5.

```
1     procedure P is
2        BAD_FORMAT : exception;
3        procedure Q is
4           begin
5              . . .
6              if S / = ' ' then raise BAD_FORMAT; end if;
7              . . .
8           end Q;
9        procedure R is
10          begin
11             Q;
12          exception when BAD_FORMAT = > -- handler body 1
13          end R;
14       begin
15          R;
16          Q;
17       exception when BAD_FORMAT = > -- handler body 2
18    end P;
```

Table 9-5:   Ada Program Fragment

In this example we see a main procedure P with two nested procedures Q and R. At lines 15-16, R and then Q are invoked and on line 11, Q is invoked by R. If Q is invoked by R and if the exception BAD_FORMAT is raised, then Q is terminated and handler body 1 on line 12 is entered. Instead if Q is invoked by P at line 16 and BAD_FORMAT is raised, then handler body 2 will receive control.

Note that since the handlers apply only to the **begin-end** part of a block, an exception in the declarative part of a block subprogram or package will always be propagated. Also note that an exception may be propagated beyond its scope, in which case it may only be handled by an **others** clause. For example:

```
procedure A is

    procedure B is
        FLOPPED : exception;
    begin
        -- sequence of statements
    exception
        when FLOPPED => raise
    end;

begin
    B;
exception
    when others =>   --handle FLOPPED if possible else raise
                  raise;
end;
```

Here we see two procedures A and B. B declares an exception FLOPPED and provides a handler for it. However, all the handler does is to raise FLOPPED out of its scope to procedure A. In A the raised exception will be handled by the **others** clause.

In contrast to CLU, in Ada one can suppress the checking for the predefined exceptions, e.g., by writing

pragma SUPPRESS(OVERFLOW_CHECK).

This tells the compiler that it needn't check for arithmetic overflow in the scope of the pragma. Of course, OVERFLOW may arise somewhere else and be propagated into this scope, or it may appear in a **raise** statement. If OVERFLOW occurs in an expression where **pragma** SUPPRESS(OVERFLOW) has been used, the results are unpredictable.

As the occurrence of an exception causes the termination of all of the procedures in the dynamic chain of calls until a handler for the exception is found, Ada offers a way for these procedures to perform a last action. If each procedure contains a handler using the word

when others => statements; **raise**;

then the statements will be executed and then the original exception will be re-raised to the next procedure of the chain.

We observe that as declarations may include the evaluation of expressions, exceptions may be raised at that time. If this occurs, then the procedure's handler will be unable to assume the existence of other declared items as execution of the declarations was aborted. To avoid this problem, Ada advises that the expressions be replaced by function calls which themselves handle the raising of any possible exceptions. However, if an exception does occur during the declaration elaboration, then an exception handler from an outer block handles it.

In conclusion, the exception handling facility may be used in many ways: for handling anticipated errors, for terminating unusual conditions, for re-trying various operations, and for perfoming any final clean-up actions. In Table 9-6 we see several small examples of each of these ways of using exceptions. In procedure DOSOMETHING, the exception HANDLE_ERROR is defined and then attached to a handler. This conventional use of exceptions is shown again to underline their fundamental use in this way. In procedure DIVIDE_CHECK, we see an example of how an exception can abort the computation of a value, which would produce an undefined result and instead return some specific value, in this case a zero. In procedure COPYOVER two files are opened and are successively read and written. When an end_of_file is encountered, the exception is raised and a final EOF character is appended to the output and the two files are closed. This is an example of using exception handling for executing a termination condition.

In retrospect, the Ada facility for exception handling does have some flaws. One deficiency is the fact that when an exception is raised, it cannot pass parameters back to its handler. This forces the programmer to communicate via global variables, which is not in the spirit of modular programming. Another problem is the fact that exceptions are propogated up the dynamic chain, searching for a handler. If the programmer has not supplied one, then the exception will be raised in modules which do not expect its occurrence, leading to difficult debugging situations. Finally, I observe that despite the credo of strong typing which is followed so closely in Ada, for exceptions the compiler is unable to lend any assistance. Further complications arise with the interaction of concurrent processes and exceptions.

```
procedure DOSOMETHING is
  HANDLE_ERROR : exception;
begin
  -- perform some set of actions
exception
  when HANDLE_ERROR => --error handling code
end;
end DOSOMETHING;

  function SECURE_DIVIDE(X, Y : REAL) return REAL is
    begin
      return X/Y;
    exception
      when NUMERIC_ERROR => return 0;
  end SECURE_DIVIDE;

  procedure COPYOVER is
  begin
    OPEN(INFILE);
    OPEN(OUTFILE);
  loop
      GET(INFILE, CHARACTER);
      PUT(OUTFILE, CHARACTER);
    end loop;
  exception
    when END_OF_FILE =>
            PUT(OUTFILE, EOF);
            CLOSE(OUTFILE);
            CLOSE(INFILE);
  end COPYOVER;
```

Table 9-6: Examples of the Use of Exceptions in Ada

Concepts Discussed in This Chapter

Catch phrases
CHECK exception
Escape exceptions
Exception handling
Failure signals
Handler
ON-condition
ON-unit

Others statement
PL/1 Prefixes
Propogation of exceptions
Raise statement
Resumption model
Signaling
SUPPRESS in Ada
Termination model

Exercises

1. Look up the PL/1 abbreviations for its ON-conditions.
2. Write a sentence which explains the meaning of each PL/1 ON-condition.
3. Write a sentence which explains the meaning of each Ada exception.
4. Determine the scope of a prefix in PL/1 when it is attached to a DO statement.
5. Determine the action taken in an ON statement when the word SNAP is encountered.
6. ALGOL68 does not have a general exception handling facility. but it does provide exceptions and default handlers for its **file** type. Look up the ALGOL68 report and discuss this facility. Be critical, especially regarding the scope of these handlers.
7. Consider the following way of producing recursion in PL/1 due to MacLaren. First, explain exactly how this program works. How will it terminate? Could you add some lines of code which would cause it to terminate without an error message?

```
FACTORIAL: PROCEDURE;
DECLARE (N, F) FIXED FIN (31) INIT (1);
ON FINISH BEGIN;
    PUT LIST (N, "FACTORIAL =", F);
    PUT SKIP
    N = N + 1;
    F = N * F;
    STOP;
    END;
STOP;
END FACTORIAL;
```

8. A common error in programs is an infinite loop. How would you suggest implementing an ON INFINITELOOP facility in PL/1, which transfers control to the ON-unit whenever the program goes into this condition?

9. Write an Ada procedure which attempts to read a record from a tape more than once if the exception TAPE_ERROR is encountered.

Chapter 10

CONCURRENCY

"Now is not this ridiculous - and is not this preposterous?

A thorough-paced absurdity - explain it if you can."

-Patience by Gilbert and Sullivan

10.1. Basic Concepts

Up until now, underlying everything we have said is the basic assumption that when we run a program, only one statement is executed at any given time. This presents no problem if the model of the computer which we intend to use is a uniprocessor of the von Neumann variety. But there are now many reasons for considering this view of computing to be out of date. Similarly, when we discussed procedures and coroutines, in both cases only one procedure (or coroutine) could be active at a given time. The language concept of the procedure (and the coroutine) is simply the next higher level of abstraction one gets by starting with a machine which permits only sequential execution. Today there are reasons to believe that multiprocessor computers will soon be readily available. To exploit their power, we must design new programming languages with features that permit the best use of the multiprocessor's concurrent computation facilities.

Actually many of today's computers are capable of carrying out different tasks at the same time. This is usually referred to as *asynchronous* operation. For example, input and output can proceed at the same time the central processing unit is executing instructions. This was the earliest form of concurrency. A more recent development is the capability of some operating systems to have several jobs all simultaneously in a state of partial completion. One job may be performing an input operation, another performing an output operation, a third using the central processing unit, while the others are waiting. Such a capability is referred to as *multiprogramming* and its purpose is to make maximum use of the computer's asynchronous capabilities. Suppose from now on we refer to the sequence of operations performed during the execution of a sequential program as a *process*. Then, on a multiprogramming computer the user jobs, the input-output programs which control the channels, and the routines for processing interrupts are all viewed as processes. If we are going to write operating systems in a high level language, then some facilities for describing concurrent execution of processes is essential.

Our future multiprocessors may come in many different forms, the processors may share a common memory and/or have some private memory, but the goal is the same. It is to offer a high degree of concurrency either for solving many different problems or for working on different parts of the same problem. The term given to such a computer architecture is *distributed computer system*. But in order to exploit the potential concurrency, one must be given a way of writing programs which: (i) allow one to naturally express the inherent concurrency of the problem, and (ii) can be translated into an efficient, concurrent machine language program. The latest progress and potential of computer hardware makes the development of higher level languages which contain features for expressing concurrency imperative.

But if the efficient use of a computer's resources was the only reason for developing concurrent features in programming languages, this might not be enough. It happens that there are several very important problem domains for which concurrency is natural and a notation for describing and designing such systems is needed. I will briefly mention three of them.

A *discrete system simulation* is one which tries to model iterations between elements of a complex network where many of the interactions occur in parallel. Examples include a manufacturing assembly line or freeway traffic flow or information flow in an organization. The purpose of a computer model is to run the simulation and to test out various hypotheses. Conventional programming languages can and have been augmented so that simulations can be more easily described; see [GPSS or SIMSCRIPT]. But a language which includes concurrency as a basic feature should allow discrete system simulations to be designed and programmed far better. For example each of the active elements of a simulation could be represented as a process. The process would be able to imitate the features of the element it represents and also would be able to interact concurrently with the other processes, as is the case in the real world.

Process control is the term applied to the automation of manufacturing processes. For example, consider an oil refinery which takes raw oil and turns it into several derivatives including gasoline. The computer program which controls this process is monitoring hundreds of sensors which report statistics on the temperature, pressure, and rate of flow in the system. Responding to those signals, the computer will send more signals to adjust speeds of machinery, valves of pipes, alarms, etc. The essential characteristic of process control programs is that everything is happening concurrently, in *real-time*, and responses are typically required immediately.

The third example, which we mentioned before, is the problem of designing an operating system. As the card reader, card punch, tapes, disks, drums, terminals, and central processing unit can all be working asynchronously, an operating system must be able to cope with requests for these resources. Some of these processes work much faster than others and the allocation of resources to maximize throughput and/or to minimize response time is a major issue. A higher level programming language with facilities for process synchronization offers a much more useful tool for building operating systems than assembly language.

My final argument for concurrency in programming languages is that it represents a new way of thinking about computing. By encouraging us to think in that way, we may discover new and better solutions to old problems and ways of solving problems which could not be solved nicely before. Thus, for all of these reasons, in this chapter we study the issue of embedding concurrency features in programming languages.

When we have two processes which pass data to one another, we call this *process communication*. We use the term *synchronization* to refer to the mechanism which controls the order in which processes execute. When the outcome of a computation depends upon the speed at which the processes are executed, then we say there is a *race condition* and that these parts of the computation are *time critical*.

One of the early languages which introduced features for concurrency was PL/1. Program parts which can be executed in parallel in PL/1 are called tasks and the form of concurrency offered is called *multitasking*. To start up a task, one proceeds in a manner similar to activating a procedure. One might write

CALL Q(parameters) TASK(X);

This statement denotes Q as a task and at run-time Q will be started. At the same time the calling procedure P will continue to execute. P and Q are not synchronized and either may complete first. Thus, PL/1 provides a mechanism so Q can inform P that it has completed. An *event variable* is a variable which is shared among two or more tasks and which has two states. These states are called *in-execution* and *terminated* but may just as well be thought of as true and false. In the task initiation above, X is an event variable associated with the activation of Q. X may be queried in P as to its value or P may execute the statement WAIT(X) which causes P to delay further execution until X is set to *terminated*. When Q is activated, it may inherit all of the variables of P if it is in P's scope. Thus, P and Q may share common data and there is no way of guaranteeing that an update operation of a common variable will complete before an access by the other procedure is made.

PL/1 also permits concurrency at the statement level. After declaring an event variable, e.g.,

DECLARE E EVENT;

one may attach the phrase EVENT(E) to an input or output statement. This indicates that the program may proceed as the statement is being executed. The program will continue to execute unless it encounters a WAIT(E) statement. Also, a mechanism exists for assigning a priority to a task, so that if several jobs are waiting to be executed, the one with highest priority is chosen.

When two processes share common data, they often must be synchronized so that one is not allowed to tamper with the data while another is using it. This is called *mutual exclusion*. Operations such as *wait* can be used to achieve mutual exclusion as it operates on a event variable which is common to the procedures. Such instructions are often implemented using a "testandset" instruction at the machine level which allows the testing and assigning of a value to be done indivisibly, i.e., without interrupt. The use of event variables aids in the design of concurrent processes. It reduces the analysis of a process to two cases, either it is waiting for an event to occur or for an event which has already occurred. The problem with event variables is that they require the programmer to consider the relative speeds of the processes. This is unfortunate as one goal of a programming language facility for concurrency should be that it reduces the analysis of a concurrent system to the analyses of a set of sequential processes. This is the main reason they have been rejected for inclusion into newer languages.

Before we look more closely at some modern techniques for describing concurrency, it will be useful to summarize what aspects of a concurrency facility are needed. The language needs

(i) a way of delineating sections of code which can be executed in parallel. We will see that these will be called processes or tasks or collateral clauses, etc.

(ii) a way of saying that a process can now be executed.

(iii) a way to guarantee mutual exclusion of shared data. There are at least two schools of thought here. One provides a linguistic mechanism which protects the shared data. The chief examples are semaphores (Section 10.2) and monitors (Section 10.3). The other requires all shared data to be communicated via messages between processes (Sections 10.4 and 10.5). Thus, communication is called message passing, though syntactically it may be viewed as parameter passing (see [Ada 80]).

(iv) a means must be provided to synchronize concurrent programs. Examples include *wait-signal* operations of monitors or the rendezvous in Ada.

(v) a way of assigning priorities to processes.

(vi) a mechanism for delaying a process for a fixed amount of time.

In the next few sections, we will take a look at how concurrency has been provided for in several languages. We will especially try to assess these languages with respect to these six issues.

10.2. Semaphores

The sequence of statements that refer to a variable which is shared by another process is called a *critical region*. If a process will always complete its critical region in a finite amount of time, it is said to *terminate*. If a process will always enter a critical region within a finite time, then we say that *fair scheduling* has been followed. We now consider a synchronizing method which provides for mutual exclusion in and completion of critical regions, and fair scheduling among processes. This mechanism is called a semaphore and it was invented by Edsger Dijkstra in 1965, [Dijkstra 68b]. First we shall discuss the semaphore in general terms and then discuss its implementation in ALGOL68.

A *semaphore* is a variable, say s, which is shared by two or more processes and allows two operations, *wait(s)* and *signal(s)*, with s being a binary-valued variable. Also associated with the semaphore is a list of processes which are waiting to be executed. The precise way in which this list is to be implemented is not specified, but it must guarantee fair scheduling. A queue is the most often used implementation for this list, and we will continue to assume its use here. Thus, a process is either executing, or waiting to be executed or blocked from executing and waiting on the queue associated with the semaphore.

If a process P uses a semaphore s, then the definitions of *wait* and *signal* are:

wait(s) : **if** $s = 1$ **then** $s := 0$
                      else place process P into the queue
signal(s) : **if** queue $\neq$ empty **then** remove a process from the
                       queue and schedule it for execution
                      else $s := 1$

Notice that as *wait* and *signal* both share the variable s, they must not be allowed to access and write the variable simultaneously. This can be implemented by using a more primitive form of mutual exclusion, the testandset instruction mentioned before. Thus we see that the ability to synchronize processes is defined by using more than one level of abstraction.

How is mutual exclusion implemented using a binary semaphore? Consider the case of two processes in Table 10-1, one which reads from, and another which writes to a common database.

procedure READER	**procedure** WRITER
begin	**begin**
. . .	. . .
wait (*mutex*)	*wait* (*mutex*)
read the database	write the database
signal (*mutex*)	*signal* (*mutex*)
. . .	. . .
end	**end**

Table 10-1:   Mutual Exclusion Using a Binary Semaphore

In Table 10-1 whenever READER or WRITER is executing its critical region, then the semaphore *mutex* = 0 and the other process is placed into the queue. *Mutex* is initialized to one. If there are n processes then each critical region can be surrounded by *wait-signal* operations using the same semaphore variable.

Now that a method for mutual exclusion has been found, the next step is to provide for two processes to signal each other. One famous example which illustrates the need for signal communication is the producer-consumer problem which we saw in Section 7.8, and solved by using coroutines. One process is producing records one at a time, while the other is consuming them one at a time. Only a one record buffer is available to hold a record which has just been produced but not yet consumed. As long as one can synchronize the producer and consumer so that the consumer only acts once a record is produced and the producer only acts when the buffer is empty, then mutual exclusion is guaranteed. Table 10-2 shows how this can be done and should be self-explanatory.

$ok := 0 ; fin := 1$
procedure PRODUCER
    while more input records **do**
        wait (*fin*)
        write a record to the buffer
        signal (*ok*)
    end
procedure CONSUMER
    loop
        wait (*ok*)
        read a record from buffer to output
        signal (*fin*)
        write the output
    repeat
end

Table 10-2: Producer-Consumer Problem Solved Using Semaphores

An alternate form of the producer-consumer problem is to assume that the buffer is large enough to hold several records. Now the producer and consumer must be synchronized so that the producer doesn't try to enter a new record into a full buffer and the consumer doesn't try to remove a record from an empty buffer. For this we generalize the semaphore from being binary-valued to what's called a counting semaphore. This is done in ALGOL68 which has a built-in mode called **sema**, modeled after the semaphore. A semaphore variable is declared, e.g. **sema** *mutex*,, and there are two operations which can then be applied.

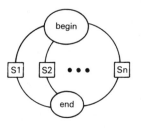

Figure 10-1:   A Collateral Statement in ALGOL68

down *mutex* : **if** *mutex* is zero **then** execution is blocked
                             else *mutex* is decreased by one

up *mutex*   : *mutex* is increased by one and all programs
                             previously halted by *mutex* are resumed.

A *collateral statement* in ALGOL68 is a list of two or more statements separated by commas and enclosed by either parentheses or **begin** and **end**.   Each program unit separated by a comma may be executed in parallel with the other units in a collateral statement.   The statement is not completed until all statements in the clause are done.   A *parallel clause* is similar to a collateral statement in ALGOL68, but it is used when the constituents of the phrase need to be synchronized.   A parallel clause is denoted by writing the keyword **par** immediately before the delimiters.   An example of semaphores in ALGOL68 is shown in Table 10-3.

This program declares a buffer of size 50 and two semaphores *numberin* and *openspots*.   Integers *i* and *j* are initialized to zero.   The parallel clause contains two phrases, one which reads into the buffer and the other which writes out of the buffer.   If there is space in the buffer, *openspots* is positive and a character is read into the correct position.   Then *numberin* is increased by one.   Similarly, if *numberin* is positive, an element in the buffer is printed and *openspots* is increased by one.

For more examples of the use of semaphores the reader should consult [Calingaert 81].   As Brinch-Hansen in [Brinch-Hansen 73] has pointed out, "The semaphore is an elegant synchronizing tool for an ideal programmer who never makes mistakes.   But unfortunately the consequences of using semaphores incorrectly can be quite serious."

```
begin
    [50] int buffer;
    int i := 0, j := 0;
    sema numberin := level 0, openspots := level 50;
    par (do down openspots;
            i := i mod 50 + 1;
            read(buffer[i]);
            up numberin;
        od,
        do down numberin;
            j := j mod 50 + 1;
            print (buffer [j]);
            up openspots
        od)
end
```

Table 10-3:   Producer-Consumer Problem Solved in ALGOL68

For example, if a programmer reverses the commands *wait* and *signal*, then more than one process may be in its critical region at the same time.   But as it is a time-dependent error, the error may not arise for a long while.   If *signal* is mistakenly replaced by *wait*, then deadlock will occur.   Another problem is that the compiler cannot know if the semaphore is incorrectly initialized, or if a shared variable is accessible outside of the critical region.   These weaknesses led   to the development of a more reliable mechanism, the monitor.

10.3. Monitors

Another programming language feature for handling synchronization is called the monitor which was introduced by Brinch-Hansen in [Brinch-Hansen 73] and Hoare in [Hoare 74].   In contrast to the semaphore, in which each process keeps the text of its critical region, a monitor collects together all the code for accessing shared data into one unit.   Its general form is similar to the SIMULA **class,**

> **monitor** name
>   **begin** declarations of data local to this monitor
>   declarations of procedures
>   initializations of local data
> **end** name

The procedures of a monitor can be used by all processes. In order to call a procedure P within a monitor, one would say

name.P (actual parameters)

The monitor guarantees that only one process may be executing a procedure in the monitor at a particular time and this procedure must complete before another process is allowed to enter the monitor. As with the modules for abstract data types, (see Chapter 8), a monitor's procedure may only access local data and actual parameters. Similarly, variables local to a monitor may not be accessed outside the monitor. A monitor may designate some procedures as local to the monitor and are thus not available outside.

When a process is granted access to a monitor, it may request access to a resource which is currently busy. A wait instruction is provided which will cause the requesting program to be delayed. To indicate that a resource is no longer needed, a signal instruction is provided. This causes a waiting process to be awakened and resumed. When a process is executing in a monitor, we may have none, one or more processes on a queue waiting for access to the monitor. At the same time we may have zero, one or more processes waiting for a condition to be signalled, using the signal operation. Note that if a process signals a condition for which no processes are waiting, then nothing happens.

The monitor has been regarded as such a useful device for describing concurrency that it has been included in at least four higher level programming languages: Concurrent-Pascal developed by Brinch-Hansen [Brinch-Hansen 75], MODULA developed by Wirth [Wirth 77a-d], Mesa developed at Xerox [Mitchell 79], and CSP/K, a derivative of PL/1, developed by Holt, et al. [Holt 78].

CSP/K:

SP/K is actually a series of languages which are increasingly larger subsets of PL/1. It has been successfully used in the teaching of PL/1. CSP/K is an extension to SP/K which permits concurrency. Processes are provided using a form of the conventional procedure mechanism. Mutual exclusion is provided by the monitor and synchronization by the WAIT and SIGNAL statements.

A process is defined by writing

NAME: PROCEDURE OPTIONS (CONCURRENT)

Multiple entry points of a concurrent procedure are defined by writing a name followed by a colon followed by the word PROCESS. For example Table 10-4, from [Holt 78], considers a problem which has two processes, one which counts the occurrence of an event, COUNT, and a second process, WATCH, which prints the value of COUNT and every so often resets the count to zero.

```
EXAMPLE : PROCEDURE OPTIONS (CONCURRENT)
    CRITICAL : MONITOR
        DECLARE (SUM) BINARY FIXED;
        DO; SUM = 0;
        END;
    COUNT : ENTRY;
        SUM = SUM + 1;
        END;
    WATCH : ENTRY;
        PUT SKIP LIST (SUM);
        SUM = 0;
        END;
    END CRITICAL;
    COUNTER : PROCESS;
        /*DO SOMETHING*/
        CALL COUNT;
        /*DO SOMETHING*/
        END COUNTER;
    WATCHER:  PROCESS;
        /*DO SOMETHING*/
        CALL WATCH;
        /*DO SOMETHING*/
        END WATCHER;
    END EXAMPLE;
```

Table 10-4: CSP/K Example

In Table 10-4, EXAMPLE names this entire concurrent program which contains one monitor called CRITICAL and two processes COUNTER and WATCHER. The variable SUM is local to EXAMPLE and may be used by the monitor and the processes. CSP/K uses the PL/1 scope rules so local variables may be used anywhere in the scope of a process or monitor unless re-declaration occurs. Before any processes begin to execute, the initialization code of a monitor is executed. Thus, in Algorithm 10-4, SUM is set to zero. Monitor entries are optional, but in this case there are two labeled entries COUNT and WATCH. Entries may have parameters and local variables. An entry may be reached by a process if it says "CALL entryname". An entry may return a value, but then it must be invoked using a function call. Note that calls from inside a monitor entry to other entries in the same or other monitors is forbidden. Unfortunately monitor procedures and entries may access global variables and procedures as defined by the PL/1 scope rules.

A WAIT statement causes the current process to be suspended, placed on a queue, and removed from the monitor. When a SIGNAL statement is executed it causes one of the processes waiting for the condition to be taken off the queue and given exclusive control of the monitor. If the queue is empty or after all processes on the queue have been resumed, the process which executed the SIGNAL statement will be resumed.

Rather than allowing simple WAIT and SIGNAL operations, CSP/K allows them to operate on condition variables which are declared in a monitor. Condition variables are automatically initialized to empty. They are the only arguments of a WAIT or SIGNAL statement. CSP/K uses a FIFO (first-in-first-out) scheduling policy. A final extension that CSP/K has made to PL/1 is to associate a priority number with a condition variable. This can be used to override the normal FIFO scheduling. Though this provides a hole in the policy of fair scheduling, it is believed to be needed, particularly for operating systems applications. For more details on CSP/K and its use see the delightful book by Holt, Graham, Lazowska, and Scott called *Structured Concurrent Programming with Operating Systems Applications.*

Concurrent-Pascal:

Concurrent-Pascal is a language developed by Brinch-Hansen which extends the language Pascal with features permitting concurrency. The main new features are processes, monitors and classes, plus the statements *init, delay* and *continue* and the data type *queue.* As before, a process is a sequential program which may be executed simultaneously with other processes. A monitor is a mechanism for encapsulating data which is shared among processes and for synchronizing access to the data. A class corresponds to the notion introduced by SIMULA and can be viewed as an abstract data type facility but without the scheduling properties of a monitor.

The form of a process is

    type process-name = **process** (formal parameters)
            variable, constant, type and
            procedure declarations;
            body
            end

A process is viewed as defining a new type. To define an instance of this type one writes **var** x : process-name. This associates the name x with the process. The statement "**init** x*(actual parameters)*" causes space to be allocated for the local variables (called private variables) of the process and begins its execution. After **init**, all parameters and private variables will exist for the duration of the program. The process may only access its own parameters and private variables. This is in contrast to the normal scope rules of Pascal which allow inheritance of variables from an outer scope. This is an important step forward, as it allows a process to be studied as a self-contained unit and viewed in a time-independent manner. It also allows and forces the programmer to explicitly state to which data the process is given access.

The form of a monitor is

type monitor-name = **monitor** (formal parameters)
          shared variables
          local procedures
          procedures with entry
          begin
            initialization code
          end .

A monitor declares a set of shared variables. It may contain procedures which are local to the monitor. Procedures which may be used by processes or procedures in other monitors are declared so by writing **entry** before their name, e.g.

procedure entry *controldisk*(**var** x : *buffer)*

As a monitor is a type, one writes

var p, q : *monitor-name;*

and then one may say

init q *(actual parameters)*

This causes storage to be allocated and the initialization code at the end of the monitor to be executed. As for a process, once the **init** statement is executed, the parameters and shared variables exist forever. A monitor or a process may be **init**'ed once. When a procedure of the monitor is executing, it has exclusive access to the permanent variables. Other calls on the monitor will be delayed in a queue for later access. Within a monitor, procedures must be declared before used, procedure definitions cannot be nested nor is recursion allowed.

When a process requests a resource that is busy, the monitor may execute a **delay** statement. This places the process in the queue, which may only hold *one* process at a time. A **continue** operation causes the process on the queue to be removed and given exclusive access to the monitor.

A Concurrent-Pascal program consists of a series of type definitions. The main program is viewed as an anonymous type which is created when the program is loaded. The **init** statements are executed, causing processes to begin execution. Table 10-5 shows one example of a complete concurrent program in Concurrent-Pascal. For more detail on the language and examples of its use, one should consult [Brinch-Hansen 73,75,77]. In Table 10-5 we have a solution to a producer-consumer problem which first appeared in [Brinch-Hansen 75]. The producer (lines 2-8) is reading records and then spooling them into a queue of buffers. The consumer process (lines 9-15) deletes records from the front of the queue. The producer and consumer are represented as processes. A record whose first component is 'E' ends the program. The monitor *cbuffer* (lines 16-25) provides the mutual exclusion and synchronization which is needed to solve this problem. This monitor insures that the producer doesn't access the queue when it is full, and the consumer doesn't access the queue when it is empty. The queue is treated circularly. Variables *front* and *rear* have the obvious interpretation on the queue. Variable *noful* is the number of full buffers, *nobuf* is the total number of buffers, which for this example is 5. When the producer calls *spool*, line 6, and if there is no room in the queue, then the producer is delayed, line 20, on the system queue. Otherwise, the new input record, *contents*, is assigned to the next free buffer, *pool(rear)*, line 21. *Rear* is updated as is *noful*.and a **continue** is executed to resume execution of the consumer if it is on the queue. When the consumer calls *unspool*, line 13, then if *noful* = 0, it is delayed. Otherwise a record is removed and assigned to *contents*. Variables *front* and *noful* are incremented appropriately. On line 37, the **init** statement begins *x, y, z* concurrently and they continue to execute until a terminating record appears.

Some final thoughts

A monitor is a mechanism which puts a wall around a collection of resources so that concurrent processes will not access those resources in unpredictable ways. It accomplishes this by providing to the programmer three facilities: (i) a means for invoking procedures in the

```
1    type  buffer  = array (1..80) of char,
2    producer  = process
3         var card : buffer
4         begin card (1) := 'N'
5           while card(1) <> 'E' do
6             begin  read (card); spool(card);
7             end;
8       end,
9    consumer  = process
10        var line : buffer
11        begin  line := 'N';
12          while line <> 'E' do
13            begin  unspool(line); write (line);
14            end
15       end,
16   cbuffer  = monitor
17        var pool = array (1..5) of buffer
18        front, rear, nobuf, noful : integer
19        procedure entry spool (contents : buffer)
20          begin  if noful = nobuf then delay;
21                 pool(rear) := contents
22                 rear := rear mod nobuf + 1;
23                 noful := noful + 1;
24                 continue
25             end;
26      procedure entry unspool (contents : buffer)
27             begin if noful = 0 then delay
28                   contents := pool(front);
29                   front := front mod nobuf + 1;
30                   noful := noful - 1;
31                   continue
32             end
33    begin  front := 1 ; rear := 1; nobuf := 5 : noful := 0
34    end
35    var x : producer, y : consumer, z : cbuffer
36    begin
37      init x, y, z
38    end.
```

Handwritten annotations: "spooling to front of queue", "reading records", "delete records from front of queue", "exclusion + synchronization"

Table 10-5: Producer-Consumer Problem in Concurrent-Pascal

monitor; (ii) a way of scheduling the various calls made by outside procedures (usually a queue); (iii) a mechanism inside the monitor which permits the suspension and continuation of procedures initiated by processes (e.g. WAIT-SIGNAL or *delay-continue*). The monitor contains local data, a set of procedures and generally some initialization statements. A user invokes a monitor procedure and if no other user is currently executing a monitor procedure, he is permitted to do so. Otherwise he is placed on the monitor queue to await his turn. The monitor concept is another step in the development of concurrency primitives. Viewed today, the examples here lack a means for non-deterministic access of alternatives. In the next section, we will see what is meant by this term. Also, though the monitor appears to successfully model the situation of concurrency on a uniprocessor with shared memory, it is less appropriate for a distributed model, as we shall see in the next section.

10.4. Message Passing

In the past few years, advances in the development of computer hardware have permitted networks of processors to become economically feasible. But this has created new problems for programming language designers. Concurrent execution is, of course, not new, and in the previous sections we have seen several methods for handling this concept in a programming language. The monitor concept as developed by Brinch-Hansen and Hoare is ideally suited for a language which is running on a single processor or else on a multiprocessor which shares a common memory. However, the monitor concept does not seem to be the natural one to use when the underlying hardware configuration consists of many separate processors each having their own local memory, but no shared memory whatsoever.

Fortunately the two inventors of the monitor have offered proposed solutions to this new problem. Brinch-Hansen has outlined a language for *distributed processes* which he presents in [Brinch-Hansen 78]. Hoare also outlines a language proposal which he calls *communicating sequential processes* in [Hoare 78]. For simplicity we will refer to Brinch-Hansen's language proposal as DP and to Hoare's language proposal as CSP.

Both DP and CSP choose the process as the fundamental unit of concurrent program execution. In this sense they remain consistent with the mechanisms we've already seen. The difference lies in the manner in which processes communicate, namely by messages which they send to each other. This basic idea closely models the loosely coupled distributed network of processors which is envisioned as the underlying hardware.

In CSP a process P sends a message to a process Q by executing a statement of the form

Q ! *action(x)* //output to process Q the message //

Process Q receives the message by having a command which looks like

P ? *action(y)* //from P receive the message //

The name *action* identifies the type of message. In this case the message has one field, whose value is supplied by process P from $P's$ variable x, and is received by process Q in $Q's$ variable y. The process Q must name both the process from which it intends to receive a message (P) and the type of message (*action*). Likewise, P must name both the intended recipient (Q) and the message type. This requirement of symmetric naming is somewhat controversial and is not required in either DP or (as we shall see later) in Ada.

In DP, Brinch-Hansen has chosen to use a more familiar form of communication, the procedure. The command

call $Q.R$ *(input # output)*

in process P causes procedure R in process Q to be executed. The actual input parameters are denoted by *input* and the parameters designated *output* can be used to return values to process P. In process Q one would find the corresponding declaration

procedure R *(input parameters # output parameters)*

One major difference between CSP and DP is the manner in which synchronization of the communicating processes takes place. In both languages one process has to wait for another process to be ready to receive a communication. Therefore, one process may have to wait for the second process to reach its corresponding output or input command. When it does and the transfer is successfully completed, in CSP both processes will continue in parallel. The difference in DP is that the calling process is *forced to wait* while the second process executes the called procedure. Only when the called procedure is completed can both processes resume in parallel.

A point of similarity between CSP and DP is their use of guarded commands to control the nondeterminism of a program. Guarded commands were first introduced by Dijkstra in [Dijkstra 75b] and have

since been adopted in many concurrent programming languages
including Ada. A guarded command enables a process to make an
arbitrary choice among several different statements by inspecting the
current values of its variables. If none of the alternatives are true,then
all the guards are said to have failed, and no corresponding statement is
executed. If one or more of the guards are true, then an arbitrary one
is chosen. For concreteness I will present the CSP form of guarded
commands.

In CSP two processes p and q are written as

$$[\ p :: \text{commands} \mid q :: \text{commands}]$$

The vertical bars denote the fact that p and q are processes and can
execute concurrently. There are two statements which can take guards,
an alternative command and a repetitive command. The alternative
command is best understood by a simple example

$$[\ x > 0 \rightarrow y := +1 \mid x < 0 \rightarrow y := -1 \mid x = 0 \rightarrow y := 0]$$

The three guards in this CSP alternative statement are $x > 0$, $x < 0$
and $x = 0$. The fact that they are alternatives is denoted by the vertical
bar. Whichever guard is true will cause y to be assigned the sign of x.

The repetitive command in CSP is denoted by placing an asterisk
immediately before the left square bracket. For example

$$i := 1;\ *[\ i <= n;\ A(i) \neq 0 \rightarrow A(i) := B(i)/A(i)]$$

This command causes the elements of the array $A(i)$ to be set to the
quotient $B(i)/A(i)$ for $i = 1,2,.....,n$ unless $A(i) = 0$ in which case the
division step is skipped.

In DP a different syntax is used for guarded commands. The two
statements which take guards are

$$\textbf{when } B1 : S1 \mid B2 : S2 \mid \ldots \textbf{ end}$$
$$\textbf{cycle } B1 : S1 \mid B2 : S2 \mid \ldots \textbf{ end}$$

The first causes the program to wait until one of the conditions B1, B2,
etc., becomes true,and it can then execute the corresponding S_i. The
cycle statement causes endless repetition of a **when** statement as long as
one or more guards is true. For both statements,if more than one B_i is
true, a nondeterministic choice of which corresponding S_i to execute is
made. In an effort to better appreciate the differences between these
two language proposals,Welsh, Lister, and Salzman in [Welsh 79] have
investigated many programs using the two notations and the reader is
encouraged to read all of the examples in their paper.

When two concurrent processes wish to communicate, they must go through two steps. The first step is called synchronization. This refers to the fact that both processes must reach the statements in their own programs which call for the exchange of information. If one reaches that point first he will wait for the other. When both have arrived at the proper points in the program, they are synchronized. Then the communication takes place. In CSP we have seen that communication is denoted by the ! and ? operators and that both processes have to explicitly name the other. To put together the notions of CSP, I will write an example program. This is one we have seen before, namely a binary search tree with two operations: find and insert.

```
P ::
    data,leftchild,rightchild (1 .. 100) integer;
    flag : boolean; flag := false; maxsize : integer; maxsize := 100;
    *[ n : integer; P ? find(n) → LOOKUP; P ! answer(flag) |
       n : integer; P ? insert(n) → LOOKUP;
       [i ≠ 0 → skip |
       maxsize < 100 → maxsize := maxsize + 1;
                       data(maxsize) := n;
                       leftchild(maxsize) := 0;
                       rightchild(maxsize) := 0;
                n < data(j) → leftchild(j) := maxsize |
                n > data(j) → rightchild(j) := maxsize]
where
LOOKUP :: i, j : integer;
    i := 1; flag := false; *[i ≠ 0; flag = false →
        n < data(i) → j := i; i := leftchild(i);
      | n > data(i) → j := i; i := rightchild(i);
      | n = data(i) → flag := true]
```

Table 10-6: A Binary Search Tree in CSP

In Table 10-6 we see three arrays defined. The *i*th element of these three arrays forms a node of a binary search tree with *data, leftchild* and *rightchild* fields. The main part of P is a repetitive loop containing two parts. In the first part we see a *find* instruction and in the second part an *insert* instruction. When a *find* is received by P, that guard is now true, and that will cause LOOKUP to be executed. LOOKUP sets the variable *flag* to either true or false and returns that to the calling process via *answer*. Examining LOOKUP we see a repetitive loop with three alternatives. The program is looking to see if *n* is already contained in the binary search tree. If *n* is less than the value of the current node, then *i* is moved to the left child, whereas if *n* is greater than the value of the current node, then *i* is moved to the right child, else *flag* is set to true and LOOKUP terminates. If *n* is not in the tree, then *i* will eventually be set to 0, and *j* will be the index of the last node that was examined. If *insert* is received, then LOOKUP is first executed followed by the segment of code below the call. In this segment, if *i* has been set to some non-zero value by LOOKUP, then *n* must already be in the tree. Otherwise, a new node must be added to the tree. This is done by increasing *maxsize* and storing the proper values in the various fields. Note that the processes of inserting and finding can proceed in parallel.

Clearly the search for concurrent language primitives is not over. Both of these language proposals (CSP and DP) have stimulated a great deal of thought about the "best" mechanisms. In the next section we will examine how concurrency is done in Ada, a language whose designers had the opportunity of studying both DP and CSP.

10.5. Concurrency in Ada

The basic concurrency unit in Ada is a form of a module called a task. Like a package, a task consists of two parts: a specification and a body. The form is shown in Table 10-7.

```
task type T is
    -- entry declarations go here
end T;

task body T is
    -- declarative part is here
begin
    -- sequence of statements
end T;
    .

    .

    .
X, Y : T; --X,Y declared as tasks
```

Table 10-7:   The Shell of a Task in Ada

As shown, a task consists of two parts, the specification part and the task body. These parts may appear separately and may be compiled separately, but the specification part must appear first. The specification part contains entry declarations. If the reserved word **type** is left off of the task defintion, then a single task is being defined rather than a task type. In Table 10-7 one sees a task type and the variables X and Y which are instantiated as objects of task type T. A task type is similar to a limited private type of an Ada package in the sense that neither assignment, equality, nor inequality are defined for objects of the task type.

For a simple example consider the tasks defined in Table 10-8.

```
procedure GO_TO_MOVIE is
    task FIND_SEATS;
    task GET_POPCORN;

task body FIND_SEATS is
    . . .
end;

task body GET_POPCORN is
    . . .
end;

begin       -- FIND_SEATS and GET_POPCORN
            -- become active here
    WATCH_MOVIE;
end;        -- at this point Ada waits for the two tasks to complete
```

Table 10-8:   An Example of Two Tasks and Their Activation

In Table 10-8 we see a procedure containing two tasks. When the **begin** is entered, both of the tasks will be activated in parallel with the procedure WATCH_MOVIE. The procedure may not complete until WATCH_MOVIE and the two tasks have completed execution. This is normal termination. Each task depends upon either a block, or on a subprogram body or on a task body. A task object depends upon the unit in which it is declared. A task which is designated by an access (pointer) value depends upon the unit where the access type is declared.

The elements of a task specification consist of entries. These are the means by which one task can communicate with another. In form, entries are similar to procedure specifications. An entry has a name and parameters. But as á procedure executes its body when called, an entry is not executed by the calling procedure but by the owning task. An

accept statement specifies the actions to be done when a call of an entry is made. The description in the **accept** statement must match the entry in the task specification. For example:

An entry declaration:
   entry PUT_SENTENCE(S : **in** STRING);

An entry call:
   MOVE_TO_OUTPUT.PUT_SENTENCE(QUOTE);

An **accept** statement:
   accept PUT_SENTENCE(S : **in** STRING) **do**
      PRINT(S);
   end PUT_SENTENCE;

An **accept** statement for an entry may only appear in the task body. Thus, a task may only execute **accept** statements for its own entries. Of course a task body may contain more than one **accept** statement. When an entry call is made, the entry call and the **accept** statement are synchronized. This happens in the following manner. In one case the calling task may reach its entry call before the corresponding **accept** statement is reached by the owning task. Then the execution of the calling task is suspended until the task body reaches the appropriate **accept** statement. The second possibility is when the task reaches an **accept** statement, but no entry call for it has been made. Then the execution of the task is suspended until an appropriate entry call is issued. These two possibilities are shown in Figure 10-2. The term *rendezvous* refers to the synchronization which takes place between the caller and the task containing the entry called. Once both the caller and the callee have synchronized, they can then communicate which they do by passing parameters from the caller to the callee. Then the body of the **accept** statement is executed. While this is done, the caller waits. Finally any **out** parameters produced by the execution of the **accept** statement are sent to the caller. Now both processes are free to resume on their own.

In Ada, one of the two communicating tasks, the calling task, knows the name of the other and names it explicitly. The second task only knows that an interaction is expected. In Hoare's CSP both processes must know each other's name. Communication there is viewed as synchronized input-output. A rendezvous in CSP requires one task to wait at its I/O operation, until the second task arrives at its corresponding I/O operation. Then they both execute the I/O operation

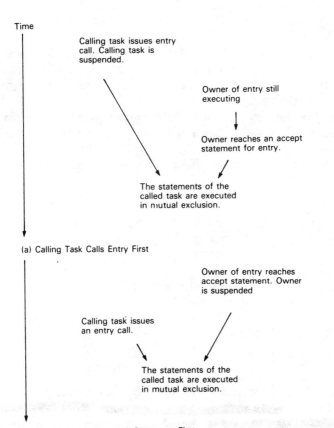

Figure 10-2: Two Possible Orders for Having a Rendezvous in Ada

and continue independently. The source and destination of the I/O must be compatible. One negative consequence of forcing the names of both processes to be known is that it forbids the use of a library routine. In Ada a task can be thought of as either a user of a service or a provider of a service. As a user, it must know the name of the service, but as a provider it needn't know the name of its user.

In Table 10-9 we see a main procedure called OVERSEE which contains a task called POURWATER in its declarative part. In the procedure's body, we see an inner block containing a second task called FILLBUCKET. Task POURWATER becomes active when the first **begin** is reached while task FILLBUCKET becomes active when the second **begin** is reached. Task FILLBUCKET contains an entry call to POURGLASS, whereas POURWATER contains a corresponding **accept** statement. The transfer of a glass will take place only when a rendezvous takes place.

A **select** statement in Ada is the means by which nondeterminism is introduced into the language. It allows a wait on one of several alternatives. A select alternative is said to be *open* if there is no preceding **when** clause or if the corresponding condition is true. Otherwise it is said to be *closed*.

```
select stmt ::= select
               [when condition = >]
               {or [when condition = >]
                     select-alternative}
               [else
                     sequence of statements]
               end select


select-alternative ::=
               accept-statement [sequence-of-statements]
               | delay-statement [sequence-of-statements]
```

It is important to understand how the conditions in a **select** statement are evaluated. First all the conditions are evaluated to determine which ones are actually open. If there are open alternatives, one is immediately selected. (There are several special cases in which a particular alternative will be immediately selected. These are detailed in the Ada manual, [Ada 80].) If no alternatives are open and there is an **else** part, then that is selected. However, if no **else** part is present, the task waits until an open alternative arises. Selection among a set of open alternatives is done by making an arbitrary choice of one of them.

```
procedure  OVERSEE is
  task POURWATER is
      entry  POURGLASS(S : in GLASS);
      entry  POURPITCHER(C : out PITCHER);
  end;

  task body POURWATER is
    begin
      accept POURGLASS(S : in GLASS) do
        . . .
      end;
  end POURWATER;
begin        -- at this point POURWATER becomes active
  declare
      task FILLBUCKET;

      task body FILLBUCKET is
        begin
          . . .
          POURWATER.POURGLASS(MINE);
          . . .
      end FILLBUCKET;

    begin        -- at this point FILLBUCKET becomes active
      . . .
    end;
    . . .
end OVERSEE;
```

Table 10-9:   Example of Ada Procedure with Task

The actual algorithm which is used to make the choice is not part of
Ada, and it should not be relied upon by any program.

Now that we have seen the basic concurrency features of Ada, let's
look at an example in Table 10-10. The task PRODCON has two
entries. GIVE and TAKE. The body contains definitions of local data
and the actions to be taken for each of the two entries. The body itself
is a single loop which contains two alternatives. The alternatives are
denoted by the SELECT statement. Each entry is protected by a guard
so that GIVE is not accepted unless COUNT < LIMIT and TAKE is
not accepted unless COUNT > 0. If GIVE is accepted, then an input
character C is assigned to the POOL. Pointers INP and COUNT are
updated appropriately. If TAKE is accepted, then a character is assigned
from POOL to D and carried out.

For a second example we re-consider again the binary search tree
example which contains two operations, insert and find. We create this
data structure as an Ada task. Here we see a task with two entries
denoting the two operations which are permitted. The definitions of the
data type BSTREE and BSTREEPTR are the same as was shown in
Chapter 8. Procedure LOOKUP searches the binary search tree pointed
at by T for data item N and either falls off the end of the tree or sets
FLAG to true. If N is not in the tree, then J is used to point to the last
node of the tree where the new node is to be attached while

```
task BSTREES is
   entry FIND(N : CHARACTER; T:BSTREEPTR;
            ANSWER : out BOOLEAN);
   entry INSERT(N : CHARACTER; T : BSTREEPTR);
end;

task body BSTREES is
   type BSTREEPTR;
   type BSTREE is
         record
            DATA : CHARACTER;
            LEFTCHILD : BSTREEPTR;
            RIGHTCHILD : BSTREEPTR;
         end record;
   type BSTREEPTR is access BSTREE;
   J,U : BSTREEPTR; ITEM : CHARACTER;
   FLAG, DIRECTION : BOOLEAN;
```

   Table 10-11:   Type Definitions for Binary Search Tree Example

```
task PRODCON is
  entry GIVE (C : in CHARACTER);
  entry TAKE (D : out CHARACTER);
end;

task body PRODCON is
  LIMIT : constant INTEGER := 100;
  POOL : array (1..LIMIT) of CHARACTER;
  INP,OUTP : INTEGER range 1 .. LIMIT := 1;
  COUNT : INTEGER range 0.. LIMIT := 0;
  begin
    loop
      select
        when COUNT < LIMIT = >
          accept GIVE (C : in CHARACTER) do
                POOL (INP) := C;
            end;
            INP := INP mod LIMIT + 1;
            COUNT := COUNT + 1;
      or
        when COUNT > 0  = >
          accept TAKE (D : out CHARACTER) do
                D := POOL (OUTP);
            end;
            OUTP := OUTP mod LIMIT + 1;
            COUNT := COUNT - 1;
      end select;
    end loop;
end PRODCON
```

Table 10-10: Producer-Consumer in Ada

DIRECTION tells us whether to attach the new node to the left or right subtree. The INSERT operation begins by merely accepting the data item N for subsequent insertion. The calling task is then free to proceed while the above task performs a LOOKUP followed by the actual insertion.

The Dining Philosophers' Problem

One problem which has become a standard for measuring the effectiveness of any programming language features for concurrency is called the dining philosophers' problem. The problem goes as follows: five philosophers spend all of their time either thinking or eating. When a philosopher gets hungry, he enters the dining room where he finds a table surrounded by five chairs. On the table are five plates and forks. In the middle of the table is a large dish of spaghetti. The philosopher sits down and picks up the fork on the left of his plate. But, as the spaghetti is so entangled, he needs two forks to get himself a portion for his plate. Therefore, he tries to pick up the fork on his right as well. If he can do this, he gets a portion of spaghetti, eats it and then puts down both forks and leaves the room. The problem is to write a computer program which will accurately simulate this form of behavior. A partial solution to this problem using Ada, by R. Williamson, follows.

Retrospective

The Ada scheme for concurrency must be viewed as an evolutionary step in the search for appropriate concurrency primitives. The mechanism is surely higher level than the notion of semaphores as is seen in Table 10-15 where a binary semaphore is easily defined using an Ada task. In Table 10-15 we see two entries WAIT and SIGNAL. In the task body we see that they will be executed one after another in an infinite loop. There are no arguments for the entries, and so all that they accomplish is synchronization. By surrounding critical code with these two operations one gets the effect of a binary semaphore. The limitation of this formulation is that only one semaphore is produced. To get a semaphore type so that one can declare variables of type semaphore, one can declare a task type instead of a task, see [Ada 79b].

Though Ada easily handles the simulation of semaphores it does not fare as well on monitors. As observed by Wegner and Smolka, [Wegner 83], using tasks alone, it is not possible to produce monitor behavior. The fundamental difficulty is the fact that **accept** statements cannot be used to simulate calls of procedures which can be suspended and subsequently resumed. However, by placing all monitor procedures into a package one can produce the required behavior. The synchronization is accomplished by tasks which are local to the package.

```
procedure LOOKUP(N:CHARACTER; FLAG:out BOOLEAN;
                 J: out BSTREEPTR, T : BSTREEPTR);
  Q : BSTREEPTR;
  FLAG := FALSE; Q := T;
loop
  if Q <> null
    then if N < Q.DATA then J := Q; DIRECTION := TRUE;
                            Q := Q.LEFTCHILD;
         elsif N > Q.DATA then J := Q;
                    DIRECTION := FALSE; Q := Q.RIGHTCHILD;
         else FLAG := TRUE; exit;
         end if;
    end if;
  end loop;
end LOOKUP;
begin
  loop
    select
      accept FIND(N:CHARACTER; T:BSTREEPTR;
                  ANSWER:out BOOLEAN);
        LOOKUP(N, FLAG, J, T);
        ANSWER := FLAG;
      end FIND;
    or
      accept INSERT(N:CHARACTER, T : BSTREEPTR);
        ITEM := N;
      end INSERT;
      LOOKUP(ITEM, FLAG, J, T);
      if not FLAG
        then U := new BSTREE(ITEM, null, null);
             if DIRECTION then J.LEFTCHILD := U;
                          else J.RIGHTCHILD := U;
             end if;
        end if;
    end select;
  end loop;
end BSTREES;
```

Table 10-12:   A Binary Search Tree Implemented as an Ada Task

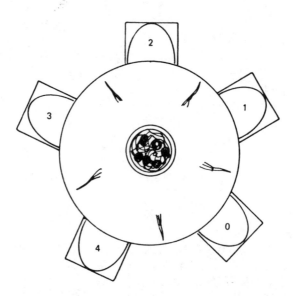

Figure 10-3:   The Dining Philosophers' Table

See [Wegner 83] for more details. Of course just being able to simulate
semaphores or monitors doesn't imply that the rendezvous mechanism
is superior. Certainly as more concurrent programs are written in Ada
and as more truly distributed systems get built, our insight about the
most appropriate language features for concurrency will improve.

```
procedure MAIN is
   -- Dining Philosophers Problem
   -- Declaration of tasks, forks, philosophers, and room go here
   FORK : array (0 .. 4) of FORKS;
   PHILOSOPHER : array (0 .. 4) of PHILOSOPHERS;
begin
      -- tasks FORK(0 .. 4), PHIL(0 .. 4) and ROOM
      -- automatically start as this block is entered.
      for I in 0 .. 4 loop
         PHILOSOPHER(I).LIFE(I : INTEGER);
      end loop;
   -- main program will terminate when
   -- all tasks terminate
end;

task type FORKS is
   entry PICKUP;
   entry PUTDOWN;
end;

task body FORKS is
   begin loop
      accept PICKUP;
      accept PUTDOWN;
   end loop;
end FORKS;

task type PHILOSOPHERS is
   entry LIFE (I1 : in INTEGER);
end;
```

Table 10-13:   Dining Philosophers, Part I

```
task body PHILOSOPHERS is
   I : INTEGER;
begin
   accept LIFE (I1 : in INTEGER) do I := I1; end;
   loop
      delay THINKTIME(I);
      ROOM.ENTER;
      FORK(I).PICKUP;
      FORK((I+1) mod 5).PICKUP;
      delay EATTIME(I);
      FORK(I).PUTDOWN;
      FORK((I+1) mod 5).PUTDOWN;
      ROOM.EXIT;
   end loop;
 end PHILOSOPHERS;

task ROOM is
   entry ENTER;
   entry EXIT;
 end;

task body ROOM is
   OCCUPANCY : INTEGER := 0;
   begin
     loop
       select
         when OCCUPANCY < 4 =>
            accept ENTER do
               OCCUPANCY := OCCUPANCY + 1;
            end;
         or
            accept EXIT do
               OCCUPANCY := OCCUPANCY - 1 ;
            end;
       end select;
     end loop;
   end;
end ROOM;
```

Table 10-14:   The Dining Philosophers in Ada

```
task SEMAPHORE is
  entry WAIT;
  entry SIGNAL;
end;

task body SEMAPHORE is
  begin loop
        accept WAIT;
        accept SIGNAL;
     end loop;
  end;
```

Table 10-15:   A Binary Semaphore in Ada

Concepts Discussed in This Chapter

Bounded buffer problem
Collateral clause
Concurrency
Deadlock
Discrete system simulation
Distributed computer system
Event variable
Message passing
Monitor
Multiprograming
Mutual exclusion

Parallel clause
Process
Process communication
Process control
Producer-consumer
Race condition
Reader-writer problem
Rendezvous
Semaphore
Synchronization

Exercises

1. Consider the following outline of a pair of procedures activated by a main program:

```
procedure MAIN
    integer x,y
    procedure P(..)
        L1 : . . .
            while x ≠ 0 do end
            x := 1
        L2 : . . .
            while y ≠ 0 do  end
            y := 1
        L3 : . . .
            x := 0;  y := 0
        return
    end P
    procedure Q(..)
        M1 : . . .
            while y ≠ 0 do end
            y := -1
        M2 : . . .
            while x ≠ 0 do  end
```

```
        x := -1
        M3 : . . .
        x := 0;  y := 0
        return
        end
        x := 0;  y := 0
    process P(..) [task]
    process Q(..) [task]
    end MAIN
```

(a) Under what set of conditions will *P* and *Q* run to completion? (b) Under what set of conditions will *P* and *Q* deadlock?

2. [Holt 78] The mathematician Dekker has shown how mutual exclusion can be accomplished using only busy-waiting and memory interlocking. Try to give an argument which shows that Dekker's algorithm actually works.

```
mutexbegin:  box(me) := true                    //try to enter//
        while box(him) do //does he also need to enter//
        if turn ≠ me
        then box(me) := false //change my mind temp//
            while turn ≠ me do //wait//
            repeat
            box(me) := true //try to enter again//
        endif
        repeat

mutexend:   box(me) := false
            turn := him                          //let him enter//
```

3. A semaphore may be implemented by using a busy-waiting technique and the mutual exclusion described in Section 10.2. Each process uses a local variable *flag,* and we assume a testandset instruction implements the comparison and decrementing of *s.* Discuss the merits/demerits of this scheme.

```
wait(s): flag := true
        while flag do
            mutexbegin
            if s > 0 then s := s - 1
                    flag := false
```

endif
mutexend
repeat

signal(s): mutexbegin
$s := s + 1$
mutexend

4. Dijkstra's use of the letters P and V for the operations on a semaphore come from the Dutch words *probern* and *verhogen.* Look up their meaning.
5. Two alternate definitions of semaphores are below. Compare them with the one given in the text.

Binary Semaphores

P(*mutex*): **if** *mutex* $= 1$ **then** *mutex* $:= 0$
                    else place the process onto the queue

V(*mutex*): **if** queue $=$ empty **then** remove a process
                    else *mutex* $:= 1$

Counting Semaphores

P(*mutex*): **if** *mutex* > 0 **then** *mutex* $:=$ *mutex* -1
                    else place the process onto the queue

V(*mutex*): **if** queue $\neq$ empty **then** remove process, run
                    else *mutex* $:=$ *mutex* $+ 1$

6. Compare events in PL/1 with semaphores. How do they differ?
7. If one mistakenly writes

wait(s)
   critical region
wait(s)

Explain what will happen in detail.
8. This book uses the initials CSP as an acronym for four different things. What are they?
9. In the Ada program which purports to solve the dining philosophers' problem, Table 10-14, you are to fill in all of the details so you have a complete Ada program. Try to

show that every philosopher will eventually get a chance to eat.

Chapter 11

INPUT-OUTPUT

"A PRINT statement does not imply that printing will occur, and a
WRITE statement does not imply that printing will not occur.
lines 1046-1048, *FORTRAN77 Manual*

Of all of the aspects of language design, input-output (or I/O) is
regarded as the most distasteful. One reason for this is likely that it is
impossible to make the design of this part of a language entirely
independent of the computer's characteristics. Some language designers
have gone so far as to put their collective heads in the sand and not
define input-output at all. The ALGOL60 team was an early sinner in
this regard, and more recently the Euclid design group has done the
same. But most language designers have faced up to the fact that it is
better to design as much of the I/O in a machine independent manner,
than to have the entire facility patched on by the language
implementors.

In this chapter I do not intend to completely summarize the input-
output facilities of one or more languages. That would not be
illuminating, plus it would require a large number of pages. The goal of
this chapter is to present the current framework in which existing I/O
facilities are modeled. I will use as examples the I/O features of the
languages FORTRAN, PL/1, Pascal, and Ada as they span a wide
spectrum of capabilities.

The earliest higher level languages tended to treat I/O on an ad hoc basis. Specific operations were designated to work for specific I/O devices. This approach has been replaced in part by the notion called a file. A *file* is an ordered collection of homogeneous data. Typically, files may be declared in a program and can be used as the target of input or output instructions. Most importantly, a file can be associated with an external device, often by listing its name in an appropriate manner on some job control cards. A file must be opened before it is used. This permits the operating system to set up buffers and to allocate the appropriate device to the requesting program. Once a file is closed the buffers are lost and the device is deallocated. When a file is closed and subsequently reopened, the file pointer is reset to the beginning of the file. Therefore, subsequent I/O operations will either re-read or re-write the first data items. The concept of a file has now gained major status as a basic concept for I/O in high level programming languages.

Each file has certain attributes which must be specified by the programmer. One such attribute is the *access mode* of the file. A file (as with a procedure's parameter) may either be read-only, write-only, or read-write.

Input Devices	Output Devices
card reader	card punch
terminal keyboard	terminal screen
paper tape	paper tape punch
magnetic tape	magnetic tape
disk pack	disk pack
console switches	console lights
graphics tablet	line printer
	drum
	floppy disk
	plotter

Table 11-1:   Some Typical I/O Devices

Another important attribute of files is the manner in which its data can be read or written. A *sequential file* is a sequence of data which must be operated on in linear order. Devices such as the card reader, line printer and magnetic tape are sequential. Sequential files are so pervasive that we will see that some languages permit only sequential files. A *random access file* (or direct access or nonsequential file) has its data accessed by name or location rather than by any enforced ordering. Table 11-1 lists some common I/O devices.

One important distinguishing characteristic of I/O is whether or not a conversion of representation occurs during the transfer. For example, input from a card reader enters as character string data but it may be converted to an internal form such as binary for integers or floating point for reals. Other types of input do not imply a representation conversion, for example reading from or writing to a file on disk. In the former case there may be considerable programmer controls for describing the conversion from internal to external form. These controls are often stated in a FORMAT statement, a concept introduced by FORTRAN, continued by PL/1, but dropped by Pascal and Ada.

We are now going to take a closer look at the I/O facilities of several programming languages. We will be scrutinizing their features primarily from the following points of view:

□ To what extent are the I/O facilities integrated into the mainstream of the language;

□ How are the machine dependencies, such as associations with external files, expressed;

□ Are the facilities simple to use, yet how capable are they of expressing sophisticated output formats?

Pascal

Pascal is an example of a language which offers only a few primitive operations for performing input-output, and so we begin with it. We shall see that an effort was made to incorporate the input-output facilities into the procedure and typing mechanisms of the language. Conceptually, input and output are viewed as streams of data which are composed of lines of text. For some devices, such as the line printer, the separation of lines is denoted by special "control" characters.

In Pascal there is the notion of a file as a sequence of data all of the same type. To declare a file one may write

type <identifier> = **file of** <type>;

and then one can declare variables of type file, e.g.,

type f = **file of** *integer;*
var $x : f;$

There are *external* and *internal* files in Pascal. External files must be listed in the program heading. The operating system and the job control cards serve to associate the external files with the names listed in the program heading. There are two standard files, called *input* and *output*, and these are taken as the default whenever a file name is omitted.

The declaration of a file f automatically introduces an associated variable whose type is the same as the file's components. This variable is called the file-buffer and it is denoted as $f\uparrow$. At any time, the only component of a file which is visible is the contents of $f\uparrow$. There are certain operations which manipulate files. Each time a single read or a write is performed on a file, $f\uparrow$ is moved forward. If $f\uparrow$ moves beyond the end-of-file, then $eof(f)$ becomes true. Also, there is an operation $reset(f)$ which moves f to the beginning of the file, $rewrite(f)$ which assigns f to the empty file, $get(f)$ and $put(f)$. The latter two operations are defined only for single components of a file. Operation $get(f)$ moves $f\uparrow$ to the next element in the file or else it sets $eof(f)$ to true and $f\uparrow$ to undefined. Operation $put(f)$ appends the value in the buffer, $f\uparrow$, to f.

Recognizing that more sophisticated I/O operations are needed, Pascal has extended the use of get and put to

> $read(f,x)$ which is equivalent to $x := f\uparrow$; $get(f)$
> $write(f,x)$ which is equivalent to $f\uparrow := x$; $put(f)$

Operations $read$ and $write$ are predefined procedures. But now Pascal breaks with convention and permits $read$ and $write$ to accept an arbitrary number of arguments. For example,

> $read\ (f_1, x_1,...,x_n)$
which is equivalent to
> **begin** $read(f_1,x_1);...; read(f,x_n)$ **end**

and similarly for $write$. The types of x_i may be either integer, real, char or any subrange of integer or char. But the input of the values of an enumerated type or of Boolean type is not permitted. Each x_i can have three components, $e:e_1:e_2$ where e is a name, e_1 is a minimum field width, and e_2 is the length of the fractional part. When an output value is written without a field-width specification, then a default width is used.

Two other operations of interest are $readln$ (read line) and $writeln$. Operation $readln(x)$ skips to the next line after x is assigned its value. Its definition in terms of the primitives is

> **while not** $eoln(f)$ **do** $get(f)$;
> $get(f)$

where $eoln(f)$ is true if the end-of-line of f has been reached. In that case $f\uparrow$ = blank.

A most convenient aspect of $read$ and $readln$ is that one need not specify exactly where the input is to be found or whether it is written using, e.g., decimal or scientific notation. The input file is a stream of data and as values are encountered they are assigned to the names in the argument list.

It is a credit to Pascal that its input-output can be summarized so concisely. The integration of I/O into the normal typing and procedure facilities make this brevity possible.

PL/1

Having seen the simplicity of Pascal, we are now ready (hopefully) to turn to PL/1. I/O in PL/1 is divided into two major groups called stream and record. As with Pascal, *stream I/O* is viewed as a contiguous sequence of homogeneous data to which conversions are applied during the transfer from internal to external device or vice-versa. *Record I/O* views the data as segmented into groups, called records, where each member of the group can be referenced by its name. No conversion is made. There are different statements for each category of I/O, as shown in Table 11-2.

Record I/O	Stream I/O	Control Statements
READ	GET	OPEN
WRITE	PUT	CLOSE
REWRITE		UNLOCK
LOCATE		DELETE

Table 11-2: I/O Statements in PL/1

Both stream and record I/O work on files. Table 11-3 shows the attributes which exist for files. In PL/1, one may declare a file name by writing, e.g.,

DECLARE MYFILE FILE;

This associates the name MYFILE with an external device whose name is transmitted to the operating system via job control cards. The default file names are called SYSIN and SYSOUT. and they traditionally referred to the card reader and the line printer. A file may be declared as being read-only, write-only or read-write using the attribute identifiers INPUT and OUTPUT. Files may be explicitly opened or closed using

OPEN FILE(name); and CLOSE FILE(name);

statements. There is one input command, GET, and one output

```
Stream I/O          Record I/O
------------        -----------------------------------
ENVIRONMENT   BACKWARDS       KEYED
FILE          BUFFERED        OUTPUT
INPUT         DIRECT          RECORD
OUTPUT        ENVIRONMENT     SEQUENTIAL
PRINT         EXCLUSIVE       TRANSIENT
STREAM        FILE            UNBUFFERED
              INPUT           UPDATE
```

Table 11-3:   File Attributes in PL/1

command, PUT, for stream I/O.   However, there are three different
types of stream I/O called list-directed, data-directed, and edit-directed.
The first two require no format statement either on input or output.
The last one does, e.g.,

GET EDIT(name list)(format list);

For list-directed I/O, one might say GET LIST(A,B,C) which causes
the next three values in the input stream to be found and assigned to
A,B,and C respectively.   Of course, there is an attempt to convert the
input values which are initially in terms of character strings, to the types
of A, B and C. If this is not possible, then the exception CONVERSION
is raised.   Saying PUT LIST(A,B,C) prints the values of A, B,and C
using default values for the width of fields.

Data-directed input, e.g.,GET DATA(A,B,C) will search for inputs of
the form A = ...; B = ...; C = ...; where the three dots indicate some
values in the input stream.   These values are converted from character
representation to the form required by the attributes of their associated
name.   On output, e.g.,PUT DATA(A,B,C) this statement causes a line
of output exactly as the input shown above.   Data-directed I/O has the
nice property that its output is acceptable as data-directed input.

There are various keywords one can attach to control printing.   These
include

PUT	print starting at the next tab position
PUT SKIP	print starting on a new line
PUT SKIP(n)	print after skipping n-1 lines
PUT PAGE	print starting at the top of the page
PUT LINE(n)	print starting at line n of the page
GET COPY	read and print the input

Note however, that if the output file to which these statements refer does not have the attribute PRINTER associated with it, then the options SKIP, LINE, PAGE and COLUMN are meaningless.

For edit-directed output we have the statement form

PUT FILE (name) EDIT (list) (format)

The list of options which can occur in the format are found in Table 11-4(a). Also listed in Table 11-4 (b), for comparison, are the new FORTRAN77 format options. The capital letters refer to the types of the values. These are used to determine the kind of conversion which must be applied. The lower case letters present further elaborations of the types, such as the number of columns in which the value will be found, or the number of digits to be placed after the decimal point. For precise definitions of these quantities the appropriate language reference manual should be selected.

An interesting variation of the FORMAT specification which PL/1 offers is the picture specification. For example if one writes

P'$$$$9.99.'

it means that any value from $0.00 to $9999.99 can be printed, with no space between the $ and the first significant digit. The $ is allowed to "drift" so that it appears immediately to the left of the first nonblank character. The complete set of options for picture specifications can be seen in Table 11-5. Using picture specifications to describe the output of data was first introduced in COBOL, [COBOL 72].

Another aspect of I/O is the handling of special situations, which in PL/1 is nicely integrated into its exception handling facility. For example the condition ENDFILE is raised when an end-of-file is reached or, NAME(file name) can be raised during a data-directed GET statement if an unrecognizable identifier is found, or KEY(filename) is raised when a key is not found as expected.

A further aspect of format specification is the ability to abbreviate its input-output instructions. With the exception of the P phrase, format phrases in PL/1 assume the general form "(r) phrase (w,d)" where r is the replication factor, phrase is either A, E, F or X, w is the total number of characters and d, if used, specifies the number of digits to the right of the decimal point. In PL/1, r, w or d may be constants *or expressions*. Finally, if a format statement is exhausted, but more names appear in the list, then the format statement is repeated.

A or A(w)	alphabetic
B or B(w)	bit string
C or C(s,t)	complex number
E(w,d) or E(w,d,s)	floating point number
F(w), F(w,d), F(w,d,p)	fixed point number
P 'specs'	picture
R(label)	trans editing to the format at label
X(w)	skip w characters or insert w blanks

(a) Format Operators in PL/1

A or Aw	character
Dw.d	real, double precision or complex
Ew.d, Ew.dEe, Ew.dDe	real, double precision or complex
Fw.d	real, double precision or complex
Gw.d.	real, double precision or complex
nH	Hollerith
Iw or Iw.m	Integer
Lw	Logical
Tc	Trans next char to or from cth pos.
bx	skip b characters.

(b)   Format Operators in FORTRAN77

Table 11-4: Format Operators in Some Languages

9	::=	blank, 0,1,...,9
A	::=	blank, A,B,...,Z
X	::=	any symbol
V	::=	assume a decimal point
S	::=	a sign (+ or -)
B	::=	insert a blank
Z	::=	replace leading zeros by blanks
*	::=	replace leading zeros by *
+	::=	insert + if item is positive
-	::=	insert - if item is negative
.	::=	insert a period
$	::=	insert a $

Table 11-5: Options for the PL/1 Picture Specification

Another very useful facility in PL/1 is the ability to perform read and write operations to character string variables instead of files. This is called the string option. A character string variable assigns an explicit order to its elements and in this way it is similar to a sequential file as in Pascal. This capability can be very useful. First an external file can be input as character data and assigned to a string. This restricts the type conversion when reading from external to internal form. Now this string can be read as often as one wishes, using a variety of formats. Also the character string can be examined using all of the language features available for string manipulation.

So far we have been speaking entirely about stream oriented I/O in PL/1. There is an alternate form called RECORD which is characterized by the fact that the data in RECORD files are maintained using the machine's internal form. No conversion is made when writing into or reading from an external device. The advantage of record I/O is the speed gained in avoiding the conversion step. Associated with record I/O are different I/O statements, READ and WRITE in place of GET and PUT. For example to open a file which allows for record I/O and which uses buffering we write

OPEN FILE (name) RECORD INPUT SEQUENTIAL BUFFERED

Besides sequential files, PL/1 has a direct access attribute called DIRECT. Records are accessed on a direct access file by key name. Direct access files are most advantageous for large files where it is necessary to process only a few of the records. Also, they are superior when the records of the file are to be processed in a random order.

The BUFFERED attribute allows the programmer more control over how the I/O is handled. In LOCATE mode the I/O instruction does not specify the source or destination of a transfer, but uses a pointer into the buffer. For example,

READ FILE (name) SET (pointer)

sets the pointer to the buffer area, so that the user of the associated based variable automatically accesses the current buffer. On output, a based variable identifies the information and the statement

LOCATE (based variable) FILE (name)

allocates an output buffer and sets the pointer associated with the based variable. Thereafter, assignments to the based variable cause information to be written into the current buffer.

As we can see the PL/1 I/O features are much more extensive than

Pascal. For many applications these features seem highly desirable.

Ada

The Ada programming language has not provided intrinsic features for I/O. Instead they have taken the view that I/O should be defined as an extension of existing facilities. So in Ada, I/O statements are produced using the facilities for generic packages, default parameters and subprogram overloading. Recalling from before, there are four basic issues which must be addressed by the I/O system. These are: (i) the declaration of internal files, (ii) the connection of internal to external files, (iii) communicating the access mode of the file, and (iv) format control. These issues have all been addressed by incorporating the I/O facility into pre-existing features of the language.

There are three standard I/O packages which are included in Ada. These are called INPUT_OUTPUT, TEXT_IO and LOW_LEVEL_IO. Within a program an input-output operation is performed on a so-called internal file. These files are named by variables and have attributes of type IN_FILE (read-only), OUT_FILE (write-only) or INOUT_FILE (read-write). These three types are all part of the generic package INPUT_OUTPUT and their operations are defined there. This is shown in Table 11-6. To get a file type of a specific kind one might write

package INTEGERIO **is new**
    INPUT_OUTPUT(ITEM_TYPE => INTEGER);

Now one can declare read-only files of integers by saying

NEWNUMBERS_FILE : INTEGERIO . INFILE;

A variable of type FILE has associated with it an unbounded index sequence which usually starts at 0. Each associated element has a positive index. An external file is represented in a program by a STRING whose interpretation is implementation dependent. The association of an internal file to an external device is dynamic. It is accomplished by the use of the CREATE or OPEN operations. For example,

CREATE(FILE => NEWNUMBERS, NAME =>"a/b/c");

associates the internal file NEWNUMBERS with the external file a/b/c whereas

NAME(NEWNUMBERS);

returns the string "a/b/c". An external device is deallocated following a CLOSE or DELETE operation. Two other built-in functions on files are

```
generic
  type ITEM_TYPE is limited private;
package INPUT_OUTPUT is
  type IN_FILE is limited private;
  type OUT_FILE is limited private;
  type INOUT_FILE is limited private;
  type FILE_INDEX is range 0 .. --defined in implementation
  procedure CREATE(FILE : in out OUT_FILE; NAME : STRING);
  procedure CREATE(FILE : in out INOUT_FILE; NAME : STRING);
  procedure OPEN(FILE : in out INFILE; NAME : STRING);
  procedure OPEN(FILE : in out OUT_FILE; NAME : STRING);
  procedure OPEN(FILE : in out INOUT_FILE; NAME : STRING);
  procedure CLOSE(FILE : in out IN_FILE);
  procedure CLOSE(FILE : in out OUT_FILE);
  procedure CLOSE(FILE : in out INOUT_FILE);
  procedure READ(FILE : INFILE; ITEM : out ITEMTYPE);
  procedure READ(FILE : INOUT_FILE; ITEM : out ITEMTYPE);
  procedure WRITE(FILE : INOUT_FILE; ITEM : in ITEMTYPE);
  procedure WRITE(FILE : OUT_FILE; ITEM : in ITEMTYPE);

  --exceptions
  NAME_ERROR : exception;
  USE_ERROR : exception;
   . . .
  private
    --declarations of private types
   . . .
end INPUT_OUTPUT;
```

Table 11-6: Package INPUT-OUTPUT in Ada, [Ada 80]

the predicate IS_OPEN and the function SIZE with the obvious interpretations. For stream I/O, SIZE gives the number of elements read or written on the file. As files are sequential, only one element is accessible at any time, and the value is returned by NEXT_READ. The next position is always incremented by a read or write operation. The sensing of end-of-file is tested by writing the condition END_OF_FILE(F) > SIZE(F) for some file F. No automatic buffering facility is provided, but it is easily possible to define such a package using arrays for the buffers.

File handling:

CREATE	OPEN
DELETE	CLOSE
IS_OPEN	NAME

Data handling

READ	WRITE

File positioning

SIZE	LAST
END_OF_FILE	TRUNCATE
NEXT_READ	NEXT_WRITE
SET_READ	SET_WRITE
RESET_READ	RESET_WRITE

Table 11-7:   INPUT-OUTPUT Operations in Ada

We mentioned before that conversion on input is from character to the form of the appropriate type (e.g. integer, real) and on output from the type's internal representation to character strings. These conversion procedures are included in the TEXT_IO package. Another aspect of TEXT_IO is its treatment of lines on stream data. Lines are viewed as logical units of arbitrary lengths which corresponds more to terminal use rather than card reader or line printer use. Ada has dropped the use of formats or picture specification. The basic I/O operations for all scalar types are GET and PUT, which are defined as overloaded subprograms. There are the usual standard input and output files. In order to deal with lines of either fixed or arbitrary lengths, there are some operators in TEXT_IO. These include NEW_LINE which inserts a line mark in a text; or SKIP_LINE which, on input, reads either forward or backward an appropriate number of line marks. GET and PUT work on either free or fixed format text. On output free format is obtained by using the value zero with a field width specification. This prints the value using a minimum number of characters. If the field width specification contains a nonzero parameter, then fixed format is assumed. Pascal uses an implementation defined default width in contrast. All this is summarized in Table 11-8 where we see the outline for the elements in the TEXT_IO package.

No predefined I/O functions can be provided for user defined types. Thus, GET and PUT are placed in generic packages that can be instantiated by the programmer for each new type he creates. Also included with TEXT_IO are functions for layout control, such as LINE, COL, SET_COL, NEW_LINE, SKIP_LINE, END_OF_LINE, SET_LINE_LENGTH, and LINE_LENGTH.

A facility exists in Ada which attempts to aid in the communication with nonstandard peripheral devices. This is a murky area in that so much is device dependent. Nevertheless, Ada has attempted to categorize the difficulties and show how they can be treated in the language. This is done in the package called LOW_LEVEL_IO. The operations in this package are done by using the predefined procedures SEND_CONTROL and RECEIVE_CONTROL and by overloading them. The purpose of SEND_CONTROL is to send control information to the physical device. Procedure RECEIVE_CONTROL is used to monitor the execution of an I/O operation by requesting control information from the device. Each procedure has two parameters, one is the device type and the second is the respective data. The visible part of the LOW_LEVEL_IO package looks like

```
package LOW_LEVEL_IO is
    -- declarations of the possible types for DEVICE and DATA
    -- declarations of overloaded procedures for these types
procedure SEND_CONTROL
        (DEVICE : devicetype; DATA : in out datatype);
procedure RECEIVE_CONTROL
        (DEVICE : devicetype; DATA : in out datatype);
    end;
```

The bodies of the two procedures must be supplied by the installation.

```
package TEXT_IO is
  package CHARACTER_IO is
    new INPUT_OUTPUT(CHARACTER);
  type IN_FILE is new CHARACTER_IO.IN_FILE;
  type OUT_FILE is new CHARACTER_IO.OUT_FILE;

  -- character input-output
  procedure GET(FILE : in IN_FILE; ITEM : out CHARACTER);
  procedure GET(ITEM : out CHARACTER);
  procedure PUT(FILE : in OUT_FILE; ITEM : in CHARACTER);
  procedure PUT(ITEM : in CHARACTER);
  -- String input-output
  -- generic package for integer input-output
  -- generic package for fixed point input-output
  -- input-output for Boolean
  -- generic package for enumeration types
  -- layout control
  -- default input and output manipulation

  function STANDARD_INPUT return IN_FILE;
  function STANDARD_OUTPUT return OUT_FILE;
  procedure SET_OUTPUT(FILE : OUT_file);
  function CURRENT_OUTPUT return OUT_FILE;
  -- exceptions
    . . .
end TEXT_IO;
```

Table 11-8:   Package TEXT_IO in Ada

Concepts Discussed in This Chapter

Files
INPUT-OUTPUT in Ada
LOWLEVEL I/O in Ada
Picture specification
Random access files
Record i/o
Sequential files
Stream i/o
TEXT_IO in Ada

Exercises

1. In Pascal, how does *reset*(f) work in case f is the empty file?

2. In Pascal, what gets printed from the statement

$$write(32+18, \text{ '='}, 50, \text{ ' IS'}, 32+18=50)$$

3. What sort of I/O is preferable for stream I/O and what sort is preferable for record I/O in PL/1? Why?

4. In Pascal the statement *readln(a, b, c)* is often assumed to mean "Read the values of a, b, and c and ignore the rest of the information on the line". What happens if a, b, and c are not all on the same line but are distributed over two lines? How will *readln* actually behave?

5. It would be nice if Pascal included facilities for random access I/O. One way to extend Pascal would be to define a new type which contained the required field definitions and associated procedures such as *get* and *put*. Expand on this hint by defining the type and the operations in Pascal which would be necessary.

6. In Pascal if a file *f* has large elements, then *read(f,x)* will take a long time as these large values must be copied from the buffer to *x*. Discuss what you might do to avoid this inefficiency if *x* is never changed.

7. Consider the following Pascal program and state if it will work and how. Try it on your own Pascal compiler.

```
var f : file of record i : integer; c : char end;
begin
     while not eof(f) do
             begin
                 write (output, f↑ . c);
                 get (f)
             end
   end
```

Chapter 12

FUNCTIONAL PROGRAMMING

12.1. What Is Functional Programming?

In this chapter we will be examining the language design aspects of the major applicative programming language LISP. I will include some tutorial material for completeness. The reader who has not had previous experience with the language would do well to read the primer by [Weissman 67] or [Winston 79] for an excellent introduction to the language. I will begin with a general discussion of functions and evaluation. This is followed by showing how programs and data can be represented via a uniform mechanism, the so-called S-expression. Then I present the LISP interpreter in LISP, to reveal both the simple semantics of this powerful language and the simplicity of writing a sophisticated program. In the later sections, I examine more detailed issues of language design relating to LISP including shallow binding, the handling of FEXPRs and FUNARGs and lazy evaluation. The treatment here has been especially influenced by John Allen's *Anatomy of LISP*, (McGraw-Hill), which is recommended to the reader who wants a more advanced discussion of these topics.

A *function* from mathematics is a rule of correspondence which associates to each member of its domain a unique member in the range. The domain and range may be finite or infinite, different or the same.

We say that a function is *partial* over its domain if there is at least one domain value for which the corresponding range value is undefined. Otherwise, we say that the function is *total*. Partial functions occur naturally in programming as we shall soon see. It will occasionally be convenient for us to represent all undefined values by the special symbol □ called *bottom*. A function is *strict* if f[. . □ . .] = □. This notation means that if any function has an argument which is the bottom element, then its corresponding range value is bottom.

A function may be presented in several ways. One way is to enumerate pairs of domain and corresponding range values, but this is unsatisfactory for domains of large size. Alternatively we can supply a rule which shows how to compute the proper range value for any value in the domain. For example,

$$plusone[x] ::= x+1$$
$$square[x] ::= x*x$$
$$absolute[x] ::= \textbf{if } x < 0 \textbf{ then } -x \textbf{ else } x$$

These rules begin to look like the functions expressible in a programming language. There is the name of the function followed by its arguments enclosed in square brackets. We will use square brackets instead of the more conventional parentheses because we will soon have more than enough parentheses used for other purposes. The use of the double-colon-equals, or ::=, should be read as "is defined as." The right-hand side of the double-colon-equals gives a rule for computing a value. When a function is presented as a rule, values are supplied to its arguments and the function is evaluated. Evaluation is a concept related to algorithms rather than to mathematical functions. We will be studying this concept later on in this chapter.

Several questions now begin to arise about defining functions. What elements are we allowed to use on the right-hand side? Can we use any arithmetic operator, or other expressions besides **if-then-else**? Can we use the names of other functions or the name of the function which is being defined? The answer to these last questions is *yes*. For example,

$$plustwo[x] ::= plusone[plusone[x]]$$
$$xsqplusx[x] ::= square[x] + absolute[x]$$

These are examples of *functional composition*, the nesting of one function call in another. An example of recursive definition of a partial function is given by the well-known factorial function

$$fact[n] ::= \textbf{if } n = 0 \textbf{ then } 1 \textbf{ else } n*fact[n-1]$$

Thus,we see that a function can be viewed as a kind of program. It has inputs and a rule for combining these inputs to produce a value. It may use other functions to help it or it may use itself recursively. No distinction need be made between functions such as plus, minus, times, which are written as infix operators using special symbols (+, -, *), and functions such as *plustwo* or *fact.* The use of functions to create programs is what we mean by functional programming.

One essential ingredient of functional programming is that the value of a function is determined solely by the values of its arguments. Thus, calls of the function using the same arguments will always produce the same value. This property is called *referential transparency.* An *applicative programming language* is one which achieves its effect by applying functions, either recursively or through composition, and for which all of its expressions obey the principle of referential transparency. The term *functional programming language* is used here as a synonymous phrase.

It is useful to consider the contrasts between an applicative and an imperative programming language. When we restrict our language to functions which obey referential transparency, then the advantage is that in any expression we may replace a function by any other function which returns the same set of values. This is a very desirable feature, for it supports program modularity. The disadvantage is that all results of these functions are new objects instead of modified versions of their arguments. This creation of new objects can be very time consuming. Value returning procedures which also alter their parameters or alter global variables are said to have *side-effects.* When larger programs are composed of such procedures, then one must think in terms of the global environment and the changes which will be made to these altered variables. Computing *by effect* is very efficient on a von Neumann machine. But it introduces the concept of variables which hold values and a global environment to which incremental changes are being made. These concepts are clumsy, complicated to model and difficult to control as programs get larger.

It is possible to write functions without side-effects (pure functions) in ALGOL60 or Pascal or even in FORTRAN. The guidelines for doing so are that there must be no use of global variables and that no value of a parameter should be changed. The return value is the *only* way of obtaining a result. But as the type of object that a function can return is severely limited in these languages, functional programming in these languages is not very useful. On the other hand we will see that some functional programming languages, e.g. LISP, offer imperative features.

The few examples of functions we have seen should point out the difference between variables in the mathematical sense and in the programming sense. In mathematics a variable is typically used to denote either a fixed value or a range of values, such as "let x be the integer whose . . ." or "for all x there exists a y such that . . . " In programming languages a variable is usually the name of an object which can change over time and is neither fixed nor necessarily ranges over all values of its type.

The thesis of functional programming is that if we base a language on pure functions with the only operations being functional composition, recursion, and the conditional expression, then we have a powerful, expressive and semantically elegant system. This no doubt comes as a shock to those who have not experienced functional programming before. And we will not have time to justify the claims of expressiveness here. But this has already been done in several places, including [Burge 75] and [Henderson 80]. Our purpose is to examine the language design issues raised by a functional programming language. This means we must look closely at how such a language is implemented. And the language which epitomizes functional programming is LISP.

12.2. The Basics of LISP

We now try to define more precisely the domain that we will permit our functional programming language to operate on. This domain is called *S-expressions* and was invented by John McCarthy for the programming language LISP; see [McCarthy 60] and [LISP]. An S-expression is constructed out of atoms and parentheses. An *atom* is a sequence of alphabetic, or numeric characters possibly intermixed. Atoms can be either *numeric*

$$876 \quad -250$$

or symbolic

HERE ARE FOUR ATOMS

Symbolic atoms are indivisible and, hence, the only operation which can be performed on them is equality testing. A numeric atom is a sequence of digits possibly preceded by a sign.

An atom is an S-expression. A list of atoms is an S-expression. A list whose elements are S-expressions is an S-expression. Actually, this is not the complete definition of S-expressions but rather of lists, a subset of S-expressions.   However, it will do for now.   Thus, some examples of lists include

SIMPLE

(ADD 2 PLUS 3)

((RUTH 9) (EDWARD 6))

The first line has one atom, the second line a list of four atoms and the third line a list with two sub-lists each of which contains two atoms. Notice how a blank is used to separate atoms.

Lists are versatile at expressing complex data structures. For example, consider expressing algebraic formulas composed of constants, variables and binary operators.

$x + y$ ::= (PLUS x y)

$2x + 3y$ ::= (PLUS (TIMES 2 x) (TIMES 3 y))

$ax^2 + bx + c$ ::= (PLUS (TIMES a (EXP x 2))(PLUS (TIMES b x) c))

$10 x y z$ ::= (TIMES 10 (TIMES x (TIMES y z)))

We see the binary operators can be replaced by mnemonics and positioned in prefix form.   Also, note how the right-hand side fully determines the association of operands to operators, whereas the infix expression does not.   Finally, we see that the level of nesting can get arbitrarily deep.

In order to manipulate S-expressions we need some primitive functions.   We will use the same names as in LISP.   Though they undoubtedly will seem strange at first, you will get used to them and you may even grow to like them. The first function allows one to select the first element of a list.   It is called *car* and when LISP was originally developed it stood for the instruction "contents of the *a*ddress *r*egister" on the IBM 704.   For example,

$car[(A)] = A$

$car[(A \ B)] = A$

$car[((A \ B) \ (C \ D))] = (A \ B)$

$car[ATOM] = \square$

We see that *car* is a partial function which is undefined for arguments which are atoms.

The second function is called *cdr* (pronounced "could-er").   Its original meaning was "contents of the *d*ecrement *r*egister" on the IBM 704.   The *cdr* of a list is the list one gets by deleting the first member.

$cdr[(A)] = NIL$

$cdr[(A\ B)] = (B)$
$cdr[((A\ B)\ (C\ D))] = ((C\ D))$
$cdr[ATOM] = \square$

The *cdr* of a one element list is the empty list, which we represent by the special atom NIL. *Cdr* like *car* is a partial function.

Using *car* and *cdr* we can select out any element of a list. For example, if the list L = ((A B) (C) (D E F)) then

$car[L] = (A\ B)$ $car[cdr[car[L]]] = B$
$cdr[L] = ((C)(D\ E\ F))$ $car[car[cdr[cdr[L]]]] = D$
$car[cdr[L]] = (C)$ $cdr[car[cdr[cdr[L]]]] = (E\ F)$
$car[car[L]] = A$ $car[cdr[car[cdr[cdr[L]]]]] = E$
$cdr[cdr[L]] = ((D\ E\ F))$ $cdr[cdr[car[cdr[cdr[L]]]]] = (F)$
$car[cdr[cdr[L]]] = (D\ E\ F)$ $car[cdr[cdr[car[cdr[cdr[L]]]]]] = F$
$cdr[car[L]] = (B)$
$car[car[cdr[L]]] = C$

The intermixing of *car* and *cdr* occurs so often that LISP offers a method of abbreviation. For example *car[cdr[x]] = cadr[x]; car[car[x]] = caar[x]; car[cdr[car[x]]] = cadar[x]; car[car[cdr[x]]] = caadr[x].* The general rule should be obvious from these examples.

The third primitive function on S-expressions is an operator which allows one to construct arbitrarily complex lists. This function is called *cons* and it takes two S-expressions *x,y* as arguments and returns a new S-expression *z* such that *car[z] = x* and *cdr[z] = y.* For example,

$cons\ [A;\ (B\ C)] = (A\ B\ C)$
$cons\ [(A);\ (B\ C)] = ((A)\ B\ C)$
$cons\ [(A);\ ((B\ C))] = ((A)\ (B\ C))$
$cons\ [A;\ NIL] = (A)$

For notation I will separate arguments of a function by the semicolon. The result of a *cons* operation is to increase the length of its second argument by one. *Cons* is a strict function which is totally defined over the domain of S-expressions union bottom. One sees that the second argument of *cons* is either a list or the special atom NIL which represents the empty list. If the second argument was an atom, e.g. *cons*[A; B] then we expect the result to be (A B), but this violates the definition of *cons*, as *car*[(A B)] = A, but *cdr*[(A B)] = (B) and not B. This anomaly will cause us to expand our definition of the domain from lists to S-expressions.

To complete our set of useful primitive functions, we need a predicate which permits us to determine if a component of an S-expression is a list or an atom. Thus *atom[x]* is true if *x* is an atom (including NIL) and false otherwise. This introduces special interpretations of the atoms T and NIL which we will understand as true and false. Now we can write an expression such as

$$makesure[x] ::= \textbf{if } atom[x] \textbf{ then } NIL \textbf{ else } car[x]$$

This transforms *car[x]* into a total function defined over all S-expressions. *Atom* is a total function.

We mentioned before that the only operation on atoms is equality testing. The function to accomplish this is called *eq*. Thus, *eq[x; y]* is true (T) if *x,y* are the same atoms or else it is false (NIL). However, if either *x* or *y* are not atoms, then *eq[x; y]* is undefined. To guard against our mistakenly using *eq* on a nonatomic argument, we often use the function *null[x]* which is true if *x* is NIL and false otherwise.

We will assume that addition (+), subtraction (-), multiplication (*), division (/) and modulo (rem) are available operators. Also we assume that the relational operators $=$, $\neq$, $<$, $\leqslant$, $\geqslant$, $>$ exist for numeric atoms. We are now ready to write some simple functions which manipulate S-expressions.

$$length[x] ::= \textbf{if } null[x] \textbf{ then } 0 \textbf{ else } length\ [cdr[x]] + 1$$

The function *length* is defined for all lists where the length of the empty list is zero and the length of (x1 x2 ... xN) is N.

> *length [(A)] = 1*
> *length [(A B)] = 2*
> *length [((A) (B))] = 2*
> *length [(A (B) (C D))] = 3*

Another useful function is *append[x; y]* where *x, y* are lists.

$$append[x; y] ::= \textbf{if } null[x] \textbf{ then } y$$
$$\textbf{else if } null[y] \textbf{ then } x$$
$$\textbf{else } cons[car[x];\ append[cdr[x];\ y]]$$

If *x* = NIL the result is *y*. Otherwise *x* $\neq$ NIL and if *y*=NIL the result is *x*. If neither of these cases hold, then the result is

cons[car[x]; append[cdr[x]; y]]

For a list x = (x1 x2 ... xN) we see that *append* produces the expression

cons[x1; cons[x2;...;cons[xN; append[NIL;y]]...]] = (x1 x2 ... xN y)

We are building up a toolbox of generally useful functions and at the same time getting some experience with functional programming. Consider a function which reverses the order of a list. Thus,

$$reverse[NIL] = NIL$$
$$reverse[(A)] = (A)$$
$$reverse[(A\ B)] = (B\ A)$$
$$reverse[(A\ B\ C)] = (C\ B\ A)$$
$$reverse[(A\ (B\ C)\ D)] = (D\ (B\ C)\ A)$$

This function can be written in several ways. Here is one way using *append*

reverse[x] ::= **if** *null[x]* **then** *NIL*
    else *append[reverse[cdr[x]]; cons[car[x]; NIL]]*

Try saying the definition out loud, or describe it on a blackboard. This effort should make it obvious that *reverse* works. Let's simulate *reverse* as it processes the list (x1 x2 ... xN). We get

$$append[reverse[(x2...xN)],\ cons[x1;\ NIL]]$$

which becomes

$$append[append[reverse[(x3...xN)],\ cons[x2;\ NIL]],\ cons[x1;\ NIL]]$$

Let's try it one more time; we get

$$append[append[append[reverse[(x4...xN)],$$
$$cons[x2;\ NIL]],\ cons[x2;\ NIL]];\ cons[x1;\ NIL]]$$

If N=3, then *reverse* [((x4...xN))] = *reverse* [NIL] = NIL and *append* [NIL; *y*] = *y* so the new expression becomes

$$append[append[cons[x3;\ NIL],\ cons[x2;\ NIL]],\ cons[x1;\ NIL]]$$

Since *cons*[A; NIL] = (A),we can reduce this expression further to

$$append[append[(x3);\ (x2)];\ (x1)]$$

which by the definition of *append* becomes

$$append[cons[x3;\ append[NIL;\ (x2)]];\ (x1)]$$

Thus,we see that the next iteration yields

$$append[(x3\ x2),\ (x1)] \quad = cons[x3;\ append[(x2);\ (x1)]$$
$$= cons[x3;\ cons[x2;\ append[NIL;\ (x1)]]]$$

$$= cons[x3; \; cons[x2; \; (x1)]]$$
$$= cons[x3; \; (x2 \; x1)]$$
$$= (x3 \; x2 \; x1)$$

This example may seem somewhat tedious, and it is, as it is designed in part to point out the inefficiency of this particular *reverse*. On a list of *n* items, *reverse* will produce *n* calls of *append*. The *i*th call of *append* will produce *i-1* calls to *cons* which means that the total number of calls to *cons* is *1+2+...+n-1* = *n(n-1)/2* plus an additional *n* calls to *cons* which are explicitly in the definition of *reverse*. This number of steps is an order of magnitude larger than we would normally expect for a reversing algorithm.

A much more efficient version of *reverse* can be gotten by introducing an auxiliary function which exhibits a well-known technique of functional programming called an *accumulating parameter*. It goes like this

reverse[x] ::= *reverse1[x; NIL]*
reverse1[x; y] ::= **if** *null[x]* **then** *y*
                  else *reverse1[cdr[x]; cons[car[x]; y]]*

Let us see how the new definition of *reverse* works on our list x = (x1 x2 x3)

reverse[x] = *reverse1*[(x1 x2 x3); NIL]
          = *reverse1*[(x2 x3); *cons*[x1; NIL]]
          = *reverse1* [(x3); *cons*[x2; *cons*[x1; NIL]]]
          = *reverse1*[NIL; *cons*[x3; *cons*[x2; *cons*[x1; NIL]]]]
          = *cons*[x3; *cons*[x2; *cons* [x1; NIL]]]
          = (x3 x2 x1)

Thus we see that the new parameter *y* is used to accumulate the answer as the elements of *x* are being examined. In fact, at any point when *reverse1* is called we observe that its arguments *x* and *y* satisfy the relation that *append[reverse[x]; y]* yields the reverse of the original list. We also observe that for a list of length *n* only *n* calls of *cons* will be made.

Consider the functions

square[x] ::= **if** *null[x]* **then** NIL **else** *cons[car[x]*car[x]; square[cdr[x]]]*
mod2[x] ::= **if** *null[x]* **then** NIL **else** *cons[car[x] rem 2, mod2[cdr[x]]]*

Square computes the list of numbers whose elements are the squares of the numbers in the original list. The function *mod2* returns a list whose entries are the remainders modulo 2 of each number in the original. These functions are not especially interesting by themselves, but they are quite similar in form. This leads us to consider defining a general function which captures these similarities. The function can have three arguments, a list *x* as before, a function and a third parameter which is a constant value:

> *map[f; x; y]* ::= **if** *null[x]* **then** *y*
>
>   **else** *cons[f[car[x]]; map[f; cdr[x]; y]]*

Using *map* we can define *square* and *mod2* as

> *square[x]* ::= *map[exp2; x; NIL]*
>
> *mod2[x]*   ::= *map[rem2; x; NIL]*

A *higher order function* is a function such that at least one of its arguments or its value is a function. The function *map* is such a function. Such functions can be extremely useful in functional programming. But one problem with allowing functions as arguments, and which is apparent from these two examples, is that we need a mechanism which allows us to name a function and its parameters. Without such a mechanism we can become confused as to which parameter of which function a variable name refers to. The solution adopted by LISP is to use lambda (λ) notation as originally introduced by the logician Alonzo Church [Church 41].

A lambda expression is an expression whose value is a function. As a function is a rule for computing a value, a lambda expression ties together its parameters with the rule. Thus.

> λ *[[x] x+5]* λ *[[x; y] 2x+3y]* λ *[[x; y; z]* **if** *eq[x; NIL]* **then** *y* **else** *z]*

are three lambda expressions. The variables *x, y, z* are said to be *bound variables*. This means they are local to the lambda expression. It is also possible to have *unbound variables* occurring in lambda expressions,

> λ *[[x] x+z]* λ *[[x; y]* **if** *eq[x; NIL]* **then** *y* **else** *z]*

In both examples *z* is an unbound variable and, hence, the question arises as to where the variable will get its value when the lambda expression is evaluated. We will be able to answer this question in the next section.

Evaluating a λ-expression includes two phases: first one evaluates the actual parameters and then associates them with the corresponding λ-variables; then the function body is evaluated. Lambda expressions can be used to avoid needless computation. For example, if we have

$$f ::= \lambda \; [[x] \; \text{fif} \; p[q[x]] \; \textbf{then} \; q[x] \; \textbf{else} \; NIL]]$$

then we see that $q[x]$ will be computed twice, once to evaluate the conditional and second, if $p[q[x]]$ is true; evaluated again as the result. This recomputation can be avoided if we write

$$f ::= \lambda \; [[x] \; q[x]]$$
$$g ::= \lambda \; [[a] \; \text{fif} \; p[a] \; \textbf{then} \; a \; \textbf{else} \; NIL]]$$

Now $q[x]$ will be evaluated once, as an argument of $g[f]$ and its value substituted for a. In other approaches to functional programming (see [Henderson 80]), people introduce a higher level of notation for this purpose called a **where** or **let** clause. Another way to avoid this recomputation is given in the exercises.

Do you recall that $cons[x; y]$ is undefined if y is an atom? In order to avoid this problem, we need to extend the definition of S-expression so that it handles more than just lists. We shall represent the result $cons[x; y]$ by the dotted pair $(x .y)$. This value is different from $(x \; y)$, which is the result of $cons[x; cons[y; NIL]]$. Dot notation adds an element of confusion because there now exists more than one way to write the same value. For example (x) and $(x . NIL)$ are equivalent as is $(x \; y \; z . NIL)$ and $(x \; y \; z)$. Whenever possible, we will prefer to use list notation.

The new and complete definition of an S-expression is

1. an atom is an S-expression;
2. if x, y are S-expressions, then the dotted pair $(x . y)$ is an S-expression.

A convenient way of viewing S-expressions is graphically as they form a set of binary trees. That can be seen in Figure 12-1.

Up to now we have been writing function definitions assuming that an **if-then-else** expression was available. We now need to formalize this to bring us back into LISP. A *conditional expression* in LISP is written as

$$[p_1 \to e_1; p_2 \to e_2; \ldots; p_n \to e_n]$$

where each expression p_i returns true or false (or undefined) and each e_i is an expression. The rule for interpreting a conditional expression is: evaluate the p_i from left to right finding the first one which returns true (T). Having found such a p_i, evaluate the corresponding e_i and that is the result of this expression. If all p_i evaluate to false, or if a p_i is evaluated to undefined, or if p_i is true and e_i evaluates to undefined,

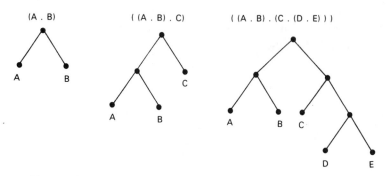

(A . B)   ((A . B) . C)   ((A . B) . (C . (D . E)))

A   B   A   B   C

                    A   B

                                                                D   E

Figure 12-1:   Graphical Representation for Some S-expressions

then the entire expression is undefined.

We can rewrite *reverse[x]* using this new form for the conditional expression

$$reverse[x] ::= [null[x] \rightarrow NIL;$$
$$T \rightarrow append[reverse[cdr[x]]; cons[car[x]; NIL]]]$$

Note the use of the atom T for true which selects the second expression automatically if *null[x]* is false.

The conditional expression forces out in the open all of the problems about order of evaluation which so far have been under the surface. If p_i is true, then there is no need to evaluate either p_j or e_j for $j > i$. Thus, we can't consider the conditional as a function with $2n$ arguments p_1; e_1; . . . ; p_n; e_n where it doesn't matter which order the arguments are evaluated. The order is important as we can see in this simple example

$$[eq [0 ; 0] \rightarrow 1; T \rightarrow car[A]]$$

If there was no order on evaluating the conditions, then this example might result in either 1 or undefined. Of course, if we allow nonstrict functions, then the result of the conditional may still be defined. The traditional **if-then-else** is a nonstrict function as seen by its axiomatic description.

if true then p **else** $q = p$
if false then p **else** $q = q$
if true then p **else** $\square = p$
if false then $\square$ **else** $q = q$

Before we conclude this section, it should be noted that there are really two kinds of undefinedness. In one case we may have a function applied to an argument for which it is not defined. Thus, immediate termination occurs with undefined as the result. In another case the function may be applied to legal arguments, but it may not terminate its computation. This is logical undefinedness, and the program can go on forever.

Summary

Now that you have become more familiar with functional programming, let's review what we have learned.

1. We have defined the set of S-expressions as the data type of our language. An important special case of S-expressions are lists which we will often use for examples.
2. We have the primitive operators: *car*, *cdr*, *cons*, *eq*, *atom* which operate on S-expressions.
3. We allow functional composition, recursion, and the special conditional expression as the only control features of our language.
4. In applying a function, all parameters are evaluated using the call-by-value rule before a function is applied to its arguments.
5. We have seen how algebraic formula can be put into fully parenthesized, prefix form called Cambridge Polish form.

The next section elaborates on points 4 and 5. First we outline the evaluation process more carefully. *Then we show how functional programs can be represented as S-expressions.* Imagine if we were going to represent an ALGOL60 program using its fundamental data structure, an array! Well, LISP provides a very natural mapping for functions into S-expressions. One consequence of this fact is that an interpreter for (pure) LISP can be written in LISP on a single page.

12.3. The LISP Interpreter

If we are to write an interpreter for LISP in LISP, then LISP functions must be expressible as S-expressions. We have already seen that an algebraic expression such as $AX^2 + BX + C$ can be written as the list or S-expression

(PLUS (TIMES A (EXP X 2)) (PLUS (TIMES B X) C))

Viewed as an S-expression this list has length 3, depth 3 and eleven atoms: PLUS, TIMES, A, EXP, X, 2, PLUS, TIMES, B, X, C. In general when we are given a function with a variable name like x or y, then we will write these variables in upper case X, Y as atoms. This complicates matters somewhat, because if we have a constant in a function, say A, it is already capitalized. To differentiate between constants and variables we will write (QUOTE A) to stand for a constant. A function's name is treated like a variable, so *car[x]* is (CAR X) and *append[x; y]* is (APPEND X Y). If we were to write (A B), A would be mistaken by the interpreter as a function, so instead we can write (QUOTE (A B)) whose result is (A B). The conditional expression $[p_1 \rightarrow e_1;...,p_n \rightarrow e_n]$ becomes (COND (p'$_1$ e'$_1$) ... (p'$_n$ e'$_n$)) where p'$_i$, e'$_i$ are the representations into S-expressions of p_i and e_i. For example, the body of *reverse* translated into its S-expression representation would look like

(COND ((EQ X NIL) NIL)
     (T (APPEND (REVERSE(CDR X)) (CONS (CAR X) NIL))))

We continue to write the constants true and false using the atoms T, NIL. If we have a lambda expression such as $\lambda\ [[x; y]\ x^2 + y]$ then it is written as

(LAMBDA (X Y) (PLUS (EXP X 2) Y))

Now we need some way of entering the function's name as well as its body. LISP provides such a mechanism called LABEL. This is necessary as a function may need to call other functions or itself. Thus, the complete *reverse* function would appear as the S-expression

(LABEL REVERSE
(LAMBDA (X) (COND ((EQ X NIL) NIL)
(T (APPEND (REVERSE (CDR X)) (CONS (CAR X) NIL))))))

Thus ,with some very simple rules we see how to represent any LISP function as an S-expression.

In order to write an interpreter for LISP, we next need a mechanism for maintaining a symbol table. The symbol table will be used to hold name-value pairs. The name may be a variable and its value a number or the name may be LAMBDA and its value a lambda expression. In LISP, symbol tables are known as *association lists* or a-lists or environments. Following [LISP], the function *assoc* takes a name and a symbol table as its arguments. It examines the table left-to-right until a name match is found and the (name . value) pair is returned. If the name is not found. the result is undefined.

$assoc[x; env] ::= [eq[caar[env]; x] \rightarrow car[env];$
$\qquad\qquad T \rightarrow assoc[x; cdr[env]]]$

Thus, if env = ((X . 10) (Y . 20) (Z . 30)) then

$assoc[Z; env] = (Z . 30), \quad assoc[W; env] = \square$

Before we look at the LISP interpreter, let's summarize our understanding about evaluation. The complete rule is

1. if the expression to be evaluated is a constant, that is if it is of the form (QUOTE S-expression), then the value is the quoted expression;
2. if the expression is a variable, return its current value in the environment;
3. if the expression is a conditional, then evaluate it as described previously;
4. if the expression is of the form $f[x_1;...;x_n]$ then

   - evaluate $x_1;...;x_n$ left-to-right;
   - find the definition of f;
   - associate the evaluated actuals with formula for f;
   - evaluate the body of f.

We are now ready to look at the LISP interpreter in Table 12-1. Before we delve into its secrets, one can't help but marvel at its simplicity. Though it's true that most LISP implementations are more complicated than what is described in Table 12-1, nevertheless, the interpreter here captures almost all of the essential details.

The LISP interpreter is composed of seven functions: *evalquote, apply, eval, pairlis, assoc, evcon* and *evlis*. These functions call each other and themselves, and they also make use of the basic LISP functions *car, cdr, cons, eq, atom,* and *null.* See Figure 12-2 for a diagram exhibiting these interrelationships.

pairlis[x; y; a] has three arguments: *x* a list of names, *y* a corresponding list of values, and *a* an association list. The association list is an S-expression containing dotted pairs of names and values. The purpose of *pairlis* is to insert the new name-value pairs defined by *x* and *y* into the list *a.* So, for example

$pairlis[(A1\ A2\ A3); (V1\ V2\ V3); ((N1.W1)(N2.W2))] =$
$\qquad ((A1.V1)\ (A2.V2)\ (A3.V3)\ (N1.W1)\ (N2.W2))$

1 evalquote[fn; x] ::= apply[fn; x; NIL]

2 apply[fn; x; a] ::= [atom[fn] → [eq[fn; CAR] → caar[x];
3   eq[fn; CDR] → cdar[x];
4   eq[fn; CONS] → cons[car[x]; cadr[x]];
5   eq[fn; ATOM] → atom[car[x]];
6   eq[fn; EQ] → eq[car[x]; cadr[x]];
7   T → apply[eval[fn; a]; x; a]];
8   eq[car[fn]; LAMBDA] → eval[caddr[fn]; pairlis[cadr[fn]; x; a]]
9   eq[car[fn]; LABEL] → apply[caddr[fn]; x; cons[cons[cadr[fn];
10   caddr[fn]]; a]]]

11 eval[e; a] ::= [atom[e] → cdr[assoc[e; a]];
12   atom[car[e]] → [eq[car[e]; QUOTE] → cadr[e];
13   eq[car[e]; COND] → evcon[cdr[e]; a];
14   T → apply[car[e]; evlis[cdr[e]; a]; a]];
15   T → apply[car[e]; evlis[cdr[e]; a]; a]]

16 pairlis[x; y; a] ::= [null[x] → a;
17   T → cons[cons[car[x]; car[y]]; pairlis[cdr[x]; cdr[y]; a]]]

18 assoc[x; a] ::= [eq[caar[a]; x] → car[a]; T → assoc[x; cdr[a]]]

19 evcon[c; a] ::= [eval[caar[c]; a] → eval[cadar[c]; a];
20   T → evcon[cdr[c]; a]]

21 evlis[m; a] ::= [null[m] → NIL;
22   T → cons[eval[car[m]; a]; evlis[cdr[m]; a]]]

Table 12-1: LISP Interpreter

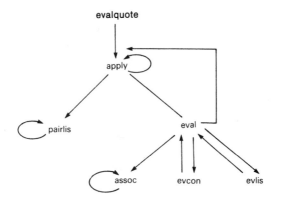

Figure 12-2: Calling Hierarchy of the LISP Interpreter

assoc[x;a] has two arguments: *x* is a name and *a* an association list. The result of applying *assoc* is it searches for the first occurrence of *x* and returns the name-value pair whose name is *x*. Thus

assoc[A3; ((A1.V1) (A2.V2) (A3.V3) (N1.W1) (N2.W2))] = (A3.V3)

apply[fn; x; a] has three arguments: a function, its arguments and an environment.   Note how *evalquote* is merely used to set the environment to NIL.   If *fn* is an atom, then it is either CAR, CDR, CONS, EQ or ATOM, or its name must be looked up in the environment. This looking up is done by calling *eval[fn;a]* and with the result reactivating *apply[eval[fn; a]; x; a]*. If *fn* is one of the primitive LISP functions, then the appropriate action is taken, either *car*, *cdr*, *cons*, *eq* or *atom*.   For example, if *fn* = CONS then *x* is a list of length two and the arguments are at *car[x]* and *cadr[x]*.   If *fn* is not an atom, then it is either a LAMBDA or a LABEL.   In the former case we have something like

  fn = (LAMBDA (X Y) (PLUS (TIMES X 2) Y)).

We must pair the lambda variables (X Y) with the actual values in *x*, so we call *pairlis[cadr[fn]; x; a]*.   Then we wish to evaluate the lambda form, *caddr[fn]* in this new environment, *eval[caddr[fn], pairlis[cadr[fn];*

x; a]]. In case *fn* is LABEL, we have something like

   fn = (LABEL 2XPY (LAMBDA (X Y) (PLUS (TIMES X 2) Y))).

Now *caddr[fn]* = (LAMBDA (X Y) (PLUS (TIMES X 2))) and *cadr[fn]* = 2XPY. The function *apply* is called

   apply[(LAMBDA (X Y)(PLUS (TIMES X 2))); X;
       ((2XPY . (LAMBDA (X Y) (PLUS (TIMES X 2)))) . *a*)]

This causes the function's name and definition to be placed into the environment, *a*, and *apply* will then evaluate it using actual arguments *x*.

   eval[e; a] has two arguments, *e* which is a form and *a* an environment. Recall that a form is a lambda expression which has been stripped of its lambda variables. If the form is an atom, then it must be a variable. Its name-value pair is located in the environment, using *assoc*, and the value is returned. If the *car* of the form is QUOTE, then the result is cadr[(QUOTE X)] = X. If the *car* of the form is COND, then we have a conditional expression handled by *evcon*. Otherwise we are evaluating a function and its arguments. The arguments are evaluated first, in left-to-right order using *evlis*. Then *apply* is called with arguments which are the function, its evaluated arguments and the new environment.

   We have mentioned the meaning of LABEL before. This is the mechanism LISP uses to load a function name and its definition into the symbol table representing the environment. By writing *label [f; λ [x; y] 2x + y]]* this has the effect of binding *f* to the function λ *[[x; y] 2x + y]]*. LABEL is a *special form* as is LAMBDA and COND. Note that LABEL is dynamic and when the environment in which the label was encountered is exited, the function name and its definition disappear. Labels may be nested within labels.

   Now let's take an example LISP function and see if we can follow what the LISP interpreter does at it tries to evaluate it. For this illustration, I will select a simple function you have seen before, the *length* function of the previous section:

length = λ *[[x][null[x]* → *0; T* → *length[cdr[x]]* + *1]]*

We will compute *length[(A B)]*. The interpreter begins with *evalquote* which invokes *apply* giving

apply[LENGTH;(A B);
((LENGTH(LAMBDA(X)(COND((NULL X)0)
       (T(PLUS 1(LENGTH(CDR X)))))))]

Note how the environment is not NIL, but the definition of *length* has been placed there. Now *apply* invokes *eval* which strips off the function name and re-invokes *apply* giving

apply[(LAMBDA(X)(COND((NULL X)0)
                     (T(PLUS 1(LENGTH(CDR X))))));
(A B);(a)]

We will let *a* stand for the complete function definition of LENGTH stored in the environment. Now *apply* discovers a LAMBDA and calls *eval* plus an inner call to *pairlis*. The latter function will associate X with the value (A B). This gives:

eval[(COND((NULL X)0)(T(PLUS 1(LENGTH(CDR X))))));
      ((X (A B)) a)]

Now *eval* will recognize that it has to evaluate a conditional expression by encountering COND. It does this by calling *evcon*.

[*eval*[(NULL X);((X (A B))a)] → *eval*[0;((X (A B))a)]
T → *evcon*[((T(PLUS 1(LENGTH(CDR X)))));((X (A B))a)]]

From the expression we see that X is not null and so the T clause will be evaluated. Then (CDR X) will be computed followed by the recursive application of *length* to the new argument (B). This will reduce to the S-expression:

(PLUS 1 (PLUS 1 0)

which yields 2 as its result.

12.4. FUNARGs and FEXPRs

Now let's examine the interpreter even more closely. Looking at *eval* and *apply* we see that if a function is supplied with too few arguments, then the result is undefined. But if it is given too many arguments, then they are ignored and the computation proceeds. Let's look more closely at the binding of lambda variables. A problem arises if we have f ::= λ[[x] x + y] and we try to compute f[2]. The 2 would be bound to *x* but no value exists for *y*. However, if we defined a new lambda function λ[[y] f[2]][1], then the computation correctly returns 3, though the binding of *y* occurs with a different λ. As *pairlis* inserts new name-value pairs onto the front of the environment, the entire environment is always available. These considerations lead to the following characterization of variables in LISP.

A variable which is bound by the latest λ is called *local.* Variables which are not bound locally are called, naturally, nonlocal. But nonlocal variables can be distinguished even further. Nonlocal variables may be either potentially bound at some point in the computation or *unbound.* Of the potentially bound variables there are two types. Names such as *car, cdr,* T, NIL we call *global* as they have a predefined meaning. Other nonlocal variables which are λ-bound somewhere in the environment are called *free* variables. Figure 12-3 shows the relationships between free, global, unbound, local, and nonlocal variables in LISP.

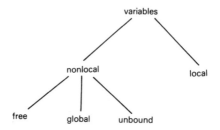

Figure 12-3:   Characterization of Variables in LISP, see [Allen 78]

In LISP, nonlocal variables are bound by finding the most recent mention of that name in the environment. This is called *dynamic binding* and it is in sharp contrast to the ALGOL60 (etc.) static binding rule. A term often used to describe free variables whose bindings are dynamically determined is *fluid variables.*

Now we consider binding as it relates to functions with function parameters and to functions whose result is a function. Consider the function

maplist ::= λ [[fn; x][null[x] → NIL;
        T → cons[fn[car[x]]; maplist[fn; cdr[x]]]]]

This function has two arguments, one that is a function *fn.* If the second argument, *x*, is not null, then *fn* is applied to the *car* of *x* and *maplist* is recursively invoked. If we were to apply *maplist[car,* ((A)(B)(C))] we would like to get

$cons[car[(A)]; \; cons[car[(B)]; \; cons[car[(C)]; \; NIL]]] =$
$cons[A; \; cons[B; \; cons[C; \; NIL]]] =$
(A B C)

But since LISP evaluates all arguments before applying a function how do we suppress the evaluation of *car*? One way is to use QUOTE to give *maplist[quote[car]; x]*. However, things get more complicated when *fn* is replaced by a lambda expression that has free variables. Any such variable is dynamically bound, but we would wish it bound to the value which was current when the functional argument was bound to *fn*. Unfortunately, it gets rebound to a different value. A solution to this problem is to associate the name of the current environment with the function and use that pair as the value of the formal parameter. This association is called a *closure* or *FUNARG*. See section 7.3 for an earlier discussion of closure. To get this process working LISP introduces the word *function* whose one argument is a representation of a function. Its purpose is to construct the closure which was current when the function instance is evaluated.

How do we alter the interpreter to handle funargs? When *eval* encounters (FUNCTION fn), it creates (FUNARGS *fn table*) where *table* is the current environment. In *apply*, FUNARGS is recognized and *table* is used to bind λ-variables. Thus.there are two environments, the *binding environment* of *table* and the current *activation environment*.

In *eval[f; a]* of the interpreter the line is added

$eq[car[f], FUNCTION] \rightarrow list[FUNARG; \; cadr[f]; \; a]$

and in *apply[f; args; a]* we add

$eq[car[f]; FUNARG] \rightarrow apply[cadr[f]; \; args; \; caddr[f]]$

The discussion given here follows [Allen 78].and the reader is advised to look there for more details.

A last word on variables and binding. The imperative based languages such as ALGOL60 advocate static binding for nonlocal variables. Thus, the meaning of free variables is fixed by the surrounding program text and,hence,they are not really free. We have seen that in the LISP interpreter, the function *assoc* finds the current value associated with any name. As the symbol table may contain more than one occurrence of the same name, the name-value pair which is retrieved is the first encountered. Each new level of the symbol table is built on top of the previous table and the previous table is saved by line 8:

eq[*car*[fn]; LAMBDA] → *eval*[*caddr*[*fn*]; *pairlis*[*cadr*[*fn*]; *x*; *a*]]

This call on *eval* creates a new table using *pairlis* and when *eval* returns the old symbol table *a* is restored.

The most general environment which LISP creates is a tree of symbol tables. The previous discussion leads one to believe that a stack is sufficient, but functional arguments and values can generate different branches. Thus, the search for a name can be very long. Moreover, Wegbreit [Wegbreit 71] has observed that variables are infrequently rebound. This implies that the number of bindings of a variable is small compared to the number of environments which may have to be examined to find a particular binding. This leads one to consider an alternative implementation of the symbol table.

An alternate strategy is to turn the symbol table inside out and for each variable name create a list of all of its bindings and the environments these bindings come from. When a new environment is created, its name is added to the environment tree. For each variable a new value is entered along with the associated environment name. To look up a name, the input must contain a branch of the tree. This branch is recursively searched until a binding is found. The new scheme is called *shallow binding* in contrast to *assoc-pairlis* in Table 12-1 which implements *deep binding*.

12.5. The PROG Feature

All the features of LISP which we have seen so far are based on the notion of functional application obeying the principle of referential transparency. Thus, we call this part of LISP, pure LISP or applicative LISP. It turns out that it can be convenient for some problems to express their solution by a series of statements which alter the values in a single, global environment. An imperative feature in a programming language is a command which is executed for its effect on the value of a variable. In an imperative language, statements are executed in the order they appear unless an explicit alteration of the flow occurs. If s_1 and s_2 are two such statements, then $s_1; s_2$ means execute s_1 and then execute s_2. We achieve the same effect in LISP by writing $\lambda[[\lambda]S_2][S_1]$. Though this lambda expression also has a value, the value of S_2, that is usually unimportant.

The main statement in imperative languages is the assignment statement, <variable-name> := <expression>. The effect of this statement is that the expression is evaluated and the result assigned to the "box" whose name is <variable-name>. In the LISP context we can view the assignment statement as a mechanism for passing values to nonlocal variables across lambda expression boundaries. This is called a *side-effect*. The most well-known example of a side-effect in LISP is the *print* function. This function evaluates its argument, yielding say *val*, prints *val* on the system output device and returns *val* as its result. Mathematically, *print* works like the identity function, but its real purpose is its side-effect.

The *prog* feature stands for the program feature in LISP. It includes a set of statements, as opposed to expressions, and a sequencing mechanism which guides their execution. A BNF description of the prog is shown in Table 12-2.

\<prog\>	::= **prog** [[\<prog variables\>]\<prog body.\>]
\<prog body\>	::= \<prog item\>\<prog body\> | \<prog item\>
\<prog item\>	::= \<label\> | \<prog form\>;
\<label\>	::= \<identifier\>
\<progform\>	::=\<applicatn\>|\<condtinl stmt\>|\<assgn stmt\> \<return stmt\> | \<go stmt\>
\<cond stmt\>	::= \<conditional expression\>
\<assign stmt\>	::= \<identifier\> (arrow) \<form\>
\<return stmt\>	::= **return** [\<form\>]
\<go stmt\>	::= **go** [\<form\>]

Table 12-2: Syntax for the LISP Prog Feature

We see in Table 12-2, a prog contains prog variables which are local and similar to λ-variables. Usually these variables are initialized to NIL. The \<prog body\> contains the imperative statements which it executes in left-to-right order. Each \<prog form\> is evaluated as would normally happen in LISP. We see that there are essentially four new statements; the conditional, **return** and **go** which alter the flow of control, and the assignment statement. As with most LISP constructs, the value of the assignment statement is the result of evaluating its right-hand side. The identifier on the left-hand side is searched for in the symbol table. The identifier may be a nonlocal variable. Once it is found, its value is replaced by the value of the right-hand side. This destroys the previous value of the identifier. This is a fundamentally different kind of binding than what we have seen so far. In λ-binding a new value is associated with a new symbol table,and the old value is not lost. But by changing the value of a nonlocal variable, the assignment statement can have a wide ranging effect.

The conditional statement is similar to LISP's conditional expression, but its semantics are somewhat different. If none of the conditions are true, then a conditional expression is undefined, but a conditional statement is defined with value NIL. The next statement in the prog body will then be executed. The **return** statement causes the prog body to be exited and a return made to the caller. As the prog body is exited, all prog variables disappear. The value of the prog is the value of the argument of the **return** statement.

The **go** statement is used in conjunction with a label which names a statement in a prog body. A label is any identifier which occurs by itself in the prog body. A label name may be the same as any λ-variable or prog variable as the interpreter can distinguish the two using their contexts. If the argument of the **go** statement is a label of a prog body, then a transfer of control is affected. But if the argument is not a label, it will be evaluated and the result will be examined to see if it is a label. If not, a re-evaluation is performed, until a label has been found. Prog bodies are examined according to the dynamic chain of their creation, for the first one to contain the label. When the transfer is performed, the appropriate environment must be restored. Note that both the nonlocal **go** statement and the nonlocal **return** are different from the ALGOL60 procedure exit. In the latter case the enclosing control environment is restored, but in the former case any dynamic environment may be restored.

equal ::= λ [[x,y] prog[
p [and[null[x], null[y]] → return[T]];
[or[null[x], null[y]] → return[F]];
[and[atom[car[x]],atom[car[y]]] →
[eq[car[x],car[y]] →
[x ← cdr[x]; y ← cdr[y];
go[p]];
T → return[F]]
T → [or[atom[car[x]],atom[car[y]]]
→ return[F]
T → [equal[car[x],car[y]] →
[x ← cdr[x]; y ← cdr[y];
go[p]];
T → return[F]]]]]]

Table 12-3:   Example of the Prog Feature

In Table 12-3 we see an example of the prog feature describing a function which determines if two lists are equal. If both lists are null, then true is returned. If only one of the lists is null, then false is returned. Otherwise we check if the car of both lists is an atom. If so and the atoms are equal then x and y are assigned to the *cdr* of their respective lists and a branch back to label p is made. If only one list has a first element which is an atom and the other does not, then false is returned. Otherwise *equal* is recursively applied to the front of both lists. If the result is true, then x and y are moved to the *cdr* of their lists, and *go[p]* is executed. Otherwise the result returned is false.

Our next consideration is the mapping of the prog statements into S-expressions so that we maintain our mapping of LISP forms onto S-expressions. A form such as

$$prog[[x_1;...;x_n]...]$$

becomes

$$(PROG\ (x1\ x2\ xN)...)$$

An assignment such as $x \leftarrow y$ becomes (SETQ X Y). We observe that SETQ must be a special form for we want to suppress the evaluation of its first argument and only evaluate its second argument. LISP allows both arguments to be evaluated if one writes instead (SET X Y). Using SET one can simulate SETQ by writing (SET (QUOTE X)(Y)). A translation of the *equal* prog body is shown in Table 12-4.

```
(LAMBDA (X Y)
    (PROG
        P(COND (AND(NULL (X) NULL(Y)) (RETURN T))
            (OR(NULL(X) NULL(Y)) (RETURN F))
            (AND(ATOM(CAR X) ATOM(CAR Y))
                (COND( EQ(CAR X CAR Y)
                    ((SETQ X (CDR X))
                    (SETQ Y (CDR Y))
                    (GO P)))
                (T (RETURN F))))
            (T (COND (OR(ATOM(CAR X) ATOM(CAR Y))
                (RETURN F))
            (T (COND(EQUAL(CAR X CAR Y)
                ((SETQ X (CDR X))
                (SETQ Y (CDR Y))
                (GO P)))
                (T RETURN F)))))))))
```

Table 12-4: Translation of EQUAL

12.6. Delayed Evaluation

Though LISP has decided to use call-by-value for all evaluations, that is by no means an unalterable decision. It is possible to consider an alternative we have already discussed earlier in Chapter 7, call-by-name. Using call-by-name implies that the unevaluated arguments are substituted for the formal parameters, and it is not until a formal parameter is encountered at execution time that the corresponding actual is evaluated. Since an actual parameter may be an expression, we must bind it to the environment which exists on entry to the procedure. This, as we've seen before, is called a closure.

The advantage of this new LISP evaluator is that it will not evaluate a parameter until it actually needs it. If an actual parameter is not used in the computation, then the computation proceeds and may well terminate even if the evaluated actual parameter leads to a nonterminating computation. The disadvantage of this scheme is its inefficiency, as every time a LISP variable that is a formal parameter is encountered, it will be re-evaluated. If the re-evaluation contains no side-effects, then these extra evaluations are unnecessary.

There is a modification of the call-by-name scheme which attempts to avoid the inefficiency. The basic idea is that once a formal parameter is evaluated for the first time, we alter the symbol table replacing the actual parameter by its value.   All subsequent references to this parameter simply retrieve the value in the symbol table. Clearly, this scheme does not work in the presence of side-effects. It is referred to as *call-by-need.*

In its most general form call-by-need or lazy evaluation will mean that the following set of evaluation rules will apply:

1. evaluating all arguments of *cons* are delayed;
2. evaluating all definitions of nested lambda expressions are delayed;
3. evaluating all arguments of user defined functions are delayed;
4. all arguments of elementary functions, all conditional tests and all functional applications are evaluated immediately.

These rules are given by Henderson in [Henderson 80]. To see the usefulness of lazy evaluation we consider a well-known problem from functional programming called *samefringe*. Given two binary trees, the problem is to write a function which determines if their leaf nodes occur in the same order, irrespective of the shape of the tree. For example, the trees represented by the lists (A B C), (A (B C)), and (A (B(C)))) all have the same fringe. The obvious way to solve this problem is to flatten the two input trees by constructing a list of their leaves. Then the two lists are checked for equality. This solution is shown in Table 12-5.

samefringe[x; y] ::= equalist[flatten[x]; flatten[y]]
equalist[x; y] ::= [null[x] → null[y];
null[y] → F;
eq[car[x]; car[y]] → equalist[cdr[x]; cdr[y]]
T → F]
flatten[x] ::= [atom[x] → cons[x; NIL];
T → append[flatten[car[x]]; flatten[cdr[x]]]]

Table 12-5:   One Solution of the SameFringe Problem, [Henderson 80]

The problem with this solution is that even if the two trees differ in their first leaf position, this program will have to traverse both of the trees to create their flattened fringes.   A superior program would prevent any such extra computation by checking the respective leaf nodes and terminating as soon as a difference is found.   And this is precisely what will happen when the function in Table 12-5 is executed using lazy evaluation.
Consider the inputs(A . (B . C)) and ((A . B) . (C . D)) to *samefringe.* After one step we get

equalist[append[flatten[A]; flatten[(B.C)]];
append[flatten[(A.B)]; flatten[(C.D)]]]

This occurs since the conditional test is forced in *flatten.*   Evaluating more we get

equalist[append[cons[A; NIL]; append[flatten[B]; flatten[C]]];
append[append[flatten[A]; flatten[B]]; append[flatten[C]; [flatten[D]]]]

Now using the definition of *append* we get

equalist[cons[A; append[NIL; append[flatten[B]; flatten[C]]]];
append[cons[A;append[NIL;cons[B;NIL]]]; append[flatten[C]; flatten[D]]]]

which, forcing the list in *append,* becomes

equalist[cons[A; append[flatten[B]; flatten[C]]];
cons[A; append[cons[B; NIL]; append[flatten[C]; flatten[D]]]]]

Now we can apply the conditional tests in *equalist* and since neither argument is NIL we get

[eq[A; A] → *equalist[append[flatten[B]; flatten[C]];*
append[cons[B; NIL]; append[flatten[C]; flatten[D]]]]
T → *F]*

which becomes

equalist[append[flatten[B]; flatten[C]];
append[cons[B; NIL]; append[flatten[C]; flatten[D]]]]

At this point we can see what is happening. Using lazy evaluation, the elements of the fringes of the trees are being checked one by one. As long as they are equal, the process continues, but once they are unequal, false is returned and the entire process completes. This avoids the unnecessary computation which could result from first constructing the fringes of both trees and then testing for equality. So lazy evaluation in this case makes for an efficient program.

Concepts Discussed in This Chapter

Accumulating parameter
Atoms
Applicative programming
Conditional expression
Delayed evaluation
Environment
Function, partial
  pure
  strict
  total
Fexprs
Funargs

Functional programming
LISP
LISP interpreter
Referential transparency
Side-effects
S-expression
Variables, bound
  unbound
  free
  local
  nonlocal

Exercises

1. Consider the following three definitions of *append*

    append[x; y] : = **if** *null[x]* **then** *y*
          else *cons[car[x]; append[cdr[x]; y]]*

    append[x; y] :: = **if** *null[x]* **then**
          if *null[y]* **then** *NIL* **else** *y*
        else if *null[y]* **then** *x*
          else *cons[car[x]; append[cdr[x]; y]]*

    append[x; y] :: = **if** *null[y]* **then** *x*
        else *appendspecial(x,y)*

    appendspecial[x; y] :: = **if** *null[x]* **then** *y*
      else *cons[car[y]; appendspecial[cdr[x]; y]]*

    Compare these versions with the version in the text. Which is the most efficient and why?
2. Design a function which computes the product of a list of integers.
3. Design a function *access[list; i]* which returns the *i*th value in the list.
4. Design a function *union[x; y]* which returns a list which is

the union of two sets represented as lists x and y.

5. What is the result of *eq[A; A]*, *eq[(A); A]*, *eq[(A); (A)]*?

6. The following LISP function computes the nth Fibonacci number

$$fib[n] ::= [eq[n; 0] \rightarrow 0;\ eq[n; 1] \rightarrow 1$$
$$T \rightarrow fib[n\text{-}1] + fib[n\text{-}2]]$$

How many calls to *fib* are made? Use the accumulation of parameters technique to write a Fibonacci program which makes only *n* calls or less of any function it uses.

7. Design a LISP function which computes the depth of a list where

depth[NIL] = 0; depth[(A)] = 1; depth[(A (B (C)))] = 3

8. How would you describe the difference between NIL, (NIL) and (NIL.NIL)?

9. Consider the function

$$f[s] ::= [atom[s] \rightarrow s;\ T \rightarrow cons[f[cdr[s]];\ f[car[s]]]]$$

Is this function partial or total? What is the value of f[A], f[(A . B)], f[(A B)]?

10. Consider the function

$$findit[x; y] ::= [atom[x] \rightarrow [eq[x; y] \rightarrow T;\ T \rightarrow NIL;$$
$$T \rightarrow cons[findit[car[x];y];\ findit[cdr[x];y]]]$$

What does *findit* do? Is *findit* partial or total. Evaluate *findit[(A.B); A]; findit[(A.(B.C)); B]; findit[(A.B); (A.B)]*.

11. Consider the LISP function

$$reverse[x;\ y] = [null[x] \rightarrow y;\ T \rightarrow reverse[cdr[x];\ concat[car[x];\ y]]]$$

and its iterative equivalent

$$reverse[x;\ y] = prog[[\ ]\ |\ [null[x] \rightarrow return[y]]$$
$$y \rightarrow concat[car[x];\ y];$$
$$x \rightarrow cdr[x]$$
$$go[l]]$$

Your job is to write a LISP function which takes recursively defined LISP functions and translates them into equivalent iterative ones.

Chapter 13

DATA FLOW PROGRAMMING
LANGUAGES

13.1. The Data Flow Model

The advancement of the speed of computers has been phenomenal over the past two decades. There have been several orders of magnitude improvement, so that now processors exist with cycle times of a few nanoseconds that can execute several million instructions in a second. Nevertheless, the demand for computing cycles has outstripped even these gains. Compute bound jobs such as weather prediction, simulation, and monte-carlo analysis can require execution speeds in the billions of instructions per second. Therefore the search for faster computers goes on.

But on one level this search is beginning to run into critical problems. As hardware designers continue to try to make elementary components smaller, they are running up against physical limitations. For example as the size of connectors is made smaller, the resistance per unit length of a conductor scales up quadratically. This requires additional circuitry, thus eliminating much of the gain. Therefore, one cannot expect to improve processor speed much more by placing components closer together. Another factor is the amount of power versus the cooling required as circuits become densely packed. This ratio has been growing very fast to the extent that the newest super-computers will have to be super-cooled in order to get them to achieve super speeds. For example, circuits built using Josephson junction technology must be cooled to only 4 degrees above absolute zero by immersion in liquid helium. In short, the approach of focusing on the central processing unit and trying to speed up its circuitry does not appear capable of sustaining the orders of improvement that have been achieved in the past.

But this is not the only means that has been investigated for achieving faster computation speeds. Other solutions have included the creation of special purpose processors such as array processors, vector machines, and multiprocessors. An array processor is a machine which uses pipelining to speed up the application of a single instruction on an array of data. This paradigm of computing is essential in many important algorithms such as the fast Fourier transform. Adding an array processor to a medium scale computer can have the effect of turning it into a "number-cruncher" for certain kinds of problems. This is a very cost-effective approach to improved computing. But one problem with this approach is that array processors are not easily programmable. Usually one must program in a baroque assembly language in order to get the array processor to perform new tasks. For essential tasks such as the FFT, the programming effort is worth it, but the complexity of programming does preclude using this approach in a more general way. Another approach to improving the speed of computers has been to "vectorize" the source code. This consists of having a post processor which takes, e.g. Fortran code, and tries to determine when an operation is being applied to a vector of values. This approach has not been especially successful chiefly because existing programming languages force programmers to strictly order their computations. and this ordering is difficult to unravel. Another approach to faster computation is the construction of a multiprocessor, that is a set of processing elements connected together and perhaps sharing a common memory. One of the serious problems here is how to schedule the computational tasks so that a near maximum of parallel operation is achieved. This approach has suffered from the appearance of bottlenecks which all but reduce the multiprocessor's speed to that of a uniprocessor and in some cases to a slow one.

What we intend to examine in this chapter is another approach to fast computing, the data flow model of computation. This model offers an entirely new way of viewing the execution of programs. Its virtue appears to be a simple and elegant way to take advantage of any parallelism which is inherent in a task without requiring the programmer to explicitly communicate it to the language translator. Up to this time only a few prototype computers for implementing this model have been built. Therefore,it is too early to know if the data flow computer will be a success. But, as it offers us a completely different way of viewing computations, as opposed to the classical von Neumann machine, I feel it is worthwhile discussing it here. Moreover,there are many interesting implications for programming language design which stem from the data flow model and that will be my primary emphasis in this chapter.

The data flow model consists of a graph of a program where the nodes represent operations and the data flows along the arcs. Consider the following program written in a conventional programming language

    1 A = P - Q
    2 B = A/P
    3 C = Q * B
    4 D = A + B
    5 E = A * B - C
    6 ANSWER = D * E

If one looks at these statements,one can easily see that the statements need not be executed strictly in the order they are listed. Though the order as given, [1, 2, 3, 4, 5, 6] is a perfectly legal execution sequence, so would be [1, 2, 3, 5, 4, 6] or even [1, 2, (3 and 4 simultaneously), 5, 6]. If we look at the data graph which is produced by this set of six statements, we can see the potential alternatives clearly exposed. In Figure 13-1(a) we see six nodes and nine directed edges. The nodes show the data item which is computed while the edges give the dependencies of one node upon another. This is nothing more than the precedence graph of that computation. In this graph an assignment statement can be executed as soon as all the nodes with arrows pointing to this node have been executed. In Figure 13-1(b) we see an equivalent representation of the data flow graph. Here the nodes represent operations and the edges carry the values which are produced. Notice that the variable names are no longer needed. It is clear from the diagram that once nodes 1 and 2 complete their operations, nodes 3, 4 and 5a may be executed in parallel. The graph in Figure 13-1(b) is the way data flow graphs are usually drawn. See [Ackerman 82] for other examples of programs and their data flow graphs.

One virtue of this data flow model is that it automatically exposes any inherent parallelism, without the need for the programmer to explicitly designate it. Note that inputs which enter a node are computed on a first-in-first-out basis. No fan-in of arcs is permitted and,hence,no data values can become interleaved with others producing improper combinations of data. Thus,we say that the data flow graph produces

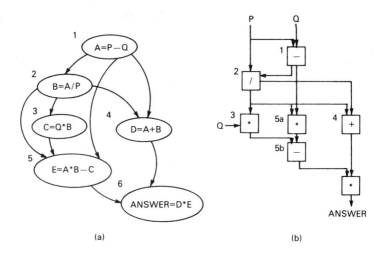

Figure 13-1:   A Data Graph for Six Assignment Statements

determinate execution.   Another advantage is the fact that there is no global data base from which values are retrieved and stored. Equivalently there are no side-effects as exist in conventional imperative programming language models.   Therefore, any errors which are produced are directly traceable to the original specification of the graph. Perhaps more importantly, these errors are always reproducible as they do not arise from race conditions as can be the case in conventional concurrent programming.   A *data flow programming language* is a higher level language which is translated into a data flow graph and subsequently run on a data flow computer.   A *data flow computer* is a machine which executes programs that are expressed in the data flow graph model.   In the next section we will look briefly at one proposed data flow machine.   Then in the following section we will get to our real purpose which is to study a data flow programming language.

So far we have only seen a primitive form of data flow graph, namely one for the evaluation of an expression.   In order to be able to handle programs of various sorts one needs to introduce more than just operation nodes.   One such node is termed a *conditional construction* and it comes in several forms.   These nodes produce selective routing of the data values as they move within the graph as shown in Figure 13-2.   In Figure 13-2 we see two small circles and two ovals.   The circles are

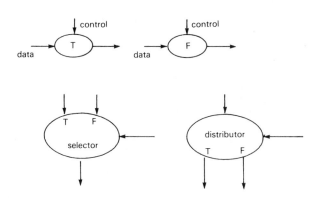

Figure 13-2: Some Conditional Nodes in a Data Flow Graph

labeled T for true and F for false. When a T node receives a true signal it opens and allows the next data item on its incoming arc to pass through. Otherwise it absorbs the data item. Similarly for the node labeled F. The oval nodes are called a *selector* and a *distributor* node. For example, the selector node has three input arcs and one output arc. Its mode of operation proceeds as follows: first a data value from the horizontal direction enters the node. This value is Boolean. If it is true, then the selector node will wait until a data value appears at the arc marked T. It will allow this value to pass through it and out the bottom. Similarly if the original data value is false, only a data item from the edge marked F will be permitted to pass through. It does not absorb the other choice. The distributor works in a similar fashion. A Boolean value is accepted from the horizontal arc. This determines whether the next input data item from the top will be passed to the edge labelled T or F. For a more complete discussion of data flow graphs and the variety of nodes needed to express a program one should read [Davis 82].

We are now ready to view a program and its corresponding data graph. This program is written in the data flow language called VAL, [Dennis 79]. VAL is more fully discussed in section 13.3. Consider the program *TEST* in Table 13-1. The procedure TEST is simple enough. Two items *a* and *b* are parameters. First the local variables *r, s* are initialized to values *b, 0* respectively. These two assignments are followed by a **do-if-iter** loop which terminates when $s = a$. Within the

```
      function TEST(a, b : integer returns integer)
        for r, s : integer := b, 0;
    do if s ≠ a then iter
        r, s := if r > 0 then  r/2, s+1
                  else  3*r, s+1 endif
      enditer
      else r endif
    endfor
  endfun
  end TEST
```

Table 13-1:   A Sample Data Flow Program

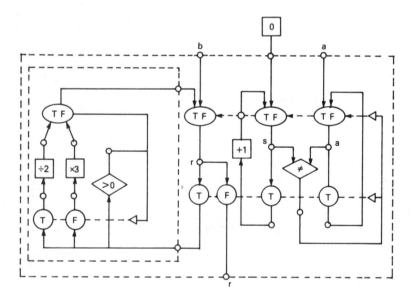

Figure 13-3:   A Data Flow Graph for Program TEST

iter clause is an **if** expression which assigns values to r, s depending upon the value of r. In either case the value of s is increased by 1 each time. When $s = a$, then r is returned as the result. (The reader is cautioned that the purpose of *TEST* is merely to demonstrate the underlying data graph structure and does not necessarily accomplish anything when viewed by itself.) In Figure 13-3 we see the corresponding data flow graph for *TEST*. There are operation nodes containing multiplication, division and plus one. There are comparison nodes performing not equal and greater-than-zero. The result of these nodes is a Boolean value. There are four selector nodes and several nodes marked T or F. Nodes marked T are "opened" when a Boolean value true is passed through them and they are "closed" otherwise. Similarly nodes marked F are normally closed unless a Boolean value F is passed though them. Initially the selector nodes are enabled to F.

We see in the data flow graph of *TEST* the two inputs and the zero value at the top. These values are entered into selector nodes and passed through. The data items marked *s* and *a* are replicated and sent into the comparison box. If the comparison box produces a true value, then three of the four circular nodes will be opened, and at the same time three selector boxes will be enabled to true. Therefore, *s* will be increased by one and *a* will be passed through the selector again. At the same time, *b* has become *r*, has passed through the node marked T and flows to the comparison box. If the value is greater than one, then true enables both the selector and permits the value to be divided by 2.

Before we examine what a higher level programming language for data flow would look like, we should consider at least one form of machine architecture which would support such a system. We note that it is not necessary to build a machine which processes data flow graphs. On the contrary, one could translate a data flow graph into a set of instructions which could be run on a conventional machine. However, doing this would lose all the advantages of parallelism which were gained by using the data flow graph model in the first place. Thus, the strategy has been to try and define directly a machine which would process these graphs.

One of the difficulties in building such an architecture is the fact that to gain maximum parallelism one has to permit more than one token to travel along an edge. This could be accomplished by having the data values carry with them identifying information, a label, that would say in what context this data item should be included. This type of architecture is called a *dynamic tagged data flow model*. Another difficulty that was uncovered is that data structures have to be treated as whole objects rather than a collection of constituent parts. This is needed to maintain the clean semantics of data flow, i.e., all operations are side-effect free. But a consequence is that the entire data structure must be copied whenever it is to be used in another setting. Also time and space consuming is the fact that as no data structure can be operated upon before it is copied, one must wait until any update operations are completed. This tends to limit parallelism. These problems have caused delays in the development of practical data flow machines.

For our purposes here, let's look briefly at one specific machine architecture. The one I have chosen is a machine which was constructed in Manchester, England by Watson and Gurd, see [Watson 82]. The high-level design is shown in Figure 13-4.

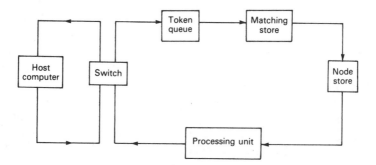

Figure 13-4: The Manchester Data Flow Machine

The machine consists of five basic components plus a conventional host computer that provides input and output services. The various components are connected in a ring as shown, and the data values with their label travel around the ring.

When a new data item is produced by a node in the processing unit, this value goes around the ring to the token queue. Here it is temporarily stored. The matching unit's job is to gather tokens together which are required for the firing of a node. When a token arrives, it looks for its other partners, and if they are not all there, it waits. The operation of the matching store is via an associative memory. Once all of the required data tokens have arrived, they proceed to the node store where it is determined what new node they need to be sent to, based upon the data flow graph. They are then sent to the processing unit where the node is executed on the appropriate data items.

13.2. Language Design Goals

In order to make best use of a data flow computer, it is desirable to have a high level language in which one can adequately express programs and for which those programs can be adequately translated into data flow graphs. If instead, people attempted to use a conventional high level language like PL/1 or Pascal and tried to produce data flow graphs, the result would be far from satisfactory as too much sequential detail is forced upon the programmer. There are several key elements, first stated by Ackerman [Ackerman 82], which influence the design of any dataflow language. These are:

- □ *no side-effects.* As we saw before when examining data flow graphs, there is no global data space of values. Each node is a self-contained function. Thus, a dataflow language must not permit side effects. We have already seen languages which permit no side-effects, pure-LISP in Chapter 12 and Backus' FP, [Backus 78].
- □ *locality of effect.* This means that the data produced at one node does not have some long-term effect somewhere else, but is used immediately afterwards. This has important consequences on the scope rules of a dataflow language.
- □ *the single assignment rule.* A variable may appear on the left-hand side of an assignment statement only once within a given program.
- □ *unusual forms of iteration* must exist, due to the insistence of no side-effects, the application of the single assignment rule, and the desire to express parallelism.

In this section, these aspects are examined in some detail so we can begin to understand why higher level data flow programming languages have the form they do.

If we look back at the six statement program at the beginning of this chapter, we see that the variables A, B, C, D, and E can be viewed merely as placeholders for intermediate computations. Though other sections of code might use the same variable name, the computation is unrelated and the logic of the program might permit these two sets of computations to be done in parallel. However, the use of the same variable name implies that a dependency exists. It is often very hard for a compiler to determine that a real dependency does not exist, (think of the problems caused by branches among the code). Though notions such as scope restrict the range over which names can have an effect, these are only partial corrections to a more pervasive problem. The conclusion in terms of language design is that instructions will have only a local effect and not a global one.

The need to ensure lack of side-effects is a more severe constraint on a programming language. The most common form of side-effect is when a procedure modifies a global variable. Therefore, a data flow programming language must disallow this. Another form of side-effect is when a procedure changes one of its parameters. Even this must be disallowed. Another problem arises when we consider the handling of structured values such as arrays and records. In conventional programming languages these structures are selectively modified, which is a side-effect. The only solution is to treat arrays and records as values and to create an entirely new structure whenever a modification is needed. The feature known as aliasing, discussed in Chapters 4 and 7, makes the problem of discovering concurrency more difficult. For example consider the procedure

```
type table = array [1 .. 100] of integer;
procedure TABLEPLUSONE(var P, Q : table);
  for i := 1 to 99 do
      Q[i+1] := P[i] + 1;
end
```

In procedure *TABLEPLUSONE* the values of P have one added to them and are then copied into Q. If this procedure were considered by a data flow processor it would appear that P and Q are distinct and, therefore, the 100 assignments can be done in parallel. However, if the procedure is invoked as "**procedure** *TABLEPLUSONE(A, A)*" then the assignments could interfere with each other. Even more complications exist and are detailed by Ackerman in [Ackerman 82].

One way of removing aliasing and side-effects in parameters is to require the call-by-value mechanism for all parameter passing. But the data flow model actually extends way beyond just a restrictive form of parameter passing. A fundamental shift is made from a programming world where people deal with objects to a world populated by values. Integers, reals, Booleans, pointers, arrays, records, and sets are all viewed as values. In the tradition of pure-Lisp, only functional applications are permitted. This has a big influence, for example on arrays, in data flow. When viewed as values, they may have non-consecutive bounds and may be altered dynamically. All array operations produce an entirely new array and thus parallel operations can be naturally performed, though at the expense of copying. Moreover, in dataflow functions are generalized so that they may return values of any type, scalar or structured.

Given the fact that the data flow language must be applicative and value-oriented, where does that leave the assignment statement? In conventional languages the purpose of this statement is to bind a location with a value to a name for later use. In dataflow, the purpose of assignment is to bind a value to a name. The value can only be accessed by that name and the use of the name is just a shorthand for the expression it represents. Thus, assignment statements are now much closer to mathematical formulas. A statement such as "A = B + C" is nothing more than an equation in the conventional mathematical sense. The relationship that A is equal to the sum of B plus C should hold throughout the scope of the names A, B, and C. In dataflow, assignment statements should be viewed as definitions of equality. In the literature languages which use this interpretation of assignment are called *definitional languages*. As Ackerman points out in [Ackerman 82], definitional languages support program verification as the assignments in the program are equivalent to the assertions which are made to verify the program's correctness. This contrasts sharply with conventional imperative languages where an assignment such as "A = B + C" must be checked for all possible flows of control through that statement. The one thing which could spoil this nice property of definitional languages is permitting the use of the same name on the left-hand side of assignment more than once. Thus, the single assignment rule is employed to maintain the benefit of this feature. Another statement which is ruled out of definitional languages is "A = A + 1". In a definitional setting it makes no sense. Note that it is not really necessary for a data flow language to insist on the single assignment rule. Instead one could permit the scope of a variable to extend to the point where it is re-used. But in practice most definitional languages do employ it.

Despite the fact that we have been insisting that a purely applicative approach is what is called for in a data flow language, it is necessary to recognize the importance of iteration. As a paradigm for expressing certain computations, iteration plays a central role. Of course, all iterations can be rewritten in a recursive format, but an iterative construction is often clearer. Therefore, a practical data flow language must somehow provide iteration. Since the variables within the body of an iteration are changed each time through the loop, and often these changes depend upon the values of the loop variables, these requirements appear to violate the single assignment rule. In fact, they do and the only consolation is that the single assignment rule can be obeyed for each cycle. Data flow language designers must determine how to insert iteration into their language while maintaining to as great a degree as possible the various constraints discussed before. Observe that the redefinition of variables can take place only before beginning each new cycle. During each new cycle the single assignment rule should be obeyed. As for a loss of parallelism, if the values in one cycle depend upon the values in a previous cycle, then parallelism is not possible. However the language designer must supply a means whereby the programmer can express the fact that cycles are independent of each other or let the compiler do it. Another reason to violate the purely applicative nature of data flow comes from the need to perform input/output, which is inevitably a side-effect.

In the next section, we will examine in some detail a data flow programming language called VAL. Our purpose will be to see how all of the issues raised here are handled in one dataflow programming language.

13.3. VAL - A Data Flow Programming Language

VAL is a higher level programming language whose design was influenced by the fact it is intended to be run on a data flow machine. It was developed by Jack Dennis and a group of researchers at MIT, [Dennis 79]. It is of special interest to us because on the one hand it incorporates many features of a modern imperative programming language. In fact, in many ways it is modeled after CLU, see [Liskov 78].

The built-in data types of VAL are **Boolean**, **integer**, **real**, and **character**. Each of the types have the conventional set of operations included in the language. New types may be constructed by the structured operators **array**, **record** and **oneof**. The first two are certainly familiar and the third comes from CLU and is a means for defining a union of data types. One aspect of types in VAL which is different than in other languages is the fact that there exists error values for each type. Moreover the structured types have some rules which are unusual as we shall see.

An array type is unusual because its bounds are not part of the type. Only the index set and the component type are part of the array definition. If one writes

type *table* = **array** *[integer]*;

the length of the array is not part of the type definition and type *table* represents all one-dimensional arrays of integers. In one sense this is an improvement over Pascal where one has to create different procedures for different size arrays.   Another advantage is that many more kinds of operations are possible.   One can add new elements at either end of an array, or concatenate two arrays or merge them or delete elements at either end.   Clearly, string manipulation can be accomplished by using arrays of type character.

In VAL two types are equivalent if their defining structures are identical.   The language is strongly typed in the sense that all type checking can be done at compile-time.   All functions supply a value of a given type and all actual parameters are checked for type agreement with the formal parameters.   There is no automatic coercion from one type to another.   Some of the special error values are **undef** for undefined, **pos_over** for positive overflow, **miss_elt** for missing array element and **unknown**.   The reason for of having these elements is that they permit the handling of run-time errors without violating the type compatibility rules.

As discussed in the previous section, the environment of VAL consists of values.   These values are assigned to variables whose value can then no longer be changed .   Thus, we say that variables are *immutable*.   A variable is immutable within its scope of access, i.e. within a function or a block.   Arrays and records are treated as if they were scalars, as if they represented a single value.   Thus, they are never modified, but entirely new arrays or records are built.   At least these building operations can be done in parallel thereby mitigating the inefficiency of having to recreate an entire array when only a few elements are altered.

As VAL is purely applicative it contains no statements, only functions and expressions. This is identical to pure-LISP.   For example in place of an **if-then-else** statement there is

conditional := **if** expression **then** expression
{**elseif** expression **then** expression}
else expression **endif**

It is possible to create an environment immediately prior to entering an expression.   This is done by the **let-in** clause which provides a list of identifier-value bindings.   All of the bindings are released at the end of the **let-in** phrase.   For example,

let *x : real; t : real*
t := a + 3.5;
x := t + 2.9;
in *t*x* **endlet**

In this example a is imported into the environment while t and x are local names. The result of the **let-in** is the expression t^*x.

An unusual feature of functions in VAL is that they can return more than one value. The way this is specified within the function is by writing a list of expressions separated by commas. At the call site one might write

> $x : real,$
> $y : integer,$
> $z : Boolean := TRIPLE(items);$

The function *TRIPLE* returns three items: a real, integer and Boolean value which are assigned to x, y, and z respectively.

Parallel expressions in VAL consist of three parts: a range specification, environment expansion, and result accumulation. For example the **forall** statement in VAL is designed so that a parallel set of statements exist in the body. The body of the **forall** contains an environment expansion area as in the **let-in** expression. The **forall** causes an execution to proceed once for each element in the body. These executions may be done in parallel. At the conclusion, a means is provided for collecting the results together, called **construct**, which permits each parallel path to generate a value which turns into an array element. There is a second way to accumulate the results in a **forall**, given by the **eval** operator. Here values generated from each path are merged into a single result immediately as they are formed. This form of merging requires a binary operator, such as **times**, and hence, the computations can be done as a balanced binary tree thereby getting (in theory) *log* performance. Finally the **forall** may produce more than one value using combinations of **construct** and **eval**. The BNF for **forall** is shown below.

> forall-exp ::=
>   **forall** value-name **in** [expression] { , value-name **in** [expression]}
>   [declaration-definition part]
>   forall-body-part {forall-body-part} **endall**
>
> forall-body-part ::= **construct** expression |**eval** forall-op expression
>
> forall-op ::= **plus** | **times** | **min** | **max** | **or** | **and**

For two small examples of **forall** consider

> **forall** J **in** $[1, N]$
>   **eval plus** J^*J+J **endall**

forall *J* in *[1, 4]*
   X : **real** := *nthpower*(**real** (*J*), *J*);
  construct *J*, *X*
endall

The first **forall** expression computes the sum of $J*J+J$ for values of J from 1 to N. The second example creates two arrays, J and X, whose indices range from 1 to 4. The first array contains the values 1 to 4. The second array contains the value of J raised to the Jth power. The real virtue of the **forall** is that each execution path is a separate and independent computation which can proceed at its own pace. Therefore, any degree of concurrency which the underlying machine is capable of achieving can be employed here. Moreover, within each of the separate paths, there may exist steps which can be performed concurrently.

It is undesirable to avoid all forms of sequential operation in a data flow language. In particular there is a need for instructions which control the sequencing of operations such as an **if-then-else** statement does in a more conventional language. In VAL there exists an **if-then-else** expression (shown before) and a form of **case** expression. Also, there exists a **for-iter** expression which is used for describing loops that cannot execute in parallel because the values produced on one iteration are used in the subsequent cycle. For these three expressions a conditional clause exists and VAL insures that no result operation can start to execute until that conditional expression completes and chooses an action to be performed. For example, the **case** in VAL is shown in Table 13-2.

In the first example in Table 13-2, X is a union of types. Within the **tagcase** P is assigned the value of expression X. Then if P has tag A or C, then the result returned is *expression1*. If P has tag B, the result returned is *expression2*. In the second example the type *list* defines a union of either empty or a record, one of whose components is of type *list*. First the variables T and U are assigned initial values. Z is the selector expression of the **tagcase**. If Z is empty, then the result is U. Otherwise an iteration is begun. T and U are assigned to $Z.rest$ and a new list formed by **make** respectively. As one can see the purpose of this segment of VAL code is to produce as the value of U the reverse of the original list.

A **for** expression in VAL has two parts: the loop initialization and the body. All loop parameters must be declared and initialized before the body is entered. The loop body is an expression which is executed repeatedly until a final result can be returned. The **iter** clauses produce

```
tagcase-exp ::= tagcase [valuename :=] expression [ ; ]
                   taglist : expression {taglist : expression}
                   [otherwise expression]
              endtag
```

```
taglist ::= tag tagname { , tagname }
```

Two examples of the **tagcase** follow:
X is **oneof** *[A :* **integer***; B :* **real***; C :* **integer***]*

```
tagcase P := X
   tag A, C : expression1
   tag B : expression2
 endtag
```

```
type list = oneof [empty : null; nonempty :
                    record [item : real; rest : list]]
```

```
for T, U : list := input, make list[empty : nil];
 do  tagcase Z := T;
      tag empty : U
      tag nonempty:
            iter T, U := Z.rest,
                  make list[nonempty : record[item : Z.item; rest : U]
            enditer
       endtag
endfor
```

Table 13-2:   The case expression in VAL

re-evaluation of the entire loop body, but with new bindings for the loop parameters. In Table 13-3 there are three examples of iteration selected from the VAL reference manual, [Ackerman 79]. The first example is the factorial function. The second example computes the greatest common divisor (gcd) of two integers using Euclid's algorithm. The last example is Newton's method for determining the square root of X.

VAL does not permit recursive functions as the implementors considered recursion too difficult to implement in conjunction with the data flow model.

A final important feature of VAL is the handling of errors. One consequence of using the data flow model is that stopping an operation in the middle is very difficult. This is because so many things could potentially be happening at once. The solution in VAL is that no operation can abort, but if something does go wrong it returns a legal error value which is predefined. Moreover this error value must agree in type with the operation result type. Then VAL defines within it certain operations for testing the presence of these error values. Eight of the error values in VAL are

pos_over,	numbers which exceed the machine capacity
neg_over,	negative numbers which exceed the machines capacity
pos_under,	numbers known to require greater precision than available
neg_under,	same as above but negative numbers
zero_divide,	result of division by zero
miss_elt,	result of trying to access an undefined array element
unknown,	an unknown number
undef,	produced for all other error conditions

The error value **undef** belongs to all types, but the others belong only to their appropriate type. One should note that for the Boolean data type, there are now three possible results: true, false, and **undef**. As a consequence, "**undef** = **undef**" results not in the value true but in **undef**.

The statements in VAL are capable of handling arguments where one or more are these error values. For example, if the conditional expression in an **if-then-else** expression is undefined then the result is undefined. Or adding a nonegative number to a **pos_over** number yields a **pos_over** result.

The real advantage of VAL is that it needs no features for describing concurrency or synchronization. The programmer does not have to supply any ordering on the computations beyond what is required by the

for Y *:* **integer** *:= 1; P :* **integer** *:= N*
  do if $P \neq 1$ **then iter** $Y := Y*P; P := P-1$
                enditer
                else Y
    endif
  endfor

for X, Y *: integer :=* **if** $abs(U) > abs(V)$ **then** $abs(U), abs(V)$
                                else $abs(V), abs(U)$
                endif
do if $X \neq Y$ **then if** $X-Y > Y$ **then iter** $X, Y := X-Y, Y$
                        enditer
                      else iter $X, Y := Y, X-Y$
                        enditer
              endif
              else X
endfor

for T *: real :=* $X;$
do **let** D *: real :=* $(X/T-T)/2;$
   in if $D < eps$ **then** T
     else iter $T := T+D;$ **enditer**
      endif
   endlet
endfor

Table 13-3:   Three Examples from VAL

algorithm. Thus, the ease of writing programs is no worse and in many instances easier than for conventional programming languages. Perhaps the greatest weakness in VAL is the lack of recursion and the nonexistent input/output. The reader is advised to consult [McGraw 82] for a more thorough analysis of VAL.

Concepts Discussed in This Chapter

Applicative languages
Data flow model
Definitional language
Determinate execution
Dynamic tagged data flow model
Selector nodes
Side-effects
Single assignment rule

Exercises

1. Investigate another data flow language other than VAL. For example consider the language called ID developed by Arvind and Gostelow.
2. Write a VAL function which implements the data structure Stack. Then do the same for the data structure Queue.
3. The selector and distributor nodes can be built using the more primitive True and False nodes. Give diagrams which show these constructions.
4. In the VAL program which computes N!, what would happen if the statements within the **iter** clause were interchanged?
5. Show how one can add a **case** statement in VAL of the form: **case** i **of** S1, . . . , Sn **endcase**.
6. Get a copy of the VAL reference manual, [VAL], and make a comparison of the typing mechanisms of Pascal and VAL.

Chapter 14

OBJECT ORIENTED PROGRAMMING LANGUAGES

Tim Rentsch

The term "object oriented" is used to describe much of the work and many of the systems being done in Computer Science today. Applied in diverse areas, this trendy phrase has come to mean different things to different people. To add to the confusion, there are often differing interpretations even within a given area. An example? Object oriented programming.

In this chapter I will discuss Smalltalk to explain the ideas of object oriented programming. No doubt other choices are possible, but Smalltalk seems to me to be the best one. For Smalltalk is the original object oriented programming language, and yet today remains the model object oriented system.

Even though I will rely on Smalltalk as the archetypal object oriented programming language, I will do more than explain the specifics of Smalltalk the programming language. I will also point out how the Smalltalk approach is an improvement over traditional programming languages. More importantly, much of what Smalltalk is, is not specific programmatic ideas but general principles relating to programming language design and, by implication, object oriented programming. I will also point out these design principles.

14.1. History

The immediate ancestor of object oriented programming is the programming language Simula. The Smalltalk programming system carried the object oriented paradigm to a smoother model. Although other systems have definitely shown some object oriented tendencies, the explicit awareness of the idea -- including the term "object oriented" -- came from the Smalltalk effort.

Smalltalk is the software half of an ambitious project known as the Dynabook. The Dynabook is a sort of computer holy grail, with the goal of being a truly personal computer. The Dynabook ultimately is expected to handle with equal facility any and all kinds of information management, and to be all (computer type) things to all people. Accordingly, Smalltalk has to carry quite a burden of expressiveness and convenience.

Alan Kay is the man chiefly responsible for the vision of the Dynabook. In the late 1960s, he did work on a preliminary version, known in that incarnation as the Flex machine. Then in the early 1970s, he went to the Xerox Palo Alto Research Center and there formed the Learning Research Group. Kay's goal was still a truly useful personal computer, with the Xerox Alto [Thacker 82] being the interim hardware for the Dynabook, and with the Learning Research Group doing Smalltalk as the software.

Smalltalk drew heavily from Flex, which in turn was an "Eulerized" [Wirth66] version of Simula. While a LISP influence is clearly evidenced in the deeper structure of Smalltalk, the *class* notion from Simula dominated the design. The language became completely based on the notion of a class as the sole structural unit, with instances of classes, or *objects*, being the concrete units which inhabit the world of the Smalltalk system. Smalltalk did not completely give up its LISP heritage; rather that heritage is felt more as a flavor of the system than as specific ideas of the programming language.

14.2. Division of Smalltalk into Programming Language and User Interface

More than a programming language, Smalltalk is a complete programming environment, all of which reflects the object oriented philosophy. Object oriented programming is so much a part of Smalltalk that it is difficult to tell where one leaves off and the other begins. For the purposes of exposition, we would like to divide Smalltalk into a programming language and a user interface. A brief discussion will make clear the distinction and remove confusion about which term means what.

Smalltalk may be thought of as comprised of four pieces, *viz.*, a programming language kernel, a programming paradigm, a programming system, and a user interface model. These pieces are fuzzily defined and not explicit within the Smalltalk system. They are basically hierarchical, though there is overlap and some convolution. Thus, the user interface is built on the programming system, which is built following the programming paradigm and using the programming language kernel.

The *programming language kernel* is the syntax and semantics as determined by the Smalltalk compiler. The *programming paradigm* is the style of use of the kernel, a sort of world view or "meaning" attached to the entities in the kernel. The *programming system* is the set of system objects and classes that provides the framework for exercising the programming paradigm and language kernel, the things necessary to make programming possible and convenient. The *user interface model* is the use and usage of the systems building material in order to present the system to the user -- in other words, the given user interface plus the user interface "flavor." The combination of these four pieces is the Smalltalk system.[1]

Using this view of the Smalltalk world, imagine a line drawn within the programming system such that the objects and classes relating to the user interface model are on one side and objects and classes relating to the programming paradigm and language kernel are on the other. We now find Smalltalk divided naturally into two parts: a user interface part, and a programming language part. We will examine each in turn for its object oriented ideas.

14.3. Smalltalk: Object Oriented Programming Language

Smalltalk embodies more than the abstract ideas of object oriented programming. Actual implementations of any programming language provide an understanding and a concreteness which is difficult to get

---

[1]Although I have presented the pieces as separate and independent, they are not, really. In fact they are inseparable and very interdependent. Not only could each piece itself not exist in a vacuum, the design for each piece influenced the design for all the other pieces, i.e., each design could not exist in a vacuum. A more faithful representation would be as interrelated aspects of the Smalltalk system. Following the note, however, I shall continue to consider them as "pieces" rather than "aspects."

from abstract concepts alone. Such is the case with Smalltalk. By detailing Smalltalk's particulars in familiar terms, we hope to more fully understand the ideal which Smalltalk hopes to express.

Although we naturally understand new ideas in terms of familiar ones, there is a danger in relying completely on this method, especially when paradigm shifts are essential to the new ideas. When the gap between the familiar and the new becomes too large, the sense of closeness breaks down, leaving only the much weaker notion of equivalence. Equivalence is not the issue; it is well known that any reasonable programming language can compute all computable functions, and hence all programming languages are, in that sense, "equivalent." We want understanding, but not at the cost of having that understanding in terms of the old model. Rather we want our understanding to allow us to think in the new model.

The plan, therefore, is to navigate two parallel courses through the exposition. The first will be explanation, in very familiar terms, of Smalltalk's essential particulars. The second will be contrasting reflection, by examples and discussion, showing the difference between the familiar explanation and the actual situation. The combination of the two will provide understanding while simultaneously shaking loose any preconceptions of the old model, allowing the essential shift in viewpoint and so appreciation for the model of object oriented programming.

14.3.1. Objects

Let's start with objects. An object in Smalltalk is really just a piece of (dynamically allocated) memory. Objects are automatically reclaimed, typically by reference counting or garbage collection, and there is some storage overhead associated with that. Mostly, however, an object is just several consecutive memory cells which together make up the state of the object.

Each object memory cell holds what is essentially a pointer (actually a unique bit string rather than a memory address) to some object in the Smalltalk system. This is different from a language like Pascal where variables serve as containers for values rather than as a means for referring to objects. All variables in Smalltalk designate objects rather than contain values. Other programming languages, such as CLU, have this property, and it is commonly referred to as *pointer semantics*.

An object remembers its state in its memory cells, the object's *instance variables*. Most commonly, these are what Smalltalk calls *named* instance variables: a particular memory cell within an object, referenced by an identifier. The identifier may appear on the left hand side of an assignment arrow, so as to store a new value (object designator). A named instance variable should remind you of a record field name in Pascal, with two exceptions. One is that an object may reference only its own instance variables, not another object's. The other is that the value held in an instance variable is an object designator, which fits into exactly one memory cell, and so an instance variable (in fact all Smalltalk variables) may refer to any object, i.e., variables are in this sense typeless. Note that this is a stronger statement than the previous one about pointer semantics.

In addition to any named instance variables, each object has a pseudo-variable named *self*. *Self* is a way of referring to the object as a whole -- an object's reference to *self* returns the object designator of the object itself. Pseudo-variables such as *self* may not be assigned into, but they may be used as ordinary variables in every other way.

In addition to named instance variables, Smalltalk objects have the capacity for anonymous instance variables, which are accessed by indexing. Such an object would have a layout in memory as shown in Figure 14-1. The Smalltalk language does not have an explicit construct which specifically does indexing; rather indexing is performed "behind the scenes" as a result of sending certain messages. In order to explain the indexing that Smalltalk provides, we must first digress to explain messages and how they are sent.

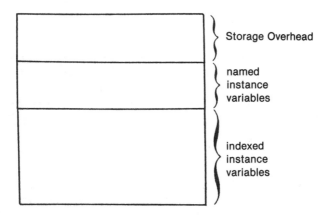

Figure 14-1:   Memory Layout for an Object with Indexed Instance Variables

14.3.2. Messages

Computation in Smalltalk occurs as a result of sending *messages* to objects. Messages are sent by giving a *receiver* followed by a *message pattern*, which is a *message selector* plus any arguments. The semantics of sending a message resemble those of calling a procedure, as we will see in more detail shortly. For now let's just take a look at the syntax[2] (given in Table 14-2) and a few examples (given in Table 14-1).

unary:	screen flash
binary:	x < y
keyword:	window moveTo: newOrigin
keyword:	self at: i - 1 put: mouse cursor - window origin
(same as)	self at: (i - 1) put: ((mouse cursor) - (window origin))
(but not)	(self at: (i - 1)) put: ((mouse cursor)-(window origin))

Table 14-1:   Examples of Message Expressions

An examination of the syntax reveals several items of interest. An object may be sent a *unary*, *binary*, or *keyword* message, corresponding to zero, one, or $>=$ one arguments. (Note that keyword messages "use up" as many keywords as possible. This is shown by the syntax for **keywordExpression**, and by the final example in Table 14-1 as well.) Second, the precedence of message sending is unary, binary, keyword, left-to-right, with the usual rule that parentheses change the order of evaluation. Third, Smalltalk is an expression language in that every message sent returns a value, which is an object designator. This returned object designator may be sent a further message, used as an argument to another message, or remembered by assigning it to one or more variables.

Objects also use messages to access and update anonymous instance variables. An object with indexable instance variables defines methods for *at: index* and *at: index put: object*, which are indexed loads and stores, respectively. Such objects also have defined a message *grow* which enlarges the area for the indexable variables of the object. Thus, the indexing mechanism is integrated into the language and uses no special

---

[2]I have taken some liberties with the Smalltalk syntax, which Smalltalk experts will recognize, but they are irrelevant to the discussion. The most significant of these liberties is the omission of *cascaded messages*, whereby several messages may be sent sequentially to a single receiver. Although helpful in terms of actual programming, cascaded messages represent syntactic sugar and are not germane to a discussion of object oriented programming.

expression   =   [variable '←'] * keywordExpr

keywordExpr   =
    binaryExpr*Receiver* [keyword   binaryExpr*Argument*] *

binaryExpr   =
    unaryExpr |
    binaryExpr*Receiver* binarySelector   unaryExpr*Argument*

unaryExpr   =   primary | unaryExpr*Receiver* unarySelector

primary   =   variable | literal | '(' expression ')'

keyword   =   identifier ':'

binarySelector   =   specialCharacter [specialCharacter]

unarySelector   =   identifier

variable   =   identifier

specialCharacter   =
    '+' | '-' | '*' | '/' | '\' | '%' | '?' | '@' | '~' | '<' | '>' | '=' | '&' | '!' | '|'

Table 14-2:   Abbreviated Syntax[3] for Message Expressions

syntax.

Indexable instance variables provide simple one-dimensional arrays, but they can also be used as a foundation to provide much more. Since *at:* and *at:put:* are sent as messages, and are in turn interpreted in terms of *basicAt:* and *basicAt:put:*, it is a simple matter to extend the indexing scheme to something more elaborate. One obvious extension is a two-dimensional array, with messages *at:at:* and *at:at:put:*. It is just as easy to provide two-dimensional arrays which take a *Point* as the single index. Smalltalk itself relies on indexable instance variables to provide classes such as *MethodDictionaries*, which are implemented as hash tables. All of these possibilities are expressed within the language using a syntax

---

[3]Meta-language usage: text in italic is comment, even when it appears as part of a meta-variable, and is not part of the syntax. As is customary, [**thing**] means an optional **thing**, [**thing**] * means zero or more **things**, and [**thing**] + means one or more **things**.

indistinguishable from the "built-in" case. This is made possible by folding indexing into the message passing model, reducing the number of concepts and unifying the language.

14.3.3. Methods

Objects respond to messages by means of *methods*. Just as sending a message is similar to calling a procedure, so a method is similar to a procedure definition. Table 14-3 gives method syntax.

method   =   messagePattern temporaryVariables methodBody

messagePattern   =
       unarySelector
   | binarySelector   variable*FormalParameter*
   | [keyword   variable*FormalParameter*] +

temporaryVariables   =   '|' [variable] * '|'

methodBody   =   [expression '.'] * ['↑' expression]

Table 14-3:   Syntax for Smalltalk Method

The syntax shows that a method has a message pattern, some temporary variables, and a list of statement-expressions which make up the method body. A *message pattern* is the message to which the method responds, including any formal arguments to the method. The *temporary variables* are just that -- variables that come into existence when the method is instantiated and disappear when the method completes. A *method body* is a specification of what actions to perform when actually responding to a message -- analogous to a procedure body.

Method execution is effected by evaluating sequentially the expressions comprising the method. As can be seen from the expression syntax given earlier, these expressions may send further messages and/or assign expression values to variables. The final expression of a method may return an explicit value by means of the ↑**expression** construction. In all cases, some value must be returned in order to preserve the expression language semantics; methods which do not explicitly return a value implicitly return *self*, the object to which the message was sent.

Sending a message in Smalltalk resembles in many ways calling a procedure in a conventional language such as Ada. Arguments are evaluated, and are passed by value. Control of the sender is suspended, and control is given to the receiver. The receiver retains control until returning to the sender, supplying a return value (a Smalltalk *reply*) as part of the return.

The difference between message sending and procedure calling is the means by which the message is bound to the corresponding method. In Ada the analagous procedure-call / procedure-body binding is done as part of the compilation process; in Smalltalk the message-receiving object binds the message, at the time of its reception, to the method appropriate for that particular object. The dynamic binding done by the message sending mechanism makes it more powerful than the conventional procedure call.

The message passing mechanism is reinforced by the sense of scope that Smalltalk exhibits. Methods exist within objects and hence may access (besides the method's temporaries) the object's instance variables, but not any other object's instance variables. The lack of globally enclosing scope means that (1) an object's methods need be concerned only with the state of that object, and (2) by symmetry, no object can affect the instance variables of another. The implication is that the central, very expressive mechanism of message passing is also the only mechanism provided.

14.3.4. Classes

Although objects behave as if they contained the message-responding methods, in actual fact they do not. Each object has one memory cell set aside which contains an object designator for the object's *class*, which contains the description for objects which are instances of the class. A class contains information such as the names of instance variables for objects of that class, and the methods which objects of the class use to respond to messages. The notion of a class will probably remind you of an abstract data type, for example what in CLU is called a *cluster*.

Classes do more than their counterparts in the abstract data type world. Classes play an active role in the Smalltalk system, serving to contain additional information and behavior appropriate to the classes instances. For example, new instances of a class need to be created -- what better place to put that behavior than in the class itself? Classes respond to the message *new* with a new instance of the class (or *new: size* for a class with indexable instance variables). A class collects such information and behavior as is common to its instances.

The preceeding implicitly assumes that classes are objects and can be sent messages just like other objects. This is certainly true, and is implied by a much more general statement -- everything in Smalltalk is an object. And every object is an instance of some class, which can be augmented to have whatever additional behavior the programmer deems appropriate. (We will see an example shortly of extending class *Integer.*)

The tendency towards extreme uniformity produces some pleasing and perhaps unexpected results. One such result is that, since stack frames and activation records are regular Smalltalk objects, the debugger can be written in Smalltalk itself, and so can be understood and adapted by the programmer. More generally, all of the behavior in the Smalltalk system is expressed using one language, and so is ultimately accessible to the programmer, both in terms of understandability and in terms of modifiability. For contrast, compare this to a conventional programming system, which typically has at least three levels of interpretation: the machine language, a high level language, and (at least one) command language interpreter.

14.3.5. Control Structures

Control structures in Smalltalk are handled by the message passing mechanism plus the predefined class *Block*. A block is a literal object (similar to an integer) which is essentially an unevaluated piece of code. (Syntax for blocks is given in Table 14-4.) Blocks may be sent the message *value* to cause evaluation (or *value: argument* for blocks that take an argument). Blocks have predefined methods for messages that do iteration, thus

$$[\; i < n \;] \quad \text{whileTrue:} \quad [\quad x \leftarrow x \; \text{transform.} \quad i \leftarrow i + 1 \quad]$$

contains two blocks, the first of which gets sent the message *whileTrue:* with the second block as an argument. The *whileTrue:* method, which is predefined in class *Block*, does what you would naturally expect, i.e., evaluates the argument (by sending the message *value*) as long as the receiver (the first block) evaluates to *true.* Blocks return as their value (in response to the *value* message) the value of the last expression in the block. Blocks may also cause the method which they are in to return a value, and so complete execution of the method, by ↑**expression** as the last expression in the block.

Blocks resemble call-by-name parameters of ALGOL-60, or anonymous

primary   =   block | variable | literal | '(' expression ')'

block   =   '[' [arguments '|'] blockBody ']'

arguments   =   [':' variable] +

blockBody   =   [expression '.'] * ['↑' expression]

Table 14-4:   Expression Syntax expanded to include Blocks

procedure parameters, but the interaction of blocks with the message sending mechanism makes blocks more powerful than either. It is a simple matter, for example, to add new control structures to those supplied by the system. A simple iteration control structure similiar to a Pascal **for** statement may be defined by adding a method to class *Integer*, as shown in Table 14-5.

```
to: upperLimit  do: block  | t |
    t ← self.
    [ t < = upperLimit ]
        whileTrue: [ block value: t.  t ← t + 1 ]
```

Table 14-5:   Control Structure added to class Integer

Interestingly, the combination of blocks and the message passing mechanism suffices to define the basic conditional control structure. Returned booleans, like $i < n$, are either *true* or *false*, instances of class *True* or class *False*, respectively. These predefined classes have methods which answer the basic conditional message *ifTrue:ifFalse:* appropriately, as shown in Table 14-6.

Class   True
...
    ifTrue: trueBlock ifFalse: falseBlock | |
      ↑ trueBlock value

Class   False
...
    ifTrue: trueBlock ifFalse: falseBlock | |
      ↑ falseBlock value

Table 14-6:   Methods for Conditional Message ifTrue:ifFalse:

When *i* responds to the message $<$ *n*, as in *i* $<$ *n*, *i* returns either *true* or *false*. When *true* is sent the *ifTrue:ifFalse:* message, it evaluates the first argument and simply ignores the second. Similarly, *false* evaluates only the second argument.

Here again we see the advantages of the strong unifying approach that Smalltalk takes. Because control structures are built using the message passing mechanism, it is easy to build new control structures that have the same appearance and status as the "built-in" control structures. Classes that implement collections, such as linked lists, sets, ordered collections, etc., implement a *do:* message that invokes a block once for each element of the collection. Also, because blocks are objects, it is possible to use them (under appropriate circumstances) interchangeably with other objects. (We will see an example of this later on, after the subclassing mechanism has been explained.) These advantages are made possible by unifying blocks into the object-message model which is consistently taken by Smalltalk.

14.3.6. Classes Compared to Abstract Data Types

The class concept was originally understood along the lines of data abstraction. Contemporary data abstraction schemes all have their roots ultimately in the class concept. But Smalltalk's runtime binding and lack of typing requirements together make possible a more flexible, more polymorphic programming language. Table 14-7 gives a simple example.

Class *Dictionary* provides a simple mechanism to insert and lookup items in a dictionary. The only requirement placed on the items inserted or looked up is that they can compare for equality (as in *element* = *item*), and that they know how to *hash* (and *rehash*) themselves. The example not only allows one definition to work for a variety of element item "types," but also allows mixing of various types within a single dictionary. Thus, the message passing mechanism -- and so the object oriented paradigm -- is more flexible than, say, generic modules in Ada.

14.3.7. Inheritance and Subclassing

A class may be extended by subclassing, which is similar to Simula prefixing. The subclass is said to inherit the behavior of the superclass, to which it may add variables, and add and/or replace methods. The memory layout of related sub- and super-classes is shown in

Class   Dictionary
indexable instance variables

...

```
insert: item  | index element |
    index ← ( item hash ) mod: ( self size ) .
    [ ( element ←  self at: index ) = nil  ]
      whileFalse: [
        ( element = item )  ifTrue: [ ↑element ].
        index ← ( index + (item rehash) ) mod: ( self size ) .
      ].
    self at: index put: item.
    ↑item

lookup: item  | index element |
    index ← ( item hash ) mod: ( self size ) .
    [ ( element ←  self at: index ) = nil  ]
      whileFalse: [
        ( element = item )  ifTrue: [ ↑element ].
        index ← ( index + (item rehash) ) mod: ( self size ) .
      ].
    ↑ nil
```

Table 14-7:   Simple Dictionary Class

Figure 14-2.

Methods as well as variables are inherited from the superclass, but here there is a difference from Simula -- all methods are what Simula calls *virtual*. What this means is that when a message is sent to an object, the method is looked for first in the object's class, then its superclass, then the super-superclass, and so on, until finally class *Object*, which is the superclass of all classes, is reached. The first corresponding method that is found when going up the superclass chain is the one used to respond to the message.

A subclass which replaces a superclass method may invoke the overridden method by means of the pseudo-variable *super*. A message sent to *super* is the same as a message sent to *self*, except that the method lookup starts at the next level up in the superclass hierarchy -- the superclass of the class in which the method sending the message to *super* resides. Thus, *super* may be used to invoke methods which would otherwise be hidden by the methods of the subclass. An example is given in Table 14-8.

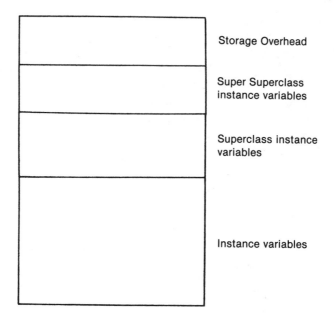

Figure 14-2: Memory Layouts of Objects related by Superclassing

| Class | Window |
| instance variables | border frame title |

     ...

```
         show | |
             frame clear.  border display.  title display
```

Class	PanedWindow
Superclass	Window
instance variables	panes

     ...

```
         show | |
             super show.  panes do: [ :pane | pane show ]
```

Table 14-8: Invoking Superclass Code with super

The *show* method of *PanedWindow*, which overrides the *show* method of its superclass, *Window*, invokes the overridden method by sending the message *show* to *super*.

Smalltalk makes possible more than just simple polymorphism. When combined with inheritance, the message passing mechanism allows factoring out of common code so that a given piece of code need appear only once. To see how this works, let's look at some code which generates and evaluates expression trees.

Object	(Some code added here)
Number	(Used as is)
Real	(Used as is)
Integer	(Used as is)
Block	(Used as is)
Expr	(New class)
DelayedLeaf	(New class)
BinaryOperation	(New class)
Plus	(New class)
Minus	(New class)
Times	(New class)
Divide	(New class)

Table 14-9: Superclass Hierarchy for Expression Tree Classes

The expression tree code introduces seven new classes, adds a tiny amount of code to class *Object*, and uses a few existing classes as is. The relevant classes and their relative place on the superclass tree is shown in Table 14-9. The actual code is shown in Figure 14-10.

The example illustrates a number of important points. First, because the expression operators are effected by sending messages, the code is completely polymorphic -- the same code suffices for integers, reals, points, or what-have-you. (As an aside, note that no additional code need be written to be able to generate expression trees, which, when evaluated, yield as values other expression trees.) Second, because of the default definition for value supplied in *Object*, objects themselves may serve as leaves of the tree, without any encapsulating "dummy" node.   Third, by fortuitous choice of the evaluation message name, *value*, it is possible to put arbitrary Smalltalk code, in the form of *Block*'s, in the leaves.   Fourth -- and this is really the point -- even though the specific construction mechanisms for non-*DelayedLeaf Expr*'s and *DelayedLeaf*'s are different, they can share the common code of the general construction methods.   This is made possible by the combination of inheritance and the message passing mechanism. Mere polymorphism is not enough -- without inheritance the crucial code in *Expr* would have to be replicated in *DelayedLeaf* (and all of the *BinaryOperation* subclasses as well), even though the code is identical at the source level. Smalltalk's approach makes possible an even stronger statement -- the same object code works for both cases.

Class   Object
    value | | ↑ self
    delayed | | ↑ (DelayedLeaf new) leaf: self

Class   Expr
Superclass   Object
    + e | | ↑ self under: Plus with: e
    - e | | ↑ self under: Minus with: e
    * e | | ↑ self under: Times with: e
    / e | | ↑ self under: Divide with: e
    under: op with: right | |
       ↑ (op new) left: (self undelayed) right: right
    undelayed | | ↑ self

Class   DelayedLeaf
Superclass   Expr
instance variables   leaf
    leaf: l | | leaf ← l
    undelayed | | ↑ leaf

Class   BinaryOperation
Superclass   Expr
instance variables   left   right
    left: l right: r | | left ← l.   right ← r

Class   Plus "similarly *Minus, Times, Divide*"
Superclass   BinaryOperation
    value | | ↑ (left value) + (right value)

Table 14-10:   Expression Tree Code

14.4. Smalltalk: Object Oriented User Interface

Smalltalk uses a few simple metaphors -- objects, activity, communication, behavior -- to express the notions of the language of programming. These same metaphors carry over into the realm of user interface. The Smalltalk programming system naturally extends the object oriented programming ideas to take advantage of those ideas in the Smalltalk user interface. By examining the user interface and the extent to which the object oriented principles apply, we will gain a more thorough understanding of the concept of object oriented-ness, as well as a deeper appreciation of the design principles underlying Smalltalk.

Smalltalk is designed and intended to be run on a personal computer similar to the original Xerox Alto. Alto-esque computers interact with the user through three component pieces: a keyboard, a display, and a mouse.

The user enters textual input using the keyboard. The keyboard is the standard typewriter-like affair, with a few extra keys for special functions. A typical computer terminal keyboard is essentially the same as the keyboard needed here.

The user observes character and graphical output on a display, which is a fairly large, moderately high resolution bit-per-pixel monitor. Smalltalk presumes three general characteristics for its display. First, the resolution of the display should be sufficient to show characters by using pixel patterns on the monitor. Second, the bandwidth of the display should be high enough so that the entire display may be repainted "instantaneously," i.e., in one frame time or about one fortieth of a second. Third, the graphic interface should be sufficiently general so that text and arbitrary graphics can be freely intermixed. (Readers interested in more details should consult [Ingalls 81b].)

Additional information is supplied by means of a pointing device called a mouse. A mouse is a small hand-held box that sits on a surface to one side of the keyboard. As the mouse is moved on the surface, feedback is generated in the form of a moving mouse cursor shown on the display. Additionally, the mouse has on it several buttons which the user may press whenever the cursor shows the desired position on the screen. In this way the mouse can be used for control and graphical input.

Smalltalk uses the display to present objects to the user. More appropriately, an object is asked -- by sending a message -- to present itself on the display. The means of choosing a graphical representation is left up to the object and so fits into the object oriented mold.

While an object could choose any manner it sees fit to interact with the display and the user, most objects in Smalltalk use the "model-view-controller" approach. This scheme composites three objects, which together act harmoniously to interface with the user. The idea here is to systematically partition the responsibility of interacting with the user so that each piece has a simpler task, and, to the extent possible, a given piece can be taken out and replaced with another one of the same kind. To achieve this end, the division is made into: (1) a model, which is the underlying reality or representation, often the object itself; (2) a view, the means by which the model interacts with an area on the display; and (3) a controller, which is the agent responsible for directing the user input to whatever other object in the system determined to be interested in the particular input (which is almost always the corresponding view or model).

Note that the "model-view-controller" perception of the world is not explicitly apparent to the user. As far as the user is concerned, he interacts with Smalltalk windows which are, in his view, the object itself. We are, however, not just concerned with what the user sees. The model-view-controller schema allows a more faithful, more explicit explanation, and so a better exposition.

The user interacts with the objects on the screen by sending them "messages" in the form of mouse position and button information and keyboard keystrokes. The messages are sent to a receiver object previously chosen from among the objects presented on the screen. Figure 14-3 shows one such screen configuration. Note that the tag on the workspace window is inverted, showing it to be the selected window.

The user selects a window to be the receiver of input messages by pointing at the window and clicking any mouse button. The sequence of events is as follows. Suppose no item is selected. When the user clicks the mouse button, a message is sent to the screen controller that the button was pushed, including the mouse coordinates at the time. The screen controller, which maintains a list of active views, asks each view in turn if it desires control for mouse button activity at the given coordinate. The view that desires control is made the active receiver and is asked to do such things as are appropriate to such an action. These decisions are of course left up to the individual object, but usually they include repainting the view and giving visual feedback indicating a selection, such as the tab title highlighting shown in the figure.

Once a particular window is chosen as the active window, it becomes the receiver for messages generated by user actions on the mouse and keyboard. The messages are sent to the window's controller, which shuttles them off either to the view or the model, or perhaps both, or whatever other object is appropriate to the particular message received.

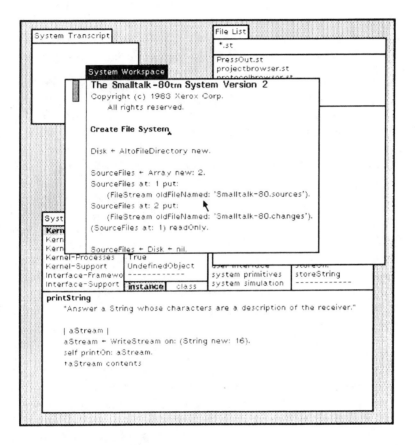

Figure 14-3: Typical Smalltalk Display

The method which ultimately handles such messages will not only perform the necessary internal state changes, but normally will also update the presentation on the screen, the updating being requested by a message to the view, since the view is responsible for the image displayed. From the point of view of the user, the objects on the screen "react" to mouse and keyboard input, or, in other words, respond to messages in the form of keystrokes and mouse clicks.

Interpreting keystrokes and mouse clicks as messages is highly restrictive when compared with the more flexible Smalltalk message sending choices. How can a more general message sending interface be crammed into the uniform "syntax" of user actions? Individual objects choose individual behavior, but a particular, simple example, that of a system workspace, should illustrate the general ideas. In addition, because of the availability of the subclassing facility and the possibility of sharing of code, it often happens that much of the behavior on one window will duplicate that of another window.

A workspace presumes the user to be primarily in an editing frame of mind. The keyboard is used to enter text which is to go into the workspace. The leftmost mouse button is used to select text (if the mouse cursor is in the main portion of the window) or to position the workspace text underneath the window (if the mouse cursor is in the painted rectangular region to the left of the window, called a scroll bar). The message that the leftmost button has been pressed is sent either to the scroll bar, which then causes the scroll to happen, or to the workspace text model, which causes a selection to take place. A keystroke message is sent to the text model, and causes the text currently selected to be replaced by the character just keyed (and the selection updated so that more typing causes insertion of text). Selection thus helps overcome one of the shortcomings of keystrokes and mouse clicks -- by selecting a piece of text it becomes an implicit argument for the next message sent (which for keystrokes is, in effect, *replace selection*).

To make other messages available to the user, a workspace uses the other two mouse buttons in conjunction with pop-up menus. A menu of choices appears when the button is pressed; the mouse is used to select a choice, which is sent as a message when the button is released.

A workspace uses the rightmost button for messages relating to the window, such as closing the window, moving the window, or changing its size. The message chosen from the menu is sent to the view. Additional parameters, such as where to position the window on a move, are gotten from the user by means of cursor shape cueing and waiting for a button click. In this case, then, the arguments are screen coordinates and are supplied with further clicks on the mouse. Messages that require no arguments, such as *close*, simply proceed.

A workspace uses the center button for messages pertaining to the text shown in the window, i.e., the model. Some messages need no arguments, and are sent by simply making the choice on the menu. Other messages need one argument and these use the selection for that purpose, as with replacing text explained previously. One of these messages is an escape hatch: the *doit* message takes the current textual selection as an argument, which is presumed to be Smalltalk source code, to be immediately compiled and executed. Thus, any message may be sent using the facility provided.

Although workspaces get by with a maximum of one textual argument, some windows need more flexibility. An example is given by the highly evolved code browser, which uses a hybrid scheme with multiple selections and a complete-the-form approach. To add a method to a class, a browser is used first to select the class which should contain the method, then to bring up a template for the method itself. The pieces of the method template are successively filled in by selecting the piece to be replaced and inserting the appropriate text. When the method is complete to the user's satisfaction, the method is added to the class using the middle mouse button to send an *accept* message. The text of the method is analyzed by the compiler, which produces the component parts such as the message selector and compiled code bytes. These parts are sent as arguments in a message to the class, gotten from another selection in the same browser, to add this compiled method to the class's method dictionary. The particulars of this scheme are interesting, perhaps, but the point is that the message sending metaphor, multiple arguments and all, is carried over into the user interface.

14.5. Design Principles

The ideas of object oriented programming evolved through a number of Smalltalk language designs to reach their current form. Smalltalk is one of the few languages that has gone through five design iterations [LRG 81]. We therefore expect the underlying design principles to be rather refined, and quite probably applicable to other styles of programming and programming languages.

The most striking design principle behind Smalltalk is that of unity. The idea is to unify diverse aspects of the language so that one concept expresses all of the various views desired. Smalltalk captures this unity, or conceptual integrity, in that there is only:

   ☐ 1 notion of simulated entity (objects)

   ☐ 1 type of reference to objects (object designators)

   ☐ 1 status for all objects

   ☐ 1 classification scheme (classing and sub-superclassing)

   ☐ 1 mechanism for processing/communication/control

☐ 1 way of invoking the message sending mechanism

☐ 1 syntax which expresses all these ideas

☐ 1 semantic interpretation (methods)

☐ 1 parameter passing mechanism

Some of Smalltalk's design principles relate directly to the object oriented notions. Smalltalk adherents argue persuasively the advantages of the message discipline and the inheritance mechanism. In particular, Smalltalk:

☐ allows very polymorphic code (and this with only little additional effort);

☐ encourages "call by desire" (in other words, a message is a request of what the sender wants, not what the receiver is expected to do);

☐ provides good default behavior;

☐ makes for understandability by using intuitive notions;

☐ facilitates modifiability -- an appropriate choice within the superclassing hierarchy allows concentration on what must be changed while ignoring what must be left alone;

☐ allows adaptability -- subclassing an existing class makes possible differential programming (the situation off "I want something just like that, except . . .").

One consequence of the message/inheritance interaction deserves mention as a design principle in its own right: factoring. Being factored means having the property of any one component being in only one place. Factoring makes possible linear code growth, while simultaneously eliminating the possibility for two identical pieces of code to get "out of sync." Factoring can actually lead to increased efficiency as well, since "multiplied use of high speed code can exert great leverage on the overall performance" [Ingalls 78, Ingalls 81b]. Factoring falls out of the message passing and inheritance mechanisms, but, object oriented or no, contemporary programming language designers should include the ability to factor as a design goal.

The Smalltalk system exhibits the less obvious but still important design principle of adopting natural metaphors. Smalltalk adopts metaphors for: (1) entities (objects), (2) processing (sending messages), (3) categorization (classes), and (4) sharing of common attributes (inheritance).

"Adopting natural metaphors" might seem strange as a design principle for programming languages. Due to Smalltalk's history as an outgrowth of the Dynabook project, the Smalltalk system is viewed by its designers not as a programming language but as a vehicle for communication and interaction with the computer. This bias give rise to what are almost meta design principles. One such design principle is the natural metaphor idea just explained. Others (taken from [Ingalls 81a]) are:

- ☐ The programming system should encompass and subsume such things as programming language, operating system, graphical user interface, and data base capability;

- ☐ All behavior in the system should be available to and modifiable by the user;

- ☐ As a corollary, the entire system should be comprehensible by a single individual;

- ☐ A few ideas should be uniformly applied at all levels of the system from user interface down to the lowest level programmatic constructs;

- ☐ "Computation should be viewed as an intrinsic property of objects uniformly invoked by sending messages." -- a gem.

Whether or not these meta design principles contribute to more conventional programming languages is subject to some debate. Certainly a more useful, more usable, more integrated computing environment is an ideal we can all look forward to. In any case, Smalltalk has contributed some important ideas to the principles of programming language design. If it turns out that the meta design principles are equally valuable, so much the better.

Concepts Discussed in This Chapter

Block
Class
Differential Programming
Factoring
Inheritance
Message
Method
Object
Pointer Semantics
Superclass (and Subclass)

Exercises

1. The value returned by the control structure added to class *Integer* shown in Table 14-5 is the initial value of the iteration variable, which is probably not what is expected in an expression language. Change the given method so that it returns the last value evaluated by the argument *block* instead. (Answer:

   ```
   to: upperLimit   do: block  | t val |
      t ← self.
      [ t < = upperLimit ]
        whileTrue: [
           val ← block value: t.
           t ← t + 1 .
        ].
      ↑ val
   ```

2. Table 14-7 shows one identifier which is not an instance variable, method argument, or temporary. Which identifier is this? (Answer: *nil.*)

3. The expression tree code given in Figure 14-10 shows four identifiers which are not instance variables, method arguments, or temporaries. What are they? What do all these identifiers have in common? (Answer: *Plus, Minus, Times, Divide* are the identifiers, and all name classes in the

system.)

4. Identifiers such as *nil* (e.g., *true*, *false*) refer to distinguished objects in the Smalltalk system. These distinguished object identifiers, as well as the names of classes in the Smalltalk system, are stored in a global dictionary so that any object may send messages to them. What other category of objects might be put in the system global dictionary? (Answer: System wide resource objects such as the *Display* or *DiskController*.)

5. The code shown in Table 14-8 does not quite conform to the method syntax given in the chapter. What's wrong with it? (Answer: there is no "." after the final expression in the method. Smalltalk syntax actually allows the final "." to be optional.)

6. Traditional meta-languages typically use either iteration or recursion, but not both, for arithmetic operators and their associated precedences. The abbreviated syntax given in Table 14-2 uses both notations, with each appealing to a particular intuitive notion about the parse tree and associated semantics. Investigate making these intuitive ideas more explicit, and explore the possible applications to improving meta-languages and semantic specifications.

References

[Ackerman 82] Ackerman, William B. "Data Flow Languages" *Computer*, IEEE, vol. 15, no. 2, Feb. 1982, 15-25.

[Ada 79a] "Preliminary Ada Reference Manual" *ACM Sigplan Notices*, 14, 6, June 1979.

[Ada 79b] "Rationale for the Design of the Ada Programming Language" *ACM Sigplan Notices*, 14, 6, June 1979.

[Ada 80] "The Ada Language Reference Manual" United States Department of Defense, December, 1980.

[Aho-Ullman 72] Aho, A., and J. Ullman. *The Theory of Parsing, Translation and Compiling* Prentice-Hall, Englewood Cliffs, N.J., 1972.

[Aho-Ullman 77] Aho, A. and J. Ullman *Principles of Compiler Design*, Addison-Wesley, Reading, Mass., 1977.

[ALGOL60] See [Naur 63]

[ALGOL68] See [Van Wijngaarden 69]

[ALPHARD] see [Wulf-London-Shaw 76]

[Allen 79] Allen, J. *The Anatomy of LISP* McGraw-Hill, New York, 1979.

[ANSICOBOL] *American National Standard COBOL (ANS X3.23-1968)* American National Standards Institute, New York, 1968.

[APL] See [Iverson 62]

[Arvind 77a] Arvind and Gostelow, K.P. "Some Relationships Between Asynchronous Interpreters of a Dataflow Language" *Formal Description of Programming Languages*, E.J. Neuhold, ed. North-Holland,

N.Y., 1977, 849-853.

[Arvind 77b] Arvind and Gostelow, K.P. "A Computer Capable of Exchanging Processing Elements for Time" *Information Processing 77*, B. Gilchrist ed., North-Holland, N.Y. 1977

[Ashcroft-Manna 71] Ashcroft, E. and Manna, Z. "The Translation of GOTO Programs into WHILE Programs" *Proceedings IFIP Congress 71*, TA-2, North-Holland, 147-152.

[Backus 57] Backus, J.W., R. J. Beeber, S. Best, R. Goldberg, L.M. Haibt, H.L. Herrick, R. A. Nelson, D. Sayre, P.B. Sheridan, H. Stern, I. Ziller, R. A. Hughes, and R. Nutt. "The FORTRAN Automatic Coding System" *Proc. Western Jt. Comp. Conf.*, AIEE (now IEEE), Los Angeles.

[Backus 73] Backus, J. "Programming Language Semantics and Closed Applicative Languages" *Proc. ACM Symposium on Principles of Programming Languages*, Oct. 1973, 71-86.

[Backus 78] Backus, J. "Can Programming be Liberated from the von Neumann Style? A Functional Style and its Algebra of Programs" *Comm. ACM*, 21, 8, August 1978, 613-641. See also in [Horowitz 83].

[Backus 78b] Backus, J. "The History of FORTRAN I, II, and III" *ACM Sigplan Notices*, 13, 8, August, 1978, 165-180.

[Barnes 80] Barnes, J.G.P. "An Overview of Ada" *Software Practice and Experience*, 10, 851-887, 1980. See also in [Horowitz 83].

[Barron 68a] Barron, D. *Recursive Techniques in Programming* American Elsevier, New York, 1968.

[Barron 68b] Barron, D. *Comparative Programming Languages*, American Elsevier, New York, 1968.

[BCPL] See [Richards 80]

[Berry 79] Berry, D. and R. Schwartz "Type Equivalence in Strongly Typed Languages: One More Look" *ACM Sigplan Notices*, 1979, 35-41.

[Birtwistle 73] Birtwistle, G.M., O-J. Dahl, B. Myhrhaug, and K. Nygaard, *SIMULA Begin* Petrocelli/Charter, New York, 1973.

[Bobrow 73] Bobrow, D., and B. Wegbreit. "A Model and Stack Implementation of Multiple Environments" *Comm. ACM*, 1, 10, 1973, 591-602.

[Bohm-Jacopini 66] Bohm, C. and Jacopini, G. "Flow Diagrams, Turing Machines and Languages with Only Two Formation Rules" *CACM*, 9,5, May, 1966, 366-371.

[Boom 80] Boom, H.J., DeJong, E. "A Critical Comparison of Several Programming Language Implementations" *Software Practice and Experience*, 10, 1980, 435-473.

[Brinch-Hansen 72] Brinch-Hansen, P. "Structured Multiprogramming" *Comm. ACM*, 15, 7, July 1972, 574-578.

[Brinch-Hansen 73] Brinch-Hansen, P. *Operating System Principles* Prentice-Hall, Englewood Cliffs, N.J. 1973.

[Brinch-Hansen 75] Brinch-Hansen, P. "The Programming Language Concurrent-Pascal" *IEEE Trans. on Soft. Eng.*, 1,2, June 1975, 199-207. See also in [Horowitz 83].

[Brinch-Hansen 77] Brinch-Hansen, P. *The Architecture of Concurrent Programs* Prentice-Hall, Englewood Cliffs, N.J. 1977.

[Brinch-Hansen 78] Brinch-Hansen, P. "Distributed Processes: a Concurrent Programming Concept" *Comm. ACM*, 21, 11, November, 1978, 934-941.

[Burge 75] Burge, W.H. *Recursive Programming Techniques* Addison-Wesley, Reading, Mass. 1975.

[BYTE 81] *Byte* Special Issue on Smalltalk, *Byte*, 6, 8, 1981.

[C] See [Ritchie 78]

[Calingaert 82] Calingaert, P. *Operating System Elements: A User Perspective*, Prentice-Hall, Englewood Cliffs, New Jersey, 1982.

[Chang 78] Chang, E., Kaden, N., Elliott, W.D. "Abstract Data Types in Euclid" *ACM SIGPLAN Notices*, 13, 3, March 1978.

[Cheatham 71] Cheatham, T. "The Recent Evolution of Programming Languages" *Proc. IFIP Cong. 1971*, C. V. Freiman, (ed.), North-Holland, Amsterdam, 118-134.

[Chomsky 59] Chomsky, N. "On Certain Formal Properties of Grammars" *Info. Control*, 2, 1959,137-167.

[Church 41] Church, Alonzo. *The Calculi of Lambda-Conversion* Princeton University Press, New Jersey, 1941.

[Clark 73] Clark, B.L. and J. J. Horning. "Reflections on a Language Designed to Write an Operating System" *ACM Sigplan Notices 8*, no. 9, 1973, 52-56.

[CLU] See [Liskov 79]

[COBOL 72] *Draft Proposed Revised X3/23 American National Standard Specifications for COBOL*, American National Standards Institute, New York.

[Cohen 70] Cohen, D.J. and Gotlieb, C.C. "A List Structure Form of Grammars for Syntactic Analysis" *ACM Computing Surveys*, 2, 1, 65 - 82.

[ConcurrentPascal] See [Brinch-Hansen 75]

[Conway 63] Conway, M.E., "Design of a Separable Transition-Diagram Compiler" *Comm. ACM*, July 1963.

[Dahl 68] Dahl, O.J., B. Myhrhaug and K. Nygaard. "The SIMULA67 Common Base Language" Publication no S-2, Norwegian Computing Center, Oslo, May 1968.

[Dahl-Dijkstra-Hoare 72] Dahl, O. J., E. W. Dijkstra, and C.A.R. Hoare. *Structured Programming* Academic Press, London and New York,

1972.

[Dahl-Nygaard 66] Dahl, O., and K. Nygaard. "SIMULA-An ALGOL-Based Simulation Language" *Comm. ACM,* 9, 9, 1966, 671-678.

[Davis 82] Davis, Alan L. and Robert M. Keller, "Data Flow Program Graphs" *Computer,* IEEE, vol. 15, no. 2, Feb. 1982, 26-41.

[de Morgan 76a] de Morgan, R.M., I.D. Hill, and B.A. Wichmann "A Supplement to the ALGOL60 Revised Report" *Computer Journal,* 19,3 1976, 276-288.

[de Morgan 76b] de Morgan, R.M. I.D. Hill, and B.A. Wichmann, "Modified Report on the Algorithmic Language ALGOL60", *Computer Journal,* 19,4, 1976, 364-379.

[Dennis 79] Ackerman, W.B. and J.B. Dennis, "VAL-a Value Oriented Algorithmic Language: Preliminary Reference Manual" Laboratory for Computer Science, MIT, Cambridge, Mass. 1979.

[Desjardins 74] Desjardins, P. and O. Lecarme "Reply to a Paper by A. N. Habermann on the Programming Language Pascal" *ACM Sigplan Notices,* 9, October 1974, 21-27.

[Dijkstra 68a] Dijkstra, E. "GoTo Statement Considered Harmful" *Comm. ACM,* 11, 3, 1968,147-148.

[Dijkstra 68b] Dijkstra, E. "Cooperating Sequential Processes" In [Genuys 68], 43-112.

[Dijkstra 75] Dijkstra, E. "Correctness Concerns and Among Other Things, Why They Are Resented" *ACM Sigplan Notices 10,* no. 6, 1975, 546-550.

[Dijkstra 75b] Dijkstra, E. "Guarded Commands, Nondeterminacy and Formal Derivation of Programs" *Comm. ACM,* 18, 8, August 1975, 453-457.

[Euclid] See [Lampson 77]

[EXTENDEDALGOL] *Extended ALGOL Reference Manual,* Burroughs Corp., Detroit, Mich., Form no. 5000128, 1971.

[Falkoff 73] Falkoff, A. and K. Iverson. "The Design of APL" *IBM Journal of Research and development,* July 1973, 324 - 334. See also in [Horowitz 83].

[FORTRAN66] *American National Standard FORTRAN (ANS X3.9-1966)* American National Standards Institute, New York, 1966.

[FORTRAN77] Draft proposed ANS FORTRAN BSR x3.9 x353/76, *ACM Sigplan Notices,* 11, 3, March 1976.

[Gannon 75] John D. Gannon and J. J. Horning. "Language Design for Programming Reliability" *IEEE Trans. Software Engineering SE-1* 2, 179-191, 1975.

[Gannon 77] Gannon, J. "An Experimental Evaluation of Data Type Conventions" *Comm. ACM 20,* 8, 1977, 584-595.

[Gentleman 71] Gentleman, W.M. "A Portable Coroutine System," *Proc. IFIP 1971*, Book TA-3 1971, 94-98.

[Genuys 68] Genuys, F. ed. *Programming Languages* Academic Press, New York.

[Geschke 75] Geschke, C.M. and J.G. Mitchell "On the Problem of Uniform References to Data Structures" *ACM Sigplan Notices*, 10, 6, June 1975, 31-42.

[Geschke 77] Geschke, C.M., J.H. Morris Jr. and E.H. Satterthwaite "Early Experience with MESA" *Comm. ACM*, 20,8, 1977.

[Goldberg 83a] Goldberg, Adele, and Robson, D., *Smalltalk-80: The Language and its Implementation*, Addison-Wesley, 1983.

[Goldberg 83b] Goldberg, Adele, *Smalltalk-80: The Interactive Programming Environment*, Addison-Wesley, to appear 1983.

[Goldberg 83c] Goldberg, Adele, (edited by Evelyn Van Orden), *Smalltalk-80: The System Protocols*, XEOS technical document, Xerox, 1983.

[Goodenough 75] Goodenough, J.B. "Exception Handling: Issues and a Proposed Notation" *Comm. ACM 18*, 12, December 1975, 683-696.

[Gordon 79] Gordon, M. "The Denotational Description of Programming Languages" Springer-Verlag, 1979.

[GPSS] "GPSS: Language Reference Manual" IBM Corporation, Poughkeepsie, N.Y. 1969.

[Gries 72] Gries, D. *Compiler Construction for Digital Computers* Wiley, New York, 1972.

[Gries 80] Gries, D. G. Levin, "Assignment and Procedure Call Proof Rules", *ACM TOPLAS*, vol. 2, no. 4, October, 1980, 564-579.

[Gries 81] Gries, D. "On Short Circuit Evaluation" Cornell Computer Science Technical Report, Cornell University, Ithaca, N.Y. 1981.

[Griswold 71a] Griswold, R. *The Macro Implementation of SNOBOL4* W. H. Freeman, San Francisco, 1971.

[Griswold 71b] Griswold, R., J. Poage, and I. Polonsky. *The SNOBOL4 Programming Language* 2nd ed., Prentice-Hall, Englewood Clifs, N.J., 1971.

[Griswold 73] Griswold, R, and M. Griswold *A SNOBOL4 Primer* Prentice-Hall, Englewood Cliffs, N.J., 1973.

[Grune 77] Grune, Dick "A View of Coroutines" *ACM Sigplan Notices*, ACM, July 1977, 75-81.

[Guttag 77a] Guttag, J. "Abstract Data Types and the Development of Data Structures" *Comm. ACM*, 20,6, June 1977, 396-404.

[Guttag 77b] Guttag, J., E. Horowitz and D. Musser "Some Extensions to Algebraic Specifications" *ACM Sigplan Notices*, 12, 3, March 1977.

[Guttag 78a] Guttag, J., E. Horowitz, D. Musser "The Design of Data Type Specifications", *Current Trends in Programming Methodology*, ed. R. Yeh, vol IV, Prentice Hall, 1978.

[Guttag 78b] Guttag, J., E. Horowitz and D. Musser "Abstract Data Types and Software Validation" *Comm. ACM*, 21,12, December 1978, 1048-1064.

[Guttag 80] Guttag, J. "Notes on Type Abstraction" *IEEE Trans. on Software Engineering*, vol. SE-6, no. 1, Jan. 1980, 13-23.

[Habermann 73] Habermann, A.N. "Critical Comments on the Programming Language Pascal." *Acta Informatica* 3, 1973,47-57.

[Hanson 78] Hanson, D. and R. Griswold "The SL5 Procedure Mechanism" *Comm. ACM*, 21, 5, 1978, 392-400.

[Henderson 80] Henderson, P. *Functional Programming: Application and Implementation* Prentice-Hall, Englewood Cliffs, New Jersey, 1980.

[Hoare 66] Hoare, C.A.R. and Wirth, N. "A Contribution to the Development of ALGOL" *Comm. ACM*, 9, 6, June 1966, 413-431. See also in [Horowitz 83].

[Hoare 69] Hoare, C.A.R. "An Axiomatic Basis for Computer Programming" *Comm. ACM,* 12, 10, 1969, 576-583.

[Hoare-Wirth 71] Hoare, C.A.R. and N. Wirth, "An Axiomatic Definition of the Programming Language Pascal" *Acta Informatica*, 2, 1973, 335-355.

[Hoare 73] Hoare, C.A.R. "Hints on Programming Language Design" Technical Report STAN-CS-73-403, Stanford University Computer Science Department, 1973. See also *Sigact/Sigplan Symposium on Principles of Programming Languages*, October 1973. See also in [Horowitz 83].

[Hoare 74] Hoare, C.A.R. "Monitors: an Operating System Structuring Concept" *Comm. ACM*, 17,10, October 1974, 549-557.

[Hoare 75] Hoare, C.A.R. "Recursive Data Structures" *Int. J. Comp. Inf. Sci.* 4, 1975, 105.

[Hoare 78] Hoare, C.A.R. "Communicating Sequential Processes" *Comm. ACM*, 21, 8, August 1978, 666-677. See also in [Horowitz 83].

[Holt 78] Holt, R.C., Lazowska, E.D., Graham, G.S., Scott, M.A., *Structured Concurrent Programming with Operating Systems Applications* Addison-Wesley, 1978.

[Horning 75] Horning, J.J., editor, "Proceedings - 1975 International Conference on Reliable Software." *ACM Sigplan Notices* 10, 6, 1975.

[Horning 79a] Horning, J.J. "A Case Study in Language Design: Euclid", *Lecture Notes in Computer Science (compiler construction)* Springer-Verlag, 1979.

[Horning 79b] Horning, J.J. "Programming Languages" *Computing*

Systems Reliability, T. Anderson and B. Randell eds., Cambridge University Press, 1979.

[Horowitz 76] Horowitz, E. and S. Sahni. *Fundamentals of Data Structures* Computer Science Press, Rockville, Maryland, 1976.

[Horowitz 78] Horowitz, E. and S. Sahni. *Fundamentals of Computer Algorithms* Computer Science Press, Rockville, Maryland, 1978.

[Horowitz 83] Horowitz, E. *Programming Languages: A Grand Tour* Computer Science Press, Rockville, Maryland, 1982. A collection of 30 papers on programming languages.

[Ingalls 78] Ingalls, D.H. "The Smalltalk-76 Programming System Design and Implementation", *Proc. 5th ACM Principles of Programming Languages Conf.*, 1978, 9-16.

[Ingalls 81a] Ingalls, Daniel H. H., "Design Principles Behind Smalltalk" *Byte*, 6, 8, 1981.

[Ingalls 81b] Ingalls, Daniel H. H., "The Smalltalk Graphics Kernel" *Byte*, 6, 8, 1981.

[Ingerman 61] Ingerman, P. "Thunks" *Comm. ACM*, 4, 1, 1961, 55-58.

[IPLV] See [Newell 64]

[INTERLISP] See [Teitelman 75]

[Iverson 62] Iverson, K. *A Programming Language* Wiley, New York, 1962.

[Jensen-Wirth 74] Jensen, K. and N. Wirth, *Pascal Users Manual and Report* Springer-verlag Berlin, 1974.

[Johnston 71] Johnston, J. "The Contour Model of Block Structured Processes" In Tou and Wegner 1971, 55-82.

[JOVIAL] "JOVIAL J73/1 Specifications", Rome Air Development Center, Air Force Systems Command, Griffis Air Force Base, New York, 13441, 1976.

[Kay 69] Kay, Alan, "The Reactive Engine" Ph.D. Thesis, University of Utah, September, 1969.

[Kay 72] Kay, Alan, "A Personal Computer for Children of All Ages", *Proc. ACM National Conference*, Boston, August, 1972.

[Kay 77a] Kay, Alan, "Personal Dynamic Media" *Computer*, March, 1977.

[Kay 77b] Kay, Alan, "Microelectronics and the Personal Computer" *Scientific American*, September, 1977.

[Kiviat 69] Kiviat, P., R. Villanueva and H. Markowitz *The SIMSCRIPT II Programming Language* Prentice-Hall, Englewood Cliffs, N.J., 1969.

[Knuth 64] Knuth, D.E. et al. "A Proposal for Input/Output Conventions in ALGOL60" *Comm. ACM*, 7,5, 1964, 273-283.

[Knuth 67] Knuth, D. "The Remaining Trouble Spots in ALGOL 60" *Comm. ACM,* 10, 10, 1967, 611-617. See also in [Horowitz 83].

[Knuth 68] Knuth, D. *The Art of Computer Programming: Fundamental Algorithms* vol. I, Addison-Wesley, Reading, Mass., 1968.

[Knuth 69] Knuth, D. *The Art of Computer Programming: Seminumerical Algorithms* vol. II, Addison-Wesley, Reading, Mass., 1969.

[Knuth 71a] Knuth, D. and R. Floyd "Notes on Avoiding GoTo Statements" *Info. Proc. Letters,* 1, 1, 1971, 23-32

[Knuth 71b] Knuth, D. "An Empirical Study of FORTRAN Programs" *Software Practice and Experience,* 1, 1971, 105-133.

[Knuth 72] Knuth, D.E. "Ancient Babylonian Algorithms" *Comm. ACM,* 1972.

[Knuth 74] Knuth, D.E. "Structured Programming with GOTO Statements" *Comp. Surveys,* 6, 4, 1974, 261-301.

[Knuth 78] Knuth, D.E. and Pardo, T. "The Early Development of Programming Languages" *Encyclopedia of Computer Science,* eds. Balzer, Holzman and Kent, 1978.

[Lampson 77] Lampson, B.W., J.J. Horning, R.L. London, J.G. Mitchell and G.J. Popek "Report on the Programming Language Euclid" *ACM Sigplan Notices,* 12,2,1977.

[Landin 64] Landin, P.J. "The Mechanical Evaluation of Expressions" *Computer Journal,* 6, 1964, 308-320.

[Landin 66] Landin, P.J. "The Next 700 Programming Languages" *Comm. ACM,* 9,3, March 1966, 157-164. See also in [Horowitz 83].

[Lemon 76] Lemon, M. "Coroutine Pascal: a Case Study in Separable Control" Tech. Rept. 76-13, Dept. Computer Science, Univ. Pittsburgh, 1976.

[Lewis 76] Lewis, P.M. II, Rosenkrantz, D.J. and Stearns, R.E. *Compiler Design Theory* Addison-Wesley, Reading, Mass., 1976.

[Liskov 77] Liskov, B., A. Snyder, R. Atkinson, and C. Schaffert "Abstraction mechanisms in CLU", *Comm. ACM,* 20, 1977, 564.

[Liskov 78] Liskov, B., E. Moss, C. Schaffert, B. Scheifler, A. Snyder "CLU Reference Manual" Computation structures group memo 161, July 1978.

[Liskov 79a] Liskov, B. et al. "CLU Reference Manual", Laboratory for Computer Science, MIT, TR-225, October, 1979.

[Liskov 79b] Liskov B., A. Snyder "Exception Handling in CLU" *IEEE Trans. on Software Eng.,* Nov. 1979, 546-558. See also in [Horowitz 83].

[LISP] See [McCarthy 65]

[LRG 81] Xerox Learning Research Group, "The Smalltalk-80 System" *Byte,* 6, 8, 1981.

[MacLaren 77] MacLaren, M. Donald "Exception Handling in PL/1" *ACM Sigplan Notices,* 12, 3, 1977, 101-104.

[McCarthy 60] McCarthy, J. "Recursive Functions of Symbolic Expressions and Their Computation by Machine, Part I" *Comm ACM,* 3, 4, 1960, 184-195. See also in [Horowitz 83].

[McCarthy 65] McCarthy, J. and Levin, S. *LISP 1.5 Programmer's Manual* 2nd ed., M.I.T. Press, Cambridge, Mass., 1965. See also [Horowitz 83] for the first 30 pages.

[McGraw 82] McGraw, James R. "The VAL language: Description and Analysis" *ACM TOPLAS,* vol. 4, No. 1, Jan. 1982, 44-82.

[McKeeman 75] McKeeman, W.M. "On Preventing Programming Languages from Interfering with Programming" *IEEE Trans. Software Engineering,* SE-1, 1, 1975, 19-26.

[Mitchell 79] Mitchell, James G., William Maybury, and Richard Sweet "Mesa Language Manual" Technical Report CSL-78-1, Xerox Palo Alto Research Center, 1979.

[Morgan 70] Morgan, H.L. "Spelling Correction in System Programs" *Comm. ACM,* 13, 2, 90-94.

[Morris 73b] Morris, J.H. Jr "Types are Not Sets" *ACM Symposium on the Principles of Programming Languages,* October 1973.

[Moses 70] Moses, J. "The Function of FUNCTION in LISP" *SIGSAM Bull.* July, 1970, 13-27

[Naur 63] Naur, P. ed. "Revised Report on the Algorithmic Language ALGOL 60" *Comm. ACM,* 6, 1, 1963, 1-17. See also in [Horowitz 83].

[Newell 64] Newell, A. ed. *Information Processing Language V Manual* Prentice-Hall, Englewood Cliffs, N.J., 1964.

[Organick 72] Organick, E. "The Multics System: an Examination of its Structure" M.I.T. Press, 1972.

[Organick 78] Organick, E., Forsythe and Plummer, *Programming Language Structures,* Academic Press, New York, 1978.

[Pakin 72] Pakin, S. *APL/360 Reference Manual* 2nd ed., Science Research Associates, Chicago, 1972.

[Parnas 71] Parnas, D.L. "Information Distribution Aspects of Design Methodology" *Proc. IFIP Congress 71* 339-344, North-Holland, Amsterdam.

[Pascal6000 79] Strait, J.P., A.B. Mickel, J.T. Easton "Pascal 6000 Release 3 Manual" University of Minnesota, January 1979.

[Pauli 80] Pauli, W. L. Soffa. "Coroutine Behavior and Implementation" *Software Practice and Experience,* 10, 3, March, 1980, 189-204.

[PL/1 76] *OS PL/1 Checkout and Optimizing Compilers: Language*

Reference Manual IBM GC33-0009-4, Fifth ed. October, 1976.

[Popek 77] Popek, G.J., J. J. Horning, B.W. Lampson, R.L. London, and J. G. Mitchell. "Notes on the Design of Euclid" *ACM Sigplan Notices* 12, 3, 1977, 11-19. See also in [Horowitz 83].

[Prenner 72] Prenner, C., J. Spitzen and B. Wegbreit "An Implementation of Backtracking for Programming Languages" In [Leavenworth 72].

[Ralston 76] Ralston, A. editor, *Encyclopedia of Computer Science* Petrocelli/Charter, N.Y., 1976.

[Rentsch 82] Rentsch, T. "Object Oriented Programming", *ACM Sigplan Notices*, vol. 17, number 9, September, 1982.

[Richards 80] Richards, M. and C. Whitby-Strevens, *BCPL - The Language and Its Compiler* Cambridge University Press, 1980.

[Ripley 78] Ripley, G.D. and F.C. Druseikis "A Statistical Analysis of Syntax Errors" *Computer Languages*, vol. 3, 1978, 227-240.

[Ritchie 78a] Ritchie, "The C Reference Manual" *The C Programming Language* Prentice-Hall, 1978. See also in [Horowitz 83].

[Ritchie 78b] Ritchie, "The C Programming Language" *Bell System Technical Journal*, July-August 1978.

[Sale 79a] Sale A.H.J. "Strings and the Sequence Abstraction in Pascal" *Software Practice and Experience*, 9, 8, 1979, 671-683.

[Sale 79b] Sale, A.H.J. "Implementing Strings in Pascal - Again" *Software Practice and Experience*, 9, 1979, 839-841.

[Sammet 69] Sammet, J. *Programming Languages: History and Fundamentals* Prentice-Hall, Englewood Cliffs N.J., 1969.

[Sammet 72] Sammet, J. "Programming Languages: History and Future" *Comm. ACM,* 15, 7, 1972, 601-610.

[Sammet 76] Sammet, J. "Roster of Programming Languages for 1976-77" *ACM Sigplan Notices*, ACM, 1976, 56-59.

[Schwartz 81] Schwartz, R. and P.M. Melliar-Smith "The Finalization Operation for Abstract Data Types" *Proc. 5th IEEE Conf on Software Engineering*, March, 1981, 273-282.

[Scott 70] Scott D. "Outline of a Mathematical Theory of Computation" *Proc. 4th Princeton Conf. on info. Sci. and Sys.*, 1970.

[Scott 71] Scott, D. and C. Strachey "Towards a Mathematical Semantics for Computer Languages" *Proc. Symp. on Computers and Automata*, Polytechnic Inst. of Brooklyn, 1971.

[Scott 72] Scott D. "Mathematical Concepts in Programming Language Semantics" *AFIPS Conf. Proc. SJCC*, vol. 40, 1972, 225-234.

[Scott 76] Scott, D. "Data Types as Lattices" *SIAM J. on Computing*, 5, September, 1976, 522-587.

[Sieworck 82] Sieworck, Daniel P., Bell, G., Newell, A., *Computer*

Structures: Readings and Examples (second edition), McGraw-Hill, 1982.

[SIMSCRIPT] See [Kiviat 69]

[Smalltalk] See [Ingalls 78]

[SNOBOL 64] D. J. Farber, R.E. Griswold, F. P. Polonsky. "SNOBOL, a String Manipulation Language" *JACM*, 11, 1, 1964, 21-30.

[SNOBOL4 71] Griswold, R., J. Poage and I. Polonsky. *The SNOBOL4 Programming Language* 2nd ed. Prentice-Hall, Englewood Cliffs, N.J. 1971.

[Steelman 78] "Steelman Requirements for DoD High Order Computer Programming Languages" U.S. Department of Defense, Washington, D.C., June, 1978.

[Stoy 77] Stoy, J.E. *Denotational Semantics - The Scott-Strachey Approach to Programming Language Theory* M.I.T. Press, 1977.

[Tanenbaum 76] Tanenbaum, A.S. "A Tutorial on ALGOL68" *Computing Surveys*, 8, 2, June 1976. See also in [Horowitz 83].

[Teitelman 69] Teitelman, W. "Toward a Programming Laboratory" *Proc. Inter. Jt. Conf. Artif. Intel.*, Washington, D.C., 1969.

[Teitelman 75] Teitelman, W. *INTERLISP Reference Manual* Xerox Palo Alto Res. Center, Palo Alto, Ca. 1975.

[Tennent 81] Tennent, R.D. *Principles of Programming Languages* Prentice-Hall, Englewood Cleffs, New Jersey, 1981.

[Tesler 81] Tesler, Larry, "The Smalltalk Environment" *Byte*, 6, 8, 1981.

[Thacker 82] Thacker, C. F., E.M. McCreight, B.W. Lampson, R.F. Sproull, and D.R. Boggs," Alto: A Personal Computer", in [Sieworck 82].

[Tou 71] Tou, J. and P. Wegner editors. "Proc. Symposium on Data Structures in Prog. Lang." *ACM Sigplan Notices*, 6, 2, 1971.

[VAL] See [Dennis 79]

[Van Wijngaarden 69] Van Wijngaarden, A. ed., B. Mailloux, J. Peck, and C. Koster "Report on the Algorithmic Language ALGOL 68" *Numerische Mathematik*, 14, 2, 1969, 79-218.

[Van Wijngaarden 75] Van Wijngaarden et al., "Revised Report on the Algorithmic Language ALGOL68", *Acta Informatica*, 5, 1975, 1-236.

[Wallis 80] Wallis, P.J.L., and B.W. Silverman "Efficient Implementation of the Ada Overloading Rules" *IPL*, 10,3, April, 1980, 120-123.

[Watson 82] Watson, Ian and John Gurd, "A Practical Data Flow Computer" *Computer*, IEEE, vol 15, no. 2, Feb. 1982, 51-57.

[Wegbreit 71] Wegbreit, B. "The ECL Programming System" *Proc. Fall Joint Computer Conference*, vol 39, 1971.

[Wegbreit 74] Wegbreit, B., "The Treatment of Data Types in EL1" *Comm. ACM*, 17,5, May 1974, 251-264.

[Wegner 68] Wegner, P. *Programming Languages, Information Structures and Machine Organization* McGraw-Hill, New York, 1968.

[Wegner 71] Wegner, P. "Data Structure Models for Programming Languages" In [Tou 71], 1-54.

[Wegner 72] Wegner, P. "The Vienna Definition Language" *ACM Computing Surveys*, 4, 1, March 1972, 5-63.

[Wegner 76] Wegner, P. "Programming Languages - the First 25 Years" *IEEE Trans. on Computers*, Dec. 1976, 1207-1225. See also in [Horowitz 83].

[Wegner 79] Wegner, P. "Programming languages - Concepts and Research Directions" *Research Directions in Software Technology*, MIT Press, Cambridge, 1979, 425-489.

[Wegner 83] Wegner, P. and S. Smolka, "Processes, Tasks, and Monitors: A Comparative Study of Concurrent Programming Primitives", Technical Report, Computer Science, Brown University, Providence, Rhode Island, 1983.

[Weissman 67] Weissman, C. *LISP 1.5 Primer* Dickenson Publishing Company, Inc., Encino, Calif.

[Welsh 77] Welsh, J., J. Sneeringer, C.A.R. Hoare "Ambiguities and Insecurities in Pascal" *Software Practice and Experience*, 7, 1977, 685-696. See also in [Horowitz 83].

[Welsh 79] Welsh, J., A. Lister, and E. Salzman, "A Comparison of Two Notations for Process Communication" *Language Design and Programming Methodology*, ed. J. Tobias, No. 79, Springer-Verlag, Berlin, 1980.

[Welsh 81] Welsh, J. and A. Lister, "A Comparative Study of Task Communication in Ada" *Software Practice and Experience*, vol. 11, 1981, 257 - 290.

[Winston 79] Winston, P. *Lisp* Addison-Wesley, Reading, Mass., 1979.

[Wirth 66] Wirth, N. and C.A.R. Hoare, "A Contribution to the Development of ALGOL" *Comm. ACM*, 9, 6, June 1966, 413-431.

[Wirth 66b] Wirth, N. and Weber, H. "Euler: a Generalization of ALGOL and its Formal Definition" *C.ACM*, Part I in 9, 1 13-23, Part II in 9, 2, 89-99.

[Wirth 71b] Wirth, N. "The Programming Language Pascal," *Acta Informatica*, 1, 1, 1971, 35-63.

[Wirth 74] Wirth, N. "On the Design of Programming Languages." *Proc. IFIP Congress 74.* 386-393, North-Holland, Amsterdam, 1974. See also in [Horowitz 83].

[Wirth 75] Wirth, N. "An Assessment of the Programming Language Pascal" *ACM Sigplan Notices*, 10, 6, June 1975, 23-30. See also in

[Horowitz 83].

[Wirth 76] Wirth, N. *Algorithms + Data Structures = Programs* Prentice-Hall, Englewood-Cliffs, New Jersey, 1976.

[Wirth 77a] Wirth, N., "MODULA, a Language for Modular Programming" *Software Practice and Experience*, vol. 7, 1977, 3-35. See also in [Horowitz 83].

[Wirth 77b] Wirth, N. "The Use of MODULA" *Software Practice and Experience*, 7, 1977, 37-65.

[Wirth 77c] Wirth. N. "Design and Implementation of MODULA" *Software Practice and Experience*, 7, 1977, 67-84.

[Wirth 77d] Wirth, N. "Toward a Discipline of Real-Time Programming" *Comm ACM*, 20, 8, August 1977

[Wirth 80] Wirth, N. "MODULA-2 Language Reference Manual" ETH, Zurich, Switzerland, 1980.

[Wulf 71] Wulf, W., D.B. Russell and A.N. Habermann, "BLISS: a Language for Systems Programming" *Comm. ACM*, 14, 12, December 1971, 780-790. See also in [Horowitz 83].

[Wulf-Shaw 73] Wulf, W. and Mary Shaw "Global Variable Considered Harmful" *SIGPLAN Notices*, 8, 2, 1973, 28-34.

[Wulf 81] Wulf, W., M. Shaw, P. Hilfinger, and L. Flon *Fundamentals of Computer Science* Addison-Wesley, Reading, Mass., 1981.

[Yemini 81] Yemini, Shaula "The Replacement Model for Modular, Verifiable Exception Handling" Report No. CSD-810204, Computer Science, University of California Los Angeles, Los Angeles, February, 1981.

[Yemini 82] Yemini, Shaula, "An Axiomatic Treatment of Exception Handling" *Proc. Ninth symposium on Principles of Programming Languages*, January, 1982.

Index

A:
abstract data type   22, 256-260
accept statement   307-310
accumulating parameter   351
Ackerman, W.   375, 383, 389, 407, 423, 426
activation record   176
Ada   23, 24, 48, 51, 52, 56, 82,
                                        86, 88, 90, 91, 95,
                                         105-107, 135-137, 154-158, 190-194,
                                        208, 216, 217, 247-250
                                         278-283, 306-319, 334-338, 407, 423

Ada Augusta,
  Countess of Lovelace   5, 6, 24
Aho, A.   37, 55, 83, 423
Aiken, H.   9
ALGOL58   170
ALGOL60   11, 21, 48, 52, 53, 82,
                                        83, 99, 166, 167, 173
                                         175, 181, 183-185, 190, 210,
                                        250, 325, 345, 423
ALGOL68   39, 87, 88, 94, 100, 143, 148, 151,

ALGOL-W   171, 215, 293-295, 423
algorithms   94, 95, 203
alias   3, 4, 7
Allen, J.   79, 213-214, 382, 407
alphabet   343, 362, 363, 423
ALPHARD   48
Alto computer   234, 423
APL   413
                            15, 16, 42, 50, 82, 112, 161,
                            168, 407, 423
applicative language   19, 345, 385
applicative order   91
applied occurrences   185
array   137-144
Arvind   407-408, 423, 424
ASCII   48
Ashcroft   104, 408, 424
assignment   81-82, 111, 381
association lists   356
atoms   346

B:
Babbage, Charles   5-7
Babylonians   3
Backus, J.   9, 19, 35, 125, 424
Barnes, J.   424
Barron, D.   78, 81, 123, 424
BASED storage   177
BASIC   24
Berry, D.   408, 424
binary search tree   239-241, 247-249, 254, 260-261
Birtwistle   250, 424
BLISS   80, 97, 221, 222
block structure   56, 166, 406-407
BNF   51-57
Bobrow   222, 408, 424
Bohm   103, 424
Boolean conditions   91-93
Brinch-Hansen, P.   23, 222, 294, 295, 296, 298, 302, 424
Burge   346, 425

C:
Calingaert, P.   294, 425
call-by-name   205-207
call-by-reference   202
call-by-text   205
call-by-value   202
call-by-value-result   202
car function   117, 347
case statement   94-96, 387-388
cast   123
catch phrase   275-276
cdr function   117, 347
Chang   244, 425
character set   47-52
Cheatham, T.   425
Check prefix   270
Chomsky, N.   58, 425
Church, A.   352, 425
Clark   42, 425
closure   bsj , 363
CLU   23, 234, 273-275, 384, 425
cluster   405
COBOL   13, 15, 331, 425
coercion   149-151
Cohen, D.   61, 425
collating sequence   48
collection variables   214
comments   37
COMMON   169-170
compiler   82-83
COMPOOL   170
concatenation   255, 256
concurrency   287-323
Concurrent-Pascal   23, 296, 298-300
conditional expr.   353
conditional statement   see if statement
cons function   117, 348
constants   86-88
context-free grammar   54
context symbol   171
Conway, M.E.   222, 425

coroutines	221-225, 229
coroutine-Pascal	222
critical region	291
CSP	302-306
CSP/K	296-298
Curry	45
D:	
Dahl, O.J.	17, 148, 221, 250, 254, 262, 425, 426
dangling else	67, 94
dangling reference	103, 135
data flow	373-392
data flow graph	378
DATA statement	92
data type	117-119, 233
enumerated	119-121
subrange	121
Boolean	123-124
character	124-127
Davis, A.	377, 426
declaration	84-85, 166
declaration elaboration	86
declaration equivalence	157
deep binding	364
definitional lang.	383
Dekker	321
delayed evaluation	368-370
Dennis, J.	20, 377, 384, 426
denotational semantics	36
Dept. of Defense	13, 23
deproceduring	220
dereferencing	80
de Morgan, R.M.	21, 426
determinism (non)	313-320
Dijkstra, E.	23, 77, 103, 148, 291, 303, 322, 42 , 426
dining philosophers	312-320
discrete simulation	288
display	180-183
dispose statment	135, 175, 189
distributed computer	288

distributed processes	302
DO loop	63, 100
Druseikis	68, 73-74, 432
Dynabook	398
dynamic scope	168
E:	
EBCDIC	48
Elliot, W.D.	425
EL1	218
EQUIVALENCE	79, 151-154
Esperanto	24
Euclid	80, 149, 172, 214, 243-247, 426
Euler	15
event variable	290
exception handling	265-285
exit statement	105
expressions	89-93
extended-ALGOL	210
extent	165-196
F:	
fair scheduling	291
Falkoff	16, 426
Farber, D.	16, 127, 433
FEXPR	205, 361-364
file	326
file buffer	328
Flon, L.	119, 144
fluid binding	169
for statement	53-54, 99-100, 131, 386, 387
format statement	327, 331
FORTRAN	9, 10, 47, 79, 82, 84, 85, 93, 102 112, 166, 169, 345
FORTRAN 77	10, 47, 49, 93, 209, 325, 332
FUNARG	361-364
functions	201, 220, 343-346

G:
Gannon, J. — 70, 426
garbage collection — 175
generic procedure — 217-220
Gentleman — 222, 426
Geschke — 42, 426
Goodenough — 267, 426
GPSS — 289, 426
Goldberg, A. — 426
Gordon — 36, 426
Gostelow — 20, 423, 424
go to statement — 101-105
Graham — 298
Gries, D. — 81, 83, 93, 426
Griswold — 16, 127, 426, 433
Grune — 223, 426
Gurd — 380, 382
Guttag, J. — 257, 260, 426, 428

H:
Hanson — 221
Henderson — 346, 353, 368, 369, 428
Hoare, C.A.R. — 10, 21, 23, 34, 35, 36, 42, 43, 82, 148, 151, 295, 308, 425, 428
Holt, R. — 40, 296, 298, 321
Horning, J.J. — 70, 426, 428, 430, 432
Horowitz, E. — 42, 140, 175, 208, 216, 254, 260, 427, 428, 429
Hume, J. — 40

I:
Ichbiah, J. — 24
IF statement — 10, 93-96
immutable — 385
imperative prog lang — 19
imports list — 172
Ingalls, D. — 419, 429
Ingerman — 205, 429
inheritance — 408-412
initialization — 86-88
input-output — 325-340

iteration   97-101
INTERLISP   204-221
interpreter   82, 355-361
Iverson, K.   15, 16, 429

J:
Jacopini   108, 424
Jensen   211, 429
Jensen's Device   206
Johnston, J.   183, 429
JOVIAL   170, 429

K:
Kaden, S.   425
Kay, A.   398, 413, 429
Knuth, D.E.   3-5, 9, 10, 42, 97, 98, 103, 105,
                                   144, 429, 430

L:
lambda variables   352
Lampson, B.   243, 430, 432
Landin   430
law of least astonishment   123
Lazowska, E.   298
Lemon   222, 430
lexically enclosing scope   166
Lewis, P.   61, 83, 430
LISP   16, 19, 82, 84, 168
Liskov, B.   35, 267. 273, 274, 275, 384, 430
Lister   304
LISP   346-372
LOW-LEVEL-I/O   337
l-value   79

M:
MacLaren   273, 431
Manchester machine   382
Manna, Z.   104, 424

McCarthy, J.	16, 346, 431
McGraw	391, 431
McKeeman, W.	38, 431
MESA	42, 275-278, 296
message passing	302-306, 402-404
Mitchell	275, 277, 298, 431, 432
MODULA	234, 237-243, 296
monitors	295-302
Morgan, H.	67, 431
Morris, J.	431
Moses, J.	431
multi-programming	288
multi-tasking	290
mutual exclusion	290

N:
name equivalence	152
narrowing	150
Naur, P.	11, 51, 431
Newell, A.	431, 432
Nygaard	17, 221, 250

O:
object oriented	397
objects	400-401
obscure export	242
ON-condition	269-270
operator priority	89-90
Organick, E.	273, 431
orthogonality	39
overloading	214-217
own variable	173, 179

P:
packages	247-250
Pakin, S.	431
parameters	202-207
Pardo,Trabb-	9-10
Parnas, D.	431

parsing	37, 55, 61
Pascal	22, 52, 86-88, 95, 100, 103, 133-134, 171, 172, 190 211, 212, 255, 327-329, 345, 384
Pauli, W.	223, 431
picture spec.	331-332
PL/1	37, 41, 170, 171, 173, 269-273, 329-334
Poage	17
pointers	132-137
Polonsky	127, 433
polymorphic	122
Popek, J.	80, 243, 432
Prenner, C.	432
procedure parameters	200
procedures	199-230
productions	54
prog feature	364-368

Q:
| qualification | 192 |
| queue | 234-236 |

R:
race condition	289
Ralston, A.	29, 432
random access	326
range constraint	155
reader-writer	292
record i/o	329
records	144-149
recursion	53, 55
referential transparency	89, 345
reliability	37
repeat statement	98
reserved words	51
Richards	432
Ripley	68, 73, 74, 432
Ritchie	432

S:
Sahni, S.   208
Sakoda   112
Sale, A.   127, 161, 432
Salzman   304
Sammet, J.   13, 25, 29, 432
scalars   123
Schwanke   213
Schwartz, R.   250, 432
scope   165-196
Scott, D.   36, 381, 432
select statement   310
semantics   35, 36
semaphores   291-295
sequential file   326
sexigesimal numbers   3
shallow binding   364
Shaw, M.   144
short circuit operator   92, 93
side-effect   89, 208, 345, 365, 381
SIMSCRIPT   289
SIMULA67   17, 85, 221, 223, 234, 250-256, 295, 398
Sieworck, D.   432
slicing   142
SL5   221
SMALLTALK   207, 397-423
Sneeringer   151
SNOBOL   16-18, 51, 82, 127-132, 168
Snyder, A.   274
Soffa   223
spaghetti stack   223
SP/K   39
static scoping   166-168
static pointer   179
STEELMAN report   24, 278
Strachy, C.   36
STRAWMAN report   24
stream i/o   329
strong typing   38
structural equivalence   152
SUBSTR function   126-127
synchronization   289

syntax graphs	57-66
string manipulation	17
SUE	41
S-expression	346

T:

Tanenbaum	151, 433
tasks	306-319
Teitelman	204, 221, 433
Tennent, R.	433
TEXT-I/O	336, 337
Thacker	398, 433
thunk	205
TOPPS	70, 74
Tou, J.	433
Tower of Babel	14
transparent export	242
trimming	143
Turing A.	9, 19, 35
type equivalence	151-154

U:

Ullman, J.	37, 55, 83
uniformity	39
universal prog. lang.	15
up level addressing	179

V:

VAL	384-391
value parameters	11
van Wijngaarden	433
variables	77-82
variant records	146-148
Vienna Def. lang.	35
Von Neumann	9, 19, 20

W:

Wagner	112

Wallis	222
Watson	380, 382, 433
Wegbreit, B.	222, 364, 432, 433
Wegner, P.	36, 316, 433
Weissman, C.	343, 433
Welsh	38, 151, 304, 433
Wexelblat	22
while statement	98, 406
widening	150
Williamson, R.	329
Winston, P.	343
Wirth, N.	21, 36, 37, 55, 57, 94, 100
	101, 138, 239, 242, 296, 434, 435
Wulf, W.	80, 97, 98, 119, 144, 176, 183,
	191, 221, 234, 435

X:

Y:
Yemini, S.	268, 435

Z:
Zahn	111-112
Zuse	9